»Not Even a Game Anymore«
The Theatre of Forced Entertainment
Das Theater von Forced Entertainment

Judith Helmer
Florian Malzacher (Eds./Hg.)

»*Not Even a Game Anymore*«

The Theatre of Forced Entertainment
Das Theater von Forced Entertainment

WITH ARTICLES BY
MIT BEITRÄGEN VON

Patricia Benecke
Tim Etchells
Matthew Goulish
Adrian Heathfield
Judith Helmer
Hans-Thies Lehmann
Florian Malzacher
Annemarie Matzke
Andrew Quick
Anke Schleper
Gerald Siegmund
Astrid Sommer

PHOTOGRAPHS BY
FOTOGRAFIEN VON

Hugo Glendinning

Alexander Verlag Berlin

Co-produced by / Ko-produziert von

Festival Theaterformen, Braunschweig / Hannover
KunstenFESTIVALdesArts, Brussel
Künstlerhaus Mousonturm, Frankfurt
Nettverk for Scenekunst, Bergen / Oslo / Trondheim
Wiener Festwochen
Productiehuis Rotterdam (Rotterdamse Schouwburg)
Volksbühne am Rosa-Luxemburg-Platz, Berlin

© by Alexander Verlag Berlin 2004
Alexander Wewerka, Fredericiastr. 8, D-14050 Berlin
info@alexander-verlag.com
www.alexander-verlag.com
Gestaltung / Design: Hartwig Otto
Umschlagfoto / Cover photo: Hugo Glendinning (aus / from: *Pleasure*)

Fotos / Photos © Hugo Glendinning
T. S. Eliot aus: *Gesammelte Gedichte*. Übersetzt von Eva Hesse.
© Suhrkamp Verlag Frankfurt 1988, „Die Brandparole"
Alexander Kluge aus: *Die Kunst, Unterschiede zu machen*.
© Suhrkamp Verlag Frankfurt 2003, „Die Sehnsucht der Zellen"

Druck und Bindung / Printing and Binding: AZ Druck und Datentechnik, Kempten
Printed in Germany (April) 2004

ISBN 3-89581-115-7

Table of Contents / Inhaltsverzeichnis

Many Thanks to ...
Herzlichen Dank an ...

Gabriela Badura, Matt Burman, Tim Etchells, Eileen Evans, Festival Theaterformen, Forced Entertainment, Hugo Glendinning, Elisabeth Gräfe, Gero Grundmann, Janine Hauthal, Christin Heinrichs, Vlatka Horvat, KunstenFESTIVALdesArts, Künstlerhaus Mousonturm, Martina Löwe, Wolfgang Müller, Nettverk for Scenekunst, Hartwig Otto, Christine Peters, Michael Philipp, Productiehuis Rotterdam (Rotterdamse Schouwburg), Anke Schleper, Heike Schleper, Benjamin Marius Schmidt, Bernhard Schreiner, Samantha Scott, Volksbühne am Rosa-Luxemburg-Platz, Alexander Wewerka, Wiener Festwochen.

1604 – Hard year and deficient in crops

1605 – Flood everywhere

1606 – Nothing recorded

1607 – Nothing written down

1608 – Hard winter

1609 – Hard winter (another one)

1610 – Elvis

1611 – The Beatles

1612 – Failure of crops and very bad, hard year

1613 – Nothing written down

1614 – Simon died

1615 – Birth of Saint Jasmine

1616 – Air strikes and 15-mile exclusion zone

1617 – Sarah's party

1618 – Moon landings

1619 – Hard year; very bad oil spillage

1620 – Saint Jasmine performs a miracle in a country called Palestine

1621 – Bad year and a plague of fainting everywhere amongst girls

1622 – Bad harvest

1623 – Nothing recorded

1624 – Partition of the country and martial law

1625 – John Lennon shot in Dallas by a gunman acting alone

1626 – A new constitution for Soviet Belgium

1627 – Strange storms and sundry omens

1628 – Nothing written down

1629 – A man saved from falling under train

1630 – A child saved in a shootout during a smash-and-grab raid

1631 – A man killed for no reason

1632 – A horse burned

1633 – Housing shortage

1634 – Nothing written down

Hidden J

Plenty of Leads to Follow
Foreword

Lauter rote Fäden
Vorwort

Florian Malzacher / Judith Helmer

Überhaupt kein Spiel mehr.
Geh zu weit. Geh zu weit. Geh zu weit.
Ränder des Spiels – wo es zum Realen zurückkehrt.

Tim Etchells

Not even a game anymore.
Go too far. Go too far. Go too far.
Edges of the game – where it comes back to the real.

Tim Etchells

Ein Mann steht auf einer schäbigen kleinen Podestbühne, umringt von hoch gestapelten Kartons, sein Oberkörper bloß, um den Bauch eine selbst gebastelte Bombe, Dynamitstange an Dynamitstange. Der Wecker auf seiner Brust tickt, zählt Minute um Minute bis zur Explosion. Nervös und stockend, etwas alleingelassen, redet er von möglichen und wünschenswerten Dramaturgien, von Bühneneffekten, guten Plots, Besetzungsproblemen, der Notwendigkeit von Kostümproben.

Hinter ihm streiten sich zwei Bäume heftig um einen Stuhl, rennen gegen Kartons. Ein nackter Mann mit Netzstrumpfhose überm Kopf springt dem Redner zur Seite, borgt sich Geld. Derweil tragen die Bäume ein Kinderhaus auf die Bühne, ein Hund rennt bellend durchs Bild … Der Traum von einem ordentlichen Theaterabend – so viel ist klar –, dieser Traum wird sich dem unglückseligen Kerl mit der Bombe, dieser Traum wird sich aber auch dem Publikum nicht erfüllen.

Und doch, zugleich: So viel Theater wie hier in *Showtime* ist im post- und postpostdramatischen Theater selten. Vorhang, Scheinwerfer, Requisiten, Pistolen, Tierkostüme, nichts fehlt. Tod, Kampf, Slapstick, Musik. Wildes Chaos und strenge, reduzierte Dramaturgie.

A bare-chested man stands on a small shabby pedestal of a stage, surrounded by piles of cardboards boxes. Tied around his waist: a belt of homemade dynamite sticks. The alarm-clock timer is ticking, counting down minute by minute towards the explosion. Alone on stage, nervous and hesitant, the man talks about possible and desirable dramaturgy – stage effects and good plots, casting problems and the necessity of dress rehearsals.

Behind him, two trees keep running into boxes as they fight over a chair. A naked man with a stocking mask over his head leaps up next to the narrator, trying to borrow some money. Meanwhile, the trees bring a children's playhouse onto the stage while a barking dog crawls around in the chaos … One thing is clear: The dream of a proper theatre show will not come true – not for the sad character with the bomb, and not for the audience.

Still, despite all this: As much theatre as there is in *Showtime* is rare in post- and post-post-dramatic theatre. Curtains, stage lights, props, pistols, animal costumes – nothing is missing. Death, conflict, slapstick and music, wild chaos and strict, reductive dramaturgy. In the year of its twentieth anniversary, the British theatre group Forced Entertainment loves and distrusts theatre in equal measure. Though propelled and swept away by it, the group is exposing theatre, pushing it to its limits, letting it falter, exploding it at times and making it implode at others. Sometimes theatre is reduced to a bare minimum, or alternatively, overloaded to the point where it might break. It is no wonder that Forced Entertainment, apart from being very successful, are also one of the most influential theatre groups in Europe. It is hardly surprising then, that they are appreciated as much by theatre lovers as they are by theorists and critics. Their theatre is not the kind reserved only for specialists and friends of discourse, but rather the kind that one can take friends along to, even those who have vowed never to enter a theatre again.

Founded in 1984 in the northern English city of Sheffield by former drama students of Exeter University, the company – with its core group consisting of Robin Arthur, Tim Etchells, Richard Lowdon, Claire Marshall, Cathy Naden and Terry O'Connor – has produced a strangely disparate range of works. They are not bound by the conventional two-hour limits of theatre – six, twelve, and even twenty-four-hour durational performances are part of their repertoire, as are videos, installations, photographs, interactive CD-ROMs, Web-based projects and reflective essays. However difficult it may be to grasp the whole spectrum of activity, *leit*motifs, *leit*interests, *leit*ideas, *leit*rules and *leit*atmospheres are clearly visible in the work.

So far, it has mainly been Tim Etchells, the group's author and director, who provided the audience with written material that might help them navigate Forced Entertainment's work. Etchells has always been the first and most

Die britische Theatergruppe Forced Entertainment, die in diesem Jahr ihr zwanzigjähriges Jubiläum feiert, liebt das Theater ebenso, wie sie ihm misstraut. Lässt sich von ihm treiben und mitreißen, ebenso, wie sie es vorführt, an seine Grenzen bringt, es scheitern lässt, mal implodierend, mal explodierend. Mal reduziert auf ein Minimum, mal überfrachtet auf ein Maximum. Kein Wunder, dass Forced Entertainment nicht nur eine der beliebtesten, sondern auch eine der einflussreichsten Theatergruppen Europas ist. Kein Wunder auch, dass Theaterliebhaber ebenso auf ihre Kosten kommen wie Theaterwissenschaftler und Kritiker. Es ist kein Theater ausschließlich für Spezialisten und Diskursliebhaber, es ist zugleich ein Theater, zu dem man all die Freunde mitnehmen kann, die sonst keines mehr betreten mögen.

Das Werk der Kompanie, die 1984 von ehemaligen Drama-Studenten der Universität Exeter in der nordenglischen Stadt Sheffield gegründet wurde, und die im Kern aus Robin Arthur, Tim Etchells, Richard Lowdon, Claire Marshall, Cathy Naden und Terry O'Conner besteht, ist ungewöhnlich disparat. Die Grenzen zweistündiger Theaterabende binden sie schon lange nicht mehr – sechs, zwölf oder gar vierundzwanzigstündige *durational performances* gehören ebenso dazu wie Videos, Installationen, Fotografien, interaktive CD-ROMs, Internetarbeiten und reflexive Essays.

Doch so schwer es fällt, den Überblick über diese Bandbreite zu behalten, so deutlich ziehen sich Leitmotive, Leitinteressen, Leitideen, Leitspielregeln und Leitstimmungen durch die Arbeit.

Bislang hat vor allem der Autor und Regisseur der Gruppe, Tim Etchells, den Zuschauern ausformulierte Anhaltspunkte gegeben, mit deren Hilfe sie sich durchs Werk hangeln konnten: Immer war Etchells der erste und wirkungsmächtigste Interpret der eigenen Arbeiten, seine Deutungen, vor allem in der Essaysammlung *Certain Fragments: Contemporary Performance and Forced Entertainment*, haben die Rezeption Forced Entertainments wesentlich geprägt. Spuren davon sind auch im vorliegenden Band zu finden, nicht nur in Etchells eigenem Beitrag, auch in vielen Zitaten und Verweisen. Und doch ist dieses Buch, das ausschließlich aus Originalbeiträgen besteht, auch der Versuch, die Grundlage für eine Betrachtung von außen, für eine unabhängige Rezeption zu schaffen.

Manche der vielen möglichen roten Fäden werden in den folgenden Kapiteln – nach Überblicken über die bisherige Entwicklung der Gruppe von Patrica Benecke und Judith Helmer – sehr explizit herausgearbeitet, andere blitzen mal hier, mal dort auf, wieder andere sind selbst schon Leitmotive des Buches geworden.

Wie die Arbeiten Forced Entertainments sehr unterschiedliche Zugänge erlauben und sehr unterschiedliche Zuschauer in ihren Bann ziehen, so soll auch dieses Buch als Einführung ebenso wie zur Vertiefung oder als Kompendium dienen. Subjektive Einblicke stehen neben journalistischen Texten, wissenschaftlichen Essays, einem Anhang mit vollständigem Werkverzeichnis und dem Versuch einer ersten umfassenden Bibliografie – und nicht zuletzt natürlich den Fotografien von Hugo Glendinning, dem langjährigen Arbeitspartner und Dokumentaristen der Gruppe.

Zu den wiederkehrenden Aspekten in diesem Buch gehören vor allem die unterschiedlichen Spielformen des Theaters, über die Forced Entertainment souverän und je nach Bedarf verfügt, und unter denen die *durational performances* mit ihrer erschöpfenden, aber auch euphorisierenden Dauer seit Mitte der Neunzigerjahre eine besondere Stellung einnehmen: Sie sind, wie Adrian Heathfield in seinem weitgreifenden Gespräch mit Tim Etchells feststellt, auch Zeichen eines stärkeren Minimalismus, klarer Regeln und Strukturen.

Diese Regeln zu beherrschen und gleichzeitig von ihnen beherrscht zu werden, das ist, so Annemarie Matzke, die besondere Leistung der Spieler von Forced Entertainment,

powerful interpreter of their own output. His analysis, especially the collection of essays *Certain Fragments: Contemporary Performance and Forced Entertainment*, contributed greatly to the reception of the company's work. Traces of his analysis are also found in this publication, not only in Etchells' own contribution, but also in many quotes and references. However, this book – consisting solely of original writing – is also an attempt at, and a basis for, an external perspective, aiming to create a context for an independent reception.

In the following chapters – after a survey of the group's development to date by Patricia Benecke and Judith Helmer – some of the many threads running through the work will be examined in detail. Others crop up here and there, while a few have themselves become leitmotifs of this publication.

Just as the work of Forced Entertainment provides varied points of entry and thus fascinates a diverse range of viewers, this book is intended as both an introduction and a compendium for in-depth investigation. It contains individual perspectives alongside journalistic pieces and scientific essays, as well as an appendix that includes a complete list of works. There is also an attempt at creating the first comprehensive Forced Entertainment bibliography. Last, but not least, the book features the photographs of Hugo Glendinning, the group's collaborator and documenter of many years.

Of the many aspects of Forced Entertainment's work discussed in this book, perhaps the most frequently talked about one is the variety of the group's performance styles. Forced Entertainment select from them with ease to suit each project's individual needs. Among their works produced since the mid-1990s, the durational performances stand out with their exhausting and at the same time exhilarating length. As remarked by Adrian Heathfield in his extensive interview with Tim Etchells, the durational works are also a sign of an increasing minimalism in Forced Entertainment's work, of clearer rules and tighter structures.

The ability to simultaneously command these rules and submit to them is, according to Annemarie Matzke, the forte of Forced Entertainment actors. It makes them performers, directors, dramatic advisers, and at the same time, players constrained and bound by the rules and dynamics of the game. The key components of these durational works, ranging from *12 am: Awake & Looking Down* to *Quizoola!* and *And on the Thousandth Night …*, are the play with the audience, repetition and difference, exhaustion and increasing familiarity, the dynamics between embodying a character and simply being oneself, stepping away from events, as well as the special relationship between prepared and improvised texts. The marathon performances however are not separate from other works by Forced Entertainment as they often originate in certain sections of shorter pieces, or else, they themselves may spark off concepts for more concise formats.

The sheer duration of these works changes the relationship with the audience, thematically bringing to the fore the foundations of theatre itself. These questions though are also true of shorter, more directed events: What does it mean to be on stage; what does it mean to sit in the dark auditorium; how does one grab attention and build it up, either to create a turning point or a false lead? The works investigate our desire for stories, and how unsuitable linear narratives are for our age, how few explanations about our world they are able to offer. Where Forced Entertainment have succeeded, far better than most contemporary theatre, is in repeatedly bringing light to the situation of the audience, strangely caught between their sense of responsibility, bearing

macht sie zu Performern, Regisseuren, Dramaturgen und Getriebenen zugleich. Das Spiel von Wiederholung und Differenz, Erschöpfung und zunehmender Vertrautheit mit dem Publikum, das In-der-Rolle-Sein und das Einfach-aus-dem-Spiel-aussteigen, aber auch das besondere Verhältnis von vorbereiteten und improvisierten Texten sind wesentlicher Bestandteil der Arbeiten von *12 am: Awake & Looking Down* über *Quizoola!* bis *And On the Thousandth Night …*

Doch stehen diese Langzeitaufführungen keineswegs isoliert – oft sind sie aus einzelnen Aspekten kürzerer Arbeiten entstanden oder liefern umgekehrt die Idee oder Initialzündung für ein gebundeneres Format.

Die schiere Dauer verändert das Verhältnis zum Zuschauer und thematisiert die Grundbedingungen des Theaters selbst. Aber auch in den kürzeren, durchinszenierten Abenden stehen diese Fragen im Mittelpunkt: Was es bedeutet, auf einer Bühne zu stehen, was es bedeutet, im Dunkeln im Parkett zu sitzen. Wie man Aufmerksamkeit aufbaut und sie entweder zu einer Pointe oder aber ins Leere führt. Wie groß unsere Sehnsucht nach Geschichten ist, und wie wenig aber eine lineare Narration in unsere Zeit passt, wie wenig sie unsere Welt erklären kann.

Vor allem hat Forced Entertainment, wie kaum ein anderes Gegenwartstheater, immer wieder die Situation des Zuschauers thematisiert, die merkwürdig zwischen Verantwortlichkeit, Zeugenschaft und Voyeurismus schwankt – oder vielleicht doch eher zwischen schlechter Zeugenschaft und schlechtem Voyeurismus. Stücke wie *Showtime* oder *First Night* machen das Verhältnis zwischen Publikum und Performer ganz direkt zum Thema, andere spielen zuweilen kaum merklich damit, den Zuschauer, wie Tim Etchells es nennt, heranzuziehen und dann wieder wegzuschubsen. Und plötzlich sieht man sich selbst zuschauen. Und ist zugleich selbst Teil der Inszenierung.

Emanuelle Enchanted
(Rehearsal / Probe)

Die Entstehung des Textes ist bei Forced Entertainment stets eng verwoben mit dem Erarbeitungsprozess als Ganzem: Nicht ein fertiges Manuskript wird in szenischer Konkretisierung umgesetzt oder auch dekonstruiert wie im zeitgenössischen Theater häufig. Die sprachlichen Elemente sind vielmehr nicht zu trennen von den anderen Bühnenmitteln: Text geht ein in Kostüme, Bühne, Gesten, Handlungsfetzen, wie umgekehrt diese in den Text einfließen, ihn prägen, ändern, konterkarieren, kommentieren. Die Heterogenität des Materials wird während des Probenprozesses

witness, and voyeurism – or perhaps rather between being bad witnesses and bad voyeurs. Performances such as *Showtime* and *First Night* deal directly with this relationship between performance and audience while others, with more subtlety, play with attracting and repelling the audience. Suddenly, one observes oneself watching, while simultaneously being part of the performance.

The process of generating text is always an important part of Forced Entertainment's way of working: It is not about staging or deconstructing a finished script as is often the case in contemporary theatre. Here, speech is inseparable from other stage elements: Text permeates the costumes, stage, gestures and plot fragments, just as these in turn inform the text, influencing, counteracting and commenting on it. The heterogeneous nature of the materials is never fully dissolved in rehearsal and causal relationships have no priority. Instead, associative consistency is often more important and a scene may be defined as a conscious confrontation between contradictory signs, frequently guided by visual or indeed rhythmic considerations.

There are many found objects in Forced Entertainment performances. Text originates from newspaper articles, film dialogues, fragments of letters or diaries. These various fragments are processed, complemented, or simply included in their original form alongside texts by Tim Etchells and those generated by performers in rehearsal. A worn-out horse costume or a gorilla head are discovered at a costume supplier, piles of clothing bought in charity shops. Toy-like props are used for improvisation in rehearsals, which are recorded on video for future reference. Nothing should be finished too hastily; fragments remaining fluid for a long time, to be tested in diverse combinations. The end result often includes passages that seem natural and un-acted next to obviously scripted texts and quotes, poetic language next to slang, curses and insults. Sentences arise as if thought up on the spot, while seemingly spontaneous elements are read out (*Speak Bitterness*) and fragmented sections are played again and again (*Club of No Regrets*). The strands of material are as heterogeneous as our urban lives, pervaded by various languages, media, cultures and images, colliding time and again in infinite combinations, which can hardly be represented by structured narratives with a beginning and an end.

nie ganz aufgehoben, kausale Verknüpfungen haben keinerlei Priorität, oft kann das Gefühl einer assoziativen Schlüssigkeit wichtiger, kann eine Szene von bewusster Konfrontation widersprüchlicher Zeichen geprägt, oder bildlichen bzw. rhythmischen Überlegungen geschuldet sein.

Vieles in den Performances von Forced Entertainment sind Fundstücke. Texte entstammen Zeitungsmeldungen, Filmdialogen, Brief- oder Tagebuchfetzen, gefundenen Notizen oder Nachrichten, die Tim Etchells bearbeitet, ergänzt oder einfach nur in eigene Texte bzw. Texte der Performer aus dem Probenprozess einfügt.

Im Kostümverleih werden ein heruntergekommenes Pferdekostüm oder ein Gorilla-Kopf entdeckt, im Second-Hand-Laden wahllos Kleiderberge gekauft. Spielutensilien für Improvisationen im Probenprozess: Material wird geschaffen und per Video-Kamera aufgezeichnet. Nichts darf zu schnell fertig werden, die einzelnen Fragmente bleiben lange im Fluss und werden in verschiedensten Kombinationen ausprobiert. Am Ende finden sich Passagen, die natürlich und ungespielt erscheinen, neben eindeutig geschriebenen Texten oder Zitiertem, poetische Rede folgt Slang, Flüchen oder Beschimpfungen. Sätze tauchen auf, als wären sie im Moment erdacht, dann wieder wird scheinbar Spontanes von Blättern verlesen (*Speak Bitterness*), werden fragmentierte Blöcke wieder und wieder gespielt (*Club of No Regrets*): Die Heterogenität des Materials ist die Heterogenität unserer städtischen Lebenswelt, in der verschiedene Sprachen, Medien, Kulturen und Bilder in unzähligen Kombinationen wieder und wieder aufeinander treffen und die durch geordnete Geschichten mit Anfang und Ende schwerlich mehr repräsentierbar ist.

Fast zwangsläufig also gehört zu den immer wiederkehrenden Motiven über die Jahre hinweg das spürbar intensive Verhältnis zur Stadt, zu einer Stadt, die weniger eine konkrete Stadt meint (beispielsweise Sheffield, wie viele Interpreten nahe legen), als vielmehr die Idee, das Gefühl von einer Stadt: Mal ist es eine ruhelose Stadt im Hintergrund, wie in *Emanuelle Enchanted*. Mal ist es, als hätten sich Darsteller und Publikum zurückgezogen, um jenseits des Lärms der Welt Rechenschaften über ihr Leben abzulegen (*Speak Bitterness*), mal als wären sie, vom Alkohol zur Zeitlupe verlangsamt, dazu verdammt, Nacht für Nacht in endlosen Wiederholungsschleifen zu verbringen (*Pleasure*), während draußen das Leben schläft oder längst wieder tobt, weil nur hier unten, in einem heruntergekommenen Club, die Nacht andauert und andauert. Die Stille des Raumes, seine indizienlose, studioartige Nüchternheit (*Speak Bitterness*) oder seine inflationäre Überladung (*Showtime*), immer aber seine merkwürdige Zeitlosigkeit, seine Nicht-Verortbarkeit prägen die Performances von Forced Entertainment – durch den Kontrast und die spürbare und zugleich abwesende Präsenz einer großen, reizüberfluteten, verlockenden, aber auch kalten und dreckigen Stadt irgendwo da draußen.

Straßen, Städte, Landschaften – das Spiel mit ‚Mapping‘-Konzepten und geografischen Strukturen zieht sich durch das Werk, wie Anke Schleper zeigt: In *A Decade of Forced Entertainment* zeichnete Forced Entertainment neben privaten Erlebnissen auch politische Ereignisse auf einer subjektiven und provisorischen Karte ein. *Ground Plans for Paradise* schuf eine abstrakte Stadt mit Hochhausblöcken aus Balsaholz und für *The Travels* suchten sie die Love Lanes, Harmony Streets, Cutthroat Alleys und Rape Lanes in ganz Großbritannien auf. Lasen Landschaften, Leute, Grundrisse wie ein Buch oder den Kaffeesatz.

Sprache ist für Forced Entertainment Landschaft und Landschaft Sprache. Und zugleich ist sie der eigentliche Ort der Melancholie, die als Stimmung so eng mit dem Werk der Gruppe verbunden ist. Gerald Siegmund nennt sie eine Sprache des Verlusts, eng verknüpft mit dem Prinzip des Theaters: dem Prinzip des andauernden Verschwindens.

Immersed as they are in this kind of urban experience, it is no surprise that throughout the years, Forced Entertainment have been revisiting the tangible and intense relationship with the city, not a specific city (e.g. Sheffield, as suggested by various observers), but rather with the idea of the urban, the feeling of a city. At times, as in *Emanuelle Enchanted*, it is a restless city, appearing in the background. At others, it is as if both performers and audience had retreated, to give account of their lives in a space away from the noise of the world (*Speak Bitterness*). Sometimes they seem doomed to enact endless narrative loops, night after night, slowed down by alcohol (*Pleasure*), while life on the outside sleeps or already rages again. Night drags on, but only deep inside the run-down club. The silence of the place – sober, unremarkable and studio-like (*Speak Bitterness*) or else completely overloaded (*Showtime*), but somehow always strangely timeless and impossible to locate – defines the performances of Forced Entertainment. It is a silence that operates in contrast to, and in the tangible absence of a vast, highly charged, tempting, but also cold and dirty city – somewhere out there.

Streets, cities, landscapes – the play with mapping concepts and geographic structures runs through the work, as shown by Anke Schleper. In *A Decade of Forced Entertainment*, next to their personal experiences, Forced Entertainment chart political events on a provisional and subjective map. For *Ground Plans for Paradise*, they created an abstract city with high-rise buildings made of balsa wood, while for *The Travels*, they sought out the Love Lanes, Harmony Streets, Cutthroat Alleys and Rape Lanes all across the U.K. They read the landscape, people and floor plans like a book or like coffee grounds.

For Forced Entertainment, language is landscape and landscape is language. At the same time, it is the true site of melancholy, a mood closely connected to the work of the group. Gerald Siegmund calls it a language of loss, closely linked to the principle of theatre: the principle of continuous disappearance.

Though the success of Forced Entertainment is mainly due to their stage work, they have in the past ten years developed a range of projects in other media. As outlined in Astrid Sommer's contribution, these projects constitute far more than add-ons: videos, Web-based work and interactive CD-ROMs (made in collaboration with Hugo Glendinning) have become a major part of Forced Entertainment work.

In their theatre works, however, the visible use of technology that marked many of the pieces in the 90's decreased and faded into a more, so to speak, subcutaneous usage. While the monitors, which still dominated Forced Entertainment's works in the 80's, have largely disappeared from the stage, the allusions to or quotes from television series and films, the question and answer format of talk shows and game shows still play an important part. The same is true of structures, such as scene montage, that are akin to flipping through television channels. In their work, one finds obvious game show scenarios with quiz questions (*Quizoola!*), news anchorpersons and show hosts sitting at desks (*Speak Bitterness, Pleasure*), but also the numerous (portrayed) animals with their plush fur and sad button eyes – as if they had, together with all the other playful props, just escaped from a children's programme, from the *Muppet Show* or a low-budget imitation Disney movie.

Children are a constant presence in the Forced Entertainment universe, though direct references to them are rare. However, their fascinated view of the world, their language, their unstoppable urge to play, as well as the spontaneous nature of their actions, the apparent absence of

Auch wenn es im Wesentlichen die Theaterabende sind, die den Erfolg Forced Entertainments begründen, so hat sich daneben in den letzten zehn Jahren eine ganze Bandbreite von Projekten in anderen Medien entwickelt, die, wie man im Beitrag von Astrid Sommer sehen kann, weit mehr sind als bloßes Beiwerk: Videos, Internetprojekte und interaktive CD-ROMs (in Zusammenarbeit mit Hugo Glendinning) sind zu einem wesentlichen Bestandteil der Arbeit geworden.

In den Theaterarbeiten selbst hingegen wurde die sichtbare Medienpräsenz in den Neunzigerjahren immer geringer und ging über in eine sozusagen subkutane Mediennutzung: Während die Monitore, die vor allem Arbeiten der Achtzigerjahre noch prägten, weitgehend von der Bühne verschwanden, blieben die Anspielungen oder Zitate aus Fernsehserien und Filmen, die Frage- und Antwortspiele aus Talk- und Gameshows und Strukturen, wie die der Szenenmontage, die zuweilen dem Prinzip des Zappings gleicht. Eindeutige Spielshow-Situationen mit ihren Quizfragen (*Quizoola!*) sind zu finden, hinter Tischen sitzende Ansager oder Moderatoren (*Speak Bitterness, Pleasure*), aber auch die zahlreichen (gespielten) Tiere mit plüschigem Fell und traurigen Knopfaugen – als wären sie, zusammen mit all den verspielten Requisiten, einer Kindersendung, der *Muppet Show* oder der Lowbudget-Imitation eines Disneyfilms entlaufen.

Ohnehin gehören Kinder fest zum Kosmos Forced Entertainments, auch wenn der explizite Verweis auf sie eher selten ist. Aber ihr faszinierter Blick auf die Welt und vor allem auf die Sprache, die Spontaneität ihrer Handlung, die scheinbar fehlende Kausalität in der Abfolge von Aktionen und Bildern, der unbändige Drang zum Spiel und die jäh einsetzende und jäh abbrechende Traurigkeit sind Elemente, die das Werk Forced Entertainments wesentlich bestimmen.

„Wie die Kinder, wie die Kinder", riefen, so berichtet Andrew Quick, Zuschauer bei einem Theaterfestival in Italien – und Quick zeigt, dass dieser durchaus positiv gemeinte Vergleich auf eine der zentralen Dynamiken in ihrer Arbeit verweist: die Dynamik des Spielens, in der der Herstellung von Regeln und Ordnung stets ihre Vernichtung folgt und der Vernichtung eine neue Regel. Eine Dynamik, die das Subjekt und letztendlich Sinn erst konstituiert.

Das Spiel spielt mit dem Risiko, versucht es zu bannen und fordert es zugleich heraus. ‚Risiko' ist ein zentraler Begriff für Forced Entertainment: Die Forderung an den Spieler, sich selbst einzubringen in die Performance, mit allem, was dazugehört: Immer wieder die gleichen Frage- und Antwortspiele, mit stets wechselnden Kandidaten. Jede Todesszene zweimal, dreimal. Wieder aufstehen, um wieder zu sterben. Immer wieder die Kartons

cause and effect in their behaviour and images, and the sudden onset or interruption of sadness – all find a strong echo in Forced Entertainment's work.

"Like children, like children", commented visitors at an Italian theatre festival, according to Andrew Quick. He shows that this comparison, positive in nature, highlights one of the central dynamics in Forced Entertainment's work: The dynamic of play – in which established rules and order inevitably get destroyed, a process, which in turn, generates a new rule. Both subject and meaning are constituted through this dynamic.

In the game, the players flirt with risk, trying to both avert and confront it at the same time. 'Risk' is a central term for Forced Entertainment:

Challenging the performer to contribute to the performance, with all of its demands – playing the same game of questions and answers again and again, but with constantly changing candidates. Every death scene twice, three times. Rising again only to die again. Piling up cardboard boxes, only to knock them over and start anew once more.

In the long and most extreme Forced Entertainment performances, thresholds are frequently reached, where the material gets very close, maybe too close to the performers themselves. They face conditions involving constant interrogation and continuous improvisation, tackling lists with no end – confessions, street names, types of silence, historical events, questions. After six hours on stage, the actors are clearly exhausted. During text improvisations, it becomes increasingly difficult for them to keep their distance from what is being said, to keep words at a distance. Their admissions, confessions and stories become less filtered as time goes on. They are still mainly fictitious and embellished but their creation, or rather, their discovery and presentation, seem earnest. More earnest and closer to the real person than many 'true' stories. *Not even a game anymore.*

The limits of play are broken or extended in many ways: through direct contact with the audience; through the blurring and ultimate collapse of distinctions between true and false, between fiction and reality; and through the passion for failure and mistakes, which are as essential to Forced Entertainment theatre as they are to Tim Etchells' conceptual universe.

Indeed, this passion led Etchells and Matthew Goulish of the Chicago company Goat Island to found the Institute of Failure, which is introduced by Goulish towards the end of the book. Forced Entertainment also challenge the limits of play by evoking in their work a huge range of events and figures from the world, a

stapeln, um sie erneut umzuwerfen. Aufzählungen ohne Ende, Bekenntnisse, Straßennamen, Arten der Stille, historische Ereignisse, Fragen. Immer wieder werden gerade in den langen und längsten Arbeiten Forced Entertainments Grenzpunkte erreicht, in denen alles sehr nah, vielleicht zu nah an die Darsteller gerät – die ständigen Verhöre, die bis in die fixierten Aufführungen als Motiv sichtbar bleiben, die permanente Improvisation. Denn nach sechs Stunden Dauerpräsenz auf der Bühne sind die Performer merklich erschöpft. Immer schwerer fällt es ihnen, bei den Textimprovisationen Distanz zum Gesagten zu wahren, sich die Worte vom eigenen Leib zu halten. Die Bekenntnisse, Geständnisse und Geschichten werden weniger gefiltert. Noch immer sind sie zum größten Teil erfunden oder ausgeschmückt, doch die Art, wie sie erfunden, besser: gefunden und wie sie präsentiert werden, scheint ernst. Ernster und näher an den Personen vielleicht als manch ,wahre' Geschichte – *not even a game anymore.*

So werden die Grenzen des Spiels im Werk auf vielerlei Weisen gesprengt oder geweitet: Durch die Aufhebung der Barriere zu den Zuschauern, durch die weniger Ununterscheidbarkeit als Unwichtigkeit der Unterscheidung von wahr und falsch, Fiktion und Realität. Durch die Leidenschaft für das Scheitern und den Fehler, die so wesentlich für das Theater Forced Entertainments, aber auch für den gedanklichen Kosmos Tim Etchells sind, dass er mit Matthew Goulish von der Chicagoer Compagnie Goat Island das Institute of Failure gründete, das Goulish gegen Ende des Buches vorstellt. Die Grenzen des Spiels sprengt Forced Entertainment aber auch durch die Welthaltigkeit der Arbeit, die Hans-Thies Lehmann mit der Welthaltigkeit Shakespeares vergleicht: Märchen steht neben Wirklichkeit, Erhabenes neben Trivialem, Tragik neben Komik.

Ein nacktes Pferd, naja: ein nackter Mann mit plüschiger Eselsmaske, ein verkehrter Zentaur, kriecht minutenlang über die schäbige Bühne

Pleasure

… mühsam aufgestützt auf eine Schnaps-flasche, kommt kaum vorwärts … Kampf gegen den Suff, die Müdigkeit, den Tod … Kampf gegen die zur Unkenntlichkeit zer-dehnte, wabernde Musik, die einmal *True Love* von Patsy Cline (oder Elvis) gewesen sein muss … so langsam, als müsste man sie an-schieben, beide, Musik und Esel, doch der kriecht weiter, tapfer, nur ein Ziel vor Augen, ein einziges Ziel, eine letzte Tat … wie der kugeldurchsiebte Sean Connery in *The Un-touchables* sich sterbend durch einen endlosen Korridor zum Telefon schiebt … damit nicht

universality that Hans-Thies Lehmann com-pares with that of Shakespeare. Fairy tales exist next to real stories from the world, the sublime next to trivia, tragedy next to comedy.

A naked horse, or rather, a naked man wearing a plush horse mask, an inverted centaur, spends minutes crawling across a shabby stage … sup-ported haphazardly by a liquor bottle, hardly moving at all … battling intoxication, tiredness, death … struggling against music slowed down to a point beyond recognition, wafting music

Club of No Regrets

that once might have been *True Love* by Patsy Cline (or Elvis) … so slow, one feels the need to push them both ahead – the music and the horse – though the man in the horse costume continues to crawl, bravely, propelled by one aim, a single aim, one last deed … like bullet-riddled Sean Connery in *The Untouchables*, dying, sliding along an endless corridor towards the telephone … so that everything would not be in vain … he crawls, ridiculous, touching, cumbersome. And nobody pays any attention – the others read their manuscripts, write curses on a blackboard, dance as if in a daze. Until after a few minutes, he reaches for the curtain, grasps it, starts pulling it again and again without any help … trying to close the curtain – this shabby,

alles sinnlos war … kriecht er, lächerlich, berührend, mühselig. Und keiner kümmert sich drum, die anderen lesen in ihren Manuskripten, schreiben Flüche auf eine Tafel, tanzen selbstvergessen vor sich hin. Bis er nach Minuten den Vorhang erreicht, ihn greift, zieht und zieht und keiner hilft … diesen Vorhang zu schließen, diesen schäbigen, zerrissenen, schmutzigen Vorhang, diesen Vorhang zu schließen, das ist das ganze Ziel, das einzige Ziel, alles mündet in diesem Ziel. Noch einmal hängt er zwischen den beiden Vorhangteilen, fast hat er es geschafft, fast ist die Musik am Ende … *„on and on it will always be"* …, er versucht, sich aufzurichten, zerrt sich nach oben, ein letztes Aufbäumen, der Vorhang fast geschlossen, die Musik setzt zum letzten, zerdehnten Tusch an – da fällt ein

Schuss. Und das Pferd kippt aus dem Blickfeld. Stille. Zettels Traum ist ausgeträumt. Die Show geht weiter.

Ergäben alle Stücke von Forced Entertainment zusammen ein Haus – so formuliert es Etchells im Programmzettel einer Idee Fassbinders folgend – dann wäre *Pleasure* das Kellergeschoss. Wären die Stücke von Forced Entertainment ein Haus, dann wäre es ein sehr großes inzwischen. Es hätte unordentliche Kinderzimmer wie *Showtime*, protestantisch nüchterne Bekenntnisbüros wie *Speak Bitterness*, Alptraumzimmer wie *Club of No Regrets*, gemütlich unterhaltsame Lounges wie *Thousandth Night*, hohe Aussichtspunkte auf dem Dach wie *Emanuelle Enchanted*. Alle unterschiedlich, alle anderen Ideen, Suchen, Aufgaben, Stimmungen verpflichtet. Und doch alle eindeutig und unverwechselbar: Forced Entertainment.

Es wäre ein merkwürdiges Haus, in dem die Bewohner verzweifelt immer wieder versuchen, gegen das Chaos anzukämpfen, ein ewiger, hoffnungsloser Kampf. Und zugleich ist dieses Chaos der eigentliche Trost in dieser Welt trauriger Hunde, Könige und Clowns, der endlosen Listen, der Verhöre und Wiederholungsschleifen. Denn nur in diesem Chaos kann man die poetischen Momente der Ruhe wirklich verstehen. Dann kommen Götter auf die Erde und für einen Augenblick scheint alles gut. Bis sie im nächsten Moment schon betrunken und grölend durch die Straßen ziehen – kein' Deut besser als die Menschen.

torn, dirty curtain – is his whole aim, his only aim. Everything culminates in this aim. One last time, he hangs between the two sides of the curtain; he has almost made it; the music has almost finished … "on and on it will always be" … he tries to raise himself, pulling himself up; one last stand – the curtain almost closed now; the music's final stretched crescendo – then suddenly, a shot rings out. The horse tumbles out of view. Silence. Bottom's dream is played out. The show goes on.

If all of Forced Entertainment's pieces formed a house, *Pleasure* would be the cellar – suggested Tim Etchells in the show's programme notes, after an idea by Fassbinder. If Forced Entertainment's works were a house, it would by now be quite a large one. It would hold untidy children's rooms like *Showtime*, bare protestant confessional offices like *Speak Bitterness*, nightmarish rooms like *Club of No Regrets*, comfortably entertaining lounges like *And on the Thousandth Night* …, and high vantage points on top of the roof like *Emanuelle Enchanted*. Each room is different, containing different ideas, quests, tasks and atmospheres. They are all, however, unequivocally and distinctly Forced Entertainment.

It would be a strange house, its inhabitants constantly struggling in an endless, desperate fight against chaos. At the same time, chaos is the only true comfort in this world of sad dogs, kings and clowns, this world of endless lists, of interrogation and repetitive loops. It is only in the midst of this chaos that one can understand the moments of poetic calm. Then the Gods come down to Earth and for a moment, all seems well. Until, a moment later, they roam the streets in a drunken, shouting mob – not one bit better than humans.

Translated by Gero Grundmann

Woman	Part two was also their heartache for the city outside. They named it & renamed it every day despite the bitter cold. They called it remarkable city, alphabet city, alphabetti city, New Milan, and the Capital City of Britain.
Man	They sat up some nites & renamed it & their love grew as they named it: the city of spires, the Kentucky Fried City, the City of Elvis King, the exploding city, the city of joy. And while they talked it rained like Ronald MacDonald outside.
Woman	That was the year the jet planes didn't fly anymore.
Man	That was the year they cancelled the Pope of the Year Pope contest.
Woman	That was the year that talks broke down in the Black City.
Man	That was the year that they shut the doors to the Institute of Believing.
Woman	In that year she called him Mr Vector & he called her Karen the Florist.

(Let The Water Run its Course)
to the Sea that Made the Promise

Marina & Lee

The Making of …
From the Beginnings to Hidden J

The Making of …
Von den Anfängen bis zu Hidden J

Patricia Benecke

Es begann weit weg von Sheffield.

It all started far from Sheffield.

Als Studenten trafen Tim Etchells und Richard Lowdon mit Deborah Chadbourn eine Verabredung: Sobald sie ihr Studium an der Universität von Exeter beendet hätten, würden sie in den Norden ziehen, um dort eine eigene Theatergruppe zu gründen. Bei ihren studentischen Arbeiten am Drama Department und einer Reihe halböffentlicher Theaterprojekte unter dem Namen Forced Entertainment lernten sie potentielle Mitstreiter kennen; die kleine Gruppe (mit Etchells und Lowdon als Autoren und Regisseuren, Chadbourn als Managerin) festigte sich und wuchs. Als es dann im Sommer 1984 wie geplant gen Norden ging, zogen Susie Williams, Robin Arthur, Huw Chadbourn und Cathy Naden mit.

Die ersten Arbeiten, vier Theaterabende, die zwischen 1984 und 1986 entstanden, waren allesamt stark vom Kino beeinflusst, dazu kamen die Bild-Dramaturgien und stark repetitiven choreografischen Systeme kontinentaleuropäischer Theatermacher wie Pina Bausch und Jan Fabre, deren Ästhetiken in Großbritannien allerdings gefiltert ankamen, neu gemischt und neu erfunden durch Aneignungsprozesse britischer Gruppen wie Impact Theatre und Hesitate & Demonstrate. Besonders Impact wurde für Forced Entertainment ein wichtiger Einfluss – mit Shows wie *A Place in Europe* und später *Songs of the Claypeople*,

As students, Tim Etchells and Richard Lowdon made an agreement with Deborah Chadbourn that once their courses at the University of Exeter were over they would move north and start a theatre company. Identifying other possible collaborators through their work as students in the Drama Department and through a handful of semi-public projects under the name Forced Entertainment, this small group (with Etchells and Lowdon as writers and directors, Chadbourn as administrator) grew slowly so that by Summer 1984, Susie Williams, Robin Arthur, Huw Chadbourn and Cathy Naden all joined them in travelling north.

The first works of the group – four theatre performances produced between 1984 and 1986 – all drew heavily on cinema, as well as on the kinds of image-based dramaturgy and highly repetitive choreographic systems which had filtered from mainland European practitioners like Pina Bausch and Jan Fabre through a remixing and reinventing process by British groups such as Impact Theatre and Hesitate & Demonstrate. Impact in particular were a big influence – with shows like *A Place in Europe* and later *Songs of the Claypeople*, which utilised electronic soundtracks, complex illusionistic stage designs, filmic

The Making of … / From the Beginnings to *Hidden J*
The Making of … / Von den Anfängen bis zu *Hidden J*
Patricia Benecke

lighting and dramatic structures based on narrative fragmentation.

Each of Forced Entertainment's first four performances based itself in a particular found cultural milieu or cinematic genre – *Jessica in the Room of Lights,* on a cinema usherette's recollected summer coming-of-age; *The Set-up*, on the clichés of gangland interrogation scenes; *Nighthawks* on a woman's journey into a landscape of American Bars; *The Day that Serenity Returned to the Ground* on science fiction scenarios about cosmonauts, accidents in inner and outer space. "It was all, quite deliberately, quoted", says Tim Etchells. "All quite removed from our everyday. The America of *Nighthawks* was a strange mix of Edward Hopper, Tom Waits, William Burroughs and Wim Wender's *Paris, Texas*. None of us had even been there. That didn't matter". What interested the group was finding these landscapes of images and voices, which they could then explore, deconstruct and eventually explode.

In the early pieces, the spectre of naturalism was perhaps never quite as far away as it seemed – *Jessica* included some Pinter-esque 'dialogue' scenes, whilst *Nighthawks* began with a 20 minute sequence of silent realist interactions in its flimsy bar-like set – drinks offered and refused, glasses polished, thrown and caught. A major brake on the naturalism in each of these pieces was the use of voiceover – poetic 'framing texts' as the group termed them: pairs of taped voices which both divided the performances into sections and, at the same time, functioned loosely to lead and mislead the audience in understanding the largely silent events onstage. This concept of frame – a text that guides or influences the perception of the action – is something that has persisted in an evolving form into the company's work more-or-less to date, changing position in the structure of the pieces and exploring new relations to the stage action. Frame

die mit elektronischen Soundtracks, komplexen illusionistischen Bühnenbildern, filmischer Beleuchtung und dramatischen Strukturen auf der Grundlage erzählerischer Fragmentierung arbeiteten.

Die ersten vier Aufführungen von Forced Entertainment beruhten auf bestimmten vorgefundenen Milieus oder Kinogenres: *Jessica in the Room of Lights* auf den Erinnerungen einer Kino-Platzanweiserin an den Sommer ihres Erwachsenwerdens; *The Set-up* auf Verhörklischees im Gangstermilieu; *Nighthawks* auf der Reise einer Frau in die Welt der *american bars*; *The Day that Serenity Returned to the Ground* auf Science-Fiction-Szenarien mit Kosmonauten und Unfällen im Welt- und Seelenraum. „Alles war ganz offensichtlich zitiert", erklärt Tim Etchells, „alles ziemlich weit vom Alltag entfernt. Das Amerika von *Nighthawks* war eine merkwürdige Mischung aus Edward Hopper, Tom Waits, William Burroughs und Wim Wenders' *Paris, Texas*. Keiner von uns war je da gewesen. Aber das war egal." Die Gruppe suchte nach solchen Landschaften aus Bildern und Stimmen, um sie zu erkunden, zu dekonstruieren und schließlich implodieren zu lassen.

Vom Gespenst des Naturalismus war man noch weniger weit entfernt, als es scheinen mochte: *Jessica* beinhaltete einige Pintereske ‚Dialogszenen', während *Nighthawks* mit einer zwanzigminütigen Sequenz stummer, realistischer Interaktionen im fragilen Bar-Bühnenbild beginnt. Getränke werden angeboten und abgelehnt, Gläser poliert, geworfen und aufgefangen. Wichtig für den Bruch mit solchen Naturalismen war der Gebrauch von *voiceovers* – poetischen ‚Rahmentexten', wie die Gruppe sie nannte: ein Stimmenpaar vom Band, das die einzelnen Abschnitte einteilte und zugleich dem Publikum ein wenig beim Verständnis der stummen Ereignisse auf der Bühne half – oder es ihnen schwerer machte. Dieses Konzept der Rahmung – ein Text, der die Wahrnehmung leitet oder beeinflusst – wurde in späteren Arbeiten immer weiter entwickelt und ist bis heute zu finden; wenngleich seine Position innerhalb der Stückstruktur stetig verändert und sein Verhältnis zum Bühnengeschehen neu erkundet wurde. Der Rahmen verschob sich von nicht manipulierbaren, ziemlich autoritären Band-Einspielungen über Video-Dialoge und Live-Monologe bis hin zu den etwas absurden, widersprüchlichen und rivalisierenden Rahmentext-Vorschlägen der isoliert agierenden Performer im Mittelpunkt von *Bloody Mess* (2004).

Die ersten Aufführungen von *Jessica in the Room of Lights* (1984) fanden in einer Kunstgalerie in der Yorkshire Arts Space Society in Sheffield statt, die auch als Probenraum der Gruppe diente. „Der Raum war das Bühnenbild: mit vergilbten Zeitungen überkleisterte Wände. Außerdem gab es Tische, Stühle, eine Menge praktischer Lampen auf der Bühne und einen Schrankkoffer voller Wasser", erzählt Richard Lowdon, Bühnenbildner und Performer. Dieses Projekt war auch der Beginn der langen und fruchtbaren Zusammenarbeit mit dem Komponisten John Avery. „John kam zu den Proben", erinnert sich Robin Arthur, „und wir machten lauter merkwürdige Sachen – wir spielten wie verrückt mit einem alten Kassettenrekorder, der Songs von The Fall oder Elektronisches wie Throbbing Gristle plärrte, und all der Lärm hielt die Energie oben. John blieb völlig cool. Dann sagte er: ‚Ich glaube, damit kann ich was anfangen.'"

Nach *Jessica* gewann die Gruppe in Großbritannien langsam an Profil. Jede Show – es folgten *The Set-up* und *Nighthawks* – tourte etwas länger als ihre Vorgängerin. *The Set-up* wurde für die National Review of Live Art ausgewählt, eine von Nikki Millican betriebene Plattform für junge Künstler, die dazu beitrug, Programmgestalter auf die Arbeit aufmerksam zu machen. „Dass wir Deborah als Vollzeit-Managerin hatten, war sicher entscheidend für die Entwicklung der Dinge", sagt Cathy Naden. „Wir haben alles erst während des Machens herausgefunden: Was es heißt zusammenzuarbeiten. Wie man Dinge organisiert. Wie man probt. Wie man was herstellt. Wie man darüber redet."

has shifted from its rather unassailable authorial position on tape through dialogue on video and monologue from live performers, all the way to the kind of absurd, contradictory and competing proposals for framing texts by the disconnected live performers at the heart of *Bloody Mess* (2004).

The first performances of *Jessica in the Room of Lights* (1984) took place in an art gallery, which also served as the group's rehearsal space, at Yorkshire Arts Space Society in Sheffield. "The room was the set: walls covered in yellowed newspaper. For the rest it was tables, chairs, a lot of practical lamps onstage and a trunk filled with water," says designer and performer Richard Lowdon. The project also began the long and fruitful collaboration with composer John Avery. "John would come to rehearsals and we'd be doing all kinds of strange stuff – going crazy with this old tape-recorder banging out songs by The Fall or electronica like Throbbing Gristle, all this noise to keep the energy up. And John would be completely unphased. 'I think I can do something to go with this' he'd say" remembers Robin Arthur.

From *Jessica* onwards the group's profile in the UK grew slowly with each of the subsequent shows, *The Set-up* and *Nighthawks,* touring slightly more than its predecessor. *The Set-up* was selected for the National Review of Live Art – an emerging artists' platform run by Nikki Millican that helped bring the group's work to the attention of programmers in the field. "Having Deborah as full-time administrator certainly made a big difference to how things progressed", says Cathy Naden. "We were working everything out as we went along. What it meant to work together. How to organise stuff. How to rehearse. How to make anything. How to talk about it". Despite the fact that the UK has precedents of innovative theatre work coming from the regions rather than London (IOU

The Making of … / From the Beginnings to *Hidden J*
The Making of … / Von den Anfängen bis zu *Hidden J*
Patricia Benecke

in Halifax, Impact in Leeds, Welfare State in Ulverston, Cumbria, Birth Gof in Cardiff) Sheffield was still something of a strange location choice for Forced Entertainment. In the early-to-mid 80s it was a depressed, ex-industrial city, still struggling with the effects of Steel Mill closures and the Miners' Strike and facing the slew of social problems that go with high unemployment. "Like many of the northern cities, Sheffield was a focus for resistance to Thatcherism. In the understanding of the time, these were socialist-controlled cities in a country that was going further and further to the right. It was an interesting location. What made it work perhaps was the way that a creative community flourished in the city – music, performance, filmmaking. People used to joke that the 'dole' (social security) was the biggest funder of the arts in Britain at that time. It was true though" (Etchells).

Although each of the early pieces was created in the spirit of group-made and group-owned work that continues to this day, directing the early performances was a rotating responsibility, with different combinations of people in charge of particular projects. Often these projects would be co-directed by teams of two to four people – some of whom might also be performing. "I think we were trying to figure out what the best way to do and discuss things might be, what our strengths and weaknesses were, what our real desires were, in terms of the work" (Lowdon). Between *Jessica* and the group's first Arts Council funded work (*Let the Water Run its Course) to the Sea that Made the Promise* in 1986, a number of decisions slowly got made by trial and error. Perhaps the most significant of these was that Tim Etchells would no longer perform and would instead direct all of the pieces, occasionally joined by different members of the group when they felt like doing so.

Beispiele für innovative Theaterarbeit, die nicht aus London, sondern aus der Provinz kam, gab es in Großbritannien durchaus (IOU in Halifax, Impact in Leeds, Welfare State in Ulverston, Cumbria, Birth Gof in Cardiff). Und doch war die Entscheidung der Gruppe für Sheffield als Standort eher verwunderlich: In den frühen und mittleren Achtzigerjahren eine Ex-Industriestadt in der Depression, noch immer dabei, die Auswirkungen der Stahlwerkschließungen und des Minenarbeiter-Streiks zu verarbeiten und konfrontiert mit einem Berg sozialer Probleme infolge hoher Arbeitslosigkeit. „Wie viele Städte im Norden war Sheffield ein Zentrum des Widerstands gegen den Thatcherismus. Nach damaligem Verständnis waren das sozialistisch kontrollierte Städte in einem Land, das ansonsten immer weiter nach rechts driftete. Also: ein interessanter Standort. Vielleicht hat es deshalb funktioniert, weil sich hier eine kreative Gemeinschaft mit Musik, Performance und Film entwickelte. Es kursierte der Witz, dass die Sozialhilfe der größte Förderer von Kunst in Großbritannien war. Aber das stimmte" (Etchells).

Obwohl jedes der frühen Stücke aus dem bis heute spürbaren Geist des Kollektivs entstand, gab es in den frühen Arbeiten bei der Regie ein Rotationsprinzip. Unterschiedliche Konstellationen von Gruppenmitgliedern übernahmen die Verantwortung für einzelne Projekte; oft führten zwei bis vier gemeinsam Regie, manche standen gleichzeitig noch selbst auf der Bühne. „Ich glaube, wir waren dabei, herauszufinden, wie man die Arbeit am besten macht. Und wir diskutierten, was unsere Stärken und unsere Schwächen waren, und was wir wirklich wollten" (Lowdon). In der Zeit zwischen *Jessica* und der ersten vom Arts Council unterstützten Arbeit (*Let the Water Run its Course) to the Sea that Made the Promise* (1986) wurden Entscheidungen oft nach dem Prinzip von *trial and error* getroffen. Die vielleicht bedeutsamste war, dass Tim Etchells nicht mehr spielen, sondern statt dessen bei

Nighthawks | The Set-up
The Day that Serenity Returned to the Ground

(Let the Water Run its Course)
to the Sea that Made the Promise
(Top / oben: rehearsal / Probe)

allen Stücken Regie führen würde. Ab und zu, wenn jemand Lust hatte, gemeinsam mit anderen Mitgliedern der Truppe.

Die großen, gemeinsamen Diskussionen blieben zwar zentraler Pfeiler der Arbeit, wurden aber ergänzt durch Treffen einer kleineren Gruppe um Etchells und Lowdon, die scherzhaft ‚Sub-Club‘ genannt wurde. In gewisser Weise war es die Formalisierung einer ohnehin bestehenden, informellen Struktur, denn Etchells und Lowdon trafen sich jeden Abend in der Kneipe, besprachen die Arbeit des Tages und schmiedeten Pläne für den nächsten. „Manchmal macht eine kleinere Gruppe schnellere Fortschritte – fasst die bisherige Arbeit zusammen, entwickelt neue Vorschläge oder schafft den Durchbruch für weitere Schritte. Es ist einfach eine Frage der Pragmatik. Und was auch immer in diesen kleineren Treffen ‚entschieden‘ wird, muss die Feuerprobe der Probenarbeit und weiterer Diskussionen der ganzen Gruppe bestehen“, erklärt Terry O'Connor, ebenfalls Absolventin des Drama-Kurses an der Exeter University, die 1986 nach ihrem Graduiertenstudium in Leeds für (Let the Water) zur Gruppe stieß.

(Let the Water) war der eigentliche Durchbruch. Der kleine Projektzuschuss des Arts Council ermöglichte zum ersten Mal ein echtes Bühnenbild: eine komplexe Struktur, beeinflusst von Formen und Ästhetik der heruntergekommenen Industriearchitektur Sheffields. Das Bühnenbild, das Lowdon und Huw Chadbourn entwarfen, bestand aus zwei Räumen mit Holzböden, vergitterten Fenstern und einer zentralen Fläche mit Säulen. Es war – wie auch in den folgenden Shows 200% & Bloody Thirsty, Some Confusions in the Law about Love und Marina & Lee – noch deutlich traditioneller als jene späterer Arbeiten und geprägt von den Diskussionen um die gewünschte Ästhetik des Stückes, die in Richard Lowdons Zeichnungen eingeflossen waren. Ansätze einer radikaleren, integraleren und organischeren Herangehensweise an das Bühnenbild waren allerdings bereits vorhanden: Zunehmend wurden Attrappen

As time went on, discussions amongst the whole group – still the mainstay of the process – would be augmented by meetings of a smaller group comprising Etchells, Lowdon and occasional others. This smaller group – known jokingly as 'sub-club' – slightly formalized an existing informal structure, in which Etchells and Lowdon would meet in the pub each night to discuss the work of the day and to make plans for the next. "Sometimes a smaller group of people can make faster progress – summarizing the work to date and making new suggestions or breakthroughs in terms of where to go next. It's just pragmatics. Anything 'decided' in these smaller meetings is always subject to the acid test of rehearsal work and yet more full-group discussions", says Terry O'Connor, another Exeter University Drama graduate who joined the group for (Let the Water) in '86 after finishing her graduate studies in Leeds.

(Let the Water) proved a real breakthrough. The small Arts Council project grant enabled them to build their first substantial set – a complex structure that drew on the forms and aesthetics of Sheffield's run-down industrial architecture. The set, designed by Lowdon and Huw Chadbourn, had two wooden floored rooms, grilled windows and a central area containing vertical pillars. This show, like the subsequent ones 200% & Bloody Thirsty, Some Confusions in the Law about Love and Marina & Lee, was designed in a more traditional way than later works would be – with discussions about the likely form of the piece feeding into Richard Lowdon's drawings and balsa-wood models. However, the seeds of a more radical, integral and organic approach to the design were already in place as early work on the projects increasingly included the construction ("bodging together", as Lowdon jokingly calls it) of actual size mock-ups of potential spaces, using found materials. "We knew that, in one sense, you only

The Making of … / From the Beginnings to *Hidden J*
The Making of … / Von den Anfängen bis zu *Hidden J*
Patricia Benecke

really begin to understand the meaning of a space once you're standing in it", says Lowdon. "A couple of times on these shows around that time we built stuff and then had the experience of thinking 'Oh my God. What is this thing? What can you do in it?'". As time went on, the group began to think of set design more and more as a kind of writing – inventing possibilities for the work by constructing environments in which they would operate.

(Let the Water) was also a breakthrough in terms of its content. "It was the first time we tackled urban experience and got into the whole industrial wasteland thing" (Naden). *(Let the Water)* was a sort of Northern English *Bonnie & Clyde* with less narrative than Forced Entertainment's earlier pieces. Etchells' disjointed and fragmentary framing text – once more from a tape recorder – describes a mythical couple's life, their relationship and death in the city, and attempts – of course in vain – to comprehend the city by giving it names: Kentucky Fried City, Fuck City, Shit City. In the performance, two women and two men (performers Arthur, Lowdon, Naden and Williams, who was later replaced by Terry O'Connor), dressed identically in second hand-clothes and sporting barbaric haircuts, play out numerous variations of their lives – including their own deaths, grievings and multiple identities – in an exaggerated physical style. At this point the group were still uncertain how to employ live, spoken text onstage without falling into naturalism. The solution, for *(Let the Water)*, was an invented nonsense language; wailings, cryings, mutterings, whisperings, and physical and aural gestures to convey a variety of emotions. In the rehearsal process for *(Let the Water)* the company first developed methods which have since become indispensable to them: a loose and sustained use of improvisation, and an open, 'see-what-comes' attitude to generating material. As a

möglicher Räume in Originalgröße aus vorgefundenem Material konstruiert (oder, wie Lowdon es nannte, „zusammengebastelt"). „Uns war klar, dass man in gewisser Weise die Bedeutung eines Raumes erst dann zu verstehen beginnt, wenn man in ihm steht", sagt Lowdon. „Es passierte in den Shows dieser Zeit einige Male, dass wir Sachen bauten und dann dachten: ‚Oh, mein Gott, was ist das? Was kann man darin machen?'" Nach und nach begann die Gruppe, die Entwicklung des Bühnenbilds als eine Art des Schreibens zu begreifen – als Entwicklung eines Möglichkeitsraumes für die Arbeit.

Auch inhaltlich wurde *(Let the Water)* zum Durchbruch. „Es war das erste Mal, dass wir uns mit der urbanen Lebenswelt auseinander setzten und in diese Industriewüsten-Kiste hineingerieten" (Naden). *(Let the Water)* war eine Art nordenglisches *Bonnie & Clyde* mit weniger narrativen Passagen als in den früheren Stücken. Etchells fragmentarischer Rahmentext – wieder vom Band – beschreibt das Leben eines mythischen Paares, seine Beziehung und seinen Tod in der Stadt, sowie die – natürlich erfolglosen – Versuche, diese Stadt zu verstehen, indem man sie benennt: Kentucky Fried City, Fuck City, Shit City. Zwei Frauen und zwei Männer (Arthur, Lowdon, Naden und Williams, die später durch Terry O'Connor ersetzt wurde) spielen in identischen Secondhand-Kleidern, mit schauerlichen Frisuren und übertriebener Körperlichkeit unzählige Variationen ihres Lebens durch – inklusive ihres eigenen Todes, ihrer Beerdigung und multipler Identitäten.

Noch immer herrschte in der Gruppe Unsicherheit, wie man Text live auf der Bühne sprechen konnte ohne in Naturalismus zu verfallen. Die Lösung für *(Let the Water)* bestand in einer erfundenen Nonsense-Sprache: mit Heulen, Schreien, Nuscheln, Flüstern und Gesten ließ sich eine Bandbreite von Emotionen ausdrücken. Im Probenprozess wurden Methoden erforscht, die seither unverzichtbar geworden sind: Improvisation und eine offene ‚Schaun wir mal'-Haltung bei der

Entwicklung des Materials, was dazu führte, dass die stilisierten und systematisch repetitiven Choreografien der vorangegangenen Arbeiten (*Jessica, The Set-up, Nighthawks, Serenity*) von rauer und roher Körperlichkeit abgelöst wurden. Die Strukturen wurden nun um die Energien und spielerischen Interaktionen zwischen den Performern herumgebaut.

In *(Let the Water)* entwickelte die Gruppe auch ihr spezifisches Verständnis von den Bedingungen von Performance. Vor allem konzentrierten sie sich auf das Verhältnis von Performern, die offensichtlich spielten, und Performern, die gerade nur zusahen oder von einer Aufgabe zur nächsten wechselten. Diese zwei Arten der Anwesenheit auf der Bühne nannten sie ,being on' und ,being off' und begannen, die Beziehung zwischen ihnen zu erkunden. So entstanden in *(Let the Water)* und nachfolgenden Projekten Passagen mit schnellen Wechseln zwischen übertriebenem Spielen bzw. Darstellen und bloßem Ruhen bzw. Zusehen. Spielerisch bewegten sie sich innerhalb von Sekunden von einem Zustand zum anderen. „Auf der selben Bühne sind zwei ,Ebenen' von Performance oder Präsenz sichtbar. Interessant daran ist, dass man so das ,Machen' der Performance und die Menschen, die sie machen, ebenso zum Gegenstand der Arbeit erklärt, wie ihren vermeintlichen Gehalt. Irgendwie wurde so der ganze Repräsentationsstil der Arbeit freigesetzt – weil jetzt der Stil selbst zur Diskussion stand" (Etchells). In enger Verbindung mit dem Konzept von ,on' und ,off' (einer Terminologie, die teilweise von Anthony Howells *The Elements of Performance Art* und den Schriften Richard Schechners und Michael Kirbys geborgt war) steht die Idee der ,performance arena' – einem Teil der Bühne, der als Ort des bewussten ,Zeigens' markiert wird, während der Bereich um oder hinter ihm (der dem Blick des Publikums offen steht, in dem die Performer aber nicht mehr ,im Dienst' sind) als menschlich und verletzlich ausgewiesen ist. In *(Let the Water)* wurden die beiden identischen Zimmer auf beiden Seiten der Bühne

result of this way of working the stylized and systematic repetitive choreographies of the previous works (*Jessica, The Set-Up, Nighthawks, Serenity*) were superseded by a rougher and more ragged physicality, and by structures built around the vital force of live, competitive, and playful performer interaction.

(Let the Water) also saw the group developing its own particular understanding of the performance situation. In particular they focused on the relationship between those performers engaged in overtly theatrical activity and those still on-stage, but simply watching or moving between tasks. Terming these two modes of being on-stage being 'on' and being 'off', they started to explore the relation between the two. *(Let the Water)* and subsequent projects included sections in which performers switched rapidly from exaggerated playing or enacting to simply resting and watching – moving back and forth between the two states, playfully, in the space of a few seconds. "This way of thinking deals with the fact that two 'levels' of performance or presence are visible on the same stage. What's interesting is that it allows the 'doing' of the performance and the people doing it to be subjects in the work, just as much as the putative content. Somehow the whole representational style of the work was freed up – because now the style itself was under discussion" (Etchells). Linked to 'on' and 'off' (terminology borrowed in part from Anthony Howell's *The Elements of Performance Art*, as well as from writings by Richard Schechner and Michael Kirby) was the idea of the 'performance arena' – a part of the stage designated as the place where something is consciously 'shown', and the area surrounding or backing it, which is still open and available to the public's gaze but in which performers are designated as off duty; human and vulnerable. In *(Let the Water)* the two identical room spaces on either side of the stage became the 'on' areas

Poland-tour / Polen-Tournee (1989)

zu *on*-Gebieten – also Arenen für die Aktionen der Performer – während der Zentralbereich mit den Säulen *off*-Gebiet war, von dem aus sie einander zusahen und kommentierten. Die Strategie der Teilung des Bühnenraums prägte die Struktur auch vieler späterer Shows: Immer wieder anders und neu erfunden, floss die Unterscheidung zwischen *on* und *off*, zwischen *performance arena* und Ruhebereich, ein in so unterschiedliche Projekte wie *Emanuelle Enchanted, Pleasure* und *And on the Thousandth Night* …

(Let the Water) stellte für die Gruppe einen Wendepunkt dar. Neben positiven Kritiken brachte das Stück eine erste große Tour durch Großbritannien sowie Einladungen ins Ausland. Doch unmittelbar darauf folgte eine Zeit der Veränderungen und der Verunsicherung: „Die unmittelbaren Genre-Dekonstruktionen, mit denen wir vor *(Let the Water)* gearbeitet hatten, waren eindeutig an ihr Ende gekommen. Aber der Weg nach vorne war nicht klar" (Etchells). Damals trennte sich der Performer Huw Chadbourn von der Gruppe, um eigene Projekte zu verfolgen. Die nachfolgende Produktion, *200% & Bloody Thirsty*, verursachte in den kommenden sechs Monaten so große Probleme, dass die Gruppe sich schließlich entschloss, eine bereits gebuchte Tour abzusagen und sich mehr Zeit zu nehmen. Diese Entscheidung kostete das Vertrauen einiger Förderer, aber dank der erklärenden Worte von Managerin Deborah Chadbourn respektierten viele die Entscheidung, mit einer Arbeit unter Niveau nicht auf Tournee zu gehen. In der Zeit zwischen der ersten, gescheiterten und der zweiten, dann doch fertig gestellten Version von *200%* verließ auch die Performerin Susie Williams die Gruppe. „Mit dem ersten *200%* gerieten wir ziemlich in Verwirrung. Wir suchten etwas und konnten es nicht definieren. Der ganze Prozess war sehr chaotisch" (Etchells). Nicht gerade hilfreich war da, dass der ursprüngliche Bühnenbildentwurf – eine hölzerne, zweietagige ‚Haus'-Struktur, die so groß war, dass sie kaum in den Probenraum in einer alten Fabrik

– arenas for enactments by the performers – whilst the central area with pillars became the 'off' area from which they'd watch each other, looking on with encouragement or laughter. This strategy of dividing stage space, in altered forms, would help structure many of the shows after this one, with the distinction between 'on' and 'off', between performance arena and 'rest area' reconfigured and reinvented to suit projects as diverse as *Emanuelle Enchanted, Pleasure* and *And on the Thousandth Night* …

The reception of *(Let the Water)* was a watershed for the group. The piece garnered favourable reviews and the first big tour in the UK as well as invitations to perform abroad. But afterwards there was a period of upheaval and uncertainty. "The straightforward genre deconstructions of the shows we'd made before *(Let the Water)* were clearly at an end but the route forwards wasn't clear" (Etchells). At this point performer Huw Chadbourn left to pursue his own projects. In the following six months, the next Forced Entertainment piece, *200% & Bloody Thirsty* hit such severe problems in rehearsal that eventually the group decided to cancel a tour that was booked, giving themselves more time to develop the project. The cancellation lost them the confidence of some promoters, but thanks to the calming efforts of administrator Deborah Chadbourn, many others respected the group's decision not to tour sub-standard work. In the break between the failed version of the performance and the second, completed version, performer Susie Williams also left the group. "We got very confused with the first *200%*. We were looking for something and we couldn't define it. The whole process was very chaotic" (Etchells). Things weren't helped by the fact that the initial set design for the piece – a wooden 'house' structure on two levels that was so big it barely fit inside the group's old factory rehearsal space – proved almost entirely unworkable. "It was

The Making of … / From the Beginnings to *Hidden J*
The Making of … / Von den Anfängen bis zu *Hidden J*
Patricia Benecke

pretty well the last time we built a set straight from a design model. Since then I think everything we've done has been mocked-up first using stuff to hand in the rehearsal room. These days, the design emerges much more as a part of the process" (Lowdon).

In 1987, Forced Entertainment saw the American artists The Wooster Group for the first time as they presented *L.S.D. (Just the High Points)*, part three of *The Road to Immortality* trilogy, which included a high-speed rewritten version of Arthur Miller's *The Crucible*. "We were excited by the work because it came from such a different aesthetic and formal place compared to so much of the work from Europe and UK that we'd been influenced by directly or from a distance" (Etchells). There was a boldness to the Wooster Group's style – they addressed the audience directly at times, even explaining the structure of the performance. "It wasn't as shrouded in atmosphere as the stuff we were used to watching" (O'Connor). The encounter with the Wooster Group coincided with a slow realization by Forced Entertainment that with *(Let the Water)* their own work had stumbled into territory that they could really call their own. If performances by their early influence Impact had been connected deeply to cinema then their own work from *(Let the Water)* on was plugged more significantly into the contemporary landscape of urban Britain and, surprisingly, into television – the medium of sets that wobble, of unconvincing fictions and channel hopping.

The completed version of *200% & Bloody Thirsty* (1988) featured framing texts from two video-angels on monitors hung above the stage. This was the company's first use of video, beginning a line of works that would explore its use in performance (from *200%* through *Some Confusions, Marina & Lee*, ending with the use of live-camera in *Emanuelle Enchanted* in 1992).

passte – sich als fast völlig unbrauchbar erwies. „Es war so ziemlich das letzte Mal, dass wir ein Bühnenbild direkt nach dem Modell gebaut haben. Seither haben wir, glaube ich, alles immer zuerst mit Sachen, die im Probenraum herumlagen, als Attrappe konstruiert. Heute entstehen die Bühnenbilder viel mehr als Teil des gesamten Prozesses" (Lowdon).

1987 sah Forced Entertainment zum ersten Mal die amerikanische Wooster Group mit ihrer Aufführung von *L.S.D. (Just the High Points)*, dem dritten Teil der *The Road to Immortality*-Trilogie mit ihrer Hochgeschwindigkeitsversion von Arthur Millers *Hexenjagd*. „Diese Arbeit fanden wir ziemlich aufregend, denn sie kam von einem völlig anderen ästhetischen und formalen Ort als die meisten Arbeiten aus Europa und Großbritannien, von denen wir direkt oder aus der Entfernung beeinflusst waren" (Etchells). Der Stil der Wooster Group hatte eine gewisse Kühnheit: Die Performer wendeten sich direkt ans Publikum und erklärten gelegentlich sogar die Struktur des Abends. „Das Ganze hüllte sich nicht so sehr in Atmosphäre wie die Sachen, die wir sonst sahen" (O'Connor).

Die Begegnung mit der Wooster Group traf zusammen mit der langsam dämmernden Einsicht, dass Forced Entertainment mit *(Let the Water)* in ein Gebiet vorgestoßen war, das wirklich ihr eigenes war. Während die Performances von Impact, die sie früher beeinflusst hatten, tief mit dem Kino verbunden waren, bezog sich ihre eigene Arbeit von *(Let the Water)* an vor allem auf die zeitgenössische Landschaft des urbanen Großbritannien und, überraschenderweise, auf das Fernsehen – das Medium flackernder Geräte, wenig überzeugender Fiktionen und des Zappens zwischen den Kanälen.

Die schließlich fertiggestellte Version von *200% & Bloody Thirsty* (1988) war gerahmt von Texten zweier Videoengel auf über der Bühne schwebenden Monitoren. Es war das erste Mal, dass die Gruppe Video benutzte und

200% & Bloody Thirsty

zugleich der Anfang einer ganzen Reihe von Arbeiten, die sich mit seinem Einsatz auseinander setzten (von *200%* über *Some Confusions, Marina & Lee* bis schließlich zur Verwendung der Live-Kamera in *Emanuelle Enchanted*).

Die Engel in *200% & Bloody Thirsty* wurden von Laien gespielt: Mark Etchells (Tims Bruder) und Sarah Singleton, eine Freundin der Gruppe, wurden, ausgestattet mit Blech-Heiligenscheinen, vor einem gemalten blauen Himmel aufgenommen. Melancholische Figuren, die in gedämpft poetischem Ton darüber reden, wie sie die Welt da unten retten und zu einem besseren Ort machen würden. Das zweigeschossige Holzhaus der gescheiterten ersten Fassung war unter dem Kitsch-Himmel der Monitore durch das rostige Metall-Skelett eines Hauses ersetzt worden, umgeben von toten Bäumen. „Das erste Haus war ein Image – das Bild eines Hauses. Das zweite Haus war ein Raum – etwas, das man besetzen konnte" (Lowdon). Und die erste einer langen Reihe hausartiger Konstruktionen, die in den Produktionen von 1987 bis 1991 die Bühnenmitte einnahmen. „Von diesem Zeitpunkt an waren es solche Häuser, die viele der Shows definierten – von dem Metallrahmen-Haus in *200%* über jenes in *Marina & Lee* und die flüchtigen Holzhäuser und -räume in *Emanuelle, Club of No Regrets* und *Hidden J* bis hin zum bemalten Kinderspielhaus in *Showtime*" (Lowdon).

In *200 %* war der ganze Boden übersät von Secondhand-Klamotten. Eine wilde, betrunkene Party am Anfang (die später in *Hidden J* zitiert wurde) gab mit ihrem Sturm von Geschrei und Bierwerfen den Ton für das lärmende, energiegeladene und komische Bühnengeschehen vor. „Es war reine Energie. Wir wollten nicht, dass die Leute fragen: ,Worum geht es?', sondern einfach: ,Was sehe ich?'" (Cathy Naden).

Der Fortschritt, den Forced Entertainment mit *(Let the Water)* und *200%* machte, blieb nicht unbemerkt. Obwohl sie sich nie als Teil

The angels in *200% & Bloody Thirsty* were played by non-actors – Mark Etchells (Tim's brother) and Sarah Singleton, a friend of the company – shot on video against painted blue skies, wearing tin-foil halos. In muted poetical conversation, these melancholic figures revealed how they wished to save the world down below and make the earth a better place. Beneath the kitsch-heaven of the monitors the two-story wooden house of the failed first incarnation of the piece was replaced with a skeletal rusted-metal house surrounded by dead trees. "The first house was an image – a picture of a house. The second house was a space – something you could occupy" (Lowdon). And it was the first in a long line of house-like constructions that would sit centre stage in Forced Entertainment productions from 1987 to 1991. "These houses were the defining objects in many of the shows from this point on – from the metal frame house of *200%*, to that in *Marina & Lee*, to the flimsy wooden houses and rooms made from basic theatre 'flats' in *Emanuelle, Club of No Regrets* and *Hidden J* right through to the painted kids' play house we used in *Showtime*" (Lowdon).

In *200%*, the floor throughout the space was strewn with second-hand clothes. The performance began with a wild, drunken party – later cited in *Hidden J* – a storm of yelling and beer throwing that set the tone for the raucous, energetic and comical action of the piece. "It was all energy. We didn't want people to ask 'What is it about?', but simply 'What do I see?'", says Cathy Naden.

The progress that Forced Entertainment made in *(Let the Water)* and *200%* did not go unnoticed. Though they would never really feel like part of Britain's mainstream theatre scene, their reception in certain parts of the theatre community, from this point on, was enthusiastic. *200%* went on a reasonable British tour, followed

The Making of … / From the Beginnings to *Hidden J*
The Making of … / Von den Anfängen bis zu *Hidden J*
Patricia Benecke

by European invitations from Belgium and Poland. The itinerant life that would come to dominate their work had begun and the next few shows only confirmed the pattern – bringing bigger tours and more foreign invitations.

After *200% & Bloody Thirsty*, the group's work moved further and further away from the single-genre deconstructions that had characterized the early performances and deeper into a territory identified by layering, juxtaposition and collage. In different ways, each of the subsequent performances (*Some Confusions in the Law about Love, Marina & Lee, Emanuelle Enchanted, Club of No Regrets,* and *Hidden J*) mixed texts and images drawn in reference to, or quoted directly from, different narrative worlds. For *Some Confusions* (1989) – which included two additional performers, Claire Marshall and Fred McVittie – the group mixed material from séances with Elvis Presley and 16TH Century Japanese Love Suicide plays. For *Marina & Lee* (1991) they made a complex mélange of raucous mock-opera, kung fu fights, Westerns and other elements, presided over by the melancholic displaced figure of Claire Marshall's Marina. For *Emanuelle Enchanted* (1992), they mixed the desperate poetical last broadcasts of an imaginary TV newsroom (the texts played directly to camera) with characters (described on cardboard signs) from TV, movies, urban myths and history. For the brutal and spectacular *Club* (1993), Tim Etchells condensed fragments of dialogue from diverse bad movies and television series into archetypal clichés, which were then announced by the heroine of the performance (and demented on-stage director) Helen X (Terry O'Connor). For *Hidden J* (1994), they collided the story of a drunken wedding in northern England with the shards of stories from Europe and Africa.

Each of these five shows were jagged, unsettling and comical at the same time, and denser

des britischen Theatermainstreams empfanden, war die Reaktion auf ihre Arbeit in manchen Teilen der Szene von diesem Punkt an geradezu enthusiastisch. *200%* ging auf eine beachtliche Tour durch Großbritannien, es folgten Einladungen aus Belgien und Polen. Das nomadische Leben, das ihre Arbeit künftig prägte, nahm seinen Anfang: die nächsten Shows bestätigten das Muster, brachten größere Tourneen und weitere Einladungen aus dem Ausland.

Zunehmend entfernte man sich jetzt von den Genre-Dekonstruktionen, die frühere Performances charakterisiert hatten, und wagte sich immer weiter auf ein Gebiet der Schichtungen, Nebeneinanderstellungen und Collagen. Auf je eigene Weise mischten die folgenden Produktionen (*Some Confusions in the Law about Love, Marina & Lee, Emanuelle Enchanted, Club of No Regrets* und *Hidden J*) Texte und Bilder, die sich auf unterschiedliche Erzählwelten bezogen oder sie zitierten. Für *Some Confusions* (1989) – an dem zwei zusätzliche Performer, Claire Marshall und Fred McVittie beteiligt waren – mischte die Gruppe Berichte von Séancen mit Elvis Presley und japanische Liebes-Selbstmord-Stücke aus dem 16. Jahrhundert. Für *Marina & Lee* (1991) entwarfen sie eine komplexe Melange aus rauer Pseudo-Oper, Kung Fu-Kämpfen, Western und anderen Elementen – überwacht von Claire Marshall als melancholischer, heimatloser Marina. Für *Emanuelle Enchanted* (1992) mischten sie die (in die Kamera gesprochenen) verzweifelten, poetischen letzten Nachrichten eines imaginären Fernsehstudios mit (durch Pappschilder skizzierten) Charakteren aus Fernsehen, Geschichte und städtischen Mythen. Für den brutalen und spektakulären *Club* (1993) verdichtete Etchells Dialogfragmente aus verschiedenen schlechten Kinofilmen und Fernsehserien zu archetypischen Klischees, die von der Heldin des Stücks (und schwachsinnigen Regisseurin auf der Bühne) Helen X (Terry O'Connor) angesagt wurden. Für *Hidden J* (1994) ließen sie die Geschichte einer betrunkenen Hochzeit in Nordengland mit

Bruchstücken von Geschichten aus Europa und Afrika kollidieren.

Diese fünf Shows waren schroff, beunruhigend und komisch zugleich, waren dichter als frühere Arbeiten und rückten die Bemühungen von Performern (und Zuschauern), aus den überfordernden, intertextuellen Räumen einen Sinn zu machen, in den Vordergrund. Zunehmende Improvisationen, die weiterhin enge Zusammenarbeit mit dem Komponisten John Avery und der forcierte Umgang mit Bühnentext prägten die Arbeit. Das besoffene Geschrei und die grammatikalisch desorganisierten Texte in *200% & Bloody Thirsty* (bereits einen Schritt näher am Livetext als der reine Nonsense in *(Let the Water)*) machten schließlich in *Some Confusions* einem komplexen, vielschichtigen Skript mit Interviews, narrativen Monologen und dramatischen Dialogen Platz, das die Arbeit gelegentlich auf die früheren Auseinandersetzungen mit dem Realismus zurückwarf. Die Reaktion auf solche Diskussionen führte in der nächsten Show, *Marina & Lee*, wieder zu einfacheren Textformen: trocken-komischen Monologen von Marshall (zu diesem Zeitpunkt bereits ein Vollmitglied der Truppe) als Marina sowie Unterhaltungen zwischen ihr (live auf der Bühne) und Richard Lowdon (auf Video). Daneben wurschtelten sich die übrigen Performer durch hektische und unverbundene, filmartige Dialoge und eine Reihe von Bühnengeständnissen (wie sie später *Speak Bitterness* füllten): Unter hellweißem Licht zogen sich die Performer bis auf die Unterwäsche aus und wandten sich ohne den ‚Schutz' ihrer absurden, notdürftigen Kostüme an das Publikum. Die Entscheidung, das umständliche theatralische Sammelsurium von Perücken, falschen Brüsten, grellen Secondhand-Kleidern, falschem Blut und gespensterhaftem Puder aufzugeben, das die Ästhetik der Truppe in den Arbeiten zwischen 1987 und 1991 oft zu uniformieren schien, war eine weitere Folge der *on/off*-Unterscheidung, die mit *(Let the Water)* begonnen hatte. Ohne Kostüme und in direkter Ansprache ans

than the previous work. What came to the fore were the attempts of the performers (and watchers) to make sense of these stressful intertextual spaces. The working processes for these shows involved increasing amounts of improvisation, continued close work with composer John Avery, and a dogged pursuit of using spoken text from the stage. The drunken yelling and grammatically disorganized live texts in *200% & Bloody Thirsty* (already one step closer to live text than the pure nonsense talk of *(Let the Water)*) eventually gave way, in *Some Confusions*, to a complex multi-layered script involving interviews, narrational monologues and dramatic dialogues, a form which at times threw the work back towards its early struggle with realism. In reaction, the next show, *Marina & Lee*, opted for simpler text forms – deadpan monologues from Marshall (by this point a full member of the company) as Marina as well as conversations between her (live on stage) and Richard Lowdon (pre-recorded on video). Alongside these texts the rest of the performers made their way through hectic and disconnected movie-like dialogues and a sequence of onstage confessions to the audience. The confessions (direct forbears to those which would later make-up *Speak Bitterness*) were performed under bright white light. To deliver these texts the performers stripped down to their underwear, addressing the audience without the 'shield' of variously absurd and provisional costumes that they wore in the rest of performance. The decision to abandon the clumsy theatrical repertoire of wigs, fake breasts, gaudy second-hand clothes, fake blood and ghostly talcum-powder that oftentimes seemed like the uniform of the company's aesthetic in the works between 1987 and 1991 was a further articulation of the on-off distinction that they had begun in *(Let the Water)*. Without the costumes, and addressing the public directly, the performers were present and vulnerable in a way that they had never really been before.

Both *Emanuelle Enchanted* and *Club of No Regrets* were milestone projects for the group and were key in establishing some of their most fundamental approaches to theatrical language. For its part, *Emanuelle* further developed Lowdon's stage-on-a-stage design first used in *Some Confusions*. For years after *Emanuelle*'s wooden floor, translucent curtain and crude wooden proscenium, there would be a procession of stages-on-stages as the group seriously undertook the task of "raising the performance itself to the level of a subject" (Etchells). *Emanuelle* also fully established the group's work with cardboard signs (begun discretely in *Marina & Lee*) and substantially developed an approach to dramaturgy that the group had long called "attempt structure". "In dramatic theatre you get the plot. A story unfolds. That's the drama. In our work from this time the drama was about the telling of the story – the struggle to articulate, the attempt to get it right …" (O'Connor). *Emanuelle*'s protagonists attempted to tell the story of one particular night of crisis and change, their struggle to tell or inhabit the story formed the drama of the piece.

In *Club* Etchells' bad movie scenes were given titles to emphasise their clichéd status – "A Just as They're About to Kiss the Telephone Rings Scene", "A Look How I Am Crying Scene" or "A Drug Trip Scene". The attempt to make sense of these fragments was organized on stage by Terry O'Connor's Helen X, a woman lost between worlds, reinventing her own story as a dark fairy tale whilst directing an increasingly frantic arrangement of the scenes, hell-bent on wringing sense from them. In the tiny box-set, a room of chalk-scrawled blackboards that sits centre of a bare stage, two confused and unwilling actors (Marshall and Arthur) are taped to

Publikum waren die Performer auf eine Weise präsent und verletzlich, die sie zuvor nicht kannten.

Sowohl *Emanuelle Enchanted* wie auch *Club of No Regrets* waren Meilensteine für die Gruppe und Schlüsselwerke beim Etablieren einiger grundlegender Methoden ihrer dramatischen Sprache. *Emanuelle* bedeutete auch eine Weiterentwicklung der ‚Bühne auf der Bühne‘, die, von Lowdon entworfen, erstmals in *Some Confusions* auftauchte. In den Jahren nach *Emanuelles* Holzboden, den durchscheinenden Vorhängen und dem rohen hölzernen Proszenium gab es eine Reihe solcher Bühnen auf der Bühne – sichtbare Manifestation des Versuchs, „die Performance selbst zum Gegenstand zu machen" (Etchells). *Emanuelle* perfektionierte auch die Arbeit mit Pappschildern (die diskret in *Marina & Lee* begonnen hatte) und entwickelte substanziell eine dramaturgische Herangehensweise, die von der Gruppe lange als „Versuchsstruktur" bezeichnet wurde. „Im dramatischen Theater bekommst du den Plot. Eine Geschichte entwickelt sich. Das ist Drama. In unserer Arbeit damals drehte sich das Drama um das Erzählen der Geschichte – das Ringen um Artikulation, der Versuch, es richtig hinzukriegen" (O'Connor). *Emanuelles* Protagonisten versuchen, die Geschichte einer Nacht der Krise und der Veränderung zu schildern – und ihr Kampf darum, diese Geschichte erzählen oder sich zu eigen machen zu können, wurde zum Drama des Stückes.

In *Club* erhielten Etchells' missratene Filmszenen Titel, die ihre Klischeehaftigkeit unterstrichen – „Eine ‚Gerade als sie sich küssen wollen, klingelt das Telefon‘-Szene", „Eine ‚Schau wie ich weine‘-Szene" oder „Eine Drogentrip-Szene". Im Mittelpunkt Terry O'Connor als zwischen den Welten verlorene Helen X, die ihre eigene Geschichte als dunkles Märchen neu erfindet, während sie als Regisseurin einer zunehmend hektischen Szenenfolge auf Teufel komm raus versucht, einen Sinn in das Geschehen zu bringen. In dem winzigen, kistenartigen Bühnenraum aus kreidebekritzelten Tafeln sind zwei verwirrte und widerwillige Schauspieler (Marshall und Arthur) mit Klebeband an ihre Stühle gefesselt und werden von einem Paar unfähiger Bühnenarbeiter/Geiselnehmer (Lowdon und Naden) brutal misshandelt und mit Spielzeugpistolen gezwungen, Helens Anweisungen zu folgen. „Man sieht andauernd das Bild und seine Konstruktion: Robin voll Blut und Richard mit der Sprühpistole, wie er ständig das Zeug auf ihn spritzt; Terry im Zentrum einer riesigen Rauchwolke und mich im Hintergrund, wie ich mit Puder diesen Effekt erzeuge", sagt Cathy Naden. Die Mischung aus Bild und Konstruktion, Schauspielern und Bühnenarbeitern, *on* und

their chairs and brutalised by a pair of incompetent stage hands/hostage-takers (Lowdon and Naden) who coerce them with toy guns to act out Helen's directions. "You constantly see the image and its construction: Robin covered in blood and Richard with the spray-gun just squirting the stuff at him; Terry at the centre of a huge plume of smoke and me in the background chucking talcum powder to create the effect", says Cathy Naden. The mix of image and construction, actors and stage hands, 'on' and 'off', effect and labour to produce it was by now a trademark of the company, and in *Club* it was deployed with maximum chaos and physical violence.

45

The Making of … / From the Beginnings to *Hidden J*
The Making of … / Von den Anfängen bis zu *Hidden J*
Patricia Benecke

Over the years Etchells' poetical texts for the performances became both more complex and more concentrated. Most of the text forms that have sustained Forced Entertainment's work to this moment – lists, questions and answers, fragmentary dialogues – were developed extensively with and for the group in this period. But at the same time, the emphasis was increasingly on simple texts and on text forms that leant themselves to speaking. From *Hidden J* through *Speak Bitterness*, *Showtime* and beyond the group pursued this direction, with improvisation as an increasingly important means either to generate new text or to add to, rewrite, remix or render 'speakable' texts that Etchells had written. "We became less interested in the idea of writing as a separate function – more interested in the kind of 'writing' that one does either improvising or in condensing or ripping off stuff that's already written. Written texts were often thrown into the mix, but at least from *Hidden J* onwards, people were reading them in different sequences during improvs or cutting backwards and forwards between texts they had in rehearsal, just trying to find combinations or juxtapositions of stuff that worked" (Etchells). Just as design had become an organic part of the process, so writing too became an activity that happened at the same time and in the same room as everything else. "Writing could mean sitting at the computer and working alone, but it could also mean improvising with the group, or it could mean my passing a note with a few lines on it to someone on-stage, it could mean editing transcripts of rehearsals from videotape. Writing wasn't precious in a lot of the pieces after *Hidden J*. It was just something that got done" (Etchells).

In 1994, *Hidden J* reached similar extremes of chaos and violence as its predecessor *Club*, only this time linguistically. The stage was a dimly lit crude steel-pipe construction site with heaps

off, Effekt und Arbeit am Effekt, war inzwischen zum Markenzeichen der Truppe geworden. In *Club* wurde sie mit einem Maximum an Chaos und körperlicher Gewalt genutzt.

Im Lauf der Jahre wurden Etchells' poetische Performancetexte immer komplexer und konzentrierter. Die meisten Formen, die in der Arbeit von Forced Entertainment bis heute prägend geblieben sind (Listen, Fragen und Antworten, fragmentarische Dialoge), wurden in dieser Zeit mit und für die Gruppe entwickelt. Zugleich aber lag der Schwerpunkt zunehmend auf eher simplen Texten und Textformen, die sich zum Sprechen eigneten – eine Richtung, die von *Hidden J* über *Speak Bitterness, Showtime* und darüber hinaus verfolgt wurde. Improvisation wurde zunehmend wichtig, entweder um neuen Text zu generieren oder um Etchells' Texte zu ergänzen, umzuschreiben, neu zu mischen oder ‚sprechbar' zu machen. „Wir interessierten uns immer weniger für das Schreiben als separaten Prozess – und immer mehr für einen Schreibprozess, der sich beim Improvisieren oder beim Kondensieren oder Stehlen ergibt. Dazu kamen häufig geschriebene Texte, aber spätestens seit *Hidden J* wurden sie während der Probenimprovisationen in verschiedenen Reihenfolgen oder mit Sprüngen vor und zurück gelesen, um funktionierende Kombinationen oder Gegenüberstellungen zu finden" (Etchells). Genau wie das Bühnenbild ein organischer Bestandteil des Prozesses geworden war, wurde auch das Schreiben eine Aktivität, die zur gleichen Zeit und im gleichen Raum stattfand wie alles andere. „Schreiben konnte heißen, dass man am Computer saß und allein schrieb, aber es konnte auch heißen, dass man mit der Gruppe improvisierte, oder dass ich jemandem auf der Bühne eine kurze Notiz zuschob oder aber Probenaufzeichnungen vom Videoband abschrieb. Schreiben war in vielen Stücken seit *Hidden J* nichts Wertvolles, es war einfach etwas, das getan wurde" (Etchells).

1994 erreichte *Hidden J* ähnliche Extreme von Chaos und Gewalt wie sein Vorgänger *Club*, nur diesmal rein sprachlich. Die Bühne war eine spärlich beleuchtete Stahlrohrkonstruktion mit Haufen in die Ecke geworfener Kostüme und Kulissen. Zu Beginn klettert Claire Marshall über die Rohre, setzt sich auf einen Stuhl vorne und hängt sich ein Pappschild mit der Aufschrift „LÜGNER" um den Hals. Dieses Schild, ein Verweis ebenso auf die Schilder in *Emanuelle* wie auch auf die öffentlichen Erniedrigungen von Kollaborateuren im Europa der Nachkriegszeit oder während Chinas Kulturrevolution, deutet mögliche Streitigkeiten zwischen den Performern und ihren Geschichten an. Sobald Marshall sitzt, betritt der Rest des Personals die Bühne und beginnt ohne Hast in der Bühnenmitte ein rohes Holzhaus aufzubauen. Die Tatsache, dass ein Publikum zuschaut, scheint ihnen nicht allzu viel auszumachen. Als das Haus fertig ist, katapultiert Lowdons Aufforderung an den Tontechniker hinter der Bühne – „Musik bitte" – die Gruppe mitten in eine wilde Party innerhalb und außerhalb des eben aufgebauten Konstrukts. Es gibt Kämpfe, betrunkene Tränen und dumme Witze – eine Show wie eine Achterbahnfahrt. *Hidden J* brachte die Widersprüche der verschiedenen Erzählstränge an eine Grenze, da jeder der fünf Performer seiner eigenen Geschichte folgte. Doch gerade der Kontrast zwischen den ausgespielten Fragmenten reflektierte poetisch und chaotisch zugleich die Katerstimmung im England der Mit-Neunzigerjahre vor dem Hintergrund der Balkankrise und afrikanischer Bürgerkriegsmassaker (Ruanda). Selten war Forced Entertainment so explizit politisch gewesen.

Zusammen mit der *performance-lecture A Decade of Forced Entertainment* von 1994 war *Hidden J* (das Anleihen bei vielen älteren Shows machte) auch eine Bestandsaufnahme der ersten zehn Jahre. Und es war die letzte Show dieser Art: Die Gruppe fühlte, dass sie mit der Collagetechnik und der Konfrontation unterschiedlicher Materialien an eine Grenze gekommen war. Nun wollte sie neue Strategien suchen.

of costumes and props thrown in the corners. At the start of the performance, Claire Marshall clambers over the pipes, sits down on a chair at the front and puts a cardboard sign round her neck bearing the word "LIAR". This sign, a reference to those used in *Emanuelle*, as well as to the public humiliations of collaborators in post-Nazi Europe or during China's Cultural Revolution, indicates the possible discrepancies between the performers and their stories. Once Marshall is seated, the rest of the cast enter and in not-too-hurried a fashion proceed to build the crude wooden house that will stand centre stage. The fact that an audience are watching doesn't seem to bother them too much. With the house completed, a request from Lowdon to the offstage sound operator for "music please" throws the group into a wild party enactment that weaves in and out of the structure they have built. There are fights, drunken tears and dumb jokes and the rollercoaster of the show begins. *Hidden J* pushed the divergence of narrative strains to the limit, with each of the five performers following their own story. Nevertheless, the resulting contrast of played-out fragments reflected the hung-over mood of England in the mid-'90s in a poetic-chaotic way, with the Balkan crisis and massacres in African civil-wars (Rwanda) as a background. Forced Entertainment had rarely been so explicitly political. Together with their 1994 performance-lecture entitled *A Decade of Forced Entertainment, Hidden J*, which borrows from many of the old shows, was a stock-take of their first ten years. It was also the last show of its kind. The group felt that they had taken the collage and collision of material to its limit and were eager to develop new strategies.

Translated by Benjamin Marius Schmidt

Richard	Ladies and gentlemen, the place is, er, here and the time is late and I have six questions in a sealed envelope. Terry, are you ready to answer the questions?
Terry	Yes.
Richard	Have you ever been to earth?
Terry	Yes.
Richard	What was it like?
Terry	It was noisy.
Richard	And what's the best thing that can happen to a person on earth?
Terry	They could fall in love, or they could find a lot of money, in a bag, or they could find something they were happy with.
Richard	And what's the worst thing that can happen to somebody on earth?
Terry	People die.
Richard	What's the most worst thing that happened to you on earth?
Terry	I lost control over my bladder at a birthday party ... and then I fainted and then I had to be taken home wearing someone else's knickers ...
Richard	Terry, are you OK?
Terry	I'm alright.

Pleasure

Bloody Mess

Always Under Investigation
From Speak Bitterness *to* Bloody Mess

Immer unter Beobachtung
Von Speak Bitterness *bis* Bloody Mess

Judith Helmer

Auf das älteste und einfachste Grundprinzip des Theaters – ein Schauspieler vor einem Publikum – kann man nicht unbedarft zurückgreifen, nicht ohne die Komplexität dessen zu begreifen, was wir meinen könnten, wenn wir sagen ‚Schauspieler' und ‚vor'.

Tim Etchells

To fall back on theatre's oldest and simplest arrangement – an actor in front of an audience – is not something one can do lightly, not something one can do without understanding the complexities of what we mean when we say 'actor' and what we mean when we say 'in front of'.

Tim Etchells

Mitte der 90er Jahre, nach einer Dekade intensiver Theaterarbeit, begann Forced Entertainment die Bühne explizit zur Versuchsanordnung für die Bedingungen des Theaters selbst zu machen. Man etablierte Strategien, Tricks und Regeln, nur um genau diese dann zu brechen, zu parodieren oder zum Scheitern zu bringen. Aufführungen dauerten nun bis zu vierundzwanzig Stunden, bestanden aus nichts als unzähligen Beichten oder wurden zu überdimensionalen Quizshows. In Videos von Tim Etchells vergaßen die Schauspieler ihren Text, und bei den CD-ROMs, die in Zusammenarbeit mit Hugo Glendinning entstanden, musste sich der Betrachter die Bilder selbst zu Geschichten zusammensetzen. „Wir wussten, dass im Tanz mit und um die Erwartungen, die mit Form und Ort verbunden sind, die Möglichkeit für Bedeutung lag" (Etchells).

Eine der wichtigsten Strategien dieser forcierten Untersuchungen des Theaters aber wurde die Entwicklung der *durational performances*. Die erste, *12 am: Awake & Looking Down* (1993), bestand aus einer einzigen *Emanuelle Enchanted*-Sequenz – gestreckt über elf

Since the mid-1990s, after a decade of intensive theatre work, Forced Entertainment have increasingly turned the stage into an investigative platform for theatre itself. In successive performances, they established strategies, tricks and rules simply to break them, parody them or make them falter. Some of the group's performances began to last for up to twenty-four hours, while others consisted of nothing but innumerable confessions or oversized quiz shows. In the video works of Tim Etchells, actors forgot their lines and in the CD-ROMs that were made in collaboration with Hugo Glendinning, viewers were left to piece together narratives on their own. "We knew that in the dancing with and around the expectations inherent in form and sense of place lay the possibility of meaning" (Etchells).

A key strategy in the company's investigation of theatre has been their development of durational performances. The group's first durational work was *12 am: Awake & Looking Down* in 1993, consisting of a single sequence from *Emanuelle Enchanted* extended for a period of eleven hours. In the piece, the stage is piled high with costumes and cardboard signs – minimal means used by the performers to suggest character after character, figures ranging from ALIEN GIRL to BILLY MAUDLIN and THE GHOST OF A CHILD KILLED ON TUESDAY. "It took us a long time in the rehearsals for *Emanuelle Enchanted* to get the game with the signs as simple as it is", states Claire Marshall. "It was frustrating that you get such a little of it in the show". The idea to play this one game for an extended time only arose later, in response to an invitation to present a new work at the National Review of Live Art, which in 1993 was hosted at the ICA, London. In *12 am: Awake & Looking Down,* Forced Entertainment cut theatre's guiding principles back to the basics and exposed them as an assembly line production of narratives and meanings. At the same time though, this assembly line – and therefore, the performance – still worked, its simplicity and duration becoming its strong points. Having lived and worked together for years, the Forced Entertainment performers' instincts were honed so that they were now able to quickly grasp opportunities and moods as they arose on stage, and then either intensify or counteract them. This dynamism between the actors in real time was the driving force behind the durational performances.

What was truly exciting about the eleven-hour performance full of fast-paced costume changes was the impact it had on the performers themselves. *12 am* and the subsequent durational performances (*Speak Bitterness, Quizoola!, Who Can Sing a Song to Unfrighten Me?* and *And on the Thousandth Night …*) brought a new intensity to the performers' vulnerability. "You are on stage all the time, you do the thing all the time, you get very tired, you get very frustrated in a way with the rules and that makes you do

Stunden. Auf der Bühne haufenweise Kostüme und Pappschilder, mit denen die Performer in schier endlosem Wechsel Minimal-Charaktere von NEUNJÄHRIGER SCHÄFERJUNGE über BILLY MAUDLIN bis GEIST EINES AM DIENSTAG GETÖTETEN MÄDCHENS andeuten. „Wir haben in den Proben zu *Emanuelle Enchanted* ewig gebraucht, um es so einfach hinzubekommen, wie es ist", erinnert sich Claire Marshall. „Es war frustrierend, dass dann so wenig davon in der Show auftauchte." Die Idee, deshalb einfach einmal nur dieses eine Spiel zu spielen, dafür aber sehr sehr lange, entstand dann 1993, als Forced Entertainment vom ICA eingeladen wurde, eine neue Arbeit beim National Review of Live Art in London zu zeigen.

In *12 am: Awake & Looking Down* stutzte Forced Entertainment das Theater auf seine grundlegenden Prinzipien zusammen und stellte es als Fließbandproduktion für Geschichten und Bedeutungen bloß. Und nahm es zugleich fundamental ernst: Weil es funktionierte, so einfach, so lange. Durch das jahrelange enge Zusammenleben und -arbeiten in der gegenseitigen Wahrnehmung geschärft, konnten die Performer die sich im Spiel ergebenden Möglichkeiten und Stimmungen instinktsicher aufgreifen, weitertreiben oder ihnen gegensteuern. Diese Echtzeit-Dynamik zwischen den Spielern war der Motor der *durational performances*.

Das eigentlich Aufregende am elfstündigen Kostümwechsel im Schnelldurchlauf aber war, was mit den Performern selbst passierte. Die *durational performance* (wie später auch *Speak Bitterness, Quizoola!, Who Can Sing a Song to Unfrighten Me?* und *And on the Thousandth Night …*) brachte eine neue Intensität der Verwundbarkeit. „Du stehst durchgehend auf der Bühne, du machst das die ganze Zeit, du wirst sehr müde, dich frustrieren die Regeln irgendwie und genau deshalb stößt du auf andere, interessante Sachen" (Robin Arthur). Nicht von einer durchgehenden Rollendarstellung gedeckt und zudem durch Erschöpfung gezwungen, die Eigendarstellung teilweise aufzugeben, wurden private Momente öffentlich. In Tim Etchells' Essay *On Risk and Investment* heißt es: „Hingabe kommt, wenn wir so komplex und persönlich getroffen sind, dass wir uns jenseits der Rhetorik in Ereignisse begeben." Doch die Performer, die man ausgelaugt und schlecht abgeschminkt nach der Vorstellung beim Bier traf, waren nicht die, die man während der vielen Stunden auf der Bühne kennen zu lernen geglaubt hatte: „Sie hatten einem so oft erzählt, dass sie nicht spielten, dass sie hofften, man hielte es für Realität, wenn sie es doch taten. Sie gaben vor zu lügen und gaukelten Wahrheit vor. Oft täuschten sie auch vor, sie selbst zu sein."

Nach dem wohlgeformten Chaos früherer Shows wie *Hidden J* oder dem *Club of No Regrets* interessierte man sich nun zunehmend für – im Gruppenjargon – *single idea shows*. Das collagierende Zusammentragen von gefundenem und erfundenem Material wurde auf lediglich ein einziges Prinzip, die Handlung auf eine einzige Aktion beschränkt.

In der langen Fassung von *Speak Bitterness* – der folgenden *durational performance* – werden so autobiografische Fiktionen in Serie produziert: Acht Spieler (Sue Marshall, Tim Hall und Tim Etchells, der erstmals wieder selbst auf der Bühne agierte, ergänzten den Performergrundstock) sitzen frontal zum Publikum an einem langen Tisch und verlesen Schuldbekenntnisse aller Art: vom Genozid über Betrug bis zum Schnüffeln in fremden Tagebüchern. Anzüge und Business-Kostüme geben den Performern einen offiziellen Habitus, die Texte werden von Zetteln abgelesen, so bleiben selbst intimste Bekenntnisse auf Distanz zum Sprecher. Es wird offen gelegt und bewusst ausgestellt, dass es sich nur um eine stellvertretende Geste handelt, eine Darstellung, die keine Rolle braucht, die zwischen Text und Performer vermittelt.

Zunächst sei manchem Mitglied der Gruppe die Idee, dem Publikum einfach nur gegenüber zu sitzen und stundenlang etwas vorzulesen, unvorstellbar gewesen, erzählt Claire Marshall. Doch die lange Version von

different, interesting things", says Robin Arthur. The lack of cover, normally provided by role or character in 'regular' theatre shows, and the exhausting nature of the performance deny any form of self-promotion or protection. Private moments are made public, as Etchells says in his essay *On Risk and Investment*: "Investment comes when we're beaten so complex and so personal that we move beyond rhetoric into events". However, the drained performers one met for a drink after the show, some of their makeup still showing, seemed far removed from their image on stage. "They told you so many times they weren't acting that when they did act, they hoped you'd think it real. They pretended to tell lies, they pretended to tell the truth. And often they pretended to be themselves".

Following the well-crafted chaos of earlier shows, such as *Hidden J* or *Club of No Regrets*, now the group's interest shifted to – in their own jargon – "single idea shows". The collage-like assembly of found and invented material was confined to a single principle. The long version of *Speak Bitterness*, for example – next in line of the group's durational works – generated a continuous stream of autobiographical fiction. Eight players (Sue Marshall, Tim Hall and Tim Etchells, who returned to acting with this show, complementing the core group) faced the audience from their seats at a long metal table. Reading out a plethora of confessions, they moved from one guilty secret to another, admitting everything from genocide to fraud and reading other people's diaries. In their suits and business-like dresses, the performers exuded an 'official' air which separated them from the intimate confessions they read from sheets of paper. As the performance progressed, it was absolutely clear that what the audience saw was a representative gesture, a performance that did not need to construct characters in order to mediate between text and performer.

Claire Marshall remembers that initially many members of the group thought that the idea of sitting in front of the audience and reading to them for hours was impossible to imagine. In spite of these doubts, however, the durational version of *Speak Bitterness* at the NRLA in Glasgow was a great success and the shorter theatre version which followed it in 1995 turned out to be Forced Entertainment's great breakthrough. The group was invited to international festivals, such as Munich SpielArt, and Triple X Amsterdam, as well as to major European theatres, such as the Schouwburg in Rotterdam. Many of these visits marked the beginning of long-term collaborations with promoters and curators that have supported the company ever since. Other invitations followed and soon established Forced Entertainment as a key guest at the most renowned theatre festivals and independent venues. In the process, the group had gained an international audience that was keen to follow its development.

The confessions of *Speak Bitterness* (which had been briefly prefigured in the taped text for *(Let the Water Run its Course)* and in live sections of *Marina & Lee*) solidified everyday phenomena as source material for their artistic practice. Confessions of abandon and sins that abound in television talk shows and call-in radio broadcasts, as well as the false admissions of guilt that engulf the police after highly publicised murders or bomb attacks, all highlight society's almost Foucaultian need to confess.

Indeed, public admissions of 'private' inadequacies, weaknesses and mistakes have proved so resonant that they have made frequent reappearances in the work of the group, often functioning as a kind of direct and intimate dialogue with the audience. In a series of soliloquies in the twenty-four hour performance, *Who Can Sing a Song to Unfrighten Me?* (1999), the actors confess their fears of darkness, spiders,

Speak Bitterness wurde beim NRLA in Glasgow zum großen Erfolg, und die kurze Theaterversion, die 1995 folgte, führte zum endgültigen Durchbruch: Internationale Festivals wie SpielArt in München und Triple X Amsterdam sowie große europäische Theater wie die Rotterdamse Schouwburg luden die Sheffielder ein – der Beginn einer oftmals langjährigen Verbundenheit mit Förderern und Kuratoren, die die Gruppe seither unterstützen. Weitere Einladungen und Koproduktionen folgten und Forced Entertainment wurde zum festen Gast der wichtigsten Theaterfestivals und freien Theaterhäuser. Ein internationales Publikum wuchs, das die Entwicklung der Gruppe interessiert mitverfolgte.

Mit den Beichten von *Speak Bitterness* (die bereits kurz als Tonbandtext in *(Let the Water Run its Course)* und in *Marina & Lee* verwendet worden waren) fand, wie so oft bei Forced Entertainment, ein alltägliches Phänomen den Weg in die künstlerische Arbeit. Fernseh-Talkshows und Call-in-Radiosendungen, in denen Leute von ihren Verfehlungen und Sünden erzählen, aber auch das Phänomen, dass die Polizei nach Morden oder Bombenanschlägen von falschen Schuldgeständnissen überhäuft wird, zeugen vom fast foucaultschen Bedürfnis der Gesellschaft, zu beichten.

Öffentliche Geständnisse ‚privater' Unzulänglichkeiten und Schwächen erwiesen sich als so fruchtbar, dass sie seither immer wieder auftauchten, oft als intimer Dialog mit dem Publikum, wie etwa in der 24-Stunden-Performance *Who Can Sing a Song to Unfrighten Me?* (1999): In Solopartien beichten die Spieler ihre Ängste vor Dunkelheit, Spinnen, davor kein guter Ehemann oder Performer zu sein. Solch ein Geständnis kann sehr durchdacht ausfallen, ein Miniatur-Stück mit Spannungsaufbau und wohlgesetzten Pointen. Oder es kann, spät in der Nacht, von einem durch Müdigkeit und Erschöpfung geschwächten Spieler so ehrlich und unvermittelt erscheinen, dass der Zuschauer glaubt, einen Einblick in die Person zu bekommen. „Ich habe das immer

12 am: Awake & Looking Down

sehr spät in der Vorstellung gemacht", berichtet Robin Arthur, „zu dem Zeitpunkt sitzt du nur noch da und sagst, was dir gerade in den Sinn kommt. Normalerweise ist das etwas Wahres, weil es eben einfacher ist, die Wahrheit zu erzählen als sich etwas auszudenken."

Eine sehr spezifische Art des Sprechens bestimmte nach den Beichten von *Speak Bitterness* auch die folgenden *durational performances*. Und wie in *Speak Bitterness* war die Form in *Quizoola!* (1996) einem Fernsehformat entliehen: der Quizshow. Tim Etchells hatte auf die Aufforderung, ein Stück für das Londoner ICA zu schreiben, mit einer langen Liste von Fragen reagiert, aus der später das Frage- und Antwort-Spiel *Quizoola!* entwickelt wurde. Immer wieder driftet innerhalb der sechsstündigen Aufführung das lustvolleifrige Quizshow-Imitat in Richtung Verhör,

of not being a good husband or a good performer. These confessions can, on the one hand, appear to be intricately crafted and, like miniature plays, contain tension and well-placed turning points. Performed late at night by a tired actor weakened by exhaustion, however, these improvised texts can also appear honest and immediate enough for the audience to believe that they have gained insight into a real person. "I've always done the fears list very late in the show", says Robin Arthur, "and at that point you just sit there and say the first things that come to your mind, which are true usually, because it's easier to tell the truth than to make up fiction".

Following the confessions of *Speak Bitterness* specific forms of speech also governed

56

Always Under Investigation / From Speak Bitterness to Bloody Mess
Immer unter Beobachtung / Von Speak Bitterness bis Bloody Mess
Judith Helmer

subsequent durational performances. Like *Speak Bitterness, Quizoola!* was also based on a television format, that of the quiz show. Tim Etchells had been asked to write a piece for the ICA in London. He responded to the request with a long list of questions which was later developed into the question and answer game *Quizoola!* (1996). Throughout the six-hour performance, the flamboyantly intense quiz show repeatedly drifts off into an interrogation of the contestant, or switches to jovial banter, or acquires the atmosphere of a show trial. In *Quizoola!* there is no differentiation between questions that test knowledge, vocabulary tests and probing or invasive questions – instead, the interaction between the two performers is as diverse in the scope of questions as it is in spontaneous answers. Truth and lies are indistinguishable.

Forced Entertainment had discovered the potential of the quiz show format some time before, in their regular theatre work, as they were drawn to and interested in the ambiguity of mixing truth and fiction that's created by the game of questions and answers. Says Etchells: "We like the layers that questions open up – how you're never quite sure, as a watcher, if the answers are from performer or 'character'; how you can't be sure of the truth or the reality of the answers". The group had used this kind of structure before in *200% & Bloody Thirsty* and *Club of No Regrets*. More significantly perhaps, the conceptual map that the group had drawn of its work and its country in *A Decade of Forced Entertainment* featured questions from a decade of 'end-of-the-year quizzes'. In this performance, Richard Lowdon interviews Terry O'Connor about the group's work, an activity which rapidly turns into an aggressive investigation. Lowdon subjects O'Connor to a sadistic quiz again during *Pleasure* (1998). Dressed only in her underwear, O'Connor stands centre stage in front of the curtain, from where she has to answer

peinliche Vorführung des Befragten oder in die Atmosphäre eines Schauprozesses. Wissensfragen, Vokabeltest und Bohren in der Privatsphäre – das Spektrum der Fragen im Spiel der zwei Performer ist so weit wie das der spontanen Antworten: ununterscheidbar ob wahr oder gelogen.

Die populäre Spielform Quiz hatte Forced Entertainment schon früher für sich entdeckt, angezogen von der mehrdeutigen Mischung aus Wahrheit und Fiktion dieses Frage- und Antwortspiels. Etchells: „Wir mögen die Schichten, die durch Fragen freigelegt werden – dass du als Zuschauer nie wissen kannst, ob die Antworten von dem Performer oder von seiner Rolle stammen; dass nie sicher ist, ob die Antworten wahr, ob sie echt sind." Schon in *200% & Bloody Thirsty* und in *Club of No Regrets* finden sich solche Rhetoriken. Und bezeichnenderweise gehören zu dem Szenario, das die Gruppe in *A Decade of Forced Entertainment* von ihrem Land und ihrer Arbeit entwarf, Fragen aus einem Jahrzehnt von ‚end-of-the-year quizzes'. Darin führt Richard Lowdon mit Terry O'Connor ein Interview über die Arbeit der Gruppe, das schnell zur aggressiven Investigation wird, und auch in *Pleasure* (1998) unterzieht Lowdon O'Connor einem sadistischen Quiz: Nur mit Unterwäsche bekleidet, steht sie in der Mitte der Bühne vor dem Vorhang und muss Fragen nach der peinlichsten bis zur angenehmsten Situation ihres Lebens beantworten. Schließlich kommt es zur „Goldenen Frage": „Warum ist das moderne Leben Schrott?" Ein Glas Whiskey auf dem Kopf balancierend denkt O'Connor lange und angestrengt nach und bleibt die Antwort doch schuldig. Lowdon gibt eine Version des Willhelm Tell und schießt mit verbundenen Augen auf O'Connor, die tot zu Boden sinkt. Was als harmlose Unterhaltung begann, führt zum ultimativen Ende von Spiel: dem Spiel, tot zu sein.

Die stundenlangen Spiele nach einfachsten Regeln beeinflussten so auch die durchinsze-

nierten, mit einer Spieldauer von rund ein-
einhalb Stunden ‚kurzen' Theaterstücke dieser Periode. Und es gab Mischformen, wie das
1999 entstandene, vierundzwanzig Stunden
dauernde *Who Can Sing a Song to Unfrighten
Me?*, wo sich inszenierte und choreografierte
Szenen abwechseln mit simplen Spielen, von
denen eines wiederum selbst so interessant war,
dass es zu einer eigenen *durational performance* wurde: *And on the Thousandth Night
…* (2000), ein Marathon angefangener und
abgebrochener Geschichten.

Hatte Forced Entertainment jahrelang
mit fünf Performern gearbeitet, so änderte
sich das nach *Showtime* (1996) und *Pleasure*
(1997). In der nächsten Performance, *Dirty
Work* (1998), standen nur noch Robin Arthur,
Claire Marshall und Cathy Naden auf der
Bühne, dafür waren bei *Who Can Sing a Song
to Unfrighten Me?* gleich vierzehn Performer
beteiligt. Seither hatte jedes Stück eine unterschiedliche Performer-Konstellation. Feste
Mitglieder der Gruppe ließen Projekte aus,
und neue Gäste kamen für einzelne Arbeiten
dazu. „Diese Veränderungen entstanden aus
einer Mischung von pragmatischen und
künstlerischen Gründen", erklärt Tim Etchells.
„Wir wollten mal größere und mal kleinere
Arbeiten machen. In anderen Fällen brauch-
ten Leute Raum für andere Dinge – Privatleben, andere Projekte oder für Kinder. Wenn
man mit langem Atem überstehen möchte,
muss man flexibel sein." Seit 2001 entwickelte
Tim Etchells gleich mehrere eigene Solostücke
wie die kurzen Arbeiten *Down Time, Starfucker* oder die abendfüllende *performance
lecture Instructions for Forgetting.*

Diese Veränderungen in Größe und
Form der Gruppe entsprangen nicht nur dem
Bedürfnis nach künstlerischer Neuorientie-
rung, weg von der Anlage ‚Fünf Leute in einer
Black Box', sondern auch einem grundsätz-
lich veränderten Arbeitsprozess gegenüber
den früheren Jahren. Verbrachte die Gruppe
anfangs buchstäblich Tag und Nacht gemeinsam, Freizeit und Arbeit kaum unterscheid-
bar, zog man nach ein paar Jahren wieder aus

questions that include everything from the most
embarrassing situation in her life to the most
pleasurable one. Then she is hit with the "gold-
en question": "Why is modern life rubbish?"
O'Connor thinks long and hard about this but
does not answer, all the while balancing a glass
of whiskey on her head. Lowdon in turn shoots
at her – he is blindfolded, his William Tell-like
act causing her to sink to the ground as if dead.
What begins as harmless entertainment leads
to the ultimate end of play – death on stage.

The long performances constructed around
simple rules also influenced the well-structured
'short' performances (lasting roughly an hour
and a half) that the company continued to make
in this period. They also made shows such as
Who Can Sing a Song to Unfrighten Me? in 1999
which lasted twenty-four hours. This piece is a
kind of a hybrid between the two different strands
of Forced Entertainment shows in the sense that
it moves between directed and choreographed
scenes and others of simple play. One improvised section from this show was deemed so
interesting that it became a durational performance in its own right – *And on the Thousandth Night …* (2000), strucured as a marathon
sequence of initiated and interrupted narratives.

The phase of working with the fixed cast
of five performers was brought to a close following *Showtime* (1996) and *Pleasure* (1997). The
cast of the next performance, *Dirty Work* (1998),
consisted only of Robin Arthur, Claire Marshall
and Cathy Naden, while *Who Can Sing a Song
to Unfrighten Me?* assembled fourteen actors on
stage. From this point on, each performance has
had a different configuration of performers, with
members of the core company skipping projects
and new guests joining in for particular crea-
tions. "The changes have come about through
a combination of pragmatics and artistic desires",
says Tim Etchells. "Sometimes we wanted to do

Always Under Investigation / From *Speak Bitterness* to *Bloody Mess*
Immer unter Beobachtung / Von *Speak Bitterness* bis *Bloody Mess*
Judith Helmer

58

larger or smaller works at particular times. In other cases, people needed space for other things – private lives, other work projects or kids". Starting in 2001, Etchells himself created a number of solo performances – short works such as *Down Time* and *Starfucker* and a full-length performance lecture *Instructions for Forgetting*.

What these changes in the size and shape of the group reflect are its practical needs as well as its desire to find new creative perspectives. The change is not simply about an end to Forced Entertainment's established model of 'five people in a black box studio', but arises instead from the evolution of a fundamentally different work process. In the early years, the group had been literally inseparable, spending night and day in an indistinguishable mix of work and play. But after a few years, the members of the company have abandoned the two houses in which they had all lived together and rediscovered a sense of privacy. "We got easier on ourselves", as Claire Marshall puts it. "We don't have to be in the studio all the time". Tim Etchells' son Miles was the first baby born into the company. "That was in 1992. And suddenly we discovered weekends". Equally remarkable as the *work* of Forced Entertainment is the fact that the core group has stayed together for such a long time. The stability of the core group highlights their empathic social interaction and their ability to accommodate each other's diverse needs.

Extended touring commitments of Great Britain and Continental Europe brought with them the desire and need for more technical and administrative support. In 1996, Deborah Chadbourn moved from her position as Administrator to the newly created role of General Manager and was joined in the Forced Entertainment office by new Administrator, Verity Leigh. By the time Deborah left the company in 1999, the office also included a Production Manager, soon to

den zwei gemeinsam gemieteten Häusern aus. Und es gab wieder mehr Privatleben: „Wir haben uns das Leben etwas einfacher gemacht," erzählt Claire Marshall. „Wir müssen nicht mehr die ganze Zeit im Studio sein." Das erste Baby der Company war Tim Etchells Sohn Miles. „Das war 1992. Und plötzlich entdeckten wir, dass es Wochenenden gibt." So bemerkenswert wie die Arbeit von Forced Entertainment ist auch die Tatsache, dass die Kerngruppe über eine so lange Zeit hinweg zusammen geblieben ist. Die Stabilität des Gruppenkerns zeigt, dass der Umang miteinander sensibel genug ist, um unterschiedlichste Bedürfnisse zu akzeptieren.

Mit ausgedehnten Touren innerhalb Großbritanniens und dann – zunächst ausnahmsweise – auch durch Kontinentaleuropa wuchs das Bedürfnis nach technischer und administrativer Unterstützung. 1996 wechselte Deborah Chadbourn von ihrer Position als Administratorin zu der neu geschaffenen Stelle der Geschäftsführerin, unterstützt von Verity Leigh, die ihre alte Stelle übernahm. Als Chadbourn im Jahr 1999 die Gruppe verließ, wurde zusätzlich ein Produktionsmanager angestellt, bald unterstützt von einer Marketing-Chefin und

einem Bildungsbeauftragten: Ein Team von vier Leuten als Forced Entertainment-Management und -Unterstützung. Seit 1993 betreibt die Kompanie ein eigenes Probenstudio mit Büroräumen in der UNIT 102 im Sheffield's Cultural Industries Quarter, der Work Station – einem Ort, an dem ihre Arbeiten entstehen und zuweilen auch gezeigt werden.

Auch die Probenphasen veränderten sich, um den Veränderungen im Privat- und Arbeitsleben der Kompaniemitglieder gerecht zu werden. Manche nahmen sich eine Auszeit um Kinder zu bekommen, alle sind inzwischen auch in andere künstlerische Projekte involviert. Richard Lowdon entwirft Bühnenbilder für Ensemble wie das Vincent Dance Theatre, Cathy Naden schreibt Drehbücher und Robin Arthur geht in Deutschland, wo er derzeit lebt, eigenen Theaterprojekten nach. Vor allem aber ist Tim Etchells mit seinen Essays, Erzählungen und Vorträgen in der Öffentlichkeit als Einzelperson und ‚Kopf' von Forced Entertainment immer sichtbarer geworden. Unter solchen Umständen muss die Probenzeit gut planbar sein – auch für hinzukommende Gäste. *First Night* gibt dafür ein gutes Beispiel: Erst wurde in vier Arbeitsperioden von vier bis sechs Wochen in Sheffield geprobt, dann das Ergebnis – als *work in progress* – einem kleinen Publikum präsentiert. Nach einigen Monaten Unterbrechung wurden die Proben dann bis zur Premiere in Rotterdam wieder aufgenommen.

Ab den frühen 90er Jahren etablierte sich das lose Schema, neben ‚großen', neuen Stücken für Tourneen auch kleinere, nicht unbedingt bühnentaugliche Projekte zu entwickeln. Mehrere Galerie-Installationen, wie *Ground Plans for Paradise* (1994) mit Hugo Glendinning oder die ortspezifische Arbeit in einer Bibliothek, *Dreams' Winter* (1994), entstanden. Eine Drei-Jahres-Förderung durch das Art Council gab den nötigen Planungsspielraum für neue Arbeiten, beispielsweise eine Bustour durch das nächtliche Sheffield und später durch Rotterdam (*Nights in this*

be joined by a Marketing Administrator and an Education Officer, bringing the group's full-time management and support team to a total of four people. Since 1993, Forced Entertainment have run their own rehearsal studio in UNIT 102 in The Workstation building, part of the Sheffield's Cultural Industries Quarter – a space in which they have made and, on occasion, presented work.

The logistics surrounding the rehearsal process also changed to accommodate shifts in the personal and work lives of the company members. Some of them took time off to have children and all of them have in the meantime become involved in other projects. Richard Lowdon designs sets for companies such as the Vincent Dance Theatre, Cathy Naden is writing screenplays and Robin Arthur works on his own theatre projects in Germany, where he is currently based. Most prominent however, through his solo works, essays, novels, lectures and collaborations with other artists, Tim Etchells has emerged as the public 'figure head' of Forced Entertainment. With all these diverse commitments of Forced Entertainment members as well as the varying schedules of guest performers, good project management has become essential for rehearsals. *First Night* provides a good case study, being rehearsed in Sheffield during four work periods of four to six weeks each. The project was presented – as work in progress – to a small audience halfway through this process and then rehearsed again for a further period some months later, leading directly to the premiere in Rotterdam.

From the early '90s onwards, a pattern developed in which 'big' touring productions were developed alongside smaller projects not necessarily appropriate for stage performance. The group created several gallery installations, such as *Ground Plans for Paradise* (1994), made in collaboration with Hugo Glendinning (1994) and a site-specific piece for a library *(Dreams' Winter*, also 1994). At this point, a three-year Arts Council grant to the company provided the security to plan ahead for new work, which included nocturnal coach tours of Sheffield and later Rotterdam (*Nights in this City*, 1995 and 1997). This Arts Council grant has been renewed continually since the year 2000.

In addition to installations and site-specific projects, the company – in collaboration with photographer Hugo Glendinning and digital author Mary Agnes Krell – also started experimenting with other media. Leaving the viewer to explore his own narratives by piecing together fragments of fiction was already an important element of Forced Entertainment performances and now, a series of new works on CD-ROM raised this challenge to a new level. *Frozen Palaces* (1997), the group's first CD-ROM, features still images of rooms in a large desolate house. Inside these photographic spaces, a range of events take place – with parties, murders and love scenes enacted in an atmosphere of seemingly frozen time. A similar approach defines *Nightwalks* (1998), in which viewers are invited to navigate a confusing cityscape composed of photographic stills and the play with genre clichés – typical of Forced Entertainment – drives the CD-ROM *Spin* (1999). Forced Entertainment's works on CD-ROM – all marked by an eerie sensation of being awake in a sleeping city – play with well-known elements used in computer games and popular cinema. The medium of the CD-ROM enables the separation of enactment and reception, both in terms of time and sense of place. The viewer is free to explore virtual spaces, without being locked into a predetermined sequence or timescale. In a further exploration of interactive potential, the group's Web-based project, *Paradise* (1998), allows viewers to select one of

City, 1995 und 1997). Seit 2000 wird die Art Council-Förderung regelmäßig verlängert.

Neben den Installationen und ortsspezifischen Projekten begann Forced Entertainment in Zusammenarbeit mit dem Fotografen Hugo Glendinning und Mary Agnes Krell als *digital author* mit anderen Medien zu experimentieren. Den Zuschauer seine eigenen Geschichten aus fiktionalen Fragmenten erkunden zu lassen – was schon in den Theaterarbeiten von Forced Entertainment ein wichtiges Gestaltungsmerkmal war – wurde durch die technische Verfügbarkeit der CD-ROM zu einer besonderen Herausforderung. In ihrer ersten digitalen Arbeit, *Frozen Palaces* (1997), sind es fotografierte Räume eines großen, desolaten Hauses, in denen sich bei scheinbar stehen gebliebener Zeit verschiedene Ereignisse abspielen: Partys, Morde, Liebesszenen. Eine ähnliche Zugangsweise verfolgen auch *Nightwalks* (1998), ein Spaziergang durch eine verwirrende Stadtlandschaft aus Fotostills, und das Forced Entertainment-typische Spiel mit Genre-Klischees in *Spin* (1999). Alle CD-ROMs der Gruppe sind geprägt durch das eigenartig befremdliche Gefühl, in einer schlafenden Stadt als Einziger wach zu sein, und spielen mit altbekannten Versatzstücken aus Computerspielen oder Kinofilmen.

CD-ROMs entkoppeln Orte und Zeiten der Darstellung von denen der Rezeption. Der Betrachter kann frei von vorgegebenen Abläufen virtuelle Räume erkunden, gehalten nur von einer Struktur, die von Forced Entertainment stets so konzipiert ist, dass sie keine einheitliche Narration nahe legt.

Noch stärker auf die Interaktion ausgerichtet ist das Internetprojekt *Paradise* (1998): der Betrachter kann selbst eines von tausend Häusern in einer virtuellen Stadt mit einem eigenen Text besetzen oder einfach durch die Stadt streifen und lesen, was andere vor ihm geschrieben haben.

Zwischen 1997 und 2003 drehte Forced Entertainment eine Reihe von Videos, kurze und lange, darunter etliche Solowerke von Etchells oder Zusammenarbeiten mit dem Fotografen Hugo Glendinning. Nur das erste dieser Projekte, *DIY*, ist relativ unabhängig von der Arbeit auf der Bühne: Eine poetische Reise in das Leben Joe Ortons, umkreist vom Performancekünstler Michael Atavar. Mit *Filthy Words & Phrases* (1998) entstand dagegen eine filmische *durational performance*, die durchaus auch live denkbar wäre: Cathy Naden schreibt – in einer Referenz auf ihre Rolle im Bühnenstück *Pleasure* – sieben Stunden lang auf eine Schultafel obszöne Begriffe, Körperteile oder -funktionen, wobei ihre Stimmung zwischen Faszination, Langeweile und Erschöpfung schwankt. Die von den fünf festen Forced Entertainment-Performern an anonymen Plätzen wie Flughafenhallen oder Hotellobbys vor der Kamera gebeichteten Ängste in der Fünfkanal-Videoinstallation *Hotel Binary* (2000) sind ebenso eindeutig eng verwandt mit dem von der Bühne bekannten Gedankenkosmos und Darstellungsstil der Gruppe.

Auch die Idee einer Inszenierung im Kopf des Zuschauers durch bloßes Erzählen, wie sie *Dirty Work* zugrunde lag, nutzte Etchells 2001 für einen Film: In *Starfucker* tauchen weiße Schriftzüge aus dem schwarzen Hintergrund auf und verschwinden wieder – Slogans ersetzen Bilder, fragmentarische Szenenbeschreibungen zusammenhängende Handlung – und alles wird zusammengehalten durch die Musik John Averys. Im gleichen Jahr entstanden mit *My Eyes Were Like the Stars* und *Kent Beeson Is a Classic & an Absolutely New Thing* zwei Videos von Etchells. Im ersten Fall ist Naden (absichtlich) zu betrunken, um ihren Text zu sprechen, im zweiten Fall ist der Schauspieler Kent Beeson (unabsichtlich) dazu nicht in der Lage, weil er ihn nicht gut genug gelernt hat. In diesen Videos manifestiert sich das Scheitern der Performer durch ihr fortwährendes Kommentieren der eigenen Unfähigkeit, durch ihre Unterbrechungen und verzweifelten Wiederholungen. Die Distanz zwischen dem Sprechenden und seinem Text, das Risiko des

thousands of buildings in a virtual city and then link it to a personal text or simply browse the city in search of the remarks others have left behind.

Between 1997 and 2003, Forced Entertainment also produced a series of works on video – both long and short – many of which were solo projects by Etchells or his collaborations with photographer Hugo Glendinning. Only the first of these projects, a short film titled *DIY* – which is a poetic investigation into the life of Joe Orton, framed by the performance artist Michael Atavar – exists far from the aesthetic and formal concerns established in the group's stage work. In contrast, *Filthy Words & Phrases* (1998) captures a durational performance on video which would work just as successfully as a live show: Referencing her role in the stage work *Pleasure*, performer Cathy Naden spends seven hours writing obscenities on a blackboard – slang descriptions of everything from body parts to sex acts and bodily functions, while her mood oscillates between fascination, boredom and exhaustion. Meanwhile, confessions of personal fears (first seen in *Who Can Sing*) are featured in the five-channel video installation *Hotel Binary* (2000), which records Forced Entertainment's five core performers in anonymous locations, such as airport concourses and hotel lobbies, as they improvise their texts.

In 2001, Etchells utilised the form of the performance *Dirty Work* in his short video *Starfucker*. As was the case in *Dirty Work*, *Starfucker* exists for its viewers simply through narration. Throughout the video, lines of text appear on the screen, fading in and out of black – slogans instead of images, fragmented scenes instead of a continuous plot – all linked by John Avery's score. The same year also brought two videos by Etchells, *My Eyes Were Like the Stars* and *Kent Beeson Is a Classic & an Absolutely New Thing*.

The former features Naden, obviously (and intentionally) so drunk that her attempts to address the camera come to nothing, while in the latter the actor Kent Beeson is (unintentionally) unable to get his lines right due to lack of preparation. The actors' failure to perform manifests itself in both videos as they make comments about their own inability, interrupt their delivery halfway through the line and desperately repeat the same section of text over and over. The distance between narrator and text, the risk of failure when at a decisive moment, exposing the actors in their exhausted state – are all characteristic motifs in Forced Entertainment's work. "They talked about 'trying to get themselves into trouble.' An antidote to the skills and strategies they'd build up, a way of avoiding their own conventions" (*A Decade of Forced Entertainment*).

What really interests the group are concepts, themes, atmospheres and styles of delivery. How those will be produced is only of secondary importance and was a reason why, in the '90s, the group changed its name from the original, Forced Entertainment Theatre Co-Operative, to simply, Forced Entertainment. "We were happier working under the shorter name. We are an ensemble of artists and we do whatever we like. Some of it will be theatre, some of it will be video, Internet, etc. It doesn't matter to us in which of these areas we are working, we just want to make the work" (Etchells).

It is interesting to note, however, that from 1997 onwards, when Etchells and the group began to make their own videos, CD-ROMs and Web-based projects, their references to and stage use of video and other technical equipment started to decline. The earliest works, such as *Jessica in the Room of Lights* (1984), *The Set-up* (1985) or *Nighthawks* (1986) had been heavily influenced by film, with imagery that seemed to pay

Versagens im Moment der Aufführung, die Bloßstellung der Schauspieler in der Erschöpfung – alles Motive, die typisch sind für Forced Entertainment: „Sie sprachen davon ‚sich Ärger zu verschaffen'. Eine Art Gegenmittel zu dem Können und den Strategien, die sie anhäufen, eine Möglichkeit, die eigenen Konventionen zu umgehen" (*A Decade of Forced Entertainment*).

Es sind Themen, Stimmungen, Darstellungsstile und Konzeptionen, die die Gruppe in erster Linie interessieren. In welchem Medium sie umgesetzt werden, ist zweitrangig. Aus diesem Grund hatte man auch in den Neunzigerjahren die Bezeichnung Forced Entertainment Theatre Co-Operative auf Forced Entertainment verkürzt: „Uns war es angenehmer unter dem kürzeren Namen zu arbeiten. Wir sind ein Künstlerensemble, und wir tun, was immer wir wollen. Einiges davon wird Theater sein, anderes Video, Internet usw. Wir wollen einfach nur die Arbeit produzieren, in welchem Bereich wir uns dabei bewegen, ist uns gleich" (Etchells).

Interessant aber ist, dass seit Tim Etchells und die Gruppe ab 1997 begonnen haben, eigene Filme, CD-ROMs und Internetprojekte zu produzieren, die Verwendung von Videos und Technik selbst abzunehmen scheint. Ganz frühe Arbeiten wie *Jessica in the Room of Lights* (1984), *The Set-up* (1985) oder *Nighthawks* (1986) waren stark beeinflusst vom Film, in ihren Bildern fast eine Hommage an ein Genre und/oder eine Dekonstruktion seiner Klischees. Später benutzte man auf der Theaterbühne Mikrofone, Musikanlagen und Videos. Texte wurden von Tonbandstimmen gesprochen oder über Mikrofone verstärkt. Videos verschwanden nicht gänzlich aus den Stücken, aber man setzte sie deutlicher vom Spiel im Hier und Jetzt ab. Spielen etwa die Engel in *200% & Bloody Thirsty* (1987) noch als integraler Teil der Live-Performance mit, flimmern dagegen die Home-Videos in *Disco Relax* (1999) wie Fremdkörper über die Monitore. In seinem Solo *Instructions for Forgetting* (2001) benutzt Etchells Video-Ausschnitte, die

er von Freunden zugeschickt bekommen hatte – offensichtlich *home-movie*-Material, Ausschnitte aus ihrem Leben, Landschaften oder künstlerischer Arbeit – anstelle von extra für die Aufführung aufgenommenen Videos. Indem er sie kommentiert, kennzeichnet er dabei klar ihren Status als Objekte von außerhalb.

Instructions for Forgetting gehört zu jener Linie von Arbeiten, die Etchells „poetische" oder „intime Dokumentation" nennt und die 1994 mit der *performance lecture* *A Decade of Forced Entertainment* begann und über *Instructions* bis zu *The Travels* (2002) mit seinen Beschreibungen von Reisen der Performer zu verschiedenen Orten Großbritanniens führt. In der kurzen, poetisch-dokumentarischen Performance *Down Time* (2001) thematisiert Etchells die verstrichene Zeit zwi-

homage to certain genres and/or that attempted to deconstruct cinematic clichés. Subsequent stage performances (for example *200% & Bloody Thirsty* or *Emanuelle Enchanted*) employed microphones, sound and audiovisual material, whilst texts came from video and pre-recorded tapes. Although in later works video never disappeared completely from the stage, it was now clearly separated from events in the 'here and now' of the performance. So whilst the angels of *200% & Bloody Thirsty* (1987) were still integral to the live performance, the home videos of *Disco Relax* (1999) were reduced to a marginal flickering stage presence. Significantly, Etchells' 2001 solo performance *Instructions for Forgetting* uses video clips donated by friends – home movie documents of their lives, landscapes and art projects – rather than staged and directed videos, made especially for the piece. By commenting on the clips, Etchells highlights their status as objects emanating from elsewhere.

Instructions for Forgetting forms a part of what Etchells has called a strand of poetic or "intimate documentary" in Forced Entertainment's work. Begun in 1994 with the performance lecture *A Decade of Forced Entertainment,* this small track of works runs through *Instructions* to the 2002 production *The Travels,* which comprises accounts of the performers' journeys to various locations throughout the UK. In the short poetic documentary performance and video *Down Time* (2001), Etchells concentrates on a quality which distinguishes theatre from other media – time elapsing between recording and replaying. A mute video screen shows Etchells deep in thought. As the tape plays, he tries to remember his thoughts on the theme of "goodbyes". While real and pre-recorded times collide, thoughts refuse to manifest themselves in speech and at times all attempts at reconstruction fail.

However strong Forced Entertainment's interest in film and video has been, and despite their evocative series of CD-ROMs and installations, the group maintained its strong affinity for established theatre traditions. Their intention not to be confined to a single art form did not change their focus on theatre itself. Time and again, Forced Entertainment constructed stages on stage, complete with heavy red velvet curtains, crude proscenium arches, a scaffolding framework, spotlights, exaggerated costumes and theatrical makeup.

Despite their obsession with the play of proximity and distance between performers and audience, the group almost always worked in the simplest stage arrangement – audience at one end, actors at the other – often with a raise separating the two. In this way, traditional spatial

schen Aufzeichnung und Wiedergabe eines Videos als eine das Theater von den anderen Medien unterscheidende Qualität. Ein Monitor zeigt seinen Kopf, denkend. Live versucht er sich an seine Gedanken zum Thema ‚goodbyes' zu erinnern. Reale und aufgezeichnete Zeit kollidieren, Gedanken verweigern sich der Übersetzung in Sprache und natürlich scheitert der Versuch der Rekonstruktion.

So sehr sich Forced Entertainment für den Film zu interessieren begann, so oft CD-ROMs und Installationen als Medium für das eigene künstlerische Schaffen gewählt wurden, so stark blieb die Affinität zum Theater und seiner Tradition. Schwere rote Samtvorhänge, rahmende Gerüste, Scheinwerfer, Kostüme und Schminke: immer wieder baute Forced Entertainment Bühnen auf der Bühne.

Trotz ihrer Faszination an dem Spiel mit Nähe und Distanz zwischen Performern und Publikum arbeitete die Gruppe immer mit der einfachsten Bühnenanordnung – Publikum auf der einen Seite, Schauspieler auf der anderen – oft durch eine Rampe getrennt. Die traditionelle räumliche Trennung blieb gewahrt und wurde manchmal sogar noch durch parallel zur Rampe aufgestellte Tische, etwa in *Speak Bitterness* und *The Travels* verstärkt. Die Grenze schien zu verleugnen, dass es die Möglichkeit zur Intimität gibt, auch wenn sie sie gerade erlaubte.

Ganz bewusst wollte man den Theaterraum mit all seinen kulturhistorischen Belegungen nicht aufgeben, wie Cathy Naden beschreibt: „Wir wollten das Mainstream-Theater irritieren. Wir wollten genau in diesen Häusern bleiben, um zu zeigen, dass es eine Alternative zu den Arbeiten gibt, die hier normalerweise gezeigt werden." Die jüngeren Arbeiten *First Night* und *Bloody Mess,* mit ihren größeren Ausmaßen, scheinen genau diesen Aspekt zu unterstreichen. Beide sind sie komplexe Untersuchungen des Theaters selbst, seiner Zeit- und Erkenntnisökonomien, seines Publikums und dessen Erwartungen.

» Continued on page 72

» Fortsetzung auf Seite 72

64

Always Under Investigation / From Speak Bitterness to Bloody Mess
Immer unter Beobachtung / Von Speak Bitterness bis Bloody Mess
Judith Helmer

Some Confusions in the Law about Love

Marina & Lee

Emanuelle Enchanted

Club of No Regrets »

opposition was maintained and even enhanced at times – in projects like *Speak Bitterness* and *The Travels* – by tables placed parallel along the edge of the raise, or as a barrier that seemed to deny the possibility of intimacy even as it made it possible. A conscious effort was made to maintain the theatre as a space, together with all its cultural and historical connotations. Cathy Naden explains: "We wanted to infiltrate the mainstream theatres. We wanted to stay in those spaces, saying that there is an alternative to the work that's normally seen there". The recent larger-scale works, *First Night* and *Bloody Mess,* seem especially fixated on this issue, as they both present complex investigations of theatre itself, its temporal and cognitive economies, its audience and their sets of expectations.

Eine Geschichte, die Forced Entertainment immer wieder gebeten wurde zu erzählen, ist ihre eigene. Es ist Teil ihrer Philosophie, über die Arbeit auch zu sprechen. „Wir wollten teilhaben an der Entstehung des Diskurses über unsere Arbeit. Auf allen Ebenen. Wir hatten kein Bedürfnis zu schweigen oder mysteriös zu sein", meint Cathy Naden. „Ein wichtiger Bestandteil unserer Arbeiten war immer, dass Tim über sie schreibt."

Theaterkurse an Universitäten und Schulen gehörten zu den ersten, die sich für einen direkten Einblick in die inneren Arbeitsstrukturen von Forced Entertainment interessierten. Neben Interviews, Artikeln und Tim Etchells' Essayband *Certain Fragments* von

Bloody Mess

1999 gibt die Gruppe in Workshops und Publikumsgesprächen bereitwillig Auskunft über ihre Arbeit. Das National Sound Archiv der British Library in London verfügt seit 1999 über ein Forced Entertainment-Archiv mit Videos nicht nur der fertigen Shows, sondern auch von unzähligen, ungekürzten Probenmitschnitten.

Immer unter Beobachtung ist die Arbeit von Forced Entertainment nicht nur von außen. In ihrem Zentrum untersucht sie – von *Jessica* bis *Bloody Mess* –, was Theater ist. Untersucht, was wahr ist und was Spiel. Untersucht, was die Welt ausmacht, in der wir leben. Untersucht, wer wir selbst sind, wer wir sein wollen und wer wir vorgeben zu sein.

One story Forced Entertainment has been asked to tell many times is its own. Discussing work is part of the group's ethos. "We wanted to play a part in making the discourse around the work. At all levels. There was no desire to be silent or mysterious", says Cathy Naden. "A big part of making the work has always been Tim writing about it". Theatre classes at schools and universities were among the first who wanted to gain direct insight into Forced Entertainment's inner workings. Etchells disseminated numerous vital texts in interviews and articles, as well as a collection of essays, *Certain Fragments: Contemporary Performance and Forced Entertainment,* which he published in 1999. The group is also conducting workshops and public talks in which they speak openly about their work. The British Library in London now holds a Forced Entertainment archive in its National Sound Archive – established in 1999, it includes not only recorded stage performances but also numerous unedited rehearsal videos.

The work of Forced Entertainment is always under investigation – not just from outside. At its core, the group's work – from *Jessica* to *Bloody Mess* – investigates theatre itself, exploring the nature of truth and play. The work probes our world for clues to who we are, who we would like to be and who we pretend to be.

Translated by Gero Grundmann

Is that story too much, Tim?
Or too sad?

I'm happy to try writing again
if you'd like something else ...

Gary Carter writing to Tim Etchells for
Instructions for Forgetting

First Night

As if Things Got More Real
A Conversation with Tim Etchells

Als ob die Dinge wirklicher würden
Ein Gespräch mit Tim Etchells

Adrian Heathfield

ADRIAN HEATHFIELD Wenn ich an die verschiedenen komplexen Verschiebungen denke, die sich im Laufe der letzten 20 Jahre in eurer Arbeit ergeben haben, dann ist eine wichtige Entwicklung eure Beschäftigung mit *durationals*, also mit Werken von langer zeitlicher Dauer. Aber ich frage mich, ob diese Werke nicht auch im Licht der Veränderungen gesehen werden sollten, die in den kürzeren Theaterstücken stattgefunden haben. Bis in die frühen 90er Jahre hinein habt ihr Theaterstücke gemacht, die von der Form her äußerst eklektisch waren. Die Ästhetik beruhte auf dem Zusammenprall verschiedener Genres, Stile und Sprachen. Jetzt scheint es, dass die Theaterarbeit weniger sprunghaft, stärker minimalistisch und elementar geworden ist. Das Interesse an der Wucherung von Bedeutungen und fiktionalen Möglichkeiten ist immer noch groß, aber all das findet innerhalb sehr eng definierter Regeln oder Strukturen statt. *The Voices* zum Beispiel ist im Wesentlichen eine Serie von Monologen: eine sehr sparsame dramatische Struktur. Jeder Text funktioniert durch ein äußerst eingeschränktes Set von Dynamiken, innerhalb derer es eine Art exzessiver Produktion von Ideen gibt.

TIM ETCHELLS Ja, die zweite größere Phase unserer Arbeit, vielleicht von *Marina & Lee* über *Emanuelle Enchanted* bis zu *Club of No Regrets* und *Hidden J,* drehte sich um Collage, um die

ADRIAN HEATHFIELD Thinking of the various complex shifts that have taken place across the body of your work over the last twenty years, one significant development has been the pursuit of long durational works. But I wonder if these works should also be seen in the light of changes taking place in the shorter theatrical pieces. Through the early nineties you were making theatre works that were highly eclectic in form. The aesthetic was based on the clash of different genres, styles and languages. Now it seems that the theatre work has become less jumpy, more minimal and elemental. There is still a strong interest in the proliferation of meaning and fictional possibilities, but this takes place within very tightly defined rules or structures. Take *The Voices*, for instance, which is essentially a series of monologues: a very sparse theatrical structure. Each text works through a highly constrained set of dynamics, within which there is a kind of excessive production of ideas.

TIM ETCHELLS Yes, the second major phase of our work, perhaps from *Marina & Lee* through *Emanuelle Enchanted* to *Club of No Regrets* and *Hidden J,* was centred on collage, on the brutal juxtaposition of images, languages and things. Those shows, which really established our reputation, were structured in a way that owed a lot to the metaphor of TV channel-hopping. Each

As if Things Got More Real / A Conversation with Tim Etchells
Als ob die Dinge wirklicher würden / Ein Gespräch mit Tim Etchells
Adrian Heathfield

of them had many sections, often constructed on different-but-related principles; they used diverse theatrical languages, soundtracks, video on stage, and a lot of imagery, obviously quoted from very different places. In the end I think we tired of this mega-mix method, or reached a limit with it, and in response we became interested in a more focused approach; taking one thing, one language, one element, and then pursuing it to its ultimate end logic. The shift is also about time and depth – we need time to pursue ideas and forms now, to investigate, to get to the bottom of a particular idea. We're not so ready to set something up quickly and then move on.

HEATHFIELD That middle period of your work was very interested in the play of surfaces. I guess the difference, for example, between the use of the cardboard signs and dressing up in *Emanuelle* and the same materials and form in *12 am: Awake & Looking Down*, the durational work, is that where *Emanuelle* says things about naming, dressing, identification, *12 am* engages us with them concretely through a lived performance practice.

ETCHELLS Yes, when you push at an idea for longer – when you live with it – there's a deeper engagement, something that's almost a little beyond the theatre economy. In *First Night* the performers have these fixed showbiz smiles – very painful, very exaggerated – for most of the show. It is not just an image we do for ten minutes. The smile is world, a condition – as performer and as audience you're forced to live in and encounter that world in its depths and contradictions and possibilities.

I guess, as far as structure goes we've always had a suspicion of the 'pull a convenient new trick from the box' approach. Even when we were back in the channel-hopping mode I think we always knew that dramaturgically you have

brutale Gegenüberstellung von Bildern, Sprachen und Dingen. Diese Shows, die eigentlich erst unseren Ruf begründet haben, waren auf eine Weise strukturiert, die stark von der Metapher des Zappens beeinflusst war. Jede von ihnen hatte viele Abschnitte, die oft nach dem Prinzip ,anders, aber verwandt' konstruiert waren. Sie benutzten verschiedene dramatische Sprachen, Soundtracks, Bühnenvideos und eine Menge Bildmaterial, das ganz offensichtlich aus verschiedensten Zusammenhängen zitiert wurde. Letztlich wurden wir dieser Mega-Mix-Methode überdrüssig, glaube ich, oder wir kamen damit an eine Grenze. Und als Reaktion begannen wir, uns für eine fokussiertere Herangehensweise zu interessieren: ein Ding, eine Sprache, ein Element zu nehmen und es bis zur letzten Konsequenz zu verfolgen. Diese Verschiebung hat auch mit Zeit und Tiefe zu tun – wir brauchen jetzt ausreichend Zeit, um Ideen und Formen nachzugehen, um sie zu untersuchen, um einer bestimmten Idee auf den Grund zu gehen. Wir sind jetzt nicht mehr so schnell dazu bereit, etwas auf die Beine zu stellen um dann sofort zu etwas anderem überzugehen.

HEATHFIELD In dieser mittleren Periode eurer Arbeit hattet ihr ein großes Interesse am Spiel der Oberflächen. Ich vermute, der Unterschied beispielsweise zwischen der Verwendung von Pappschildern und Verkleidungen in *Emanuelle* und denselben Materialien und Formen in der durational *12 am: Awake & Looking Down*, besteht darin, dass *Emanuelle* Aussagen über das Benennen, Verkleiden, Identifizieren macht, während *12 am* uns daran konkret durch eine gelebte Performance-Praxis teilhaben lässt.

ETCHELLS Ja. Wenn du eine Idee länger vorantreibst – wenn du mit ihr lebst –, dann entsteht ein stärkeres Engagement, etwas, das fast ein wenig jenseits der Theaterökonomie liegt. In *First Night* behalten die Performer das fixierte Lächeln des Showbiz – sehr schmerzhaft und stark übertrieben – während fast der gesamten Show bei. Es ist nicht nur ein Bild für zehn Minuten. Das Lächeln ist Welt, ist eine Bedingung – als Performer und als Zuschauer bist du gezwungen, in dieser Welt zu leben und dich ihr mit all ihren Tiefen, Widersprüchen und Möglichkeiten zu stellen.

Ich nehme an, was die Struktur angeht, haben wir immer mit dem Verdacht gelebt, einfach ‚einen praktischen neuen Trick aus der Kiste zu ziehen‘. Selbst als wir im Modus des Zappens waren, wussten wir, glaube ich, immer, dass man dramaturgisch gesehen die Dinge von den Argumenten und Systemen her auflösen muss, die man strukturell von Anfang an aufgestellt hat. Ein Werk, das auf Bildern oder Bewegungen beruht, kann nicht in letzter Minute durch eine bewegende Rede einer neuen Person auf der Bühne einfach oder befriedigend ‚gelöst‘ oder abgeschlossen werden … Es handelt sich eher darum, dass wer mit dem Schwert lebt, durch das Schwert umkommen wird. Die Sprache, mit der du anfängst, gewinnt im Laufe des Stückes an Gewicht. Es ist ein Prozess der Investition. Seit einiger Zeit sind wir damit recht strikt geworden – und die Ökonomien der Stücke sind dementsprechend zunehmend singulärer geworden. Es macht das Leben für uns schwerer, und in gewisser Weise macht es das Leben auch für die Zuschauer schwerer.

HEATHFIELD Das ist genau das, was mich interessiert. Was wird durch die Ausdehnung der Zeit, die in den *durationals* stattfindet, gewonnen? Sie sind schwieriger, vermute ich, weil wir an Konventionen des Betrachtens gewöhnt sind, die unser Gefühl für die angemessene Dauer eines Theaterstückes konditionieren. Aber in einem Großteil der *durationals* geht es bei dieser Taktik darum, Zeit selbst zu einem explizit empfundenen Gegenstand der Arbeit zu machen. Als Zuschauer ist man in der Lage, den Einfluss von Zeit zu erfahren, wie sie durch die gezeigten Ideen hindurch wirkt. Zeit wird so in der Relation zwischen Performer und Zuschauer erfahren, und das kann Resonanzen und Einsichten um die Themen Verkörperung, Gedächtnis,

to solve things in terms of the argument and systems that you have proposed structurally from the outset. An image- or movement-based work isn't easily or satisfactorily 'solved' or concluded by the last minute arrival of a moving speech from a new person on stage … It's a question of live by the sword, die by the sword. The language you start with gains weight over the time of the piece. It's a process of investment. We've become quite strict about this in recent times – and the economies of the pieces have consequently become increasingly singular. It makes life harder for us, and in some ways it makes life harder for the audience as well.

HEATHFIELD It's the hardness that interests me. What is it that is given by the extension of time that takes place in the durational work? They are harder, I guess, because we are used to conventions of spectatorship that condition our sense of an appropriate time for a theatre work. But also like much durational work this tactic is about making time itself an explicitly felt subject in the work. As a viewer you are able to experience the affect of time as it works through the presented ideas. So time becomes felt in relation, between the performer and the viewer, and that can bring with it resonances and realisations around embodiment, memory, mortality, loss, failure that are difficult to access and comprehend.

ETCHELLS I don't know. I think people initially resist if you offer them a pared down vocabulary/economy. They think, "Oh please, give me something new!" but at a certain point, if you're clever inside the boundaries you create, I think the audience really come with you – the watcher accepts and understands the limit and starts to work inside it, too.

I think there's a sense also in which the longer pieces are easier in fact rather than harder. And

As if Things Got More Real / A Conversation with Tim Etchells
Als ob die Dinge wirklicher würden / Ein Gespräch mit Tim Etchells
Adrian Heathfield

that's connected to dramaturgy, too. Theatre forces one to deal with the ergonomic shape of an hour and a half – the pattern of 'start', 'middle' and 'end' that produces a satisfactory feeling of closure. But in the longer works we're freed, to some extent, from the tyranny of this economy. Things can be what they are. Climaxes don't have to be produced, resolutions are not needed. It is what it is. The pushing to the limit frees one as a maker and also as a watcher.

HEATHFIELD Alongside the testing of ideas by pushing them to their limit, there is also often a test of the performer's physical and psychological limits. The durational works are very exposing for the performers; they place them under sustained scrutiny, and they can be physically exhausting, taxing the performer's memory, focus, ability to stay live and connected.

ETCHELLS The durational pieces demand a very different job from 'acting'. Most of our theatre shows are pretty well scored by the time we come to do them in public. We are really aware that we are running a machine; however loose and imagistic and playful it is, it is still a machine: In an hour and forty minutes it takes the audience on a certain kind of journey. It has an architecture, and as a performer you are ultimately a servant of that architecture. Whereas in the long pieces it is much more open to your live, arbitrary, whimsical, or perverse choices. It is certainly open to your mood. In fact the long pieces demand that you contribute now, live, fast, as a maker, of decisions and of moments, in a way that the theatre work, once it is touring, doesn't.

HEATHFIELD However open, these works display a very coherent sensibility, which is purchased through twenty years of improvising together. The performers have a rich history and a shared vocabulary.

Sterblichkeit, Verlust und Scheitern mit sich bringen, die schwer zugänglich und schwer verständlich sind.

ETCHELLS Ich weiß nicht. Ich glaube, die Leute haben einen anfänglichen Widerstand dagegen, wenn man ihnen ein reduziertes Vokabular oder eine solche Ökonomie anbietet. Sie denken dann: „Oh, bitte, gib mir was Neues!" Aber ab einem gewissen Punkt, wenn du innerhalb der Grenzen, die du aufstellst, clever bist, gehen die Zuschauer wirklich mit – der Betrachter akzeptiert und versteht die Einschränkung und beginnt seinerseits, innerhalb dieser Einschränkung zu funktionieren.

Ich glaube, in gewisser Weise sind die längeren Stücke tatsächlich sogar einfacher. Und das hat ebenfalls mit Dramaturgie zu tun. Das Theater zwingt einen dazu, mit der ergonomischen Form von anderthalb Stunden umzugehen – dem Muster von ‚Anfang', ‚Mitte' und ‚Schluss', das ein befriedigendes Gefühl von Abgeschlossenheit hervorruft. Aber in den längeren Stücken sind wir bis zu einem gewissen Grad von der Tyrannei dieser Ökonomie befreit. Die Dinge sind, was sie sind. Es müssen keine Höhepunkte produziert werden, Lösungen werden nicht benötigt. Es ist, was es ist. An diese Grenze vorzustoßen, befreit einen als Macher und als Betrachter.

HEATHFIELD Neben dem Austesten von Ideen, indem man sie bis an ihre Grenzen treibt, gibt es oft auch einen Test der körperlichen und psychischen Grenzen des Performers. Die *durationals* sind für die Performer sehr bloßstellend, weil sie anhaltend einem musternden Blick ausgesetzt sind. Und sie können körperlich anstrengend sein; sie stellen Gedächtnis und Konzentration des Performers auf die Probe, seine Fähigkeit, lebendig und in Verbindung zu bleiben.

ETCHELLS Die *durationals* verlangen etwas ganz anderes als ‚Schauspielen'. Die meisten unserer Theatershows sind, wenn sie zum ersten Mal an die Öffentlichkeit kommen, bereits ziemlich gut orchestriert. Wir sind uns bewusst, dass wir eine Maschine bedienen; so lose, phantastisch und spielerisch sie auch sein mag, es ist doch eine Maschine: In einer Stunde und vierzig Minuten nimmt sie die Zuschauer auf eine Art Reise mit. Sie hat eine Architektur, und als Performer bist du letztlich der Diener dieser Architektur. Wohingegen die längeren Stücke wesentlich offener für deine lebendigen, willkürlichen, launischen oder perversen Entscheidungen sind. Sie sind auf jeden Fall offen für deine Stimmung. Tatsächlich verlangen die langen Stücke, dass du im Moment etwas beiträgst, live, schnell, als Macher von Entscheidungen und Momenten, auf eine Weise, wie das in den Theaterstücken, wenn sie erst einmal auf Tour sind, nicht geschieht.

HEATHFIELD So offen sie auch sind, zeigen diese Werke doch eine sehr kohärente Sensibilität, die ihr durch zwanzig Jahre gemeinsames Improvisieren erworben habt. Die Performer haben eine reiche Geschichte und ein gemeinsames Vokabular.

ETCHELLS Es sind nicht nur ihre Fähigkeiten als Performer. Es gibt eine Art kollektives Gedächtnis, ein Repertoire an Tönen und Fragmenten und Szenen, in denen man schon einmal zusammen war. Man sieht das insbesondere in *Quizoola!*, wo eine leichte Veränderung in Stimme und Stil des einen Performers den anderen sofort an eine ganz andere Stelle katapultiert, die aus einer früheren Show her halb bekannt sein mag. Es ist nicht mehr als eine Andeutung, aber es reicht, dass der andere weiß: ‚Dahin geht es‘. So ist es auch, wenn wir bei der Arbeit an den Theaterstücken improvisieren – du kannst auf all das Zeug, das du zusammen gemacht hast, Bezug nehmen.

HEATHFIELD Abgesehen vom angesammelten Wissen der Performer um die Spielmöglichkeiten – auf welche Weise, würdest du sagen, hat sich die Beziehung zwischen Struktur und freiem Spiel im Laufe eurer Arbeit verändert?

ETCHELLS It is not just their skills as performers; there is a kind of collective memory, a repertoire of tones and fragments and scenes that you have been in together before. You see this, in *Quizoola!* especially, where a certain change in voice and approach from one performer will instantly kick the other into a new location that might be half-known from some previous show. It is no more than a hint from this one, but the other knows quickly enough: 'We're going to take it there.' That's the way it works when we're improvising to create the theatre works, too; there's this ability to work by referencing in action all the stuff you did together before.

HEATHFIELD Aside from this accumulated knowledge of the possibilities of play for the performers, how would you say the relationship between structure and freeplay has changed throughout your work?

ETCHELLS It varies enormously from project to project. But in some ways I'd say that for us now the tighter the structure or rule is the freer the play can be. The rules of *Quizoola!* or *And on the Thousandth Night ...* or of certain sections of *First Night* can really be written on a postcard. But in performative terms the possibilities are endless.

HEATHFIELD There is now a very powerful emphasis in your work on the relation between the performers and the audience, moment by moment, eye to eye ...

ETCHELLS Yes.

HEATHFIELD It is almost as if you are working under a prerequisite regarding the performers presence and their quality of engagement with the audience. If the performer is not exposed, not connected to what is happening now in the

Quizoola!

ETCHELLS Das ist von Projekt zu Projekt enorm verschieden. Aber in gewisser Weise würde ich sagen, dass für uns jetzt das Spiel umso freier sein kann, je strikter die Struktur oder Regel ist. Die Regeln von *Quizoola!* oder *And on the Thousandth Night ...* oder mancher Abschnitte von *First Night* passen wirklich auf eine Postkarte. Aber was das Performative angeht, sind die Möglichkeiten endlos.

HEATHFIELD In eurer Arbeit gibt es jetzt eine sehr starke Betonung der Beziehung zwischen Performern und Zuschauern, von Moment zu Moment, von Auge zu Auge ...

ETCHELLS Ja.

HEATHFIELD Es ist fast so, als ob ihr hinsichtlich der Präsenz der Performer und der Qualität ihrer Beziehung zu den Zuschauern mit einer bestimmten Voraussetzung arbeiten würdet. Wenn der Performer sich nicht aussetzt, wenn er nicht in Verbindung steht mit dem, was jetzt in diesem Raum geschieht, wenn er nicht völlig in der elementaren Beziehung zu den vor ihm versammelten Menschen aufgeht, dann erscheint das in den späteren Arbeiten schon wie ein Vertrauensbruch oder eine Ausflucht, ein Schritt zurück gegenüber dem, was euer Theater eigentlich fordert.

ETCHELLS In den sehr frühen Shows (*Jessica, (Let the Water)*) haben wir mehr oder weniger so getan, als gäbe es eine vierte Wand. Sehr abgeschlossen. Wenig oder kein direktes Spiel zum Zuschauer. Aber in dem Maße, wie sich unsere Arbeit entwickelt hat, begannen wir, die Zuschauer zu ‚bemerken‘ und uns wesentlich mehr mit ihnen zu beschäftigen. Fünf Jahre später redeten wir dann ziemlich häufig direkt mit den Zuschauern und schauten sie an, aber oft so, dass wir sie ausdrücklich verkannten oder ihnen einen bestimmten Dreh verpassten. Am Anfang von *Marina & Lee* beispielsweise hält Cathy Naden den Zuschauern eine merkwürdige Physikvorlesung – als ob sie deswegen gekommen wären. In

room, not entirely engaged with the elemental relation to the people that have gathered in front of them, then this seems, for the later work, like an act of bad faith or of evasion, a step back or down from what is required in your theatre.

ETCHELLS The very early shows (*Jessica, (Let the Water)*) we made more or less as if there were a fourth wall in place. Very closed off. Little or no frontality. But as the work developed we began to notice and deal with the audience a lot more. Five years later we were talking quite a lot to the audience, and we were looking at them but often very emphatically misrecognising them or spinning them. So in the beginning of *Marina & Lee*, Cathy Naden delivers a strange physics lecture to the audience – as if that's what they're here to see. At other points in the same piece the audience are addressed as if they were present at a show-trial, or as if they were in some thriller movie, or at an opera. We talk about these as processes of misrecognition – and as a fictionalisation of the audience. Putting the audience in a fictional place by addressing them wrongly.

More recently in pieces like *The Travels* or my solo *Instructions for Forgetting* or in the durational works like *Thousandth Night,* the audience are addressed much more simply – without this kind of fictionalisation or misrecognition, just as the people who are there, the people who've come along to see you, to hear about something.

Over the years perhaps what you can see there is a slow stripping of pretence in relation to the audience. A greater and greater acknowledgement of the theatre situation. We come closer to them. We want them closer to us!

HEATHFIELD Would you say that connection with the audience, that stripping of pretence, has changed the tonal nature or emotional content

As if Things Got More Real / A Conversation with Tim Etchells
Als ob die Dinge wirklicher würden / Ein Gespräch mit Tim Etchells
Adrian Heathfield

of the work? There is, I think, less lyrical romanticism, less melancholia, more inhabitation of exposure, failure and embarrassment, a tremendous interest, as in *First Night*, in staying inside difficulty …

ETCHELLS I think the work is less romantic, less melancholic because it is less concerned with some 'poetical' elsewhere and more concerned with the here and now.

The point about difficulty is interesting, too. There's been a real development in terms of that. In some of the earliest shows that deal with the audience – like *Emanuelle*, or *Speak Bitterness,* or *Showtime* – our position with respect to them was rather concerned or worried! We wanted them to be alright. We wanted them to let us off the hook. Richard starts *Showtime* explaining nervously how a piece of theatre ought to work. He's worried about it. It's like his little prayer that everything is going to be OK. Or in *Emanuelle* the performers stand in front of the translucent curtain to present their story with the expression of frightened rabbits – as if they'd prefer not to be here but that somehow they have to say this. These are nice people and they haven't got a problem with the audience, they just would like to square things with them. You could say that of *Speak Bitterness* in a certain way, too.

Later on in the work things get a bit more difficult. You get a set of shows where the performers know that the audience are there and the desire to please has turned into bitterness. The general attitude to the audience in these later pieces can be quite abusive, and some negative assumptions are made playfully about them – that they're drunks, that they're just interested in tits and ass, that they're stupid …

HEATHFIELD The performers appear to be much more subject to some kind of testing or scru

anderen Momenten im selben Stück werden die Zuschauer angesprochen, als wohnten sie einem Schauprozess bei oder wären in einem Thriller oder in der Oper. Wir nennen das Prozesse des Verkennens, eine Fiktionalisierung des Publikums. Die Zuschauer an einen fiktionalen Ort versetzen, indem man sie falsch anspricht.

In jüngerer Zeit, in Stücken wie *The Travels* oder in meinem Solo *Instructions for Forgetting* oder in den *durationals* wie *Thousandth Night*, werden die Zuschauer viel direkter angesprochen – ohne diese Art von Fiktionalisierung oder Verkennung, einfach als die Menschen, die gekommen sind, um dich zu sehen, um etwas zu hören.

Über die Jahre kann man vielleicht eine Art langsames Ablegen der Verstellung gegenüber dem Publikum beobachten. Ein zunehmend stärkeres Anerkennen der Theatersituation. Wir kommen den Zuschauern näher. Wir wollen sie näher bei uns haben!

HEATHFIELD Würdest du sagen, dass die Verbindung mit den Zuschauern, das Ablegen des Verstellens, den Ton oder den Gefühlsgehalt der Werke verändert hat? Es gibt jetzt, glaube ich, weniger lyrische Romantik, weniger Melancholie, mehr Wohnen im Ausgesetztsein, im Scheitern, in der Peinlichkeit, ein enormes Interesse, wie in *First Night*, in Schwierigkeiten stecken zu bleiben …

ETCHELLS Ich glaube, die Arbeit ist weniger romantisch, weniger melancholisch, weil sie weniger mit einem ‚poetischen‘ Anderswo beschäftigt und stärker im Hier und Jetzt verankert ist.

Der Punkt mit den Schwierigkeiten ist ebenfalls interessant. In dieser Hinsicht gab es eine echte Entwicklung. In einigen der frühesten Shows, die sich mit dem Publikum auseinander setzten – wie *Emanuelle* oder *Speak Bitterness* oder *Showtime* – war unsere Haltung gegenüber den Zuschauern bemüht oder gar besorgt! Wir wollten, dass es ihnen gut geht. Wir wollten, dass sie uns vom Haken

First Night

lassen. Richard beginnt *Showtime* mit einer nervösen Erklärung, wie ein Theaterstück funktionieren sollte. Er macht sich Sorgen darüber. Es ist wie ein kleines Gebet, dass alles gut geht. Oder in *Emanuelle* stehen die Performer vor dem durchscheinenden Vorhang und präsentieren ihre Geschichte mit dem Ausdruck verängstigter Hasen – als ob sie lieber nicht hier wären, aber das hier nun mal irgendwie sagen müssten. Es sind nette Leute, und sie haben kein Problem mit den Zuschauern, sie würden nur gerne vorher ein paar Dinge mit ihnen klären. Dasselbe könnte man in gewisser Weise auch von *Speak Bitterness* sagen.

Später werden die Dinge etwas schwieriger. Da bekommt man eine Reihe von Shows vorgesetzt, in denen die Performer wissen, dass das Publikum da ist, und der Wunsch, ihnen zu gefallen, ist zu Bitterkeit geworden.

tiny: They are more objectified, and the audience are objectified in response to this. This is work that is deliberately voyeuristic, acknowledging the looking that is going on, playing with its power relations.

ETCHELLS It's as if those shows are saying to the audience, "You are making us do this, you want us to entertain you" …

HEATHFIELD … and then, "What is it that you really want?"

ETCHELLS Yes. "We have to smile like this because of you, and although we're doing what you apparently want us to do, we don't like it". And the ways in which 'we' don't like it become more

First Night

and more clear. In shows like *First Night* or *Pleasure* or *Disco Relax* it looks like the performers are having a hard time controlling their disdain for the public. Of course it should be clear that in these works we invent some personas with bad attitudes! It is not us. It is a set of theatrical foils that are fun to play with. What is interesting is that the durational work never has that negative energy, that sense of picking a fight, it is only present in the later theatre work.

HEATHFIELD Do you think this is a response to the theatrical frame?

ETCHELLS Yes. There's a tyranny to theatre. You have to do your show in an hour and a half, and theatre is full of expectations – facts that we are

Die allgemeine Haltung gegenüber dem Publikum in diesen späteren Stücken kann ziemlich beleidigend sein. Es werden spielerisch einige negative Annahmen über die Zuschauer gemacht – dass sie betrunken sind, dass sie nur an Titten und Hintern Interesse haben, dass sie dumm sind …

HEATHFIELD Die Performer scheinen in viel stärkerem Maße einer Art Test oder Musterung ausgesetzt zu sein: Sie sind stärker objektifiziert, und in Reaktion darauf sind auch die Zuschauer stärker objektifiziert. Diese Arbeit ist absichtlich voyeuristisch und erkennt die Blicke und ihre Machtverhältnisse an.

ETCHELLS Es ist, als würden diese Shows den Zuschauern sagen: „Ihr bringt uns dazu, dies zu tun; ihr wollt, dass wir euch unterhalten" …

HEATHFIELD ... und dann: „Was wollt ihr eigentlich wirklich?"

ETCHELLS Ja. „Wegen euch müssen wir so lächeln, und obwohl wir das tun, was ihr anscheinend wollt – uns gefällt es nicht." Und die Art, wie ‚uns' das nicht gefällt, wird immer deutlicher. In Shows wie *First Night* oder *Pleasure* oder *Disco Relax* sieht es so aus, als ob es den Performern schwer fallen würde, ihre Verachtung für das Publikum im Zaum zu halten. Natürlich sollte es klar sein, dass wir in diesen Stücken einige Charaktere mit negativer Einstellung erfinden! Das sind nicht wir. Es ist eine Reihe von Theaterfolien, mit denen zu spielen Spaß macht. Interessanterweise haben die *durationals* nie diese Art negativer Energie, dieses Gefühl, Streit zu suchen. Das findet sich nur in der späteren Theaterarbeit.

HEATHFIELD Glaubst du, das ist eine Reaktion auf den Rahmen des Theaters?

ETCHELLS Ja. Theater ist in gewisser Weise tyrannisch. Du musst deine Show in anderthalb Stunden abziehen, und das Theater ist voll von Erwartungen. Dagegen rennen wir an. Natürlich sind es gerade diese Einschränkungen, die Bedeutung ermöglichen. Und wir können sie ebenso lieben wie wir sie hassen.

Charakteristisch für die längeren Arbeiten – *Who Can Sing a Song to Unfrighten Me?*, das lange Geschichten-Erzähl-Stück *Thousandth Night*, *12 am* und *Quizoola!* und, in etwas geringerem Maße, auch *Speak Bitterness* – ist eine großzügigere und menschlichere Haltung gegenüber denen, die zuschauen, und gegenüber der Handlung im Allgemeinen. Das hat damit zu tun, dass das Publikum kommen und gehen kann, dass es keinen Druck gibt, eine bestimmte Art von Theaterdramaturgie zu erzeugen.

Diese Arbeit komponieren wir in einem ganz anderen Modus, und als Performer sind wir auf eine ganz andere Weise präsent. Wir spielen ein Spiel, in dem wir sagen: „Dies ist eine Regel, der wir uns unterwerfen werden."

First Night

88

As if Things Got More Real / A Conversation with Tim Etchells
Als ob die Dinge wirklicher würden / Ein Gespräch mit Tim Etchells
Adrian Heathfield

bashing against. Of course, those limits are what makes meaning possible. And we can love them just as much as we hate them.

The long works – *Who Can Sing a Song to Unfrighten Me?*, the long storytelling piece *Thousandth Night, 12 am* and *Quizoola!*, and, to a slightly lesser extent, *Speak Bitterness* – are characterised by a more generous and humane attitude to those who are watching, and to the activity in general. This is to do with the fact that the audience can come and go, that there is not a pressure to create a particular kind of theatrical dramaturgy.

Making this work, we are composing in a very different mode, and as performers we are present in a very different way. We are playing a game in which we say, "This is a rule that we will subject ourselves to". The audience are subject to these rules, too, in a way, because the work lasts so long; they have come to share their time with you. So in a way their presence is less a demand to be entertained as an audience and more a gesture of individuals supporting you while you are busy with your task.

HEATHFIELD Failure, which has been such a large part of your aesthetic, is anticipated in this context; because of the extended duration, representations are subject to the disarray of improvised action, the aleatory nature of human processes.

ETCHELLS Yes, absolutely. The invitation in, say *Thousandth Night*, is to come and watch us try to play a game of telling all the stories in the world for six hours, and the emphasis is on words like 'try', 'play' and 'game'. We fail of course. The stories are often shambolic, always incomplete. Whereas you know if we made a theatre length show out of that, for an hour and a half, then we would mainly want to be telling 'good' stories.

Das Publikum unterliegt in gewisser Weise ebenfalls diesen Regeln, weil die Stücke so lange dauern. Die Zuschauer sind gekommen, ihre Zeit mit dir zu teilen. Deshalb ist ihre Gegenwart in gewisser Weise weniger ein Verlangen, als Publikum unterhalten zu werden, als vielmehr eine Geste von Einzelpersonen, die dich unterstützen, während du mit deiner Aufgabe beschäftigt bist.

HEATHFIELD Das Scheitern, das einen so großen Teil eurer Ästhetik ausmacht, wird in diesem Zusammenhang vorweggenommen. Wegen der ausgedehnten Dauer sind die Repräsentationen dem Wirrwarr improvisierter Handlung unterworfen, der aleatorischen Natur menschlicher Prozesse.

ETCHELLS Ja, absolut. Die Einladung etwa in *Thousandth Night* besteht darin, zu kommen und uns zuzuschauen, wie wir versuchen, ein Spiel zu spielen, das darin besteht, sechs Stunden lang alle Geschichten der Welt zu erzählen. Und die Betonung liegt auf Worten wie ‚versuchen‘ und ‚Spiel‘. Wir scheitern natürlich. Die Geschichten sind oft chaotisch, immer unvollständig. Wohingegen wir natürlich, wenn wir daraus eine Show von Theaterlänge machen würden, anderthalb Stunden lang, hauptsächlich ‚gute‘ Geschichten würden erzählen wollen.

HEATHFIELD Ihr würdet also die Regeln, die die Handlung leiten, in einer Theatershow eher verstecken, während ihr in den *durationals* froh seid, wenn die Systeme der Arbeit offen liegen?

ETCHELLS Für ein Theaterstück würden wir die Regeln nicht notwendigerweise verstecken. Aber wir würden die Dramaturgie innerhalb dieser Regeln an engerem Zügel führen müssen.

HEATHFIELD In den *durationals* ist es nicht das System selbst, welches das Interesse des Zuschauers aufrechterhält, sondern das Spiel, das innerhalb dieses Systems stattfindet?

ETCHELLS Ja. Das ist es auch, glaube ich, was diese langen Stücke sehr warm macht. In den *durationals* herrscht tendenziell eine gewisse Transparenz; es ist innerhalb von zehn Sekunden klar, unter welchen Regeln die Performer operieren. Es ist nicht sehr ‚künstlerisch‘; jeder kann diese Spiele spielen, jeder kann im Publikum sitzen und folgen. Das ist das Interessante an der stärker regelbasierten Arbeit, im Theater wie in den *durationals*. Sie sagt: „Alles, was ihr sehen werdet, kann von der folgenden, sehr sehr einfachen Regel abgeleitet werden." Man hat dann keines der Probleme wie bei der Lektüre von Gedichten oder surrealistischer Literatur, wo auf künstlerische Weise eine absurde Sache an die nächste gereiht wird. Diese Dinge entstehen eigentlich nicht in einer Arbeit mit klaren Regeln – weil dann der Mechanismus der Regel die Arbeit für dich erledigt. Ich glaube, wir denken so auch für die Theaterstücke. Dass die Handlung oft das Ergebnis einer Regel ist, einer einzigen, haarsträubenden, einmal aufgestellten Annahme.

HEATHFIELD Das heißt, dass es in diesen Stücken neben dem, was gesagt oder bedeutet wird, auch um die Natur menschlichen Spielens geht. Insbesondere in den *durationals* scheint es etwas Anthropologisches zu geben.

ETCHELLS Ja. Man kann Menschen zuschauen. Man kann zusehen, wie sie mit schwierigen Situationen umgehen. Man sieht all ihre Tricks und Strategien, um damit fertig zu werden, um sich immer wieder neu zu erfinden, um zu sein.

HEATHFIELD Eine starke Dynamik in eurer Ästhetik ist die Wertschätzung dafür, die Arbeit gegenüber dem Zufall, dem Unfall, dem Ereignishaften, dem Augenblick des Geschehens zu öffnen. Diese Öffnungen sind nicht notwendigerweise unstrukturiert, aber sie sind bis zu einem gewissen Grad unkenntlich, bevor sie geschehen.

ETCHELLS Ja. Vielleicht ist das eine weitere Verschiebung in der Arbeit: Wir arbeiten

HEATHFIELD So you would bury the rules that govern the action more in a theatre show, whereas in the durational shows you are happy for the work's systems to remain exposed?

ETCHELLS For theatre we wouldn't necessarily bury the rules. But we'd have to keep a tighter reign on the dramaturgy inside them.

HEATHFIELD For durational work it is not the system itself which keeps the spectator's interest, but the play that takes place inside it?

ETCHELLS Yes. This I think is also what makes those long pieces very warm. There tends to be a transparency about the durationals; it's clear within ten seconds what rule the performers are operating under. It's not very 'artistic'; anybody can play these games, anybody can sit in the audience and follow. That is what is interesting about the more rule-based work, either for theatres or for durationals; they say, "Everything you are going to see can be derived from the following very very simple rule". You then have none of the problems with reading poetics or surrealism, where one weird thing has been put next to another in an artistic way. Those things don't really arise in work where the rules are clearer – because the mechanism of the rule is doing all the work for you. I think we think that way for the theatre works, too. That the action is often the product of a rule, or of one single outrageous set-up assumption.

HEATHFIELD This means that what is also in question in these pieces, aside from what is said or signified, is the nature of human play. There seems to be something anthropological about the durational works especially.

ETCHELLS Yes. You get to see people. You get to watch people. You get to see them coping with difficult situations. You get to see all their tricks and strategies for coping, for inventing and reinventing themselves, for being.

HEATHFIELD A strong dynamic within your aesthetic is valuing the opening of the work to chance, to the accident, to eventhood, to the moment of a happening. These openings are not necessarily unstructured, but they are to some extent unknowable before they happen.

ETCHELLS Yes. Perhaps this is another one of those shifts in the work; we're increasingly working with things where the rule that produced this moment is somehow evident and consequent to everything else that's happening. To be honest, weird imagistic combinations of disconnected things have never really been our style; even shows like *Club of No Regrets* or *Marina & Lee* have pretty strict economies about what kinds of moments are allowed and how they may be produced. In terms of the making process, in rehearsal we often start off working with no idea what we're doing, no idea what we are talking about, what we are looking for; the process is just waiting for things to happen in the studio, trying to uncover things by accident, by trial and error, by intuition and just stupidity. Having done so, having found some things that are interesting, then you start looking for logics, and for rules; to remove what is arbitrary.

HEATHFIELD I wonder if you could talk about these 'crafted accidents' in relation to your understanding of beauty and the beautiful.

ETCHELLS In terms of the things that I really like in our work and in other people's work, I am very attracted to things that are what they are, and I am very attracted to moments where what's happening is what's happening. (Laughs.) A certain kind of 'it is what it is what it is what it is'.

zunehmend mit Dingen, in denen die Regel, die diesen Moment hervorgebracht hat, irgendwie offenkundig ist und aus allem anderen, was geschieht, hervorgeht. Ehrlich gesagt waren absurde, phantastische Kombinationen unverbundener Dinge nie wirklich unser Stil; selbst Shows wie *Club of No Regrets* oder *Marina & Lee* haben ziemlich strikte Ökonomien in Bezug darauf, welche Arten von Momenten erlaubt sind und wie sie produziert werden dürfen. Was den Schaffensprozess angeht, beginnen wir in der Probe die Arbeit oft ohne eine Ahnung, was wir tun, ohne eine Ahnung, wovon wir reden, wonach wir suchen. Der Prozess besteht darin, einfach auf der Probebühne darauf zu warten, dass etwas geschieht, im Versuch, Dinge durch Zufall, durch Versuch und Irrtum, durch Intuition oder schiere Dummheit zu entdecken. Wenn wir das getan haben, wenn wir Dinge gefunden haben, die interessant sind, dann beginnt man, nach Logik und nach Regeln zu suchen und das Arbiträre zu entfernen.

HEATHFIELD Ich frage mich, ob du diese ‚herbeigeführten Zufälle' in Bezug zu deinem Verständnis von Schönheit und dem Schönen bringen kannst.

ETCHELLS Was unsere Arbeit und die Arbeit anderer betrifft, so finde ich Dinge attraktiv, die sind, was sie sind. Und ich finde Momente attraktiv, in denen geschieht, was geschieht. (Lacht.) Eine Art von ‚Es ist, was es ist, was es ist, was es ist'.

Für mich hat das Theater eine inhärente Hässlichkeit, weil es immer versucht, etwas mit dir zu machen. Es will etwas. Deshalb würde ich das Wort ‚theatralisch' in pejorativem Sinn verwenden: etwas, das zu stark versucht, dich zu beeinflussen, und das sich dabei selbst verzerrt. Ich finde eine Theaterpraxis sehr attraktiv, die den Dingen Zeit und Raum lässt, das zu sein, was sie sind; wo sie nicht über einen gewissen Punkt hinaus forciert werden. Es gibt eine Art von Schönheit in dieser Arbeit,

As if Things Got More Real / A Conversation with Tim Etchells
Als ob die Dinge wirklicher würden / Ein Gespräch mit Tim Etchells
Adrian Heathfield

die mich interessiert. Ich denke an Jérôme Bel oder an Edit Kaldors *Or press esc* oder sogar an die Stücke von Richard Maxwell. Es gibt eine Art Dramaturgie der Anti-Dramatik.

Was Schönheit in der Arbeit angeht – mich interessiert Schönheit nur dann, wenn man zusehen kann, wie sie gemacht wird. In jeder unserer Shows hoffe ich wirklich, dass wir etwas Schönes erreichen; aber dazu muss man den Leuten zugesehen haben, wie sie eine Menge anderer Dinge versuchen, wie sie sich bemühen und scheitern, wie sie sich zum Narren machen. Erst wenn man es nicht mehr erwartet, entsteht an den unwahrscheinlichsten Orten vielleicht etwas Schönes. Bei der Arbeit an *Bloody Mess* gibt es eine Performerin in einem Gorilla-Anzug. Das ist natürlich super für Komödie. Aber ich möchte auch, dass diese Person schön ist. Oder traurig. Oder auch tragisch. Oder die größte Intellektuelle des Stücks.

HEATHFIELD Das klingt so, als wäre Schönheit eine Qualität, die ein Performer nicht beabsichtigen kann, sondern etwas, das vielleicht durch seine Mühe hervorgebracht wird, fast gegen seinen Willen. Für dich hat das Schöne also viel mit unbewusstem Spiel zu tun; es ist etwas, das aus gescheiterten Bemühungen entsteht.

ETCHELLS Ja, das ist teilweise richtig. Ich habe ein Problem mit Absicht und mit Schönheit, insbesondere wenn beide kombiniert werden. Die Absicht, schön zu sein … die Schönheit eines Bildes … Ich tendiere dazu, mir solche Dinge anzusehen und zu sagen: „Ja, das ist sehr schön. Das nächste bitte!" Es ist alles sehr schön. Aber es ist zu leicht für das Auge und das Hirn, glaube ich. Es ist spektakulär, und ich glaube, die Welt hat davon genug. Mich interessiert Schönheit nur, wenn ich die Arbeit sehen kann, die zu ihrer Produktion aufgewendet wurde. Die Ökonomie, mit der ein solches Bild produziert wird, sollte einer Kritik unterzogen werden. Ich habe kein Interesse an unreflektierten oder unkritischen

For me, there's an inherent ugliness in theatre because it is always trying to do something to you. It wants something. So I would use the word theatrical in a derogatory sense: something that is trying too hard to affect you and is distorting itself by doing this. I am very attracted to theatrical practice where things are given the time, the space, and the place to be what they are, and not forced beyond a certain point. There is a kind of beauty in this work that interests me. I'm thinking of Jérôme Bel, or of Edit Kaldor's *Or press esc,* or of Richard Maxwell's plays even. There's a kind of dramaturgy of anti-dramatics.

Concerning beauty in the work – I'm only interested in the beautiful in so far as it can be seen to be made in front of you. In any show we make I really hope we can get to something beautiful, but you have to have watched people try a lot of other things, struggle and fail, make fools of themselves. Maybe when it is not expected anymore, something beautiful is made from the most unlikely place. In the work on *Bloody Mess* we have a performer in a gorilla suit. It is great for comedy, of course. But I'd like that person to be beautiful. Or sad. Or tragic, too. Or the biggest intellectual of the piece.

HEATHFIELD It sounds like beauty isn't a quality that can be intended by a performer, but something that they might produce through their labour, almost despite themselves. So for you the beautiful is very connected to unconscious performance; it is something that emerges from a failed aspiration.

ETCHELLS Yes, that is partly true. I have a problem with intention and with beauty, especially when the two are combined. The intention to be beautiful … the beauty of an image … I tend to look at things like that, and say "yes, that's very beautiful. Next please!" It's all very beautiful. But it's easy on the eye and the brain, I think. It's spectacular, and I think the world has enough of that. I am only interested in beauty if I can see the work put in to make it. The economy by which such an image is produced should be put under a critique. I am not interested in un-self-conscious, or non-critical uses of theatrical or performative language to produce effects – that's Hollywood or the television news. That is mostly what beautiful theatre or beautiful dance is: seductive, and not questioning the rhetorics of its own power. And so I think (or I hope) that when there is anything beautiful in our work then it is made in a way that problematises the theatrical language and process that produced it.

HEATHFIELD This kind of beauty wouldn't be owned by anyone then, either by the performers or by you, the director?

ETCHELLS Where our protagonists fuck up or fail, and consequently produce something quite beautiful, it's not a beauty that necessarily belongs to Forced Entertainment.

What we tend to do is to create a set of personas who have then, it appears, created the show. We kind of blame it on them – there is a deferral of authorship. So, at one level *First Night* is presented as the work of the personas – the incompetent, grinning vaudevillian imbeciles whose show is a disaster. We defer the authorship, the intention, the failure to 'them'. Whereas when you look at Robert Wilson it looks like Robert Wilson, like what he wanted. Robert Wilson signs it. You know that what you are looking at was his idea; to put a ten metre tall foot coming down on a miniature house in wonderland or something. Whereas we would always create a bunch of personas – fools and incompetents or maniacs, who thought that a ten metre tall foot and a little house was a good idea.

Verwendungen dramatischer oder performativer Sprache, um Effekte zu erzielen – das ist Hollywood oder Fernsehnachrichten. Schönes Theater oder schöner Tanz ist meistens: verführerisch, ohne die Rhetorik seiner eigenen Macht zu hinterfragen. Und deshalb glaube (oder hoffe) ich: Wenn es etwas Schönes in unserer Arbeit gibt, dann ist es so gemacht, dass es die dramatische Sprache und den Prozess problematisiert, der es hervorgebracht hat.

HEATHFIELD Diese Art von Schönheit würde niemandem gehören, weder den Performern noch dir, dem Regisseur?

ETCHELLS Wo unsere Protagonisten es vermasseln oder scheitern und in der Folge etwas wirklich Schönes produzieren, dann ist das eine Schönheit, die nicht notwendigerweise Forced Entertainment gehört.

Wir tendieren dazu, ein Set von Charakteren zu erschaffen, die dann, so scheint es, die Show erschaffen. Wir schieben ihnen gewissermaßen die Schuld zu – es gibt eine Verschiebung von Autorschaft. Auf einer Ebene wird *First Night* also als das Werk der Charaktere präsentiert – der inkompetenten, grinsenden Varieté-Idioten, deren Show ein Desaster ist. Wenn man sich hingegen Robert Wilson anguckt, dann sieht das aus wie Robert Wilson, wie das, was er wollte. Robert Wilson unterschreibt es. Du weißt, das, was du siehst, war seine Idee; einen zehn Meter großen Fuß auf ein Miniaturhaus im Märchenland treten zu lassen oder was auch immer. Wohingegen wir immer einen Haufen Charaktere erschaffen würden – Idioten und Unfähige oder Besessene, die meinen, dass ein zehn Meter großer Fuß und ein kleines Haus eine gute Idee sei.

HEATHFIELD Ein Haufen Stellvertreter?

ETCHELLS Ja. Und diese Stellvertreter sind oft dickköpfig, dumm oder von manischen Vorstellungen besessen. Vielleicht lachen wir und

92

As if Things Got More Real / A Conversation with Tim Etchells
Als ob die Dinge wirklicher würden / Ein Gespräch mit Tim Etchells
Adrian Heathfield

das Publikum über sie und ‚ihre' verrückten und idiotischen Ideen: Wie dämlich ist es in *Showtime*, dass der Typ meint, eine Dose Heinz-Spaghetti auf seinen Bauch zu leeren, würde für eine gute Sterbedarstellung reichen. Wir schieben also diesem Set von Charakteren und ihren Entscheidungen die ‚Schuld' an den Repräsentationsstrategien, den Unfällen und den chaotischen Strukturen zu. Während wir im Hintergrund geschäftig herumschleichen und alles irgendwie zum Laufen bringen. In *Showtime* geben wir dieser notorisch schlechten Idee mit den Spaghetti so viel Raum und Aufmerksamkeit, dass es gegen Ende tatsächlich verdammt schön ist. Und funktioniert.

HEATHFIELD Eure Verwendung von Stellvertretern interessiert mich sehr, sowohl in Bezug auf die psychologischen Modelle, mit denen ihr in den Stücken arbeitet, wie auch in Bezug auf das, was eure Arbeit über Identität aussagt. Es gibt in der Performance-Kunst eine starke Tradition von Künstlern, die durch Performance ihr Selbst erkunden und erproben. Eure Arbeit hat so viel in Fiktion investiert, dass sie dieser Tradition autobiographischer und zeugnishafter Arbeit ziemlich entgegengesetzt scheint. Und doch fungieren diese Stellvertreter in gewisser Weise als Orte persönlicher Erprobung für die Performer. Während es offensichtlich Orte sind, an denen die Performer die vielfältigen Möglichkeiten fiktionaler, alternativer ‚Ichs' durchspielen können, sind die Charaktere, die sie annehmen, doch auch Szenen psychologischer Erweiterung und Projektion.

ETCHELLS Wären wir in der Lage, eine Show zu machen, in der uns der Inhalt tatsächlich direkt gehören würde? Ich tue das in meinem Solostück *Instructions for Forgetting*, und die Truppe tut das mehr oder weniger in *Decade* und *The Travels*. Diese Arbeiten haben einen gewissen dokumentarischen Strang. Aber in der ‚eigentlichen' Theaterarbeit besteht eine starke und wiederkehrende Taktik von uns darin, Autorschaft zu verschieben und die

HEATHFIELD A bunch of surrogates?

ETCHELLS Yes. And those surrogates are often wrong-headed, stupid, or driven by manias. Perhaps we, and the audience, laugh at them and the crazy or naff ideas 'they' come up with: How daft it is in *Showtime* that one guy thinks that opening a tin of Heinz spaghetti out onto his belly will help him do a good impersonation of dying. So we 'blame' the representational strategies and the accidents and the chaotic structures on this set of personas – on their decisions –, and in the background we're busy sneaking around and getting all of it, somehow, to work. So in *Showtime* we give that chronically bad idea with the spaghetti so much space and so much commitment that by the end it is actually fucking beautiful. And it works.

HEATHFIELD Your use of surrogates interests me a lot, in terms of the psychological models you are working with in performance and what your work says about identity. There is a strong tradition in performance art of the artist exploring and testing their self through performance. Being so invested in fiction, your work would seem quite counter to this tradition of autobiographical and testimonial work, and yet there is a way in which these surrogates function as personal test sites for the performers. Whilst they are obviously places in which the performers get to play the multiple possibilities of fictional alternate selves, the personas they adopt are also scenes of psychological extension and projection.

ETCHELLS Could we make a show in which we effectively owned the content in a straightforward way? I do this in my solo piece *Instructions for Forgetting*, and the company does this more or less in *Decade* and *The Travels*. There is a little documentary strand to these works. But in the theatre work 'proper', a strong recurring tactic

93

of ours is to defer authorship, and to let the surrogates introduce levels of incompetence or misguided inventiveness for us.

As to the status of those personas in relation to the performers themselves, it is interesting; most of the theatre work we do gets made through improvisation, and of course you can't improvise something that doesn't come from you in some way. It always belongs to you; what you do is always lodged in and coming from your body, your psyche, however refracted or distorted it is. You could probably count in years the amount of time the performers of Forced Entertainment have wandered around on stages in very open improvisation, 'being' or playing whatever they like. We have been so stuck or so bored sometimes that they could have fucking done anything and it would've made it into a show! And yet, of course, any decision that anybody makes out there in improvisation is always inevitably within the frame of their own actual persona. So if you looked at an amalgamation of all the different Robin Arthurs that have appeared in the shows, or the different Cathys, Terrys, Claires and Richards, you can see them as a set of alternative selves, versions. And if you printed them all on the same film, each would occupy the same sort of space, the same zone on the film. For each of the performers there is a relation of ownership and investment in those figures, however cynically or stupidly they get made. You always live in and through them for a year or more, touring, performing. The you of you is always going to be muddled up in there.

HEATHFIELD And as a performer it is always really you that is on the line in a performance.

ETCHELLS Absolutely. You could say that the creation of surrogates, as a structural and compositional strategy for us, in no way shields the

Stellvertreter für uns Ebenen der Inkompetenz oder fehlgeleiteter Findigkeit einführen zu lassen.

Was den Status dieser Charaktere in Bezug auf die Performer selbst angeht, ist das interessant. Ein Großteil unserer Theaterarbeit entsteht durch Improvisation, und natürlich kann man nichts improvisieren, was nicht auf irgendeine Weise von einem selbst kommt. Es gehört immer dir; was du tust, wohnt immer in deinem Körper, deiner Seele. Von dort kommt es, wie gebrochen oder verzerrt auch immer. Wahrscheinlich sind es ganze Jahre, die die Performer von Forced Entertainment damit verbracht haben, in sehr offener Improvisation auf Bühnen herumzuwandern und einfach 'zu sein' oder zu spielen, was immer sie wollten. Manchmal waren wir so festgefahren oder so gelangweilt, dass sie verdammt nochmal alles hätten tun können und es hätte seinen Weg in die Show gefunden! Und doch findet natürlich jede Entscheidung, die jemand dort draußen in der Improvisation macht, unvermeidlich innerhalb des Rahmens seiner eigenen, tatsächlichen Person statt. Wenn man sich also ein Amalgam all der verschiedenen Robin Arthurs anschaut, die in den Shows aufgetreten sind, oder der verschiedenen Cathys, Terrys, Claires und Richards, dann kann man sie als ein Set alternativer 'Ichs', als Versionen sehen. Und wenn man sie alle auf denselben Film belichten würde, nähme jedes dieselbe Art von Raum, denselben Abschnitt auf dem Film ein. Bei jedem der Performer gibt es eine Beziehung des Besitzens und der Investition in diese Figuren, wie zynisch oder dumm auch immer sie gemacht sein mögen. Du lebst immer ein Jahr oder länger in ihnen und durch sie, auf Tour, in der Performance. Dein Du ist da immer mit verworren.

HEATHFIELD Und als Performer stehst immer du selbst auf dem Spiel.

ETCHELLS Absolut. Man könnte sagen, dass das Erschaffen von Stellvertretern für uns als

Dreams' Winter

strukturelle und kompositionstechnische Strategie die Performer in keiner Weise vor der vollen Gewalt des Blicks des Publikums schützt. Es hilft ihnen nicht dabei, vom Haken zu kommen. Das Publikum durchschaut sie immer, und diese Charaktere sind immer nur ein schwacher, teilweiser Schutz. Es gefällt uns, wenn diese Stellvertreterfiguren so aussehen, als könnten sie kaum noch weiter existieren, als müsste ihre Maske gleich abgenommen werden. Gegen Ende von *First Night* sagt Cathy zum Publikum: „Wir machen heute Abend nicht weiter. Ihr seid es nicht wert. Verpisst euch!" Das kann ein unheimlicher Moment sein. Weil Cathy es so spielt, als würde sie es meinen. Als ob die Maske weg wäre.

performers from the full force of the audience's gaze. It doesn't help them get off the hook; the audience is always seeing through them, and those personas are always a thin protection, always partial. We like it when those surrogate figures look like they can barely extend or persist any longer, like the mask of them must be abandoned. Toward the end of *First Night* Cathy is saying to the audience: "We're not doing any more tonight. You're not worth it. Fuck off!" That can be a scary moment. Because Cathy plays it like she means it. As if the mask is gone.

HEATHFIELD So your attraction here is to the possibility of a moment of truth, or the possibility of revealing a true self, not the truth itself.

As if Things Got More Real / A Conversation with Tim Etchells
Als ob die Dinge wirklicher würden / Ein Gespräch mit Tim Etchells
Adrian Heathfield

ETCHELLS Yes, we like to play as if things got more real. But for the most part, in the theatre works, it is 'just' dramaturgy.

HEATHFIELD It is not just effect for effect's sake, though: You are interested in staying inside particular kinds of emotional difficulty.

ETCHELLS Yes, but the achievement of this difficulty is still extremely strategic and manipulative, within a set of concerns and frames, especially when you compare it to the ways that visibility, exposure or 'realness' operate in the durational works. Everything that you strategise in order to cause an effect in the durational performances is inevitably outweighed by all of the other things that are happening that you cannot control. The durationals put the performer in the public gaze for unreasonably long amounts of time, and in structures where whatever you have planned can't really sustain or cover you for very long. You see people in the durationals, silent, or stumbling, not playing, annoyed, or just sitting there thinking. You cannot control the signification of what you are doing and how you are read under these conditions.

HEATHFIELD The play is closer to rehearsal, more like everyday human games …

ETCHELLS It's actually more-or-less a rule for the durationals: Not everything has to be (or even can be) of consequence, it can be about passing the time. There is consequence and inconsequence. There is less compunction and more good-spiritedness about the performers' participation in the durationals, when compared to the theatre shows. The durationals are more relaxed, more playful.

HEATHFIELD What is your relationship to the theatre audience's need to laugh?

HEATHFIELD An der Möglichkeit eines Momentes der Wahrheit fasziniert euch also die Möglichkeit, ein wahres Selbst zu enthüllen, und nicht die Wahrheit selbst.

ETCHELLS Ja, es gefällt uns, so zu spielen, als ob die Dinge wirklicher würden. Aber meist ist das in den Theaterstücken ‚nichts' als Dramaturgie.

HEATHFIELD Aber es ist nicht einfach ein Effekt um des Effektes willen: Ihr habt ein Interesse daran, in gewissen Arten von emotionalen Schwierigkeiten stecken zu bleiben.

ETCHELLS Ja, aber diese Schwierigkeit zu erreichen, ist doch ein extrem strategischer und manipulativer Vorgang; er findet innerhalb eines Sets von Rücksichten und Rahmungen statt, insbesondere wenn man ihn damit vergleicht, wie Sichtbarkeit, Ausgesetztsein oder ‚Wirklichkeit' in den *durationals* funktioniert. Alles, was du in den *durationals* als Strategie entwirfst, um einen Effekt zu erzielen, wird unweigerlich aufgewogen von all den anderen Dingen, die passieren und die du nicht kontrollieren kannst. Die *durationals* setzen die Performer ungebührlich lange dem öffentlichen Blick aus, und in Strukturen, in denen alles, was du geplant hast, dich nicht wirklich lange erhalten oder schützen kann. Du siehst in den *durationals* Menschen stumm, stockend, nicht spielend, verärgert oder einfach dasitzen und nachdenken. Du kannst die Bedeutung dessen, was du tust, und wie du unter diesen Bedingungen gelesen wirst, nicht kontrollieren.

HEATHFIELD Das Stück ist näher an der Probe, es ist mehr wie die alltäglichen menschlichen Spiele …

ETCHELLS Das ist für die *durationals* tatsächlich mehr oder weniger eine Regel: Nicht alles muss (oder sogar kann) von Konsequenz sein. Es kann auch einfach darum gehen, Zeit verstreichen zu lassen. Es gibt Konsequenz und Inkonsequenz. Bei den Performern gibt es weniger Hemmungen und mehr gute Laune bei der Teilnahme an den *durationals* im Vergleich zu den Theatershows. Die *durationals* sind entspannter, spielerischer.

HEATHFIELD Wie stehst du zum Bedürfnis des Theaterpublikums zu lachen?

ETCHELLS Ich weiß nicht. Ich könnte viel darüber reden und es kritisieren. Aber zugleich glaube ich, dass wir die Komödie wirklich lieben. Es gefällt uns, ‚sie alle auf unsere Seite zu ziehen'. Wir sprechen tatsächlich über ‚Gags', darüber einen Gag zum Funktionieren zu bringen. In dem, was wir tun, gibt es einen Strang von ‚experimentellem Theater' und ‚Performance'. Aber es gibt für mich auch eine klare Verbindung zu Tommy Cooper, zu Morecambe & Wise, zu John Cleese.

Manchmal verwechseln Zuschauer und Kritiker die Intentionen und Handlungen der Charaktere mit unseren eigenen. Die lange Szene in *First Night* etwa, in der Terry eine Liste der Dinge macht, an die die Zuschauer nicht denken sollten, wird oft als absichtlich langweilig oder provokativ beschrieben. Wohingegen es, für mich zumindest, hauptsächlich eine komische Szene ist (und natürlich eine poetische), aber eben eine Komödie von uns über einen Teil der Performance dieser Charaktere, der entsetzlich langweilig ist. Man beschreibt die Szene vielleicht am besten als eine Komödie über Langeweile. Sie ist nicht langweilig. Es gibt an ihr nichts Langweiliges. Wenn ich sie langweilig fände, hätte ich sie rausgeschmissen. Sie flirtet mit den Menschen, spielt ein kleines Spiel rund um Langeweile und Provokation, aber wenn man sie sich wirklich ansieht, dann gibt es alle fünfzehn Sekunden einen Scherz. Alles sehr strategisch, alles sehr platziert.

HEATHFIELD Diese Fehllektüre fasziniert mich, weil sie von einer sehr buchstäblichen Sensibilität herrührt, die das Humorvolle und Vergnügliche nur dann versteht, wenn es in konventionellen Formen geliefert wird …

ETCHELLS I don't know. I can talk a lot about critiquing it. But at the same time I think we really love comedy. We like to 'get them all on our side'. We really talk about 'gags'. Getting the gag to work. There's an 'experimental theatre' and a 'performance' lineage to what we do. But there's also such a clear line for me to Tommy Cooper, to Morecambe & Wise, to John Cleese.

Sometimes audiences and critics can confuse the personas' intentions and actions with our (Forced Entertainment's) own. So the long scene in *First Night* where Terry makes a list of things the audience should try not to think about is often described as deliberately boring and provoking. Whereas I think, for me at least, it is basically a comedy scene (and a poetic one, of course) but a comedy by us about a part of the personas' performance that is disastrously boring. The scene is perhaps best described as comedy about boredom. It is not boring. There is nothing boring about it. If I thought it was boring I would have thrown it out. It is toying with people, playing a little game around boredom and provocation, but when you really look at it there's a joke every fifteen seconds. All very strategic, all very placed.

HEATHFIELD The misreading of this fascinates me, because it comes from a very literalist sensibility that only understands the humorous and the pleasurable when they are delivered through conventional forms …

ETCHELLS Yes, it is true of quite a lot of the shows: There is a surface, and people can take it very literally. It was the same with *Pleasure*, which had a morose, underwater, melancholic feel, but at the same time to me, it was a very funny show, you really had to laugh at the absurd and preposterous negativity of it.

HEATHFIELD Your dark humour can be very black.

As if Things Got More Real / A Conversation with Tim Etchells
Als ob die Dinge wirklicher würden / Ein Gespräch mit Tim Etchells
Adrian Heathfield

ETCHELLS There has always been this desire in the work to put really low, chronically funny comedy, next to or in the middle of really vicious tragedy, and to keep swirling them together. So much of our work is about that economy of meaning shifts, of transformations.

To us, I think, the comedy, absurdity and joyousness of the material is really important. I don't like it when people only see the melancholic, the fucked up and the failed, when actually there is usually a kind of gleefulness in the work, even in the moroseness. Robin falling around and drinking through the pantomime horse's eye while his trousers are down around his ankles. It is agonising and desperate, but it is also very stupid and funny and rather glorious in its excessive indulgence of that mood. I remember Alan Read saying about *Showtime* – he was grinning from ear to ear – "Some of the cheapest jokes in London are here, tonight at the ICA." He loved it. We loved to hear that.

HEATHFIELD The other contradiction that you are very often drawn to is between the intense and the empty. As in *Filthy Words & Phrases*, where thousands of obscene phrases are chalked on a blackboard by a lone performer. Each act of writing, each phrase is psychologically charged, densely meaningful, but the context in which this takes place is almost totally blank.

ETCHELLS Much of our comedy is based on the absurdity of 'representing' the complexities of very charged ideas and emotions. In *Filthy Words & Phrases*, we list the words for very charged sexual things, in *Who Can Sing*, we're putting on stupid costumes to represent a camel or crocodile, or a tree, or in *(Let the Water)*, we play a game with tomato ketchup thrown around to represent blood in a series of violent deaths. In each case it is a very double statement; about the inherent failure in the system of rep-

ETCHELLS Ja, das trifft für ziemlich viele der Shows zu. Es gibt eine Oberfläche, und die Leute können sie sehr wörtlich nehmen. Es war dasselbe mit *Pleasure* mit seiner trübseligen, melancholischen Unterwasseratmosphäre, aber zugleich war es für mich eine sehr witzige Show. Man musste über die absurde und bizarre Negativität des Ganzen wirklich lachen.

HEATHFIELD Euer schwarzer Humor kann sehr düster sein …

ETCHELLS In unserer Arbeit gab es immer den Wunsch, wirklich niedere, notorisch witzige Komödie neben oder inmitten wirklich harter Tragödie zu platzieren und beide durcheinander zu wirbeln. Ein Großteil unserer Arbeit dreht sich also um diese Ökonomie der Bedeutungsverschiebungen, der Transformationen.

Für uns ist die Komödie, die Absurdität und Vergnüglichkeit des Materials wirklich wichtig. Es gefällt mir nicht, wenn die Leute nur das Melancholische, das Abgefuckte und Gescheiterte sehen, wo es doch in Wirklichkeit normalerweise eine Art von hämischer Freude in unserer Arbeit gibt, selbst in der Trübseligkeit. Wie Robin umherstolpert und durch das Auge des Pferdekostüms trinkt, die Hosen um die Knöchel. Das ist quälend und verzweifelt, aber es ist auch sehr dumm und witzig und ziemlich glorreich in der Art, wie es sich exzessiv dieser Stimmung hingibt. Ich erinnere mich, wie Alan Read über *Showtime* sagte, mit einem Grinsen bis über beide Ohren: „Einige der billigsten Scherze Londons sind heute Abend hier im ICA." Er liebte es. Wir liebten es, das zu hören.

HEATHFIELD Der andere Widerspruch, zu dem es euch oft hinzieht, ist der zwischen dem Intensiven und dem Leeren. Wie in *Filthy Words & Phrases*, worin tausende von obszönen Sätzen von einem einsamen Performer mit Kreide auf eine Wandtafel geschrieben werden. Jeder Akt des Schreibens, jeder Satz ist psychologisch aufgeladen, gedrängt bedeutungsvoll, aber der Kontext, in dem dies stattfindet, ist fast gänzlich leer.

ETCHELLS Viel von unserer Komik beruht auf der Absurdität, die Komplexitäten hoch aufgeladener Ideen und Emotionen ‚repräsentieren' zu wollen. In *Filthy Words & Phrases* listen wir die Worte für hoch aufgeladene sexuelle Dinge auf, in *Who Can Sing* ziehen wir dumme Kostüme an, um ein Kamel oder ein Krokodil oder einen Baum zu repräsentieren, oder in *(Let the Water)* spielen wir ein Spiel, in dem wir Tomatenketchup in der Gegend herumwerfen, um in einer Reihe gewaltsamer Todesfälle Blut zu repräsentieren. In jedem dieser Fälle ist es eine sehr doppelbödige Aussage: über das Scheitern, das jedem Repräsentationssystem innewohnt, und zugleich über den Spaß und das Vergnügen darin. Sie genießen das Spiel. Sie sind darin erfinderisch. Sie geben sich ihm hin und haben ihren Spaß daran. Und dieser Spaß, dieses Vergnügen ist wirklich wichtig.

Übersetzt von Benjamin Marius Schmidt

resentation, and, at the same time, about the inherent fun and pleasures in it. They enjoy the game. They are inventive in it. They surrender to it and are pleased by it. And the pleasures are really important.

Filthy Words & Phrases

Bent cops beat a confession out of a suspect; dentists make unnecessary extractions; surgeons make incisions and remove diseased tissue.

Great Battles from History are presented.
Hastings. Agincourt. The Somme.
The Battle of Gettysburg.
The Battle of Stalingrad. Ice. Mud. Body parts.

In a field, a horse is blinded.
Somewhere, a cow is slaughtered.
Dogs bait Badgers.
Kids shit in an abandoned flat.
A strange snow starts to fall.

Dirty Work

And on the Thousandth Night ...

Shakespeare's Grin
Remarks on World Theatre with
Forced Entertainment

Shakespeares Grinsen
Anmerkungen zum Welttheater
bei Forced Entertainment

Hans-Thies Lehmann

Seltsam genug: Forced Entertainment erinnert, immer wieder, an Shakespeare. Und dies, obwohl von einer direkten Anlehnung oder Ähnlichkeit offenbar überhaupt keine Rede sein kann. Das postdramatische Theater der Truppe um Tim Etchells ist denkbar weit entfernt vom großen Drama, von den monumentalen Schlachtszenen und Wortgewittern, Monologen, beißenden politischen Streitreden, den lyrischen, romantischen, komischen oder düster-tragischen Bühnen-Stimmungen, an die man beim Namen Shakespeare denkt. Vielmehr findet man auf dem Grat zwischen Theater und Performance, den Forced Entertainment bespielt, eine höchst gegenwärtige szenische Formel, die nichts zu tun zu haben scheint mit der dramatischen Logik des elisabethanischen Autors: fragile und fragliche, flüchtig scheinende, momentan konstruierte Subjekte statt runder Charaktere; durative Ästhetik der Langzeit-Performance anstelle narrativer Spannungssteigerung, situatives Spiel mit der Theatersituation statt Errichtung eines fiktiven dramatischen Universums. Und dennoch drängen solche Gefühle und Eindrücke, wie sie sich mit dem Namen Shakespeare verbinden, immer wieder an die Oberfläche, wenn man den witzigen und melancholischen, skurrilen, absurden,

Curiously enough, Forced Entertainment reminds one over and over of Shakespeare. This is true, although an obvious imitation or similarity cannot be spoken of. The post-dramatic theatre of the troupe gathered around Tim Etchells is far removed from the great drama, the monumental battle scenes and verbal thunderstorms, monologues, biting political polemics, lyrical, romantic, comic, and darkly tragic stage atmospheres that one associates with Shakespeare. One discovers a resolutely contemporary scenic formula on the line between theatre and performance that Forced Entertainment play out, which apparently has nothing to do with the Elizabethan author's dramatic logic: fleeting, fragile and questionable subjects constructed in an instant instead of rounded characters; a durative aesthetic of long haul performance instead of a rise in narrative tension; situational playing with the theatre itself instead of the construction of a fictive dramatic universe. Nevertheless, the feelings and impressions often associated with Shakespeare's name rise to the surface during Forced Entertainment performances, moving as they are by the depth of their feeling as well as intelligently thought out, witty and melancholy, bizarre and absurd.

Shakespeare's Grin / Remarks on World Theatre with Forced Entertainment
Shakespeares Grinsen / Anmerkungen zum Welttheater bei Forced Entertainment

Hans-Thies Lehmann

It is not just that allusions to Shakespeare crop up occasionally in the troupe's discourse – that *Macbeth* is mentioned, or that the performance *And on the Thousandth Night* … sometimes commences with the tale "once upon a time there was a king who had three daughters", or else that allusions are made – decipherable as a repetitive motif in their theatrical performances – to the masks and mistaken identity motifs in *Midsummer Night's Dream* and other comedies. It is rather a matter of a lingering, indirect and deeper correspondence, not something to be directly grasped, but rather approached.

… all the stage is a world …

The impression of an open world without borders, even if sometimes cloaked in fog or surrounded by prison walls – this impression is nearly always present in Shakespeare's theatre. Empires of thought and matter – wide and inexhaustible, endless in their various aspects, from those encompassing the world to the most banal – are travelled by this theatre with the breath of *Welt-Zeit* (world time), back and forth, between fairy tales and reality, dream and triviality, the cosmos and the inn, between Lear and Falstaff, the sublime and the inebriated, tragic and comic. No restrictive unity of style, no atmosphere without ambiguity. Nothing seems to be ruled out here. It is just the kind of feeling one has when watching Forced Entertainment, for here too, the theatre is reaching effortlessly across the most varied areas imaginable, amalgamating wit, black humour, fear, and melancholy. Banality joins in with the most profound feelings (or vice versa), everyday life seems such that everyday life (*Alltag*) turns out to be really a "day in space" (*Tag im All*, Rolf Dieter Brinkmann). Story and digression, endless reporting and interruption produce a feeling of *Welt-Fülle* (fullness of the world), which is a rare enough occurrence –

durch ihre Gefühlstiefe berührenden und zugleich so intelligent reflektierten Theaterabenden von Forced Entertainment beiwohnt. Es geht dabei nicht darum, dass im Diskurs der Truppe Hinweise auf Shakespeare gelegentlich auftauchen, *Macbeth* erwähnt wird, die Performance *And on the Thousandth Night* … zuweilen mit der Geschichte beginnt, dass es – „es war einmal" – einen König gab, der drei Töchter hatte, oder Anspielungen auf das Masken- und Vertauschspiel im *Sommernachtstraum* und anderen Komödien als wiederkehrendes Motiv der Aufführungen zu dechiffrieren sind. Es geht um eine zugleich indirektere und tiefere Korrespondenz, die eher umkreist als dingfest gemacht werden soll.

… all the stage is a world …

Der Eindruck offener, grenzenloser Welt, auch wenn sie manchmal neblig verhangen oder von Kerkermauern umschlossen ist – dieser Eindruck ist fast immer präsent im Shakespearetheater. Weit und unerschöpflich in der Unendlichkeit ihrer Aspekte, vom weltumspannenden bis zum banalsten, sind die gedanklichen und materiellen Reiche, die dieses Theater mit dem großen Atem einer *Welt-Zeit* bereist, kreuz und quer zwischen Märchen und Wirklichkeit, Traum und Trivialität, Kosmos und Kneipe, Lear und Falstaff, Erhabenheit und Suff, Tragik und Komik. Keine begrenzende Stileinheit, keine eindeutige Atmosphäre. Nichts scheint ausgeschlossen. Gerade ein solches Gefühl aber stellt sich auch bei Forced Entertainment ein, auch hier quert das Theater mühelos die verschiedensten Bereiche, amalgamiert dabei Witz, schwarzen Humor, Angst und Melancholie. Das Banale mischt sich in die tiefsten Gefühle (oder umgekehrt), das Alltägliche erscheint so, dass Alltag wirklich ein „Tag im All" wird (Rolf Dieter Brinkmann). Erzählung und Abschweifung, endloses Berichten und Unterbrechen erzeugen das Gefühl einer Welt-Fülle, die sehr selten ist, sehr britisch vielleicht, weil einer Geschichte reicher (shakespearescher) Theaterlust entspringend. In *Dirty Work* werden die dreckigen Menschheitskatastrophen von Atomkrieg, Attentat und Bürgerkrieg mit absurden und komischen Alltagserzählungen verbunden, das Tödliche wird von einfachen Personen leise erzählt. Clownerie und tödlicher Ernst vermischen sich, wenn in *First Night* eine Spielerin von der Bühne herab individuellen Zuschauern Krankheiten andichtet oder ihren baldigen Tod prophezeit. Und es tritt ins Bewusstsein, wie sehr das Sich-Einlassen auf die Theatersituation Phantasie und Realität miteinander vermischen, wie ein Moment kindlicher Naivität in Abgründe der Lebenserfahrung führen kann.

Das Shakespeare-Theater hatte wie kaum ein anderes die Möglichkeit, ‚Welt' in ihrer unbegrenzbaren Fülle und letzten Sinnleere zugleich auszusagen. Es stand unter Leitworten wie *„totus mundus agit histrionem"* und *„all the world's a stage"*. Das war in den glücklichen Zeiten, als die Bretter der Bühne noch die Welt bedeuten konnten. Und es überrascht, wenn es in unserer Zeit Forced Entertainment immer wieder gelingt, sich im Spiegel einer solchen Theateridee, wenn auch verschoben und verzerrt, zu verdoppeln und Bühne tatsächlich noch einmal Welt bedeuten zu lassen. Das Obszöne und Gewaltsame, das Lyrische und der decouvrierende Witz, Philosophie und Blödelei stehen nebeneinander, vermischen sich, beleuchten sich wechselweise. ‚Welt' aber heißt hier nicht die von einer (vierten) Wand abgeschlossene Totalität einer Fiktion, sondern eine zum Publikum hin offene, eine wesentlich mögliche, von Potentialität durchzogene Welt.

... und eine Zeit ...

Zeit, Medium und Elixier aller Theatererfahrung, erscheint im Shakepeare-Theater weder als kontinuierliche Linie, noch als mythisch oder religiös überwölbte Ordnung, sondern gleichsam als unordentliches Wortknäuel aus Zeitfäden: Theater als Zeit-Ball. Darin kreuzen und verwickeln, parodieren

grounded perhaps in a very British history of rich Shakespearean theatrical pleasure. In *Dirty Work,* the filthy catastrophes of humanity, such as atomic war, assassination, and civil war, are conjoined with absurd and comical stories from everyday life. The deadly is narrated softly by simple people. When, from her position onstage, a female player in *First Night* ascribes illnesses to or prophesizes the future death of individual audience members, clownery and dead earnestness are mixed. And it is striking how much fantasy and reality are melded while one submits to the theatre situation, how moments of childlike naiveté can lead into the greater depths of life experience.

In Shakespeare's theatre, as in no other, it was possible to express 'the world' in all of its unbound fullness and final lack of meaning. It operated under the principles described with key phrases like *"totus mundus agit histrionem"* and "all the world's a stage". Those were the happy days when the boards of the stage were still able to mean the world. And it is a surprise when – mirroring this idea of theatre, however shifted and distorted in our own day – Forced Entertainment succeed in making the stage mean the world once more. The obscene and the violent, the lyrical and the revealing joke, philosophy and plain silliness stand next to each other, mix and illuminate each other. Here, 'world' does not mean the walled-off (by a fourth wall) fictional totality, but a world open to its audience, an essentially possible world, pregnant with potentiality.

... and a time ...

Time, the medium and elixir of all theatre experience, appears in Shakespeare's theatre neither as a continuous line nor as a mythical or religious order, but rather as a disorderly knot containing words, made out of threads of time as it were:

Shakespeare's Grin / Remarks on World Theatre with Forced Entertainment
Shakespeares Grinsen / Anmerkungen zum Welttheater bei Forced Entertainment
Hans-Thies Lehmann

theatre as a ball of time (*Zeit-Ball*) as I would like to call it. In this, the different arcs of time belonging to the crown and to the people criss-cross each other and get caught in each other, parodying and obscuring each other, as do those of the animal and human worlds, nature and the state, the stars and the dynasties, time of the generations of the old families and that of the individual body and psychology. Just as Shakespeare generates this contradictory, multi-layered view, so in another way, a sense of disparity, ambiguity, and discontinuity has been inserted into the theatre of Forced Entertainment. Instead of employing a fictional *Welt-Zeit*, the post-dramatic insistence on constituting onstage time and space is realized in their work with the use of jumps, breaks and gaps of time, with variations and loops of repetition. In one moment, the Forced Entertainment performance points to contemporary history and real or imagined universal catastrophes; in the next, it points to the individual's most intimate pleasures and fears in life. In Shakespeare, the sublime progressions and lyrical flights to ever greater depth always touch base with an everyday realism. While the rays of Shakespeare's language explode in all directions and produce *Welt-Zeit*, continually referring to the time of the theatre event itself, Forced Entertainment meanwhile deepen the imploding *Welt-Fülle* (fullness of the world) by playing with the various layers of reality present in the theatre process. Hence their continual skipping over the traditional dramatic-theatrical means: "Why waste time with psychology, character exposition, even plot and development, if all anyone must know has been written on a show card … While on the one hand, it is a theatre in a shrunken state, a reduction bordering on the grotesque, on the other hand it is an explosion juggling with the means of the theatre until there's almost nothing left. If one wants, it can be termed deconstruction too" (Peter Laudenbach, *Frankfurter Allgemeine Zeitung*).

und verdecken sich wechselweise die unterschiedlichen Zeitbögen der Krone und des Volks, der Tier- und Menschenwelt, der Natur und des Staats, der Sterne und der Dynastien, Zeit der Generation der Geschlechter, des individuellen Körpers und der Psychologie. In die Form des Theaters von Forced Entertainment sind nun auf andere Weise Disparatheit, Vielschichtigkeit und Diskontinuität der Zeit eingesenkt. Die postdramatische Insistenz darauf, vor aller fiktiven Welt-Zeit eine eigene Raum-Zeit der Bühne zu konstituieren, realisiert sich hier durch Sprünge, Brüche, Lücken der Zeit, Variationen und Wiederholungsschleifen. In einem Moment weist das Spiel auf Zeitgeschichte und reale oder phantasierte Katastrophen, im nächsten auf intimste Fragen nach Lust und Ängsten des individuellen Lebens. Auch die erhabenen Steigerungen und lyrischen Vertiefungen bei Shakespeare berühren immer den alltagsnahen Realismus. Wo aber bei Shakespeare die Strahlen der Sprache in alle Richtungen explodieren und so Welt-Zeit erzeugen, die immer wieder auf die Zeit des Theatervorgangs selbst führt, vertieft Forced Entertainment die implodierende Welt-Fülle durch das Spiel mit den Realitäts-Schichten des Spielvorgangs. Daher das andauernde Überspringen der tradierten dramatischen Theatermittel: „Weshalb Zeit mit Psychologie, Figurenzeichnung, gar Handlung und Entwicklung verlieren, wenn alles, was man über eine Figur wissen muss, auf einem Plakat Platz hat. … Einerseits ist das eine Art Schrumpfzustand des Theaters, eine in die Groteske führende Reduktion, andererseits ist es eine Explosion, die die Mittel des Theaters durcheinanderwirbelt, bis kaum noch etwas von ihnen übrig ist. Wer will, darf das auch Dekonstruktion nennen" (Peter Laudenbach, *Frankfurter Allgemeine Zeitung*).

Das Besondere an diesem Theater ist die Orientierung der gesamten Spielanlage auf die Beziehung zwischen Spielenden und Zuschauenden, auf die Abgründe und die lustigen und provozierenden Möglichkeiten, die das konti-

Pleasure

nuierliche und intensive Bespielen der ‚Theatron-Achse' mit sich bringt, das fortwährende Ausspielen der Potentialitäten des Theaters als Situation. Darin lebt aber ein charakteristisches Motiv des Shakespearetheaters fort: exemplarische Gestalt des großen Theaters der dramatischen Narration, das Spiegel und Zerlegung seiner Epoche ist, gilt es auch als Inbegriff des vitalsten Kontakts zwischen den Akteuren und dem bunt gemischten, um die *prone stage* des Globe Theatre sich drängenden Publikum. Das elisabethanische Theater war auf seine Weise in jedem Moment im Gespräch mit dem Publikum, antizipierte, erfüllte, enttäuschte dessen Erwartungen, ließ sich auf das Spiel mit ihm ein. Niemals zog es sich in die *splendid isolation* der formalen Vollkommenheit zurück. Wie ist, so fragt die Theaterarbeit von Forced Entertainment, heute solch ein Zusammenhang

What's special about this kind of theatre is the orientation of the whole theatre situation towards the relationship between players and audience, to the abysses and humorous, provocative possibilities, which emerge from the continuous and intense playing on the *theatron-axis*, a constant playing-out of the potentialities of theatre-as-a-situation. Inherent here is the continuation of a characteristic motif of Shakespearean theatre – the grand, exemplary theatre of dramatic narration, mirroring and stripping bare its own day and age: the extraordinarily vital contact between the actors and the motley assemblage of persons making up an audience, crowding around the prone stage of the Globe Theatre. The Elizabethan theatre was in its own way engaged in a continuous conversation with its audience, anticipating, fulfilling, disappointing

108

Shakespeare's Grin / Remarks on World Theatre with Forced Entertainment
Shakespeares Grinsen / Anmerkungen zum Welttheater bei Forced Entertainment
Hans-Thies Lehmann

expectations, playing a game with them. It never withdrew into the splendid isolation of perfection of form. Forced Entertainment's theatre work asks: how can such a connection and communication be created between the theatre and its audience today? And they find an answer, constantly reformulated creatively: By turning the scenic tensions into contact with their visitors, by slipping them inside each other. In *And on the Thousandth Night …*, stories are commenced, then continuously interrupted – the direction of energy is constantly switched. At times, following the interruption of a particularly good story, one waits desperately for it to be taken up again, so that it might get another chance. At other times, the stories become a matter of indifference, as one fixes one's attention on the 'drama' of small acts of mutual aggression and support, of coalitions and collective inspiration, which arises between the actors, as they play this game of interruptions.

Roles – Playing – Identity

Any reflection about Forced Entertainment leads to the question of the Subject, to the play with identity. The very arrangement of seven 'kings' and 'queens' telling stories for hours allows everybody to be a 'king' or a 'queen' and thus makes the monarch's (the individual's) role a serial one. Identity as role-playing, as function, as communication (within the scene, with the audience) becomes the question of the Subject asked scenically. Tim Etchells: "… Identity on stage is now rarely a fixed point. More often … the performers are seen as sharing a constituency of texts in which their own part or parts must be worked out, or in which their role is ever fluid – subject to play and to change …" ("Diverse Assembly: Some Trends in Recent Performance", in Thomas Shank: *Contemporary British Theatre*). The actors and their playing

von Theater und Zuschauer möglich? Und sie finden darauf eine Antwort, kreativ immer wieder neu formuliert: fortwährend die innerszenische Spannung auf den Kontakt zu den Besuchern umzuwenden, beides ineinander zu schieben. Geschichten in *And on the Thousandth Night …* werden, über viele Stunden hin, immer wieder begonnen und unterbrochen – und fortwährend wechselt die energetische Richtung: Einmal wartet man fast verzweifelt darauf, dass der schöne Ansatz einer Geschichte noch einmal wieder aufgegriffen wird, eine neue Chance erhält; dann aber werden die Geschichten gleichgültig, weil man sich ganz auf das ,Drama' der wechselseitigen kleinen Aggressionen, Hilfestellungen, Koalitionen und gegenseitigen Inspirationen konzentriert, das im Spiel der Akteure miteinander und mit der Unterbrechung zum Ausdruck kommt.

Rollen – Spiel – Identität

Jedes Nachdenken über Forced Entertainment führt sogleich auf das Spiel mit der Identität, auf das Subjekt. Schon die Idee, sieben ,Könige' und ,Königinnen' über Stunden hin erzählen zu lassen, lässt jeden Menschen König oder Königin sein und macht die Rolle des Monarchen (des Individuums) seriell. Identität als Spiel von Rolle, Funktion, Kommunikation (innerszenisch und mit dem Publikum) wird zur szenisch aufgeworfenen Frage nach dem Subjekt. Tim Etchells: „Identität auf der Bühne ist heute nur selten ein Fixpunkt. Viel eher … haben die Darsteller einen gemeinsamen Textfundus, aus dem sie ihre eigene Rolle oder Rollen erarbeiten müssen, oder in dem sich die Rolle – Spiel und Veränderung ausgesetzt – in ständigem Fluss befindet." („Diverse Assembly: Some Trends in Recent Performance", in: Thomas Shank: *Contemporary British Theatre*) Damit werden, so Etchells, Spieler und Spielraum „Möglichkeitsräume". Formuliert ist das in Hinblick auf die neuere Performance allgemein, aber lesbar besonders als Beschreibung der eigenen Theateridee. Forced

Entertainment erprobt, wohin das Fehlen konstanter Rollenfiktion führt und entdeckt eine unerwartet komplexe Situation. Die betonte Ausstellung der Spieler als die realen Personen, die sie sind, führt nämlich nicht einfach zum Durchbruch des ‚Authentischen' durch die Theaterfiktion, vielmehr wird ihr reales Tun als Schauspieler selbst zu einer Rolle. Die Spieler referieren auf Fiktionen, Figuren und im nächsten (oder sogar gleichen) Moment auf ihr Spielen selbst, sie spielen Spielende und Gespielte.

Das kann ganz locker geschehen, wenn sie sich serienweise in erfundene oder reale Figuren nur dadurch verwandeln, dass sie vor sich selbst oder dem Mitspieler eine simple Papptafel halten („Eine Frau mit Vergangenheit", „Zwei Liebende (die nicht sprechen)" usw.) und so Fantasien freisetzen. Oder es wird in beinahe bedrohlicher Weise durch die Ambiguität von Spiel, Fiktion und ironischem Spiel im Spiel (und mit dem Publikum) die Unfassbarkeit der persönlichen Identität, die Unzugänglichkeit des Realen gesteigert. Wir gleiten in eine Schräglage der klassischen Frage nach Schein und Sein – aber nicht über die Thematisierung (den Inhalt) eines Dramas, sondern über das Formprinzip des Theater-Spiels. Die Zuschauer werden durch die besondere Art der Kommunikation mit dem Publikum in ebenso tiefer Weise mit den Verwirrungen der Identität konfrontiert wie im Theater der frühen Neuzeit – bildet doch in Shakespeares Stücken immer wieder der Zweifel über Schein und Sein ein wesentliches Spiel-Ferment. Zumal in Shakespeares Komödien und Romances besteht das menschliche Subjekt aus eigentlich nichts anderem als (oft genug verdoppelten und vervielfachten) Verkleidungs- und Rollenspielen. Jede Figur verfängt sich in Textfäden, die sie nicht wirklich selbst zu entwirren vermag und die sich schon gar nicht zum einheitlich gewobenen Porträt fügen. Radikal instabile Identität ist ein zentrales Motiv des Spiels, und ist wiederum untrennbar von Lust und Notwendigkeit des Rollenspiels. (Die Frau, tatsächlich gespielt

space become "zones of possibility", according to Etchells. This statement was formulated to describe the general scene of new performance, but also stands as a description of Forced Entertainment's own particular notion of theatre. Forced Entertainment's work asks where the elimination of fixed fictional roles can lead and in attempting to answer, discovers an unexpectedly complex situation. The emphasis placed on the actors themselves, as real people, doesn't lead to an emergence of 'authenticity' in theatre fiction, but instead, the actors' real actions lead to a new kind of 'role': The players refer to fictions, to characters, but in the next minute (or even at the same time) they are referring to their own playing. They play somebody playing and being played.

This can easily occur when they serially transform themselves into invented or real figures by holding up a cardboard sign, in front of themselves or their co-players ("A Woman with a Past", "Two Lovers (Not Speaking)", etc.), thus letting the imagination run free. Or else, the incomprehensibility of personal identity and the inaccessibility of the real are increased in an almost threatening way by the ambiguity of playing, fiction and ironic play within the play and play with the audience. We're sliding here toward the slope inherent in the classical question of appearance and reality – not by the thematization (content) of a drama, but by the performance's principle of form. This special form of communication with the audience confronts them with confusions of identity as pronounced as those of the theatre of the early modern era – for in most of Shakespeare's plays, doubt about appearance and reality occurs as a chief fermentative element. In Shakespeare's comedies and romances in particular, the human subject consists of not much more than disguises and role-playing, often in duplicated and multiple forms. Each character is caught up in text

Shakespeare's Grin / Remarks on World Theatre with Forced Entertainment
Shakespeares Grinsen / Anmerkungen zum Welttheater bei Forced Entertainment
Hans-Thies Lehmann

threads, from which they cannot get disentangled and which do not conform to a tightly woven, unified portrait. Radically unstable identity is one of the central motifs of playing, and is in turn inseparable from the pleasure and necessity of role-playing. (In the play, the woman, played actually by a man, disguises herself as a man to win over a man, while at the same time another woman falls in love with the woman who seems to be a man …) In the post-dramatic theatre of Forced Entertainment, there is not a direct thematization (by fable, by dramaturgy, by speech) of such Shakespearean confusions, but the instability of identity becomes immediate experience thanks to the structure of insecure perception built into the theatrical process itself – by means of which identity is turned into an object of doubt and reflection in another way.

Forced Entertainment consciously play with the impossibility of pure honesty. A peculiar and puzzling ambiguity regarding the person onstage is established by playing with, aspiring to, parodying and withdrawing honesty. At the end of the performance, the audience may leave with the uncertain feeling of having known the actors as actual acquaintances, and yet the actors remain at the same time inaccessible, unreachable as stage personae: In the lobby afterwards, they seem to be sympathetic people, but their stage existence is more questionable. Thus the 'characters' of Forced Entertainment are illuminated in a Shakespearean doubtfulness. The beauty of the Shakespearean characters consists of their fluid, increasingly nuanced, rhetorically adept speech-making – they seem to be speaking out their guts, literally – yet the result of their revealing themselves in this way is a radical inaccessibility of their inner being. This leads to the recurring problem with every reading and staging of Shakespeare: how to interpret his *dramatis personae*. The traces of their identity get lost in the

von einem Mann, verkleidet sich im Spiel als Mann, um einen Mann zu gewinnen, während sich zugleich wiederum eine Frau in den scheinbaren Mann verliebt …) In der postdramatischen Theaterpraxis von Forced Entertainment kommt es zwar nicht zu einer direkten Thematisierung (durch Fabel, Dramaturgie, Rede) solch shakespearescher Verwirrungen, aber die Instabilität der Identität wird unmittelbare Erfahrung durch die Struktur der verunsicherten Wahrnehmung im Theatervorgang selbst, über die dann Identität in anderer Weise Gegenstand von Zweifel und Reflexion werden kann.

Bewusst spielt Forced Entertainment mit der Unmöglichkeit reiner Ehrlichkeit. Weil sie gespielt, angestrebt, zugleich parodiert und entzogen wird, teilt sich eine eigentümliche Rätselhaftigkeit der Bühnen-Personen mit. Jeder macht vielleicht die Erfahrung, dass er am Ende der Performance das undeutliche Gefühl hat, die Spieler wie tatsächliche Bekannte zu kennen – zugleich aber sind sie gerade dadurch als szenische Figuren ungreifbar: Sympathische Menschen im Foyer nach der Vorstellung, umso fraglicher in ihrer Bühnenexistenz. So leuchten die 'Charaktere' von Forced Entertainment in shakespearescher Zweifelhaftigkeit. Die Schönheit der Shakespeare-Gestalten beruht darauf, dass sie sich so ausgiebig, nuanciert und rhetorisch gesteigert aussprechen, ihr Inneres förmlich ausschütten scheinen – und dass trotzdem ihre Darstellung gerade in einer radikalen Unzugänglichkeit ihres Inneren resultiert. Was dazu führt, dass sich das Problem der Auslegung seiner *dramatis personae* bei jeder Lektüre und Inszenierung Shakespeares immer wieder neu stellt. Die Spuren möglicher Identitäts-Zuschreibungen verlieren sich in der Komplexität und womöglich beabsichtigten Undeutlichkeit der Textstrukturen. Bei Forced Entertainment ist die undurchsichtige Komplexität des Ich nicht mehr ein Thema, das in einer dramatischen Fiktion ausgeleuchtet wird, sondern Substanz eines postdramatischen Spieltyps mit seiner ganz eigenen Theatralität,

And on the Thousandth Night ...

bei dem an die Stelle der Dichte des Dramas die Fülle der Verweise auf die Lebensumwelt, Medien und persönlichen Lebensprobleme, Popkultur und Politik tritt. Florian Malzacher über *Emanuelle Enchanted*: „Nachrichten, Geschichten, Ängste und Träume dringen herein wie wirre Stimmen im nächtlichen Funkverkehr: Figuren tauchen auf, verschwinden wieder, ihre Identitäten sind wechselhaft, vielleicht beliebig. (…) Jeder Zuschauer ist in die Verantwortung genommen, aktiv zu sehen, sich selbst beim (nicht selten voyeuristischen) Schauen zu beobachten und seine eigenen Verknüpfungen, seine eigene Inszenierung herzustellen. Und so zum alleinigen Kronzeugen und Interpret der Aufführung zu werden – eine Aufgabe, aus der ihn hier kein allwissender Dramatiker oder Regisseur entlässt" (*Frankfurter Rundschau* 14. 2. 2001).

complexity and in an arguably intentional ambiguity of the dramatic text. The impenetrable complexity of the ego is not illuminated by Forced Entertainment as a theme in a dramatic fiction, but becomes the very substance of their post-dramatic type of performing, that has its own theatricality, whereby various allusions to the context of daily life, media, personal problems, pop culture and politics replace dramatic density. Florian Malzacher on *Emanuelle Enchanted*: "… News, stories, fears, and dreams float in like confused voices on the radio at night: characters pop up, disappear once more, their identity malleable, perhaps arbitrary … Every member of the audience has the responsibility to see actively, to observe himself while he is (often voyeuristically) watching, and to make his own

And on the Thousandth Night ...

connections, his own stage production. Thus, to become the performance's only crown-witness and interpreter – a task no all-knowing playwright or director can take away from him …" (*Frankfurter Rundschau*, 14 February 2001).

Children and Clowns

Renate Klett (*Die Zeit*) once nicely observed that what the troupe around Tim Etchells offered was a "mixture of acting, performance, and live act", an "elevated children's theatre for adults", emphasizing the moments of theatre naiveté that always come through despite the refinement and complexity of Forced Entertainment's stage productions. This naiveté is not easily explicated, for in the theatre, the programmatic pres-

Kinder und Clowns

Schön hat Renate Klett (*Die Zeit*) einmal die „Mischung aus Schauspiel, Performance und Live Act", die die Truppe um Tim Etchells bietet, ein „überhöhtes Kindertheater für Erwachsene" genannt und damit die bei aller reflektierten Raffinesse und Komplexität der Aufführungen doch immer spürbaren Momente ihrer Theater-Naivität bezeichnet. Diese Naivität ist nicht leicht erklärlich, denn die programmatische Präsenz der Schauspieler als reale Personen ist ja theaterästhetisch durchaus unnaiv. Sie ist gespielt, damit die Grenze zwischen Gespieltem und „Authentischem" umso ungewisser werde. Doch ein shakespearescher Gestus des „einfachen" Theaters, des Direkten, Tabulosen, auch der Volksbelustigung schlägt immer wieder durch.

Die Vorliebe für die schlichten, traditionellen Theater- und Showelemente trägt dazu bei: möglichst abgeschabte Vorhangdraperien wie im Dorftheater von einst, Königskronen aus Pappe, simple Schiefertafeln, ungelenk beschriftete Schildchen, die die Spieler zur (trügerischen, zweifelhaften) Identifizierung hochhalten, übergroße Tiermasken usw. Gerade eine solch bunte Vielfalt der Stil- und Wirklichkeitsebenen macht aber auch die singuläre Erinnerung aus, die man vom Shakespeare-Theater zurückbehält. Das Grobgezimmerte, in dem sich das Subtile einnistet; die theaterhaft falsche Übertreibung, von der der große Stil der Mimen kaum zu trennen ist; die offensichtliche Illusionstechnik, die vom Zuschauer erwartet, durch das Naive hindurch das Komplexe zu erspüren: so lässt sich eine im traditionellen Theater wie in der *theatrical performance* relevante Dimension von Zirkus- und Showelement beschreiben. So viel Theater: die Requisiten wie aus dem Kinderzimmer, die eiligen Kostümwechsel, die Masken, das Markieren eines sterbenden Angeschossenen, der endlos jammert, während ihm die ‚Gedärme‘ hervorquellen – durch auf den Bauch gepresste Spaghetti in Tomatensauce dargestellt (in *Showtime*). Die um den nackten Oberkörper gebundene Zeitbombe, die alberne Verkleidung als Bäume, barfüßige Könige mit roten Roben oder eine traurige Performerin mit Hundemaske – all das hat den ironischen Stil englischer Theaterkultur, verrät seine Herkunft von lange her: aus der Shakespeare-Zeit.

Ja, und die Clowns. Die Akteure von Forced Entertainment verstehen es zu agieren wie *stand-up comedians*, Showmaster oder wie im Slapstick-Film, sie beherrschen die Register der Theater-Komik. Bei Shakespeare sind die Clowns-Szenen ein wichtiges Mittel, niemals eine zu schmale Eingrenzung des Spiels auf die ernste Handlung zuzulassen. Um Welthaltigkeit zu steigern, wird die Sphäre der tragischen Bühne immer wieder auf alle Aspekte des Lebens hin aufgerissen: das Grausame und das Groteske, das Triviale und Primitive

ence of the actors, as real persons is not at all aesthetically naive. It is played out onstage so that the boundary between playing and 'authenticity' becomes increasingly unclear. But nonetheless, a Shakespearean quality of 'simple' theatre – direct, without taboos, as popular amusement – always gets through. Adding to this effect is Forced Entertainment's preference for unpretentious and traditional elements of show and theatre: the most dilapidated drapery employed as a stage curtain, like the one a village theatre might use, cardboard crowns, old-fashioned blackboards, small, clumsily written signs used by the actors for the purpose of (misleading, dubious) identification, oversized animal masks, etc. It is precisely this multiplicity of stylistic and realistic levels in Shakespeare's theatre that one retains as a unique memory. Roughly hewn elements, in which subtlety takes root; theatrically fake exaggeration, which is a vital part of the grand style of the mime; the obvious technique of illusion that expects an audience to perceive complexity through the naïve – the circus and show elements of traditional theatre and theatrical performance may be thus described. This much theatre: props like those in a child's room, a rushed change of costume, masks, a dying man, who ceaselessly laments his fate, while his spilled 'intestines' – represented by spaghetti in tomato sauce – are pressed to his belly (in *Showtime*). A time-bomb tied to a naked upper torso, preposterous tree costumes, barefoot kings in red robes, or a sad female performer wearing a dog mask – everything done in an ironical style prevalent in the English theatre culture, betraying its origin from long ago: the age of Shakespeare.

And the clowns. The actors of Forced Entertainment understand how to play as stand-up comedians, show masters, or like those in a slapstick film. They have mastered theatre comedy in all its registers. The Shakespearean

Shakespeare's Grin / Remarks on World Theatre with Forced Entertainment
Shakespeares Grinsen / Anmerkungen zum Welttheater bei Forced Entertainment

Hans-Thies Lehmann

clown scenes are important as a means of preventing the play from becoming too narrow by concentrating only on serious action. The spheres of the tragic stage are torn wide open to allow in all aspects of life, thus increasing the amount of the world contained in it: cruel and grotesque, trivial and primitive, sublime and lyrical. Clownish elements manifest themselves throughout the theatre of Forced Entertainment. In *Quizoola!*, two players wearing clown makeup, take turns interrogating each other, with an occasional cruelty that soon destroys any one-sided fixation on a single mood. Melancholy, shock, laughter, satirical distance are all interchanged. Being a professional 'alienator' (even in the Brechtian sense) was always a clown's peculiarity, whereas the traditional actor tended to dissolve himself into, merge completely with the role. The clown's comedy is the mask of sadness. His actions seem meaningful despite his apparent unworldliness and naiveté, offering stuff for reflection through tears and laughter. It is exactly this quality that reappears over and over again in Forced Entertainment. In calling up the most common situations onstage and in their addresses to the audience aimed as provocations, the distance between playing and seriousness, between malignant comedy and empathetic melancholy, collapses. Shakespearean clown theatre.

Theatre of Language

The theatre work of Forced Entertainment thrives on the quality of its gestic performance and the atmosphere and aura created by its players while they build up ambiguous contact with the audience. It is from this experience that we understand anew certain themes of Shakespeare: those of role, identity, childish and awestruck *Welt-Fülle*, an undifferentiated mix of comedy and tragedy, the above and the below. But at the

ebenso wie das Sublime und Lyrische. Clowneske Elemente durchsetzen auch das Theater von Forced Entertainment. Die gegenseitige Inquisition zweier Spieler in Clownsschminke in *Quizoola!*, einem teilweise grausamen Lebens-Quiz, zerbricht jede einseitige Fixierung auf eine Stimmung. Melancholie, Schock, Gelächter, satirische Distanznahme wechseln einander ab. Es war immer die Besonderheit des Clowns, professioneller Verfremder zu bleiben, während der traditionelle Schauspieler dazu tendiert, sich in der Rolle aufzulösen. Die Komik des Clowns ist die Maske der Trauer, sein Tun, bei aller scheinbar naiver Weltfremdheit, wird als bedeutsam ausgestellt, der weinenden und lachenden Reflexion dargeboten. Genau dies kehrt bei Forced Entertainment immer wieder: im Nennen der schlichtesten Gegebenheiten, in den provozierenden Adressen an das Publikum bricht der Abstand zwischen Spiel und Ernst, bösartiger Komik und solidarischer Melancholie immer wieder zusammen. Shakespearisches Clownstheater.

Theater der Sprache

Die Arbeit von Forced Entertainment lebt aus der Qualität der gestischen Performanz, der Atmosphäre und Aura, die die Spieler erzeugen, um jenen vieldeutigen Kontakt mit dem Publikum aufzubauen, in dessen Erfahrung wir die shakespearischen Themen neu erfassen: Rolle, Identität, kindlich zu bestaunende Welt-Fülle, Ununterscheidbarkeit von Komik und Tragik, Oben und Unten. Zugleich aber geht es hier wie beim alten Theater-Vater vor allem um Sprache und Rede. Sie macht das tiefsinnige szenische Spiel mit Identitäten möglich. Bei Shakespeare sind es die vielschichtigen Metaphern, die rhetorischen Finessen, die Abundanz und dann wieder die präzis zugespitzte Dialogik der Rede, die ein Universum heraufbeschwören – weniger die dramatischen Fabeln, die meist aus anderen Quellen geborgt waren. Das elisabethanische Theater der Rede kam mit wenigen Requisiten aus, die Bühne war recht nackt. Im Wesentlichen musste, was man die Wortkulisse nennt, mit Hilfe der Phantasie der Zuschauer den szenischen Raum gestalten – Theater des Wortes. Vertrauen in die Evokationskraft von Sprache, von nur angedeuteten Geschichten, Worten und Namen charakterisiert auch die Arbeit von Forced Entertainment. Es geht um ein Sprech- und Worttheater, das aus tiefer Skepsis gegen die Bilder, zumal die kurrenten Medienbilder herrührt. Der Grund für diese Präferenz liegt auf der Hand. Dieses Theater verlegt ja, wie bemerkt, den eigentlichen Raum der Erfahrung nicht dahin, wo die Fiktion einer dramatischen Welt und die Phantasie des Zuschauers zusammentreffen, sondern vielmehr in jenen gemeinsamen realen Raum, der zwischen der Welt der Spieler und des Publikums vermittelt. Wenn postdramatisches Theater an die oberste Stelle nicht die dramatische Fiktion, sondern die situative Gemeinschaft des Theaterabends setzt, dann muss gerade die Dimension der sprachlichen Symbolisierung, der Ansprache und des Austauschs von Sprechen und Hören zum entscheidenden Katalysator der theatralen Kommunikation werden. Mögen sie noch so sehr verfremdet, fragmentiert, zäsuriert werden – Sprache und also Narration sind noch im Prozess ihrer Dekonstruktion der Kern des Theaters von Forced Entertainment – ganz ‚traditionell', ganz shakespearesch.

Ohne Drama, Theater

Erliegt man bei diesen Assoziationen nur einer nostalgischen Verkennung? Oder weisen sie in das Herz einer Theatralität, in der sich das Welttheater-Modell von einst, das Drama, am Beginn der bürgerlichen Neuzeit manifestierte, und die wiederum aufscheinen kann, durch und durch verwandelt, in der Gegenwart, einer Zeit nach der normativen Gültigkeit der dramatischen Figuration, einer Zeit am Endrand der bürgerlichen Gesellschaft, Kultur, Kunst? Keineswegs verhöhnt Forced Entertainment das Theater, wie man in

same time, it is particularly a matter of language, of speech, just the way it was in the theatre of the old father of the theatre. This makes a profound scenic play with identity possible. In Shakespeare's case, it is more a matter of his many-levelled metaphors, rhetorical finesse, the abundance and yet preciseness of his pointed dialogues, conjuring up a universe – and far less a matter of his dramatic fables, which, for the most part, have been borrowed from somewhere else. The Elizabethan theatre of speeches was able to get by with few props. The stage was rather naked. They mostly got by shaping their scenic space by exercising the audience's imagination: the theatre of the word. Faith in the evocative power of language, in stories just hinted at, in words and names, have all been characteristic of the work of Forced Entertainment. A theatre of speech, of the word, fuelled by a deep-seated scepticism about pictures, especially current media ones. The reason for this preference is obvious. This type of theatre does not seek to locate the space of experience on the line where the fiction of the dramatic world and the audience's imagination meet, but instead seeks to mediate between the real player's world and the audience. If post-dramatic theatre gives highest priority to the situational community of the performance and not to dramatic fiction, the dimensions of linguistic symbolization, address, exchange, speaking and hearing, will become the catalysts of theatrical communication. However estranged, fragmented and broken up, language and narration remain at the centre of Forced Entertainment's theatre, even during the process of their deconstruction – very 'traditional,' very Shakespearean.

Without Drama, Theatre

Do our Shakespearean associations signify that we have succumbed to nostalgic misperception?

Shakespeare's Grin / Remarks on World Theatre with Forced Entertainment
Shakespeares Grinsen / Anmerkungen zum Welttheater bei Forced Entertainment
Hans-Thies Lehmann

Or do they lead to the very heart of theatricality, which made itself manifest long ago, at the beginning of the bourgeois modern era, when our model of world-theatre – modern drama – was born? Could it not be that such theatricality – after a long period of normative dramatic figuration – has finally reappeared, completely transformed, at the borderline of bourgeois society, culture, art, in a post-dramatic shape? Forced Entertainment do not render theatre ridiculous, as some critics have occasionally claimed, but instead, reject only the conventional theatre with its worn-out dramaturgy. And Forced Entertainment theatre meets with the Elizabethan one as though pulled to a magnet of opposite charge – whereby it is difficult to say if this meeting emerged by the inner logic of performing or through dialogue with a particular British theatre tradition. This much is clear: What the Elizabethan theatre had done by means of fables, dramatic knotting-up of plot skeins, allegory, and tragic and comic conflict brought to extremes, can perhaps be communicated today by the theatre's own rigor and wit in their broken and post-dramatic forms. The lyricism of the theatre returns in the shape of an intimate contact with the audience and a melancholy atmosphere; tragic action is replaced and transformed by the act of playing with the very possibility of its existence as well as by speaking about dying and suicide, fright, and fears, in ways that may or may not be personal; the cosmic *Welt-Gefühl* (world feeling) emerges here not from spaciousness and variety of simulation, but from the intensely experienced world of the stage; the tension of the intrigue is now replaced with the attention that actors and audience pay to each other. In an age of unlimited information and ceaseless stories coming from the media, theatre cannot get in touch with reality if it remains satisfied with producing and reproducing only what amounts to scenic rep-

Kritiken gelegentlich lesen konnte, es lässt aber das konventionelle Theater mit seinen ausgelatschten Dramaturgien gelassen am Rand seines Weges liegen. Und dabei trifft es wie mit der elektrischen Spannung des Gegenpols auf den Elisabethaner – kaum entscheidbar, ob aus der Logik des Spiels und/oder aus einem bewussten Dialog mit ihrer spezifisch britischen Theatertradition heraus. Was sich in Fabeln, dramatischer Verknotung von Handlungsfäden, in Allegorien und zugespitzten tragischen oder komischen Konflikten im elisabethanischen Theater formulieren konnte, gelangt nun über die Strenge und den Witz des Theaters selbst, seiner gebrochenen postdramatischen Form, zur Mitteilung. Der Lyrismus des Theaters kehrt wieder in der Intimität des Publikumskontakts und der melancholischen Atmosphäre; tragische Handlung wird ersetzt und transformiert durch das Spielen mit ihrer Möglichkeit und immer wieder durch ein – zweifelhaft persönliches – Sprechen über Sterben und Selbstmord, Schrecken und Angst. Das Weltgefühl des Kosmos entsteht nicht aus Weite und Vielfalt des Fingierten, sondern des intensiv erlebten *environments* der Bühne; die Spannung der Intrige wandelt sich ins Miterleben der gespannten Aufmerksamkeit, die sich Akteure gegenseitig und den Zuschauern zuwenden. Theater kann im Zeitalter umfassender Information und pausenloser medialer Erzählerei keine Berührung mit Wirklichkeit erzielen, wenn es immer wieder nur mehr oder minder gelungene szenische Ab(zieh)bilder von Realität nach geläufigen Anordnungen produziert und reproduziert. Aber es können durch Theater Situationen hergestellt werden, in denen als Struktur und Formgesetz, als ‚Haltung' der Spieler und durch eine Atmosphäre all jene Motive wieder erscheinen, die einmal als Drama und Symbol, Fiktion und Welt-Bild existieren konnten. Shakespeare, den Wiedergänger, erkennen wir dort, wo qua Form in einem Theater jenseits der dramatischen Norm die tiefen und treibenden Motive seines Dramas aufgenommen und aufgehoben sind: Humor und Obszönität, Gewalt, Grausamkeit, die Angst um den Leib, Krankheit, Tod, Sterben, Drohung, Verletzung, Einsamkeit. Und jene Komplizenschaft von Publikum und Bühne (Hamlet oder Richard III, wie sie das Publikum verschwörerisch in ihre Machinationen einweihen), die den Aufführungen von Forced Entertainment das sonderbar „Verschwörerische" (Renate Klett) des Publikumsbezugs verleiht. Forced Entertainment stellt sich als Double des wesentlichen Shakespeare-Theaters dar. Das Double verneint, verspottet und liebt doch das klassische Modell und es verkleidet es so lange und so vielgestaltig, dass man es nicht wiedererkennt, jedoch immer wieder daran erinnert wird. Wie sehr lieben sie das Umkleiden, den Klamottentausch, Hinein- und Hinausschlüpfen in/aus Kostümen. Darin lesen wir auch ihr Verhältnis zum alten Theater: wie ein Kleiderständer, eine Art mit Lappen behängte Vogelscheuche wird das Drama immer neu zugehängt, vollgehängt, fast unsichtbar gemacht unter den Schichten unterschiedlicher Spielanzüge aus der Postmoderne, und doch kommt es immer wieder in den Blick, lugt momentweise hervor in jenen Momenten ‚dazwischen', wenn die eine Verkleidung abgehängt wird, die neue noch nicht angebracht ist: Shakespeares Grinsen.

resentations and clichés of reality, according to well-known conventions. However, situations can be created by the theatre in which those motifs – that once existed as drama and symbol, fiction and *Welt-Bild* (picture of the world) – can reappear as structure and law of form, as the players' 'attitude', and as atmosphere. A re-incarnated Shakespeare can be seen where theatre form transgresses dramatic norms, where it gathers up the deep and driving motifs of his drama: humour and obscenity, violence, cruelty, fear of bodily harm, illness, death, dying, threat, wound, loneliness. And we find the Shakespearean complicity between the audience and the stage (Hamlet or Richard III, conspiratorially informing the audience of their machinations) that give the Forced Entertainment performances this strange feeling of "conspiracy" (Renate Klett) in regard to the audience. Forced Entertainment is, in some ways, a double of the essential Shakespearean theatre. The double negates, mocks and loves its classical model, disguising it for so long and in so many ways that it becomes unrecognizable; and yet, despite this, the double resembles its model again and again. How very much they love to change clothes, to exchange clothes, slipping in and out of costumes. We can see here their relationship to the old theatre: the drama is continuously covered up, hung full, rendered almost invisible under many layers of postmodernist playing suits – like a clothes rack, a kind of scarecrow covered in rags. And yet, it always returns to view, and we get a glimpse of it peeping out during moments "in between", when one disguise is hung up and the next has yet to be donned: Shakespeare's grin.

Translated by Marc Svetov

While you're with us here tonight we'd like to ask you to try not to think about the workings of your body. Your heart pumping blood, your lungs breathing oxygen. Twitches, shudders, shrugs, nervous mannerisms. Discomfort. Try not to think about discomfort. Or deceit, deception and despair. And desperation. And mistakes. And mishaps, misdemeanours and miscellaneous errors. Try not to think about your pulse. And time. And space, and seconds passing and minutes passing. Try not to think about sleeping, or dreaming. And bad dreams that haunt you for the rest of the day. Try not to think about car crashes, holes in the road, dust, ash and smoke. And fire. Don't think about fire and sand and ash and fear, and trembling. While you're with us here tonight please try not to think about fear and trembling.

First Night

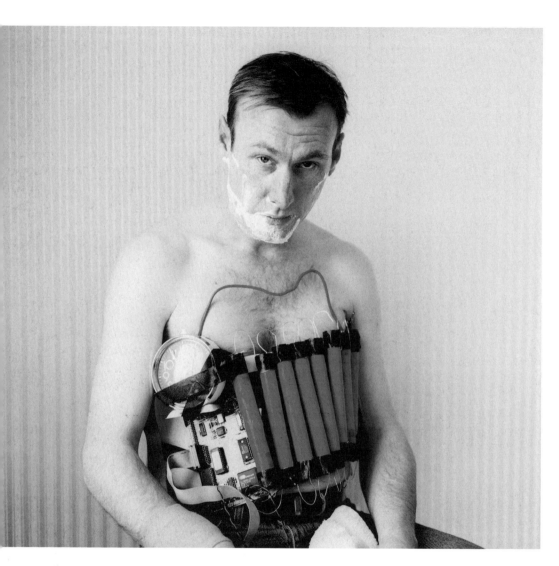

Showtime
(Pre-production)

There is a Word for People Like You: Audience
The Spectator as Bad Witness and Bad Voyeur

Es gibt ein Wort für Leute wie euch: Publikum
Der Zuschauer als schlechter Zeuge und schlechter Voyeur

Florian Malzacher

Es gibt ein Wort für Leute wie euch, und dieses Wort heißt Publikum.
Zuschauer kommen ins Theater, vielleicht um etwas zu sehen, das sie anstößig fänden, wenn sie es im wirklichen Leben sehen würden … Vielleicht seid ihr heute Abend hierher gekommen, weil ihr etwas sehen wollt, das ihr nur privat bei euch zuhause getan habt, oder vielleicht etwas, von dem ihr wünscht, dass ihr es privat bei euch zuhause getan hättet, oder etwas, von dem ihr träumt, dass ihr es privat bei euch zuhause tun würdet. Ein Publikum will in der Dunkelheit sitzen und sehen, wie andere Leute es tun. Nun, wenn ihr den Eintritt bezahlt habt – dann viel Glück!
Von dieser Seite des Teleskops aus sehen die Dinge jedoch etwas anders aus – ihr seht alle sehr klein aus und sehr weit weg, und ihr seid ziemlich viele. Es ist wichtig, daran zu denken, dass ihr mehr seid als wir. Wenn es also zum Kampf kommt, werdet ihr ohne Zweifel gewinnen.

Dass die Zuschauer in der Überzahl sind, das sollten sie – wie Richard Lowdon im Eröffnungsmonolog von *Showtime* nervös und mit einer tickenden Bombe um den Bauch bittet – nicht vergessen. Denn es bedeutet: Sie haben Verantwortung für das, was auf der Bühne geschieht, sie könnten es stoppen wenn nötig,

There is a word for people like you, and that word is audience.
An audience comes to a theatre perhaps to see something which if they saw it in real life, they may find offensive… Perhaps you've come here this evening, because you want to see something you've only done in the privacy of your own homes, something perhaps you wished you'd done in the privacy of your own homes or something that you dreamed about doing in the privacy of your own homes. An audience likes to sit in the dark and to watch other people do it. Well, if you've paid your money – good luck to you.
However, from this end of the telescope things look somewhat different – you all look very small, and very far away and there's a lot of you. It's important to remember that there are more of you than of us. So, if it does come to a fight, you will undoubtedly win.

The audience should not forget that they are in the majority, as Richard Lowdon reminds them – nervously and with a ticking bomb tied to his belly – in the opening monologue of *Showtime*. For that means: They are responsible for what happens on stage and could stop it if necessary.

There is a Word for People Like You: Audience
Es gibt ein Wort für Leute wie euch: Publikum
Florian Malzacher

But: they might also ignore the performance and trample on it.

The trivial fact that in theatre – as opposed to other art forms – the production inevitably takes place within the same space and time as the reception puts the audience in a risky position: that of sharing the responsibility of being a part of the whole. It is this phenomenon that has been of particular interest to Forced Entertainment, at least since the early '90s and that has played at least an incidental part ever since. In their works, dying is put on the stage and performers are pushed to reveal their most intimate secrets, fantasies and desires. They stand naked before us – desperately searching for some dignity or happiness – while we look on, the ever-present spectators, witnesses, voyeurs.

The shift in focus from communication that takes place within the play or across the stage to communication that takes place within the theatre itself – between actors and audience – has been a central concern for theatre reformers of all kinds. Such a shift has political ambitions. For it reveals that the theatre situation itself has always been a mirror of social models, be it the polis meeting at the Athenian theatre, the Baroque king forming the centrepiece of the play, or the awakening bourgeoisie building national theatres.

Since then, many fights have been fought with (or for) the audience; they have been shouted at, insulted, engaged, put on stage themselves or even surprised on the street. There is no longer any guarantee that the dramatic convention separating actors from the audience will be honoured. Even though the audience may no longer feel so threatened in their seats, their importance, as observers, has been recognized more than ever, even in mainstream theatres. For the most part, today's theatre isn't trying to break down the barriers between actors and audience, but is instead striving to empower the

sie könnten es aber auch unachtsam zertrampeln. Allein die banale Tatsache, dass im Theater, anders als in den anderen Künsten, die Produktion unabdinglich in derselben Raumzeit stattfindet wie die Rezeption, bringt das Publikum in eine heikle Lage: mitverantwortlicher Teil eines Ganzen zu sein.

Es ist dieses Phänomen, das Forced Entertainment spätestens seit Anfang der Neunzigerjahre besonders interessiert und das seither in den meisten ihrer Arbeiten zumindest beiläufig thematisiert wird: Sterben wird vorgeführt, Menschen werden gedrängt, Privatestes zu offenbaren, verzweifelt suchen sie nach einem Bisschen Würde, nach etwas Glück, stehen nackt vor aller Augen – immer sind wir anwesend, als Zuschauer, als Zeugen, als Voyeure.

Die Achsenverschiebung von einer dramen- oder bühneninternen zu einer intratheatralen Kommunikation mit dem Publikum eint seit rund hundert Jahren Theaterneuerer aller Couleur. Sie zielt auf das Politische. Denn sie macht sichtbar, dass – egal ob die Polis sich im Athener Theater traf, ob der barocke König zum Fluchtpunkt der Inszenierung wurde oder ob sich das erwachende Bürgertum Nationaltheater baute – die Theatersituation immer auch Spiegel gesellschaftlicher Modelle war.

Seither sind viele Gefechte um (oder für) den Zuschauer ausgetragen worden; er wurde angeschrieen, beschimpft, einbezogen, saß selbst auf der Bühne oder wurde auf der Straße vom Theater überrascht. Keinerlei Garantie, dass jener theatrale Pakt noch eingehalten würde, der den Darsteller vom Publikum trennt. Auch wenn die Sicherheitslage des Zuschauers sich inzwischen wieder entspannt hat – die Rolle des Beobachters ist bis in die Stadttheater hinein aufgewertet wie nie zuvor. Dabei geht es längst meist weniger um die Überwindung der Rampe als Grenze, als vielmehr – durch die Verschiebung der Utopie vom konkret Räumlichen ins abstrakt Semiotische – um die Ernennung des Zuschauers zum „unumschränkten Herrscher über alle möglichen Semiosen" (Erika Fischer-Lichte).

Showtime

Nicht zum aktiven Handeln wird das Publikum im Theater aufgefordert, sondern zum aktiven Sehen und Denken. Wo Brecht vom ‚aktiven Zuschauer' als Gegenstück zum aristotelischen ‚Furcht und Mitleid'-Konzept noch erwartete, dass er das Gezeigte konkret als Modell auf die Gesellschaft übertragen sollte, soll dieser Zuschauer nun Sätze und Bilder mit sich selbst in Verbindung setzen, sie verknüpfen, ergänzen zu seinen eigenen Geschichten statt einer geschlossenen, linearen Narration zu folgen. Solchermaßen aktiviert und zum Herrscher ermächtigt, trägt er eine merkwürdige Verantwortung für das, was er sieht:

Du bist für all das, was du siehst, ebenso verantwortlich, wie für das, was du tust. Das Problem bestand darin, dass man nicht immer

spectator as the "sovereign master over all possible kinds of semiosis". (Erika Fischer-Lichte)

The audience is asked not so much to act, but rather to see and to think actively. In Brecht's theatre, the 'active spectator' – the polar opposite to the Aristotelian concept of 'fear and pity' – was expected to apply what was shown on stage as a concrete model to society. The contemporary audience, meanwhile, is asked to relate texts and images to themselves, to make connections between often disparate elements, to supplement what they've seen and heard on stage in order to make their own stories, rather than follow a closed, linear narrative. Thus activated and empowered, the spectator has a peculiar responsibility for what he sees:

There is a Word for People Like You: Audience
Es gibt ein Wort für Leute wie euch: Publikum
Florian Malzacher

You are as responsible for everything you see as you were for everything you do. The problem was that you didn't always know what you were seeing until later, maybe years later, it just stayed stored in your eyes.

It was Tim Etchells himself who in his collection of essays, *Certain Fragments,* placed this quote from the notes of Vietnam War reporter Michael Herr in the context of the work of Forced Entertainment: "We always loved the idea in this – of one's responsibility for events only seen". It is the responsibility of a person who happens to witness an event, an accident, a crime, an injustice, or even a love scene, a scene of reconciliation, or simply an everyday event. It is the responsibility of seeing – and of having an attitude towards what is seen.

For Etchells, the spectator thus becomes a witness – the counter model to the idea of a passive being in Guy Debord's *The Society of the Spectacle,* who is taken to "have no idea and no claim to anything" and who "watches always only so as not to miss the sequel". The spectator in the theatre is not alone, the way he is in front of the TV; he is not watching a finished work of art or a film; instead, the spectator is a part of the event, existing within the same space and time. Active presence in a common situation.

Avant-garde theatre has developed many strategies to foreground this aspect of time spent together and thus to sensitize the audience to the visible emergence of each evening as unique and new. These strategies – pitched against the routines of performing and seeing – range in the work of Forced Entertainment from improvised passages in the shorter works through Brecht-like effects of estrangement all the way to the real physical exhaustion and hyper-awareness in the durational performances lasting six, twelve, or even 24 hours. The audience are bound up in these strategies, in this "dramaturgy of

wusste, was man sah, erst später, vielleicht Jahre später; es blieb einfach in deinen Augen gespeichert.

Tim Etchells selbst stellt in seinem Essayband *Certain Fragments* dieses Zitat aus den Aufzeichnungen des Vietnam-Kriegsberichterstatters Michael Herr in den Zusammenhang mit der Arbeit Forced Entertainments: „Wir haben die Idee dahinter immer gemocht – eine Verantwortung für Ereignisse, die man nur gesehen hat". Es ist die Verantwortung desjenigen, der zum Zeugen eines Geschehens wird, eines Unfalls, eines Verbrechens, eines Unrechts – aber auch einer Liebesszene, einer Versöhnung oder einfach eines alltäglichen Vorganges. Es ist die Verantwortung des Sehens – und der Haltung, die gegenüber dem Gesehenen eingenommen wird.

So wird der Zuschauer für Etchells zum Zeugen – und zum Gegenmodell jenes passiven Wesens in der *Gesellschaft des Spektakels,* von dem mit Guy Debord angenommen wird, dass es „von nichts eine Ahnung und auf nichts Anspruch hat", das „stets nur zuschaut, um die Fortsetzung nicht zu versäumen". Der Theaterzuschauer sitzt nicht allein vorm Fernseher, er betrachtet kein fertiges Kunstwerk oder einen Film, er ist Teil eines Geschehens, im selben Raum, zur selben Zeit. Aktive Präsenz in einer gemeinsamen Situation.

Das avancierte Theater hat vielerlei Strategien entwickelt, diesen Aspekt gemeinsam verbrachter Lebenszeit zu betonen und so den Zuschauer für das sichtbare Entstehen jedes einzelnen Abends als einmaligen und neuen zu sensibilisieren: Strategien gegen die Routine des Spielens und die Routine des Sehens, die bei Forced Entertainment von improvisierten Passagen in kürzeren Stücken über nahezu Brechtsche Verfremdungseffekte bis zur realen körperlichen Erschöpfung oder Überdrehtheit in den *durational performances* von sechs, zwölf oder gar vierundzwanzig Stunden reichen. Der Zuschauer hat Teil an diesen Strategien, an dieser – wie Kattrin

Deufert im Hinblick auf John Cage sagt – „Dramaturgie der Präsenz". Er spürt die Anspannung, die Ermüdung oder den sportiven Ehrgeiz, besonders schlagfertig oder poetisch zu sein – und er spürt sich selbst, angespannt, ermüdet oder sportiv ehrgeizig durchzuhalten. Er ist Zeuge, aber nicht außen stehend. Er ist Teil des Geschehens, er fühlt sein Gewicht:

Zeuge eines Ereignisses zu sein bedeutet, auf grundlegend ethische Weise gegenwärtig zu sein, das Gewicht der Dinge und den eigenen Platz darin zu empfinden, selbst wenn dieser Platz momentan einfach der eines Zuschauers ist. (Etchells)

Die Performancekunst der sechziger, siebziger Jahre hat solche Überlegungen zur Position des Zuschauers als Teil eines Ereignisses in vielerlei Hinsicht thematisiert und auf die Spitze getrieben. Auch die Bezeichnung ‚Zeuge' statt ‚Zuschauer', die Etchells auf die Theaterarbeit Forced Entertainments überträgt, stammt aus dieser Zeit: Chris Burden etwa verwendete sie im Hinblick auf die Anwesenden bei seiner berüchtigten Performance *Shoot* von 1971, als er sich aus fünf Metern Entfernung mit einem Gewehr in den linken Oberarm schießen ließ.

Sechsundzwanzig Jahre nach Shoot *bleibt die Unterscheidung zwischen Zuschauer und Zeuge vital und provokativ, weil sie uns daran erinnert, erneut zu fragen, an welchem Punkt Kunst ins Gewicht fällt und wo sie ihre Spuren hinterlässt – in der realen Welt oder in einer fiktionalen – und auf wem sie ihre Last niederlegt. Das Kunstwerk, das uns zu Zeugen macht, macht uns in erster Linie unfähig, mit dem Nachdenken, Reden und Berichten über das, was wir gesehen haben, aufzuhören. Wir finden uns, wie die Leute in Brechts Gedicht, die Zeuge eines Verkehrsunfalls geworden sind, immer noch an der Straßenecke stehen und diskutieren, was geschehen ist, getragen von unserer Verantwortung gegenüber den Ereignissen.* (Etchells)

presence", as Kattrin Deufert puts it in reference to John Cage. When the audience perceive the tension, exhaustion, or sports-like competitiveness to be particularly witty or poetical, for instance, they themselves might begin to feel tense, exhausted, or competitive. They are witnesses, but they are not outsiders. They are part of the event and so they feel its weight:

To witness an event is to be present at it in some fundamental ethical way, to feel the weight of things and one's place in them, even if that place is simply, for the moment, as an onlooker. (Etchells)

The performance art of the '60s and '70s focussed in many ways on the notion of the audience as part of the event and took it to extremes. Moreover, the use of the term 'witness' rather than 'spectator' to describe audience members, which Etchells sometimes uses when talking about the theatre work of Forced Entertainment, stems from this era: Chris Burden, for example, used it for those present at his infamous performance, *Shoot* (1971), in which he had himself shot with a gun in his left arm, from a distance of 5 meters.

Twenty-six years after Shoot, *the audience/witness distinction remains vital and provocative since it reminds us to ask again the questions about where art matters and where it leaves its mark – in the real world or in some fictional one – and on whom it leaves its burden. The artwork that turns us into witnesses leaves us, above all, unable to stop thinking, talking and reporting what we've seen. We're left, like the people in Brecht's poem who've witnessed a road accident, still stood on the street corner discussing what happened, borne on by our responsibility to events.* (Etchells)

Theatre is supposed to engage us, demanding an involvement beyond the moment of the event;

There is a Word for People Like You: Audience
Es gibt ein Wort für Leute wie euch: Publikum
Florian Malzacher

not unlike witnesses in legal proceedings, bound by an ethical tie to what they have seen. One could propose though, that the witness in the performances of Forced Entertainment is not a good witness, and cannot ever be a good witness. In this failure lies the audience's unique political dimension.

For even though in *Speak Bitterness*, for example, the witness is positioned as a supposedly neutral observer, with a clear view of all that takes place, and even though his gaze from within the brightly lit audience is legitimate, it is also true that this gaze is taxed beyond its capacities: The sheer amount of what is heard, with every sentence a confession, cannot be processed, neither quantitatively nor qualitatively. In this situation, distinguishing between true and false, meaningful and meaningless, is simply not possible:

We're guilty of dice, of teletype and needles. We spread true rumours and wrote false receipts. On game shows we cheated and on quiz shows we lied. We lay at home with the flu and a hangover. We made the heartbreak face and then we smiled. We stank of chlorine and fists fell on us like the rain. We doctored photographs, carefully erasing figures und substituting stone works, pillars and curtains to make it look like George Michael had stood on the balcony alone. We sacked the town, we painted it red. We slipped through customs at Nairobi International, without even being seen. We were exiled kings, useless princes. We revamped our image, we were really working class. We made the crowd blush, we were driven by demons whose names we couldn't even spell. We were white collar criminals, haunted by our pasts. We told Mrs. Gamble that Helen was with us when she wasn't. We were ex-cons trying to go straight. We thought that Freud was probably right about laughter. We had no moral compass, or if we did have one, it had been badly damaged during the frequent

Theater soll uns beschäftigen, involvieren über den Moment des Ereignisses hinaus, so wie der juristische Zeuge sich beschäftigt, sich beschäftigen muss über den Moment des Ereignisses hinaus. Doch der Zeuge in den Aufführungen Forced Entertainments – so kann man einwenden – ist kein guter Zeuge, kann kein guter Zeuge sein. Gerade darin liegt seine spezifische, auch politische Qualität.

Denn zwar wird er etwa in *Speak Bitterness* in die vermeintliche Position des neutralen Beobachters gebracht, er hat eine klare Sicht auf alles, und sein Blick im erhellten Zuschauerraum ist ein völlig legitimer – aber eben auch ein völlig überforderter: Die Menge des Gehörten – jeder Satz ein Geständnis – ist nicht verarbeitbar, quantitativ wie qualitativ. Eine Unterscheidung in wahr und falsch, in sinnvoll und sinnlos ist nicht möglich:

Wir sind schuldig des Würfelspiels, der Fernschreiben und der Nadeln. Wir verbreiteten wahre Gerüchte und stellten falsche Quittungen aus. Bei Game-Shows haben wir betrogen und bei Quiz-Shows gelogen. Wir lagen zuhause mit Grippe und Kater im Bett. Wir machten ein Gesicht zum Herzerweichen und lachten dann. Wir stanken nach Chlor, und Fäuste regneten auf uns nieder. Wir fälschten Fotografien, löschten sorgfältig Personen aus und ersetzten sie mit Mauerwerk, Säulen und Vorhängen, um es so aussehen zu lassen, als wäre George Michael allein auf dem Balkon gestanden. Wir plünderten die Stadt, malten sie rot an. Wir schlüpften ungesehen durch den Zoll in Nairobi International. Wir waren Könige im Exil, nutzlose Prinzen. Wir legten uns ein neues Image zu, wir waren wirklich Arbeiterklasse. Wir brachten die Menge zum Erröten, wir waren von Dämonen getrieben, deren Namen wir noch nicht einmal buchstabieren konnten. Wir waren Verbrecher mit weißem Kragen, heimgesucht von unserer Vergangenheit. Wir sagten Mrs. Gamble, dass Helen bei uns sei, als sie es gar nicht war. Wir waren ehemalige Hochstapler, die versuchten, ein ehrliches Leben zu führen. Wir meinten, dass Freud mit dem Lachen wahrscheinlich Recht

Speak Bitterness

hatte. Wir hatten keinen moralischen Kompass, oder wenn wir einen hatten, dann war er in den häufigen elektrischen Stürmen ernsthaft beschädigt worden. Wir waren der Ketzerei und des Hörensagens schuldig. Wir wendeten den Rücken der Wand zu …

Hunderte von Beichten lassen ihm die Wahl, entweder alle durch sich hindurchfließen zu lassen oder bei einzelnen zu verweilen, sie zu realisieren und somit andere zu versäumen. Aktiv zu werten und auszuwählen, ist seine einzige Chance – und an ihr muss er scheitern.

Was bleibt, ist ein Gefühl des Mangels.

Einerseits. Andererseits ist das Sehen in den Stücken Forced Entertainments auch eine Lust, ein Reiz, dem man schwer widerstehen kann: Der Zuschauer ist nicht nur der (schlechte) Zeuge in *Speak Bitterness*, er ist in vielen Stücken auch ein Voyeur. Ein Voyeur, dessen Blick aus dem Dunkel heraus etwas Unerlaubtes und Hierarchisierendes hat. Doch auch der Voyeur in den Aufführungen Forced Entertainments ist kein guter Voyeur, kann kein guter Voyeur sein. Immer wieder wird ihm die Dreistigkeit seines Blickes vor Augen geführt, genauer: sein Blick überhaupt erst zu einem dreisten gemacht. Er wird in die Situation (und manchmal regelrecht in die Rolle) des Voyeurs gebracht und damit konfrontiert, diese Situation entweder zu mögen oder als unangenehm zu empfinden. Meist aber beides zusammen.

Was bleibt, ist ein Gefühl des Zuviel.

In *Hidden J* tritt Claire Marshall allein auf die Bühne. Sie nimmt ein Pappschild von dem Stuhl, auf den sie sich setzt, hängt es sich um den Hals: ‚LÜGNERIN'. Sie rutscht sich auf dem Stuhl zurecht, schaut in die Augen des Publikums. Sitzt da, als wäre sie nach einem Streit von den anderen dazu verurteilt, sich öffentlich zu demütigen, schon vor Beginn des eigentlichen Stücks.

Oder: Das minutenlange Jaulen Robin Arthurs in *First Night*, wenn Richard Lowdon ihn (unter unserem Lachen und Unwohlsein) minutenlang im Schwitzkasten hält und dabei

electrical storms. We're guilty of heresy and hearsay, of turning our backs to the wall …

Hundreds of confessions leave the witness with the choice: either to let them all flow through him, or to focus on individual ones and in doing so, to miss others. Active choice and evaluation is his only option – and in this he must fail.

What remains is a feeling of lack.

On the one hand. But on the other hand, watching the performances of Forced Entertainment is also a pleasure, a temptation that is hard to resist. The spectator is not only the (bad) witness, as in *Speak Bitterness*; in many shows, he is also a voyeur. A voyeur whose gaze from the dark has an illegitimate quality, one that establishes hierarchies. But even the voyeur in the performances of Forced Entertainment is not a good voyeur, and cannot ever be a good voyeur. Again and again, the impertinence of his gaze is mirrored back at him or, to be more precise: his gaze is made impertinent. He is frequently placed in the position of (and at times even directly addressed as) the voyeur and confronted with either liking or disliking this situation. Mostly both.

What remains is a feeling of excess.

In *Hidden J*, Claire Marshall steps onto the stage, alone. She takes a piece of cardboard from a chair and puts it around her neck: 'LIAR'. She sits on the chair and returns the audience's gaze. It's as if she's had some sort of a falling out with the others and was sentenced to public humiliation before the play had even began. Or: In *First Night*, Robin Arthur yelps for several minutes as Richard Lowdon restrains him in a stranglehold, taking time to drink a glass of water. All the while, the audience are both laughing and feeling uneasy. These kinds of humiliations work only with the cooperation of the audience. Thus, the feeling of responsibility for the events in the work of Forced Entertainment always comes with a feeling of guilt – the guilt of missing

130

There is a Word for People Like You: Audience
Es gibt ein Wort für Leute wie euch: Publikum
Florian Malzacher

something, overlooking something, mishearing something on the one hand, and the guilt of seeing too much, the fascination of the gaze, on the other. (It is not surprising that this touches on the motifs of the Biblical eviction from paradise and the Freudian primal scene.)

According to Freud, the pleasure in watching – scopophilia – is necessarily an active one. It is what drives small children's desire to watch private or forbidden things. In *Showtime*, we get drawn into Cathy Naden's elaborate fantasy of her possible suicide and as we listen intently to each word with a mixture of horror and fascination, our pleasure in this indiscretion is satisfied, only to be thrown in our faces in the next moment when one of the trees shouts at us:

What the fuck are you looking at? What the fuck is your problem? Fuck off! Voyeurs! There's a fucking line and you've just crossed it. Where's your human decency? Call yourself human beings? Why don't you fuck off, piss off, cock off, wankers, voyeurs. Fuck off. Go on, pick up your things, pick up your coats and your fucking bags and bugger off just fucking cocking buggering walk off!

Etchells describes this strategy as letting the spectator come close only to push him away again. But the gaze from the darkness towards the stage and the hierarchies it establishes can be inverted. In that case, the spectator himself is turned from a witness or voyeur into the object of the gaze. In *First Night*, for instance, the characters on stage – who are supposed to be dependent on the viewer's goodwill – soon throw their apparent humility in the viewer's face by flashing their provocative and incessant smiles; then, as if this weren't enough, they directly attack him in the very place where it hurts most: his own mortality.

Another dimension of the game is revealed: death. Other works by Forced Entertainment

seelenruhig ein Glas Wasser trinkt. Demütigungen, die nur durch die Mitwirkung des Publikums funktionieren.

Das Gefühl der Verantwortung für das Gesehene resultiert bei Forced Entertainment immer auch aus einem Gefühl der Schuld – Schuld des Versäumens, des Übersehens, des Überhörens einerseits, Schuld des Zuviel-Sehens, der Faszination des Blickes andererseits. (Kein Wunder, dass man hier an Motive der biblischen Paradiesvertreibung und der Freudschen Ur-Szene rührt.)

Die Lust, zu sehen, die Skopophilie, ist, folgt man Freud, notwendig eine aktive. Sie ist der Motor für kleine Kinder, Privates oder Verbotenes sehen zu wollen. Wenn wir immer mehr in die ausführlichen Selbstmordbeschreibungen Cathy Nadens in *Showtime* hineingezogen werden, wenn wir angespannt jedem Wort lauschen, mit einer Mischung aus Grusel und Faszination, so wird diese Lust am Indiskreten nur befriedigt, um uns im nächsten Augenblick massiv darauf hinzuweisen – in diesem Fall angeschrien von einem Baum:

Was glotzt Ihr, verdammt noch mal? Was ist Euer verdammtes Problem? Verpisst Euch! Voyeure! Es gibt, verdammt noch mal, eine Grenze, und Ihr habt sie überschritten. Wo ist Euer menschlicher Anstand? Wollt Ihr Menschen sein? Verpisst Euch doch, verfickt Euch, verwichst Euch, Wichser, Voyeure. Verpisst Euch. Los, holt Eure Sachen, holt Eure Mäntel und Eure verdammten Taschen und macht Euch aus dem Staub, verdammt, verfickt, verflucht, haut einfach ab!

Den Zuschauer an sich heranlassen, um ihn dann wieder wegzuschubsen, so beschreibt es Etchells. Aber der hierarchisierende Blick aus dem Dunkel heraus auf die Bühne kann umgekehrt werden. Dann wird der Zuschauer selbst vom Zeugen oder Voyeur zum Objekt des Blicks und des Spiels: Erst wird ihm in *First Night* die Demut der Bühnenfiguren, die doch eigentlich von seinem Wohlwollen abhängig sein sollten, durch ihr provozierendes Dauerlächeln förmlich um die Ohren gehauen, dann wird er auch noch ganz direkt angegriffen, dort, wo es ihn am tiefsten trifft: bei seiner eigenen Sterblichkeit.

Eine andere Dimension tritt ins Spiel, der Tod. Der Tod, mit dem man auch in anderen Arbeiten Forced Entertainments immer wieder konfrontiert wird – doch spätestens in *First Night* bleibt kein Raum für Missverständnisse: Immer ist es der eigene Tod, auf den man letztlich zurückgeworfen wird, auf die eigene *last night*. „Das Spezifische am Theater ist", wie Heiner Müller sagt, „eben nicht die Präsenz des lebenden Zuschauers, sondern die Präsenz des potentiell sterbenden."

Und so stellt sich Cathy Naden vor uns hin und deutet uns einzeln heraus: „Du hast einen Knoten in der linken Brust". „Autounfall". „Krebs". Und Du: „Nierenversagen". „Selbstmord". „Lungenentzündung". Eine Mischung aus Wahrsagung und Drohung, eine Verwünschung vielleicht. In jedem Fall eine unangenehme Situation, die uns in unserem ‚echten' Leben zu bedrohen scheint. Das Theater wird übergriffig, holt uns hinein ins Spiel. Wir fühlen uns real bedroht und spielen zugleich, für einen Moment zumindest, eine Rolle im Stück; die Rolle eines Menschen, der bald sterben wird. Es ist die Rolle unseres Lebens.

Einerseits. Andererseits – alles ein Spiel. Jedenfalls ist es fast schon wieder eine Beruhigung, wenn wir wenig später von der gesamten Mannschaft einfach nur beleidigt und beschimpft werden. Das sind wir schließlich gewohnt. Spätestens seit Handke.

Schlechte (weil überforderte) Zeugen, schlechte (weil nicht genießende) Voyeure und schlechte (weil sich innerlich wehrende) Mitspieler: verschiedene Strategien, uns unserer Zuschauersituation bewusst zu machen. Die Unruhe, die sie erzeugen, weist tief in das Wesen des Theaters: hin auf seine Eigenschaft, politisch zu sein. Denn in einer Zeit, in der die Künste sich wieder mehr und mehr um das Politische bemühen, das der Politik selbst

have repeatedly staged this confrontation with death – but in *First Night*, there is no potential for misunderstanding: It is always one's own death, one's own *last night* that one has to face. "What is specific about theatre", Heiner Müller used to say, "is precisely not the presence of the living spectator, but rather the presence of the potentially dying one".

And thus Cathy Naden stands in front of us and points us out individually: "You've got a lump in your left breast". "Car crash". "Cancer". And You: "Kidney failure". "Suicide". "Pneumonia". Her gesture is a mixture of prophecy and threat, possibly a curse, but in any case, it creates a disagreeable situation, which seems to threaten us in our 'real' life. Theatre oversteps its boundaries and engulfs us in the game. We feel truly threatened, while at the same time, playing a role in the drama, at least for an instant; the role of a human being who is about to die. It is the role of our lives.

On the one hand. On the other hand – it is all a game. It is almost comforting when only a little bit later, we are being insulted and abused by the whole crew. We are used to that, after all. At least since Handke.

Bad witnesses (because we are taxed beyond our abilities), bad voyeurs (because we are not enjoying it) and bad players (because we resist it from inside) – roles constructed through the various strategies that make us aware of the theatre situation. The uneasiness these strategies produce points – in a profound way – to the nature of theatre itself, to its political quality. For in a time when the arts are again becoming increasingly more concerned with the political, which seems to evade the grasp of politics itself, it is precisely the theatre that has been put on the defensive. But while on the one hand theatre seems to have lost its role as the medium in which society communicates about itself, on the other hand we are

There is a Word for People Like You: Audience
Es gibt ein Wort für Leute wie euch: Publikum
Florian Malzacher

again becoming increasingly aware of the way in which the political is specific to the theatre more than to any other art form: not so much in its content as in its structure. "The tendency and content can only be right if the form is also right", Benjamin said. And that means, as Hans-Thies Lehmann puts it pointedly, that "the political effect of theatre is to be found in 'the how' of its representation". The central and essential 'how' of theatre is the very time that actors and spectators spend together in the same room. Indeed, theatre is politically strong at precisely the moment when we realise its unique place in the arts; as the medium which is able to offer us a direct confrontation with oneself as a part of a collective. When Richard Lowdon points this out to us in *Showtime* or when individuals are isolated from the crowd in *First Night*, then we, as spectators, are consciously becoming social beings.

Political theatre is a theatre that asks the audience to adopt a particular attitude or course of action. But in purely content-oriented, intentional ('contentist') theatre, this attitude quickly gets lost in a cheap consensus and an identification with the ethical actions and attitudes on stage. Indeed one's own attitude will never make the journey from the theatre hall to real life. Instead, it will be acted out in the drama, producing catharsis and with it, contentment. The identification with the 'Good' is enough in itself and leads to nothing but a good feeling, replete with a notion that one has already acted (in a good way). This argument forms the basis of Brecht's critique of Aristotle. But nowadays, even Brecht's notion of the theatre as a model for actions in the outside world does not work any more. Brecht's model has become a mere affirmation or mirror of reality and as such, fails as a valid political argument in the same way the bourgeois theatre failed before Brecht began to revolutionize it.

In Forced Entertainment too, we do find concrete indications of social realities: Games of

zu entgleiten scheint, ist ausgerechnet das Theater in die Defensive geraten. Doch während dem Theater einerseits seine Rolle als Selbstverständigungsmedium der Gesellschaft abhanden gekommen ist, gerät zeitgleich wieder in den Blick, auf welche Weise gerade ihm vor allen anderen Künsten das Politische eignet. Nämlich nicht primär in seinen Inhalten, sondern in seiner Struktur. „Die Tendenz, der Inhalt kann nur stimmen", sagt Benjamin, „wenn auch die Form stimmig ist". Das bedeutet, wie Hans-Thies Lehmann zuspitzt: „Im Wie der Darstellung ist die politische Wirkung des Theaters zu suchen." Das zentrale, das wesentliche Wie im Theater aber ist die gemeinsam verbrachte Zeit von Zuschauern und Akteuren im selben Raum. Politisch stark ist das Theater vor allem da, wo deutlich wird, dass es nach wie vor der einzige künstlerische Ort der direkten Konfrontation mit sich selbst als Kollektiv sein kann. Wenn wir von Richard Lowdon in *Showtime* direkt darauf hingewiesen werden, aber auch, wenn in *First Night* Einzelne aus der Menge isoliert werden, dann werden wir als Zuschauer bewusst zu einem gesellschaftlichen Wesen.

Politisches Theater ist ein Theater, das den Zuschauer zu einer Haltung oder gar zum Handeln anregen möchte. Doch im rein inhaltlichen, intentionalen („inhaltistischen') Theater erschöpft sich diese Haltung schnell im wohlfeilen Einverständnis und der Identifikation mit den ethischen Handlungen und Haltungen auf der Bühne. Die eigene Haltung wird, quasi kathartisch, sofort abreagiert und verpufft ohne aus dem Parkett hinaus ins Leben gerettet zu werden. Die Identifikation mit ‚dem Guten' ist sich selbst genug und führt zu nichts als einem guten Gefühl, das suggeriert, man habe bereits (gut) gehandelt. Das war schon Brechts Kritik an Aristoteles. Aber inzwischen funktioniert auch Brechts Vorstellung vom Theater als Modell für Handlungen außerhalb des Theaters nicht mehr; das Modell ist selbst zur affirmativen Wirklichkeitsabbildung geworden und scheitert als politisches Argument genau da, wo das bürgerliche Theater

First Night

scheiterte, bevor Brecht es zu revolutionieren begann.

Auch bei Forced Entertainment haben wir durchaus konkrete Hinweise auf gesellschaftliche Realitäten: Beichtspiele und Verhöre verweisen auf bekannte Foucaultsche Machtdiskurse, Bildfragmentierungen und Blickführungen auf die Strukturierung unserer Wirklichkeit durch die Medien, sadistisch aggressive Gewaltspiele auf Unterdrückung, Leid, Lust durch Brutalität. Aber es sind Schnipsel, Zitate, Fragmente, Stimmungen. Figuren-, Rollen-, Handlungsfetzen, keine konsistenten Handlungen, Rollen und Figuren. Ohne nachvollziehbare Kausalität und Narration können wir kein übertragbares Modell destillieren. Im Theater von Forced Entertainment gibt es keine Handlungs-

confession and questioning point to Foucauldian power discourses; fragmented imagery and directed gaze point to the structuring of our reality by the media; sadistic-aggressive games of violence point to repression, suffering, and taking pleasure in brutality. But these are snippets, quotes, fragments, moods. Shards of characters, roles, actions, but no consistent actions, roles, or characters. Without consistent causality or narration, we are unable to distil a model that might be transferred to the outside world. There is no recipe for action in the theatre of Forced Entertainment. No solution, no closure, no salvation.

The theatre we dreamed of was concerned with ethics and identity; it was deeply and always

There is a Word for People Like You: Audience
Es gibt ein Wort für Leute wie euch: Publikum
Florian Malzacher

political but, in embracing the fractured ambiguous landscape (social, cultural, psychic) of the '80s and '90s in Britain, we knew it had to forgo the suspect certainties of what other people called political theatre, that it had to work the territory between the real and the phantasmic, between the actual landscape and the media one, between the body and imagination. We worked with a growing confidence that a reliance on intuition, chance, dream, accident and impulse would not banish politics from the work, but ensure its veracity – a certainty that old rules did not apply. (Etchells)

Maybe nowadays political theatre is mostly this: a theatre that forces the spectator – as witness, voyeur and player – to feel the "weight of things" and his presence "in some fundamentally ethical way"; a theatre that shows him that he needs to have an attitude – and that at the same time denies him this option. Through unsettling, irritation, interruption, this kind of political theatre creates a space of possibility and thus produces a 'pressure for attitude' – while at the same time, refusing to function as an object upon which this attitude or even action might be expended.

In *Instructions for Forgetting*, Tim Etchells tells the anecdote of a young girl, attending a play. At a key moment in the performance, she and the other children in the audience are asked to clap their hands in order to bring a fairy back to life. The girl claps vigorously and is disturbed to notice that her mother makes only a half-hearted effort: Is she reluctant to help the fairy? Some time later, in real life, the girl's aunt dies, and the girl wonders if it would be worth trying to revive her aunt through such clapping. The girl decides against it: It probably would not help.

The art work resists and at the same time points to the world that it can no longer repre-

anweisungen. Keine Lösung, keine Auflösung, keine Erlösung.

Das Theater, von dem wir träumten, hatte mit Ethik und Identität zu tun, es war zutiefst und immer politisch, aber da es die fragmentierte, ambivalente Landschaft (sozial, kulturell, psychisch) der 80er und 90er in Großbritannien umschloss, wussten wir, dass wir die verdächtigen Gewissheiten dessen, was andere Leute politisches Theater nannten, aufgeben mussten, dass wir im Territorium zwischen dem Realen und dem Phantasmatischen arbeiten mussten, zwischen der tatsächlichen Landschaft und der Medienlandschaft, zwischen dem Körper und der Vorstellung. Wir arbeiteten mit dem wachsenden Vertrauen, dass sich auf Intuition, Zufall, Traum, Unfall und Impuls zu verlassen die Politik nicht aus der Arbeit vertreiben, sondern ihre Wahrhaftigkeit garantieren würde – eine Gewissheit, dass alte Regeln keine Gültigkeit hatten. (Etchells)

Vielleicht also ist heutiges politisches Theater am ehesten gerade dies: ein Theater, das den Zuschauer als Zeuge, Voyeur, Mitspieler „das Gewicht der Dinge" und seine Präsenz „auf eine grundlegend ethische Weise" fühlen lässt, das ihm zeigt, dass er eine Haltung beziehen muss – und ihm diese Möglichkeit im selben Augenblick verweigert: Durch Verunsicherung, Irritation, Unterbrechung schafft es einen Möglichkeitsraum und erzeugt so einen ‚Haltungsdruck' – ohne selbst als konkretes Objekt dieser Haltung oder gar eines Handelns zu taugen.

Tim Etchells erzählt in *Instructions for Forgetting* die Anekdote von einem kleinen Mädchen, das in einem Theaterstück zusammen mit anderen Kindern aufgefordert ist, zu klatschen, damit die Elfe wieder zum Leben erweckt wird. Es klatscht mit aller Kraft – und stellt beunruhigt fest, dass die Mutter nur halbherzig bei der Sache ist: Will sie der Elfe nicht helfen? Als wenig später im richtigen Leben die Tante des Mädchens stirbt, überlegt es, ob der Versuch lohnen würde, sie durch

Klatschen wieder zum Leben zu erwecken. Das Mädchen entscheidet sich dagegen: Es würde wohl nichts nützen.

Das Kunstwerk verweigert sich und verweist zugleich auf die Welt, die es nicht mehr repräsentiert: Weil dieses Theater nicht mehr primär inhaltlich funktioniert, kann der Druck nicht ausagiert werden, die Form verhindert die Identifikation und wird so zum eigentlich Politischen. „Das Problem ist", um es mit Michael Herr zu sagen, „dass man nicht immer weiß, was man gesehen hat".

sent: Since this theatre does not work primarily on the level of content, the pressure for attitude that it produces cannot be acted out; the form prevents identification and thus the work becomes political. To use the words of Michael Herr, "The problem is that you don't always know what you were seeing".

Translated by Benjamin Marius Schmidt

We lived in a city where happy endings were not popular, and so, without pens, we preferred to write messages on the walls in our blood.

We wrote   DOWN WITH CHILDHOOD and NO MORE MR. NICE GUY.

We wrote   TWO HAPPY DOGS SWIMMING IN A FROZEN RIVER.

We wrote   STOP PLAYING GAMES OR I'LL FUCKING KILL MYSELF.

No one knows if our messages got through.

Emanuelle Enchanted

Showtime

Bloody Play
Games of Childhood and Death

Bloody Play
Das Spiel von Kindheit und Tod

Andrew Quick

Spielen als Zustand, in dem Bedeutung im Fluss ist, in dem Möglichkeiten aufblühen, in dem Versionen sich multiplizieren, in dem die Grenzen der Realität verschwimmen, sich verbiegen, brechen. Spielen als endlose Transformation, Transformation ohne Ende und niemals reglos. Wäre das reines Spielen?

Tim Etchells

Als Spiel tritt die Gewohnheit ins Leben, und in ihr, ihren starrsten Formen, überdauert ein Restchen Spiel bis ans Ende.

Walter Benjamin

Play as a state in which meaning is in flux, in which possibility thrives, in which versions multiply, in which the confines of what is real are blurred, buckled, broken. Play as endless transformation, transformation without end and never stillness. Would that be pure play?

Tim Etchells

Habit enters life as a game, and in habit, even in its most sclerotic forms, an element of play survives to the end.

Walter Benjamin

1989 besuchte ich die Aufführung von Forced Entertainments *200% & Bloody Thirsty* auf einem internationalen Theaterfestival in Polverigi, einem kleinen italienischen Ort in der Nähe Anconas. Die Aufführung an diesem heißen Sommerabend hatte einen außergewöhnlichen Effekt auf das Publikum, das, während die verschiedenen alkoholtrunkenen und brabbelnden Krippenspiel-Versionen vor unseren Augen vorbeirauschten, zunehmend unruhig wurde: Zahlreiche Menschen verließen den Veranstaltungsort, nur um wenig später zurückzukehren und das Gesehene lautstark mit mitgebrachten Freunden zu diskutieren. Die Stimmung war aufgeladen, aber nie aggressiv. Die Gesten des Publikums zeigten

In 1989, I was with Forced Entertainment when they performed *200% & Bloody Thirsty* at an international theatre festival in Polverigi, a small village near Ancona, Italy. The performance on that hot summer evening had an extraordinary effect on the audience that filled the venue. As each drunken and babbled version of the Nativity sped by, the spectators became increasingly restless. Numerous people left the venue only to return a little later to carry on watching the performance. On their return, they would discuss loudly what they were seeing with friends they had brought back with them. The atmosphere, although highly charged, was never aggressive.

140

Bloody Play / Games of Childhood and Death
Bloody Play / Das Spiel von Kindheit und Tod
Andrew Quick

The audience's gestures reflected a certain astonishment, rather than animosity; the tone of their voices suggested an inquisitiveness, rather than the hurried arrival at damning judgment. As I sat there, amidst this tumult, I remember thinking that it had to be the enactment of drunkenness that was the cause of such intense consternation, a drunkenness that, to Italian ears and eyes, must have been very alienating. Talking with friends after the performance, I was surprised to hear that it was not the representation of excessive drinking (or the potentially blasphemous depiction of Christ's birth) that was the basis for their disquiet, although they identified this behaviour as being distinctly 'English'. Instead, they pointed to the performers' excessive energy, to the evident *delight* in enacting drink-induced revelry. "*Come bambini*", my friend said, "*come bambini*": "Like children, like children."

Looking back on Forced Entertainment's work over the last twenty years, this analogy seems a strangely appropriate place to start a discussion of their practice. I say strange, because, when the comparison with children's behaviour was made in relation to *200% & Bloody Thirsty*, I took it to be a mild form of censure. On reflection, I am sure that I was mistaken, that the equation of childishness with criticism was the consequence of my own prejudicial thinking. In fact, the child-like delight in performing drunken abandon identifies one of the most crucial dynamics at work in all of Forced Entertainment's performances to date: that of play. As I will explore in the following pages, play takes on many forms in their performance work and is never limited to the literal representation of children and their specific modes of playing.

This is not to say that the paraphernalia and activities of childhood (its toys, Wendy houses, songs, games and dressing up routines) are absent in the company's numerous performances. From the earliest pieces, such as *(Let*

eher Erstaunen als Feindseligkeit, ihre Stimmen klangen nicht nach vorschneller Verurteilung, sondern nach Neugierde. Ich erinnere mich, wie ich inmitten des ganzen Tumults dachte, die Ursache für diese deutliche Befremdung läge wohl am gespielten Betrunkensein, ein Betrunkensein, das für italienische Augen und Ohren ziemlich befremdlich sein musste. Aber in Gesprächen mit Freunden nach der Aufführung erfuhr ich zu meinem Erstaunen, dass nicht die Darstellung exzessiven Trinkens (oder die potentiell blasphemische Darstellung Christi Geburt) der Grund dieser Unruhe war, obwohl das Benehmen durchaus als typisch ‚englisch' angesehen wurde. Stattdessen hob man die maßlose Energie der Schauspieler und ihre offensichtliche *Freude* am betrunkenen Gelage hervor: „*Come bambini*", sagte mein Freund, „*come bambini*": „Wie die Kinder, wie die Kinder".

Im Rückblick auf Forced Entertainments Arbeit der letzten zwanzig Jahre erscheint diese Analogie seltsam passend als Ausgangspunkt für eine Auseinandersetzung. Ich sage seltsam, weil ich damals den Vergleich von kindischem Benehmen mit *200% & Bloody Thirsty* als milde Zensur verstand. Aber wenn ich darüber nachdenke, glaube ich, dass ich falsch lag, und dass meine Gleichsetzung von Kindlichkeit mit negativer Kritik auf eigenen Vorurteilen beruhte. Tatsächlich verweist die kindliche Freude an der Darstellung von Trunkenheit und Verwahrlosung auf eine der entscheidenden Dynamiken in der Arbeit von Forced Entertainment bis heute: auf die Dynamik des Spielens. Wie ich im Folgenden untersuchen werde, nimmt dieses Spielen in der Theaterarbeit der Gruppe vielerlei Gestalt an und ist nie auf die tatsächliche Darstellung von Kindern und deren spezifischen Formen des Spielens beschränkt.

Damit will ich nicht sagen, dass die Utensilien und Aktivitäten der Kindheit (Spielzeuge, Puppenhäuser, Lieder, Spiele und Verkleidungen) in den Aufführungen nicht vorhanden wären. Von frühen Stücken wie *(Let the Water Run its Course)* to the Sea that Made the Promise bis hin zu *The Travels* sind Spuren von Kindheit und Elemente des Spiels in allen Arbeiten leicht zu finden. In *Showtime* etwa sind die Zeichen der Kindheit offensichtlich, sie nehmen Gestalt an in Tier- und Baumkostümen, materialisieren sich in einer von Luftballons übersäten Bühne, in Kinderliedern und Tanzeinlagen. In *200% & Bloody Thirsty* und *(Let the Water Run its Course)* findet Kindheit ihr Echo im Kampf der Darsteller mit der Sprache selbst, denn Sprechen ist problematisch in diesen von Forced Entertainment entworfenen Welten. Kommunikation findet statt durch Gesten, gutturale Geräusche und gebrochenes Englisch. So wie das Kind, das die Sprache noch nicht gemeistert hat (oder, genauer, von der Sprache noch nicht gemeistert wurde), ist der Performer unfähig, das Sprechen in zusammenhängenden und sofort lesbaren Mustern zu organisieren – man denke nur an die folgenden Zeilen vom Beginn des eigentlich Spiels in *200% & Bloody Thirsty*:

A: Oh, welch einen schrecklichen Anblick er dann bietet. Ich kann kaum hinsehen.

B: Lass uns ihn foppen. Lass uns sein Blut und seine furchtbare Kleidung stehlen.

A: Nein! Lass uns dann Himmel öffnen und ihn mit Schnee berieseln.

B: Heul! Pass es auf tote Person, weil wir dich ficken werden & bedecken.

A: Wach es auf toter Mann, weil wir ausgezeichnete und wundersame Engel sind!

B: Höre genau zu, denn wir kennen die ganzen und Details deines dämlichen Zustands.

A: Oh, Du warst auf einer fick und wilden Weihnachtsfeier und usw.

Hier ist der Betrunkene, gleich dem Kind, nicht völlig vom Ordnungssystem sprachlicher Struktur eingeschnürt. Er behandelt ihre einzelnen Elemente, die Silben, Konsonanten, Wörter und Redewendungen, wie Bestandteile eines Spiels, das in dieser Performance aus den

the Water Run its Course) to the Sea that Made the Promise* (1986) to *The Travels* (2002), traces of childhood and elements of play are easily identifiable in each of the company's works. In *Showtime* (1996), for example, the signs of childhood are self-evident, materialising in the form of animal and tree costumes, the balloon-strewn set, and children's song and dance routines. In *200% & Bloody Thirsty* and *(Let the Water Run its Course) to the Sea that Made the Promise* the condition of childhood finds its echo in the performers' struggle with language itself. Speaking is difficult in these worlds staged by Forced Entertainment. Communication takes place through the use of gesture, guttural sound and broken English. Like the child who is not the master of language (or, to be exact, is not yet mastered *by* language), the performer is unable to organise speech into coherent and immediately readable patterns. Consider the following lines, which are shouted in the first live dialogue of *200% & Bloody Thirsty*:

A: O What a terrible sight he then is, I can't to bear to look.

B: Let us play a trick on him. Let us steal his blood and awful clothes.

A: No! let us make then heavens open and shower him in snow.

B: Howl! Watch it out dead person for we will to fuck & cover you up.

A: Wake it up dead man for we are excellent and wondrous angels!

B: Listen hard for we know the all and details of your stupid state.

A: O You were at a fuck and wild man Xmas party and etc.

Here, the drunk, like the child, is not completely fastened by the discipline of linguistic structure and treats its elements, its syllables, consonants, words and phrases, as individual components

Bloody Play / Games of Childhood and Death
Bloody Play / Das Spiel von Kindheit und Tod
Andrew Quick

in a game. The game, in this performance, is to repeat drunken versions of the Nativity, which are manically enacted as a means to resuscitate a sleeping, or dying, friend who has collapsed in the cold. It is a game that makes play with the essential visceral energy of language, with its ability to create gestures and signals that cannot be reduced to, or that are always in excess of, the specific meaning that is attached to a sign. In this early work, the voice becomes a site of playful invention and the initiator of dissonance. Speech seems to muddy, rather than clarify. Here, the syntax and phrases associated with tragedy and religious rite are clumsily appropriated ("Wake it up dead man for we are excellent and wondrous angels!"). In this kind of utterance, "the architecture of language without its details" returns us to the fragile verbal landscapes of our childhood landscapes, where the plenitude that marks formative experience is unable to be contained within the limits of any systematic linguistic arrangement (*CF* 134). The protagonists who participate in the drunken game of dying and resurrection, which is the centre of *200 % & Bloody Thirsty* continually fail to master the languages of tragedy and religion. However, this failure is not experienced as loss. On the contrary, their protagonists' tireless play with the materiality of language, like that of children, displays a belief that its visceral quality is both magical and liberating. Theirs is a form of play that can momentarily provide a match for life's terrors: one that has the potential to raise even the dead (*CF* 105).

Language is often revealed as playing a game with those who attempt to master its complex workings. For example, the enduring motif in *Emanuelle Enchanted* is the struggle by the figures on stage to locate the structures and the foundations in which the play in, and of, language might be regulated: to find, as one of the protagonists plaintively requests, 'NOTIONS OF

Wiederholungen betrunkener Krippenspiel-Adaptionen besteht – manisch vollzogen um einen schlafenden oder sterbenden Freund wieder zu beleben, der in der Kälte kollabiert ist. Es ist ein Spiel mit der wesentlichen, irrationalen, aus dem Bauch kommenden Kraft der Sprache und ihrer Fähigkeit, Gesten und Signale zu erzeugen, die nicht auf die einem Zeichen zugeordnete spezifische Bedeutung reduziert werden können, bzw. ständig über diese hinausschießen. In diesem frühen Stück wird die Stimme zum Ort spielerischer Erfindung und zum Initiator von Dissonanz. Sprache dient eher zur Trübung als zur Klärung. Satzbau und Redewendungen, die eigentlich Tragödie und religiösen Ritus assoziieren lassen, werden plump angepasst: („Wach es auf toter Mann, weil wir ausgezeichnete und wundersame Engel sind!"). Durch solche Äußerungen führt uns „die Architektur der Sprache ohne Detail" (*CF* 134) in die fragilen verbalen Landschaften unserer Kindheit zurück – Landschaften, in denen die Vielfalt prägender Erfahrungen unmöglich vom Rahmen systematisch linguistischer Anordnung begrenzt werden kann. Die Protagonisten, die am betrunkenen Sterbe- und Wiederauferstehungsspiel beteiligt sind, das das Zentrum von *200% & Bloody Thirsty* darstellt, scheitern permanent an dem Versuch, diese Sprache der Tragödie und der Religion zu meistern. Dieses Scheitern jedoch wird nicht als Verlust erfahren, im Gegenteil: Das unermüdliche Spiel mit dem Sprachmaterial spiegelt den kindlichen Glauben wider, seine aus dem Bauch kommende, irrationale Qualität sei magisch und befreiend. Es ist eine Art des Spiels, die sich für einen Augenblick mit den Schrecken des Lebens messen kann, ein Spiel, das die Macht hat, sogar Tote zum Leben zu erwecken (*CF* 105).

Sprache entpuppt sich oft als ein Spiel gerade mit denen, die versuchen ihre komplexe Funktionsweise zu meistern. Das Leitmotiv in *Emanuelle Enchanted* beispielsweise ist der Kampf der Bühnenfiguren, die regulierenden Strukturen und Grundlagen von bzw. im Spiel der Sprache zu lokalisieren oder – wie eine der Protagonistinnen schwermütig fordert – „EINE AHNUNG VON BESTÄNDIGKEIT IN DIESER INSTABILITÄT" (*CF* 154) zu finden. In *Emanuelle Enchanted* werden zeitliche und räumliche Relationen als fließend und flüchtig entlarvt. Es ist eine Welt, in der sich die Wände bewegen und der fortwährende Informationsfluss ihre Bewohner zu überfluten scheint. In der Sequenz *Newsroom* verlesen die Bühnenfiguren Textfragmente, wobei sie von einer Kamera aufgenommen und auf zwei Monitore links und rechts vom Tisch des Nachrichtensprechers übertragen werden. Gerade das Bemühen des Nachrichtensprechers, Wort- und Satzfetzen von den Schmierzetteln zu lesen, führt zur Fragmentierung der Sprachsyntax:

1. *Netter Augenblick*
2. *Seine hübschen Antworten*
3. *Unlesbar*
4. *Sergeant, wer hat hier das Kommando?*

KEINE SOLCHE DATEI UMZUBENENNEN

1.
Gegenstand 1: GUTES LÄCHELN
2. *Nette Geschichte.*

Merke, erinnerst du dich? Gestorben.
Nun hör zu:

1. *eine Blinddarmoperationsnarbe und*
Alarmanlagen an Gebäuden und
die Luft so süß, dass sie dich vor dem Sterben bewahrt und
Alarmanlagen in den Autos und
vor uns liegen nur große Katastrophen und
ein Film, genannt ,Sucht noch jemand Ärger in diesem Dreckloch?'
und später ,Anna, komm zu mir Anna, du bist am anderen Ende der Welt …'
und

Inmitten dieser Flut abgehackter Äußerungen ist ,Sinn' sowohl verloren als auch begehrt für

143

FIXITY WITHIN THIS INSTABILITY' (*CF* 154). In *Emanuelle Enchanted* temporal and spatial relations are revealed to be fluid and volatile. This is a world in which walls move, in which the very flow of information seems to overpower its inhabitants. In the 'newsroom' sequences of the piece, the figures on stage read out fragments of text. These sequences are recorded by a single camera and relayed on two television monitors which are placed on either side of the 'newscasters' desk. The syntax of language becomes fragmented as the newscasters endeavour to read snatches of words and phrases from scraps of paper:

1. *nice moment*
2. *his gorgeous answers*
3. *unreadable*
4. *sergeant, who's in charge here?*

NO SUCH FILE TO RENAME

1.
Item 1: GOOD SMILE
2. *Nice Story.*

Note, remember? Died.

Now listen:

1. *an appendectomy scar and*
alarms on buildings and
the air so sweet it keeps you from dying and
alarms on the cars and
ahead of us there are only great disasters and
a film called 'anybody else in this shithole looking for trouble?'
and later 'Anna, come to me Anna, you're on the other side of the world …'
and

In the midst of the welter of these disconnected utterances, 'sense' is both lost and sought after

144

Bloody Play / Games of Childhood and Death
Bloody Play / Das Spiel von Kindheit und Tod
Andrew Quick

in the attempts of both performer and spectator to piece the fragments together. *Emanuelle Enchanted* is imbued with a feeling of crisis, in which the world's structures are falling apart and continuously being rearranged. Yet there is always a striving for structure: performed with urgency, and often desperation, by the figures on stage. This desire for structure is indicated by the numbering of the disparate sections of text, which inculcate a linear structure across elements that would otherwise remain disconnected. The practices of listing and numbering become the syntactical structures in, and through, which signification is attempted. Rather than inducing order, the structures enhance the sensation of random arrangements and the fragile nature of making connections, of the failure built into any crystallisation into meaning. As one of the figures exclaims: "this is a night of losing and finding again, of losing and of finding, of losing and then of finding once again" (*CF* 150).

Unnerving play

The function and importance of play, both to the making and performing of the work, is described by Tim Etchells, who writes of the company: "They had no dogma (or they tried to have none) – they were only interested in 'what worked' (what worked for them, in this place in history, culture and time). They tried not to get stuck in one logic – they tried to keep it moving, playful, nimble" (*CF* 53). In his essay *Play On: Collaboration and Process*, Etchells repeatedly invokes play as an activity that destabilises meaning, provokes transformations and generates something other to reality. In this writing (which must always be distinguished from the material and collaborative condition of Forced Entertainment's performance work), play is articulated as an activity that challenges the

den Versuch von Schauspielern und Zuschauern die Puzzleteile zusammenzufügen. *Emanuelle Enchanted* ist durchdrungen von einem Gefühl der Krise, davon, dass die Struktur der Welt in sich zusammenbricht und dauernd neu arrangiert wird. Dennoch streben die Bühnenfiguren beharrlich oder gar verzweifelt eine Ordnung an – darauf weist die Nummerierung hin, die den völlig unverbundenen Textabschnitten eine lineare Struktur gibt. Die Tätigkeit des Auflistens und Nummerierens wird zur eigentlich syntaktischen Strukturierung, durch die (und in der) der Versuch von Bedeutungszuschreibung stattfindet. Anstatt Ordnung herbeizuführen, verstärken diese Strukturen den Eindruck von Willkürlichkeit des Arrangements, der Zerbrechlichkeit erzeugter Zusammenhänge und vom Scheitern, das jeder Konkretisierung von Bedeutung innewohnt. Es ist, wie eine der Figuren ausruft, „eine Nacht des Verlierens und Wiederfindens, des Verlierens und des Findens, des Verlierens und dann des nochmals Wiederfindens" (*CF* 150).

Enervierendes Spiel

Die Funktion und Bedeutung von Spiel, sowohl in der Entwicklung als auch in den Aufführungen der Stücke, wird von Tim Etchells folgendermaßen beschrieben: „Sie hatten kein Dogma (oder zumindest versuchten sie keines zu haben) – sie waren nur an dem interessiert ‚was funktionierte' (was für sie funktionierte, an diesem Ort in der Geschichte, Kultur und Zeit). Sie versuchten, nicht innerhalb einer Logik stecken zu bleiben – sie versuchten, die Dinge in Bewegung zu halten, spielerisch, beweglich" (*CF* 53). In seinem Essay *Play On: Collaboration and Process* beschwört Etchells das Spielen immer wieder als eine Aktivität, die Bedeutung destabilisiert, Veränderung zeigt und etwas anderes als Realität erzeugt. In seinem Text (nicht zu verwechseln mit dem Material und den gemeinschaftlichen Prozessen in der künstlerischen Praxis von Forced Entertain-

Emanuelle Enchanted

ment) wird Spielen als eine Handlung beschrieben, die Grenzen alltäglicher Lebenserfahrungen infrage stellt und dadurch eine Welt zeigt, die durch „andauernde Erfindung, (im) andauernden Fluss" konstruiert wird. Spielen wird gezeigt als ein Streben, das an den Grenzen des Vernünftigen zerrt und so die Spieler in neue, unbekannte Territorien katapultiert. An Orte, in denen vorige Systeme des Verstehens den Spielern nicht mehr bei der Einschätzung helfen, wo sie sich befinden oder wie weit sie gegangen sind.

Etchells beobachtet, dass die enervierende Qualität des Spielens, seine Tendenz, bekannte Regeln zu brechen und neue, sich dauernd verändernde, zu schaffen, nicht nur die Darsteller, sondern auch das Publikum beeinflusst. In solchen Momenten werden die passiven Zuschauer, wie Etchells mit einem

limits of everyday experience in order to reveal a world that is constructed out of "constant invention, constant flux." Play is portrayed as a pursuit that 'worries' at the borders of the sensible, causing players to be thrown into new and unknown territories, places where previous systems of understanding are no longer useful in assessing where players are, or how far they have gone.

Etchells observes that the unnerving quality of play, its tendency to break known rules and create ever changing new ones not only affects the performer (the player), but also the audience. At such moments, Etchells intimates, in a passing reference to Brecht, passive spectators are transformed into active witnesses. Like the player, the witness struggles to find new modes of understanding in the wake of activity that breaks pre-existing rules and the principles that shore them up. The result is a radical form of anxiety that interrupts those thought processes that normalise experience, that render events knowable. "The art-work that turns us into witnesses", he writes, "leaves us, above all, unable to stop thinking and reporting what we've seen" (*CF* 18).

As my account of the events that took place in Polverigi shows, the outcome of disquiet is not silence, but the uproar that results from the clamour for discussion. The agitated behaviour of the spectators who witnessed *200% & Bloody Thirsty* in Polverigi can, perhaps, be explained by the unsettling activities of play, activities that provoked the unruly gathering of watchers and animated the vociferous debate during the performance. This, it seems, was an occasion where spectators became witnesses, where the on-stage action provoked such strong feelings of instability that people felt compelled to break the usual conventions of sitting compliantly and silently in the dark. According to Etchells, witnessing has consequences. Questioning the nature of the audience's visual desire, he asks if the spectator could "dream of a looking that had no consequence, no ethical bind, no power inherent in it, no cost?" (*CF* 65). Assuring us that we "won't find that here" – in the company's work – Etchells describes a form of searching that arises as a response to the caesura (the pause in space and time) that is opened up by the agitations of play. These pauses are explained as 'stops', and they 'make strange' (once again, a reference to Brecht). The stops in play, Etchells argues, create the space and time for contemplation and the practice of judgement. These are the moments, he writes, which are "always the time for measuring how far things had gone, how much the world had changed because of the game" (*CF* 58). The stops and 'making strange' affect the performer *and* spectator, since both are caught

beiläufigen Verweis auf Brecht andeutet, in aktive Zeugen verwandelt. Unmittelbar nach dem Bruch der Regeln und ihrer untermauernden Prinzipien folgt der Kampf des Zeugen (ähnlich dem Kampf des Spielers) um neue Formen des Verstehens. Das Ergebnis ist eine radikale Verunsicherung, die jene Denkprozesse unterbricht, die dazu dienen, Erfahrungen zu normalisieren und Ereignisse begreifbar zu machen. „Das Kunstwerk, das uns zu Zeugen macht", schreibt Etchells, „lässt uns vor allem nicht mehr aufhören zu denken und immer wieder berichten, was wir gesehen haben" (*CF* 18).

Wie meine Beschreibung der Ereignisse in Polverigi zeigt, führt Unruhe nicht zu Stille, sondern zum Aufruhr aus dem Drang heraus zu diskutieren. Die Aufregung der Zuschauer, die Zeugen von *200% & Bloody Thirsty* in Polverigi waren, kann also vielleicht mit den beunruhigenden Aktivitäten des Spielens erklärt werden, die sowohl zur spontanen Versammlung der Zuschauer als auch zur lautstarken Debatte während der Aufführung führten: Aus den Zuschauern wurden, wie es scheint, Zeugen. Das Gefühl der Instabilität, das vom Bühnengeschehen erzeugt wurde, war derart intensiv, dass sich die Leute gezwungen sahen, übliche Konventionen des Fügsam-und-still-im-Dunkel-Sitzens zu brechen.

Für Etchells hat Zeugenschaft Konsequenzen. Den Ursprung der Schaulust des Publikum hinterfragend, überlegt er, ob der Zuschauer „von einem Schauen träumen könnte, das keine Konsequenzen hat, keine ethische Verpflichtung, keine innewohnende Macht, keine Kosten?" (*CF* 65). Indem er uns versichert, dass wir das „hier", in der Arbeit der Gruppe, „nicht finden werden" beschreibt Etchells eine Art des Suchens als Antwort auf die Zäsur (die Pause in Raum und Zeit), die durch das aufwühlende Spiel entsteht. Diese Pausen werden als ‚Stopps' und (wiederum als Hinweis auf Brecht) als ‚Verfremdung' beschrieben. Das Innehalten im Spielen schafft Ort und Zeit für eine Betrachtung und Beurteilung – Augenblicke, die „immer der

Zeitpunkt waren, zu messen, wie weit es gekommen war, wie sehr sich die Welt aufgrund des Spiels verändert hatte" (*CF* 58). Diese Stopps und Verfremdungen betreffen gleichermaßen Spieler und Zuschauer, da beide im Akt der Zeugenschaft gefangen sind, wobei existierende Kriterien nicht mehr ausreichen, um Erfahrungen vollständig verstehbar zu machen. Wir nähern uns der Definition von Fremdheit als etwas, das nicht erkennbar ist, ungewohnt, unbekannt, nicht erklärbar (vom Lateinischen *extraneus,* ‚von draußen, äußerlich, fremd').

Natürlich schafft solche Zeugenschaft (eine Art des Sehens und Zuhörens, die Konsequenzen hat), wie Etchells andeutet, eine Last, die wir als ‚Verantwortung' erfahren. Das ist der ‚Preis' der Zeugenschaft: Ihr ‚Gewicht', ihre ‚innewohnende Macht', ihre ‚ethische Verpflichtung'. Verantwortung – die immer auch von einem Gefühl von Sorge durchdrungen ist – erzeugt spezifische Forderungen an das Subjekt, das sie empfindet: Wie reagieren, wie handeln, was als Nächstes tun? Doch die Anforderungen dieser Verantwortung sind eng verbunden mit dem, was beantwortet werden muss: Verantwortungsbewusstsein erzeugt die Notwendigkeit einer Reaktion, die der Situation verpflichtet ist, auf die reagiert werden soll. Das ist die Pflicht, die durch Zeugenschaft entsteht. Die Begegnung mit etwas Fremden verunmöglicht vorgeschriebene und transzendentale (*a priori*) Wege des Verstehens, ansonsten würde man ja das Ungewohnte gar nicht erst als etwas dem Wissen Fremdes (außerhalb der Wahrnehmungsgrenzen Liegendes) erfahren. So wird der Reagierende zum Handeln gedrängt, ohne sich in bekannte Regeln, in geschriebenes Gesetz flüchten zu können, da das Erlebte nicht unmittelbar kognitiv verstehbar ist. In solchen Situationen, in denen Ereignisse vorgegebene Systeme des Verstehens überschreiten, wird das Subjekt dazu gedrängt, neue Formen des Beurteilens zu erfinden, um dem, was es bezeugt, gerecht zu werden. Die Beurteilung ist in diesem Fall unprogrammatisch,

in the activity of witnessing, whereby existing sets of criteria are insufficient to render the experience completely intelligible. Here we come close to defining what is meant by strangeness: that which is not quite recognisable, which is unfamiliar, unknown, alien, not easily explained (from the Latin, *extraneus*, meaning 'from the outside, external, foreign').

Of course, as Etchells suggests, bearing witness (a mode of seeing and listening that has consequences) generates a burden, which we experience as 'responsibility'. This, I think, is the 'cost' of witnessing: its 'weight'; its 'inherent power', its 'ethical bind'. Responsibility, which is always imbued with a sense of anxiety, creates specific demands on the subject who feels it: how to reply; how to act; what to do next? However, the command that responsibility makes is intimately connected to that which needs answering. Having a sense of responsibility necessitates a response that is beholden to the situation to which one is responding. This is the obligation that witnessing creates. The encounter with something strange disables prescribed and transcendental (a priori) ways of understanding. Otherwise, the unfamiliar would not be experienced as something alien to knowledge (outside the limits of perception) in the first place. In such cases, the respondent is forced to act without recourse to known rules, to the already written law, because what is being encountered does not immediately fall within her/his cognitive grasp. In those instances where events exceed programmed systems of understanding, the subject is pushed into inventing new modes of judgment in order to account for what he/she is witnessing. Here, judgement is non-programmatic, indeterminate and contingent, although it is always made in relation to the experience that is endured. This is the literal meaning of the phrase 'to take responsibility': the ability or authority to act and to decide (make

Bloody Play / Games of Childhood and Death
Bloody Play / Das Spiel von Kindheit und Tod
Andrew Quick

judgments) on one's own, *as the situation demands.* Responsibility, in this sense, is always ethical since, as Geoffrey Bennington observes in his discussion of Derrida's thinking on politics, ethics "begins where the case does not entirely correspond to any rule, and where the decision has to be taken without subsumption". Consequently, making decisions (acts of judgment) is aligned with inventiveness, with playfulness, whereby known rules (or, to be exact, the rules of the known) are put into abeyance and new ones are created in their place and tested out.

In the specific environments of Forced Entertainment's performance making, Etchells identifies moments of abeyance as being "off the route", places where the performer gets into "trouble". This 'getting into trouble' is described as: "pushing the work so you find yourselves in a territory beyond the one you know – by following a loose associative logic, by playing with no regard, in the first place, for sense" (*CF* 52). The performers in Forced Entertainment's work are not breaking rules just for the sake of it, in order to pursue a nihilistic assault on meaning (an accusation that is often flung at experimental art practice by those that judge it to have little social or political value). Rather, Etchells is staking a claim for those aesthetic practices that take the risk of negotiating material without relying on an immediate recourse to a rule, to pre-established ways of making sense of everyday occurrences. The risk inherent in this pursuit is that it might open out the radical uniqueness of experience (the event), which is revealed when the principles that guide and support how we make sense of the world are suspended. This is the risk that is initiated by play and its related activities: the games which, as Etchells observes, are always in "dialogue with the now" (*CF* 70).

However, 'the now', since it demands that the security of knowledge is left behind (or

unbestimmt und ungewiss, obwohl sie immer Bezug nimmt auf die auszuhaltende Erfahrung. Denn das ist die wörtliche Bedeutung von ‚Verantwortung übernehmen‘: die Fähigkeit oder Autorität, alleine handeln und entscheiden (Urteile fällen) zu können – *entsprechend der Situation.* Verantwortung in diesem Sinne ist immer ethisch, da, wie Geoffrey Bennington in seiner Auseinandersetzung mit Derridas Gedanken zur Politik feststellt, Ethik „beginnt, wenn der Fall nicht vollständig mit den vorhandenen Regeln korrespondiert, und die Entscheidung gemacht werden muss ohne auf existierenden Prinzipien zu basieren". Dementsprechend ist das Treffen von Entscheidungen (der Akt des Urteilens) mit einer Erfindungsgabe und Spielfreude verbunden, die bekannte Regeln (oder, um genau zu sein, die Regeln des Bekannten) außer Kraft setzt und an ihrer Stelle neue kreiert und austestet.

In der kreativen Atmosphäre ihrer Performances lassen sich laut Etchells Momente der Unentschiedenheit verorten, ein „Abkommen vom Wege", Orte, an denen die Performer in ‚Schwierigkeiten‘ geraten: „Du treibst die Arbeit so weit voran, bis du dich an einem Ort befindest, der dir unbekannt ist, der hinter dem liegt, was du kennst – indem du einer ungefestigten, assoziativen Logik folgst, in erster Linie sinnlos spielend" (*CF* 52). Forced Entertainment bricht Regeln nicht um des Brechens von Regeln willen, nicht als nihilistischer Angriff auf Bedeutung (ein Vorwurf, der experimenteller Kunstpraxis oft von jenen gemacht wird, die glauben, sie habe nur geringen sozialen oder politischen Wert). Vielmehr erhebt Etchells Anspruch auf eine ästhetische Praxis, die das Risiko eingeht, ihr Material zu verwenden ohne unmittelbar auf bekannte Regeln oder vorgegebene Weisen alltäglicher Sinngebung zurückzugreifen. Das Risiko, das diesem Streben innewohnt, liegt darin, dass es die radikale Einzigartigkeit des Erlebens (das Ereignis), die enthüllt wird, wenn die Prinzipien unseres Weltverstehens außer Kraft gesetzt werden, aufbrechen könnte. Denn das

200% & Bloody Thirsty

150

Bloody Play / Games of Childhood and Death
Bloody Play / Das Spiel von Kindheit und Tod
Andrew Quick

momentarily abandoned), generates unease. This begins to explain why children often make play with that which they find frightening: to invoke and then, perhaps, be in control of that which disturbs them. Play might reveal and unleash the immediacy of experience, but it also allows a safe passage back into the known order of things. This is why children's play is so often bound up with repetition. According to Walter Benjamin, who has written with an enduring acuity on children and theatre, the repetitive nature of play does not "deaden" the "frightening fundamental experience". Rather, as he writes in *Toys and Play* (1928), play is identified as the mechanism through which the child enjoys her/his "victories and triumphs over and over again, with total intensity." Claiming that the adult turns to narrative "to relieve his heart from its terrors", Benjamin observes that the child resorts to the repetition of (and in) play "in order to create the entire event anew" and start "right from the beginning." Consequently, play, for Benjamin, is not an imitation, 'a doing as if'. It is "a doing the same thing over and over again …" Through repetition, he argues, the shattering nature of experience, 'the now', is transformed into habit. This process of transformation, he claims, is "the essence of play". Repetition is one of the identifying features of Forced Entertainment's work to date, although its function is not merely formal. Benjamin indicates that play has two functions, both of which are useful in exploring what might be at stake in Forced Entertainment's use of repetition. Repeated actions, as play, as game playing, disrupt everyday rules and concepts and invite the player to make contact with 'fundamental frightening experience'. Play also has the capacity to transform such experience into habit: into the learned behavioural response that has become associated with a particular situation. "For play and nothing else", Benjamin writes,

ist das Risiko des Spielens und der mit ihm verbundenen Handlungen: dass sie, wie Etchells beobachtet, immer im „Dialog mit dem Jetzt" sind (*CF* 70).

Das ‚Jetzt' mit seinem Verlangen, die Sicherheit des Wissens hinter sich zu lassen (oder zumindest vorübergehend auszusetzen), schafft jedoch Unbehagen – hier nähern wir uns einer Erklärung dafür, warum Kinder mit dem spielen, was ihnen Angst macht: Um es heraufzubeschwören und dann, vielleicht, zu kontrollieren. Das Spielen kann die Unmittelbarkeit der Erfahrung enthüllen und entfesseln, aber es erlaubt auch den sicheren Rückzug in die bekannte Ordnung der Dinge. Darum wird das Kinderspiel so oft in den Kontext der Wiederholungen gestellt.

Nach Walter Benjamin, der mit beständigem Scharfsinn über Kinder und Theater geschrieben hat, „dämpft" die dem Spielen eigene Wiederholung die „furchtbare Urerfahrung" nicht. Vielmehr wird Spielen als Mechanismus identifiziert, mit dem Kinder ihre „Triumphe und Siege aufs intensivste immer wieder durchkosten". Benjamin behauptet in *Spielzeug und Spielen* (1928), „der Erwachsene entlastet sein Herz von Schrecken", indem er sich der Erzählung zuwendet, während das Kind auf die Wiederholung des Spiels zurückgreift. Es „schafft sich die ganze Sache von neuem, fängt noch einmal von vorn an." Folglich ist für Benjamin das Spielen keine Imitation, kein ‚So tun als ob', sondern ein „Immer-wieder-tun". Durch Wiederholung wird die „erschütterndste Erfahrung", das „Jetzt", in Gewohnheit transformiert. Dies ist „das Wesen des Spielens".

Wiederholung ist bis heute eines der Erkennungsmerkmale von Forced Entertainments Arbeit, aber ihre Rolle ist keine rein formale. Für Benjamin hat das Spielen zwei Funktionen, und beide erweisen sich als nützlich bei der Erläuterung dessen, was im Falle von Forced Entertainments Wiederholungen auf dem Spiel steht. Wiederholte Handlungen, wie das Spielen, unterbrechen die alltäglichen Regeln und Strukturen und laden den Spieler ein, mit der „furchtbaren Urerfahrung" in Kontakt zu treten. Dem Spiel eignet außerdem die Fähigkeit, solche Erfahrungen zur Gewohnheit zu machen: Zu einer erlernten Verhaltensweise, die mit bestimmten Situationen verbunden ist. „Denn Spiel, nichts sonst, ist die Wehmutter jeder Gewohnheit." Und so werden wir „zuerst unserer selbst habhaft". Im Spielen beginnt die Konstitution des Subjektes. Benjamin räumt jedoch ein, dass die Transformation von Erfahrung in Gewohnheit niemals vollkommen gelingt. Denn obwohl die Praktiken des Spielens entscheidend sind für das Erlernen ‚guten' Benehmens, leben sie gleichwohl in den erlernten Reaktionen fort. Gewohnheiten mögen sich verhärten, können sich, in Benjamins Worten, zu den „unkenntlich gewordene(n) versteinerte(n) Formen unseres ersten Glücks, unseres ersten Grauens" entwickeln. Dennoch setzten sich die „Restchen" unseres Verlangens nach und unsere Freude am Spielen im Laufe unseres Lebens immer wieder durch. Gewohnheiten entwickeln sich durch wiederholte Handlungen: jene Rhythmen, durch die wir lernen. Allerdings ist Spielen ein wichtiger Bestandteil von Wiederholung und immer bereit, die Welt der Gewohnheiten zusammenstürzen zu lassen. Vielleicht ist das der Grund, warum die altmodische Tradition von Theater und Performance sich in einem Umfeld weiterhin erhält, in dem das technisch aufgezeichnete Bild eine so große Machtposition zu haben scheint. Denn Spielen ist Teil des Wesens von Performance. Und durch unsere Begegnung mit dem Spielen, mit dem Live-Ereignis, das Performance ist, testen wir die Grenzen der Gewohnheit.

Wiederholung, wie das Spielen, stellt jene Prozesse in Frage, durch die wir uns als Subjekt konstituieren, weshalb man sie mit Fragen der Ethik in Verbindung bringen kann. Die Herausforderungen, mit denen das Spielen unsere verwurzelten Denkweisen und unser ‚in der Welt sein' konfrontiert, animierten uns zum erneuten Denken und

"is the mother of every habit". Thus, it is via play, "that we first gain possession of ourselves". It is through play that the subject comes into formation. Benjamin indicates, however, that this transformation of experience into habit is never finally resolved. The practices of play, he asserts, while being crucial to learning 'good' behaviour, also continue to haunt the trained response. Habit may harden, 'congeal' and 'deform' what he calls "the forms of our first happiness and our first horror", but our residual need for, and delight in, play continues throughout our lives, well beyond childhood. Habit, it seems, comes into formation through repeated actions. They are the rhythms through which we learn. Yet, as Benjamin reminds us, play is an essential constituent of repetition, one that is always ready to bring the world of habit crashing down. Perhaps this explains why the seemingly antiquated traditions of theatre and performance continue to endure in an environment where the recorded image appears to have such a cultural stranglehold. For play is part of the ontology of performance. And it is through our encounter with play, the live event that *is* performance, that we put the limits of habit to the test.

Repetition as play, therefore, calls into question the processes through which we construct ourselves as subjects. For this reason, play might be considered to invoke the ethical. The challenges that play presents to our embedded ways of thinking and being in the world make us think and act anew: "right from the beginning", as Benjamin observes. Play demands a response that is responsible to the particularity of the situation that it produces: particularities that take us by surprise, since play is always improvisational. The same, it seems, is true for performance in those instances where the live event takes us 'off the route', where, as Etchells writes, "safe passage back to the everyday is no longer assured" (*CF* 81). These occasions re-play the trauma, the intense 'happiness' and 'horror' inherent in the inauguration of the subject itself: moments where being has not yet hardened into custom.

Consider, for example, the repeated routines that structure *(Let the Water Run its Course) to the Sea that Made the Promise*. In this piece, language is stripped down to gesture, incoherent whispers, and enacted sound effects: buzzings, harsh clicks and incessant weeping. There is something distinctly child-like in the protagonists' emotional game playing. A seated performer suddenly covers her face and, rocking violently, begins to cry. This action immediately creates a response from another performer, who is sat in a parallel space on the other side of the playing area. This game of crying builds steadily to a disturbing crescendo as the two figures compete with each other: one crying and then stopping, as if throwing down a challenge; the other, picking up this challenge and responding with an even greater emotional energy. As the game goes on, what started off as a crude and amusing imitation of emotion is transformed into a heightened state of suffering, in which the performer appears to be no longer acting. No immediate context is provided – narrative or otherwise – for this emotional explosion, beyond the simple framework of the game's rules. Yet, as the game draws to its affecting conclusion, the performer creates a situation that resonates with a raw emotional power: one that, in my remembering of it, is replete with the intensity that is 'the now.' During this moment, I cannot find solace in any form of psychological or ideological intentionality. Together with the other performers looking on from the edges of the space, I witness this helpless and inexplicable state of sorrow unburdened by explanation and I'm forced to deal only with the immediacy and materiality of its happening.

Handeln: „Noch einmal von vorne", laut Benjamin. Spielen verlangt nach einer Reaktion, die auf die Besonderheiten der Situation antwortet, die sie selbst hervorruft und die uns überrascht, da das Spielen immer improvisiert ist. Das gilt, wie es scheint, immer dann auch für Performance, wenn das Live-Ereignis uns „vom Wege abbringt", dorthin, wo mit Etchells „der sichere Rückzug in den Alltag nicht länger gesichert ist". Das Trauma, also das intensive Gefühl von ‚Glück' und ‚Grauen', das bei der Subjektwerdung unvermeidlich ist, wird in diesen Ereignissen wiederholt: jene Momente des Seins, die sich noch nicht zur Gewohnheit verhärtet haben.

Führt man sich zum Beispiel die wiederholten Routinen vor Augen, die *(Let the Water Run its Course)* seine Struktur geben, sieht man eine Limitierung der Sprache auf Gesten, unzusammenhängendes Wispern und dargestellte Sound-Effekte, wie Brummen, Klicken und unablässiges Weinen. Im emotionalen Spiel der Protagonisten findet sich etwas ausdrücklich Kindliches.

Eine sitzende Performerin verbirgt plötzlich ihr Gesicht in den Händen, wippt heftig vor und zurück, beginnt zu weinen und provoziert so die unmittelbare Reaktion eines anderen Performers, der parallel zu ihr auf der anderen Seite der Bühne sitzt. Dieses Spiel des Weinens steigert sich zu einem beunruhigenden Crescendo, das sich als Wettkampf entpuppt: Weinen und herausfordernd Innehalten, bis der andere die Herausforderung annimmt und mit noch stärkerer emotionaler Energie antwortet. Das, was als primitive und amüsante Imitation anfing, entwickelt sich zu einem intensiven Leidenszustand, in dem der Performer nicht mehr Darsteller zu sein scheint. Es gibt über die simplen Spielregeln hinaus keinen unmittelbaren Zusammenhang – etwa einer Erzählstruktur – für diesen emotionalen Ausbruch. Doch während das Spiel sich dem bewegenden Ende nähert, schafft der Performer einen Zustand ursprünglicher, emotionaler Energie, der in meiner Erinnerung gesättigt ist von einer Intensität

Bloody Play / Games of Childhood and Death
Bloody Play / Das Spiel von Kindheit und Tod
Andrew Quick

des ‚Jetzt'. Keine Form von psychologischer oder ideologischer Intention bietet mir in diesem Moment Trost. Gemeinsam mit den anderen Spielern, die das Geschehen von der Seite beobachten, werde ich Zeuge dieses hilflosen und unerklärlichen Leidenszustands. Unbelastet von Erklärungen kann ich mich ausschließlich der Unmittelbarkeit und dem Wesen des Geschehens widmen. Ich bin berührt, in jeder Hinsicht. Ich fühle in meinen Eingeweiden die irrationale Verständlichkeit der Erfahrung und dann ‚erleide' ich die Auswirkung dieser Unmittelbarkeit: Ich bin ergriffen, bewegt. Diese Bewegtheit ist nicht nur eine emotionale Deplatzierung. Man kann gleichzeitig ergriffen, bewegt und vollkommen im Einklang mit dem sein, was dieses Gefühl hervorgerufen hat: Dies ist eine Definition von Sentimentalität. Vielmehr erlebe ich diese Bewegung als eine brutale Deplatzierung meiner Selbst. Ich befinde mich in einem Zustand, in dem ich, umgangssprachlich gesagt, unfähig bin, selbstbewusst zu sagen, „ich kenne mich". Und, ebenso wie der Performer, der leise auf seinem Stuhl schluchzt, bin ich allein gelassen in dieser Stille, in dieser Pause, um mich wiederzufinden, mich zu sammeln. Dieses Sammeln verändert mich, veranlasst mich zum erneuten Nachdenken (etwas, das sich in diesem Schreibprozess fortsetzt), markiert mich, wie das Kind beim Spielen, durch die singuläre Authentizität des Geschehens.

Totes Spiel

Showtime nähert sich dem Ende und Robin Arthur beklagt die Abwesenheit jeder klassisch dramatischen Struktur in dieser theatralischen Landschaft, die von der Gruppe entworfen und seit fünfundvierzig Minuten aufrechtzuerhalten versucht wurde:

Theater sollte eine Art dramatischer Spannung haben – es sollte einen Plot haben. Es sollte einige gut gezeichnete Charaktere geben, damit die Zuschauer sich in das Bühnengeschehen

Here I am touched, in both senses of the word. I feel the visceral tangibility of the experience and then, I 'suffer' this immediacy as affect: I am moved. This movement is not only an emotional displacement for it is possible to be moved and to be utterly in synchronisation with that which has produced the emotion: This is one definition of sentimentality. Rather, I experience this movement as a savage displacement of selfhood. It is an instance, to speak colloquially, where I am unable to say with any confidence that 'I know myself'. And, like the performer quietly sobbing on the chair, I am left in the silence, in the stop, to gather myself together. After this gathering, I am changed, made to think again (a process that continues in this writing), marked once more, like the child at play, by the singular authenticity of this occasion.

Dead play

Towards the end of *Showtime*, Robin Arthur bemoans the absence of classical dramatic structure in the theatrical landscape that the company have constructed and attempted to sustain over the preceding forty-five minutes:

Performance should have some kind of dramatic tension – it should have a plot. It should have some well drawn characters so that the audience can empathise with the events on the stage ... a performance should take place over one day and it should take place off stage and it should be reported by one of the protagonists ... There should be some kind of moral, there should be some kind of purpose because if there isn't a moral it's just a lot of bloody shouting and showing off. The audience doesn't pay good money to see a lot of shouting and showing off – they want something with a purpose ... they want to be transported to a delightful place, they want to see some realistic scenery, they want to be touched, oh God they want some purpose, they want some resolution … they don't want this, they don't want this …

While making this speech, Arthur clutches his exposed torso, having previously emptied the contents of a tin of spaghetti onto his belly. These are the angry words of a dying man, who spills his make-believe guts out in making a final plea for order, purpose, intelligibility and moral resolution. Here, dying is mischievously associated with the demand for narrative cohesion, spatial co-ordination, and temporal stability. Or is it the other way around: moral clarity, linearity and the tropes of classicism/realism positioned as the structural elements that signal the conceptualisation of a particular form of dying and death? Either way, the playful scenes of unruliness, chaos and disunity that make up the previous sections of *Showtime* reveal themselves to be, at least, intrinsically connected to living, to those 'life forces' that keep the finality (the ultimate closure, the only certainty), which is death, at bay.

I say 'at least', because the disruptive activities of play that are railed against in the speech above, the "bloody shouting and showing off", cannot be limited to an interpretation that attempts to identify them solely as the effects of the operations of Eros and Thanatos, as embodiments of Freud's notion of the life and death drives. Even as Robin Arthur pleads for a recognisable dramatic structure and some semblance of intelligibility, he is beleaguered by the loud barking and noisy activities of two of the other performers: Cathy Naden, wearing a pantomimic dog's head, and Claire Marshall, dressed as a tree (both costumes are reminiscent of those used in primary school plays). Is it not possible that their playful disruption and interruption of this performance of dying point to the more radical and unsettling fact that the obscenity of death cannot be tamed by any representational means? After all, when Robin

hineinversetzen können … Eine Aufführung sollte die Dauer eines Tages haben, und sie sollte hinter der Bühne stattfinden, und sie sollte von einem der Protagonisten berichtet werden … Es sollte eine Art von Moral geben, es sollte eine Art von Absicht dahinter stecken, denn wenn es keine Moral gibt, dann ist es nur eine Menge Herumgeschrei und Angeberei. Das Publikum zahlt nicht gutes Geld um ein Menge Herumgeschrei und Angeberei zu sehen – es will etwas mit einer Absicht dahinter … es will an einen wunderbaren Ort versetzt werden, es will eine realistische Szenerie, es will eine Auflösung … es will nicht das hier, es will nicht das hier …

Während dieser Rede umklammert Arthur seinen entblößten Körper, den Inhalt einer Dose Spaghetti mit Tomatensoße auf seinem Bauch. Es sind die wütenden Worte eines sterbenden Mannes, der ein letztes Plädoyer für Ordnung, Absicht, Verständlichkeit und moralische Entschlossenheit hält, während er seine vorgeblichen Eingeweide verschüttet. Sterben wird auf verschmitzte Art und Weise mit der Forderung nach narrativer Geschlossenheit, räumlicher Ordnung und zeitlicher Stabilität in Verbindung gebracht. Oder ist es andersherum und werden moralische Klarheit, Linearität und die Formen von Klassizismus/Realismus in Position gebracht als strukturelle Elemente, die auf die Konzeptualisierung einer spezifischen Art des Sterbens und des Todes hinweisen? Egal von welcher Seite man es betrachtet, die vorangegangenen spielerischen Szenen voller Unbändigkeit, Chaos und Uneinigkeit entpuppen sich nun als, zumindest ihrem Wesen nach, eng verbunden mit dem Leben und jenen ‚Lebenskräften‘, die die Endgültigkeit (die letztendliche Stilllegung, die einzige Gewissheit) des Todes in Schach halten.

Ich sage ‚zumindest‘, weil die störenden Aktivitäten des Spielens, auf die obige Rede als „Herumgeschrei und Angeberei" zielt, nicht auf eine Deutung reduziert werden können, die versucht, eben diese Aktivitäten aus-

154

Bloody Play / Games of Childhood and Death
Bloody Play / Das Spiel von Kindheit und Tod
Andrew Quick

(Let the Water Run its Course) to the Sea that Made the Promise

schließlich als Effekte der Unternehmungen von Eros und Thanatos, als Verkörperungen von Freuds Konzept vom Lebens- und Todestrieb zu identifizieren. Selbst während Robin Arthur für eine erkennbare dramatische Struktur und einen Anschein von Verständlichkeit plädiert, stören ihn zwei Mitspielerinnen mit lautem Bellen und geräuschintensiven Handlungen: Cathy Naden, die eine Hundekopfmaske trägt, und Claire Marshall, verkleidet als Baum (beide Kostüme lassen die Erinnerungen an Grundschultheater wieder aufleben). Könnte es nicht sein, dass das spielerische Stören und Unterbrechen der Sterbedarstellung auf die fundamentalere und beunruhigendere Tatsache hinweist, dass die Obszönität des Todes mit keinem repräsentativen Mittel zu bezwingen ist? Schließlich geht der

Arthur's speech finally dissolves into silent weeping, the tree, armed with a gun, walks forwards and orders the audience to stop watching: "Close your eyes. Close your fucking eyes. You shouldn't be watching this. Close your eyes and keep them closed. Please close your eyes. Please close them." Arthur invokes a representational system in which meaning should be transparent and graspable: "The audience want to go to the bar after the show and say I GOT IT, I UNDERSTOOD WHAT IT WAS ALL ABOUT, they don't want to have to say oh er, it's what ever you want it to mean ..." In marked contrast, the tree, through its command that we avert our gaze from this scene of dying and emotional suffering, implies that the matter of death is far too intimate and

Showtime

unruly an event for objective contemplation. This death, the tree would seem to assert, is an occurrence that is unfit for our visual consumption (although forcing us to shut our eyes inevitably provokes an imaginative and unsettling contemplation of the process of dying).

According to Georges Batailles *Un-knowing and Rebellion* (1952), death is 'obscene' because it exceeds any attempt to fix it through representation. Death is always off-stage (the literal meaning of obscene is 'off-scene'), out of sight, and always beyond, and yet disturbing, consciousness. No matter how hard we look, we cannot really see death. We are unable to manage death and any attempt to 'know' it remains deliciously out of reach. This is why, Bataille maintains, although death generates feelings of terror

Baum, nachdem sich Arthurs Rede in lautloses Schluchzen aufgelöst hat, mit einer Pistole bewaffnet nach vorne und befiehlt dem Publikum wegzuschauen: „Macht eure Augen zu. Macht eure verdammten Augen zu. Ihr solltet das hier nicht sehen. Macht eure Augen zu und lasst sie zu. Bitte, macht eure Augen zu. Bitte macht eure Augen zu." Robin Arthur beschwört ein repräsentatives System transparenter und greifbarer Bedeutung herauf: „Die Zuschauer wollen nach der Show in eine Kneipe gehen und sagen ICH HAB'S, ICH HAB VERSTANDEN, WORUM ES GING, sie wollen nicht sagen müssen oh äh, es ist, was immer du willst, dass es bedeutet …" In deutlichem Gegensatz dazu unterstellt der Baum durch seinen Befehl, den Blick von der Sterbe- und emotionalen Leidensszene abzuwenden, die Angelegenheit des Todes sei ein zu intimes und widerspenstiges Ereignis, um es objektiv betrachten zu können. Er scheint darauf zu bestehen, dass dieser Tod eine für den visuellen Genuss ungeeignete Erscheinung ist (obwohl gerade der Zwang, unsere Augen zu schließen, unwillkürlich eine imaginierte und beunruhigende Betrachtung des Sterbeprozesses erregt).

Nach George Batailles *Le non-savoir et la révolte* (1952) ist der Tod ‚obszön‘, da er größer ist als jeder Versuch, ihn durch Darstellung festzuhalten. Der Tod ist immer hinter den Kulissen (im wörtlichen Sinne obscene, off-scene), außer Sicht, und immer jenseits des Bewusstseins, das er zugleich aufwühlt. Es spielt keine Rolle, wie genau wir hinschauen, wir können den Tod nicht sehen. Wir sind unfähig Tod zu bewältigen und jedes Bestreben ihn zu ‚kennen‘ bleibt köstlich unerreichbar. Darum, so behauptet Bataille, erzeugt der Tod, obschon er Gefühle des Terrors und Horrors hervorruft, Formen der Qual, an denen wir uns gleichzeitig erfreuen müssen. Durch diese Zustände der Qual können wir das erreichen, was er die „äußerste Grenze des Möglichen" nennt. Diese Erfahrungsbedingung (die er „innere Erfahrung" nennt) widersetzt sich jedem Versuch, als Wissen homogenisiert zu werden. Es ist eine Bedingung des ‚Un-wissens‘, in der sich ‚Sein‘ immer in einem Zustand des Spielens befindet: „Es (meine Vorstellung) besteht in der Aussage, dass alles Spiel ist, dass Sein Spielen ist …" Batailles Vision vom Tod als Schöpfer des „Paroxysmus von Austausch, übermäßigem Reichtum und Überfluss" erweiternd, argumentiert Baudrillard in *Symbolischer Tausch und der Tod*, dass der Tod immer größer ist als jene (religiösen, wissenschaftlichen, psychoanalytischen) Wertesysteme, die beanspruchen, seine Auswirkungen durch Kontextualisierung erklären und lindern zu können. Folglich bringt Tod, egal welchem Wertesystem er zugeschrieben wird, „jede Wirtschaft" durcheinander und „zerschmettert nicht nur den objektiven Spiegel der politischen Wirtschaft, sondern sogar den umgekehrten psychischen Spiegel

and horror, it produces forms of anguish in which we must also take a delight. It is through such states of anguish that we might encounter what he describes as "the extreme limit of the 'possible'". This condition of experience (what he describes as "the inner experience") resists any attempt to homogenise it as knowledge. It is a condition of 'non-knowledge' where 'being' is always in a state of play: "It (my conception) consists in saying that all is play, that being is play …" Extending Bataille's vision of death as the creator of "a paroxysm of exchanges, super-abundance and excess", Baudrillard argues in *Symbolic Exchange and Death* that death always exceeds those systems of value (religious, scientific, psychoanalytic) that would claim to explain and calm its effects through contextualisation. Consequently, death, no matter what system of value is ascribed to it, disturbs "every economy, shattering not only the objective mirror of political economy, but also the inverse psychical mirror of repression, the unconscious and libidinal economy". The devastating and liberating effect of embracing the terror that death produces is that it unhinges the systems of representation binding the subject together. This unbinding of the subject puts the mind (and body) into a state of disequilibrium, in a state of flux and of play. And it is here that the 'now', the child-like encounter, the extreme limits of possibility, might be experienced.

It is interesting that these descriptions of death and its effects find such an uncanny echo in Benjamin's exploration of play. For Benjamin, the adult world is one in which the devastating intensity of experience is mastered by story-telling, through the structure of narrative and the control initiated by syntax and the logics of language. These structures are the basis for the systems of representation that shore up the subject and hold it in place. The child, on the other hand, having yet to master (and be mastered

Bloody Play / Games of Childhood and Death
Bloody Play / Das Spiel von Kindheit und Tod
Andrew Quick

by) such structures, pursues play to make contact with, to (re)encounter and enjoy, the shattering condition of experience itself. Through a delicate juxtaposition of Bataille and Benjamin, is it not possible then, to think that playing becomes a form of dying and dying (or, at least, the anxiety that death produces) becomes a form of play?

The resolution stipulated in Arthur's speech is one in which the twin needs for ending and understanding are synthesised through the performance of a dramatic and yet unambiguous death. Consequently, his demand is that the closure of a performance, the one he is participating in, be framed by intelligibility and moral certainty: structures through which the reasons for dying are discernible and the lessons to be drawn from his own impending tragic conclusion are easily identified, taken up for social practice. The anxieties and ambiguities caused by play, therefore, have to be excluded. In the middle of Arthur's speech, the dog sniffs his 'wound', eliciting the exasperated response, "What are you doing – go away …". Of course, throughout *Showtime*, all attempts to instil any semblance of structure are thwarted by the uncontrollable figures and components of play. The two trees, the dog, the children's songs, the bursting of balloons, constantly interrupt the stage action, and any attempt to secure theatrical stability is repeatedly overturned. Indeed, any sense of locating and maintaining a consistent representational system is undermined in the very opening moments of the performance, in which Richard Lowdon attempts to explain the rules and expectations of theatre to the audience with a home made bomb strapped to his chest (worn at the start and at the end of the performance). Although this opening speech provokes much laughter, annihilation (however playfully) haunts the very act of imposing order and the setting out of the rules. All the events that are

der Unterdrückung, der unbewussten und triebhaften Energie". Die Umarmung des Schreckens, den der Tod auslöst, hat die sowohl verheerende als auch befreiende Wirkung, das Repräsentationssystem, das das Subjekt eingrenzt, aus den Angeln zu heben. Die Freisetzung des Subjekts versetzt den Geist (und den Körper) in einen fließenden und spielerischen Zustand des Ungleichgewichts. Hier kann dieses ,Jetzt', diese kindliche Begegnung, die äußerste Grenze der Möglichkeiten, erfahren werden.

Interessanterweise finden diese Beschreibungen des Todes und seiner Auswirkungen ein geradezu unheimliches Echo in Benjamins Untersuchung des Spielens. Für ihn ist die Welt der Erwachsenen eine, in der die verheerende Intensität der Erfahrung durch Geschichtenerzählen gemeistert wird, mittels ihrer Erzählstruktur und der Kontrolle der Sprache durch Syntax und Logik. Diese Strukturen sind die Basis des Repräsentationssystems, das das Subjekt stützt und seine Position sichert. Das Kind andererseits – das jene Strukturen erst noch meistern (und von ihnen gemeistert werden) muss – spielt, um mit den erschütternden Bedingungen der Erfahrung selbst in Berührung zu kommen, um ihnen (wieder) zu begegnen und sich an ihnen zu freuen. Wäre es also, mittels einer etwas delikaten Nebeneinanderstellung von Bataille und Benjamin, nicht vorstellbar, dass Spielen eine Art des Sterbens und dass Sterben (oder zumindest die durch den Tod erzeugte Furcht) eine Art des Spielens wird?

Die in Arthurs Rede geforderte Lösung synthetisiert das doppelte Bedürfnis von (Be)enden und Verstehen durch die Darstellung eines dramatischen und dennoch unzweideutigen Todes, weshalb seine Forderung folgerichtig ist, dass das Ende der Aufführung – jener nämlich, bei der er selbst mitwirkt – von Verständlichkeit und moralischer Gewissheit gerahmt sein solle. Es ist die Forderung nach Strukturen, in denen einerseits die Gründe für das Sterben wahrnehmbar sind, andererseits die Lehre, die aus dem drohenden

Some Confusions in the Law about Love
(Rehearsal / Probe)

Who Can Sing a Song to Unfrighten Me?

subsequently witnessed take place in the humorous shadow of death: both his and the audience's, since the bomb, if it were real, would destroy everybody. The clock attached to Lowdon's chest constantly draws our attention to the real-time, the 'present-ness', of the ensuing action, as it counts down to the heard, but unseen, explosion that concludes the performance.

The tree's demand that we shut our eyes and stop watching Arthur's dying scene implies that something crucial is overlooked in those instances where death is naturalised, where death is pinned down at the service of dramatic function. Indeed, both of Arthur's prolonged and theatrical deaths are imitated by the trees who, as if mocking the crude attempt to be in the moment of dying, also apply spaghetti to their cartoon-like trunks. Here death and play are brought together, a combination that undermines both the attempt to make death sensible and the hope that its anxieties can be dampened through any formal resolution. Death, like the excessive energies of play, destructures. There are no final answers, only the demand that we respond to the questions pro-

tragischen Ende gezogen wird, einfach erkannt und in die soziale Praxis integriert werden kann. Furcht und Zweideutigkeit, die durch das Spielen verursacht werden, müssen also ausgeschlossen werden. Mitten in Arthurs Rede schnuppert der Hund an dessen ‚Wunde' und provoziert so ein verärgertes „Was machst du da – geh weg". So werden selbstverständlich alle Versuche in *Showtime*, einen Anschein von Struktur zu erwecken, durchgängig von unkontrollierbaren Figuren und Spielbestandteilen vereitelt: Zwei Bäume, der Hund, die Kinderlieder, das Zerplatzen von Ballons unterbrechen fortwährend das Bühnengeschehen und zerstören jeden Ansatz theatraler Stabilität. Jedes Gefühl, ein logisches Repräsentationssystem verorten und aufrechterhalten zu können, wird schon zu Beginn der Aufführung untergraben, wenn Richard Lowdon versucht, dem Publikum mit einer selbstgebastelten Bombe um den Bauch die Regeln und Erwartungen im Theater zu erklären. Trotz des Gelächters folgt die Vernichtung (wie spielerisch auch immer) der Herstellung von Ordnung und Regelwerken stets auf dem Fuße. Alle Ereignisse, denen man von da an als Zeuge beiwohnt, stehen im humorvollen Schatten des Todes – sowohl dem des Performers als auch des Publikums, da die Bombe, wäre sie echt, alle treffen würde. Die Uhr auf Lowdons Brust lenkt ständig unsere Aufmerksamkeit auf die reale Zeit, auf das ‚Gegenwärtig-Sein' der folgenden Aktionen, da sie den Countdown hin zur Explosion anzeigt, die zwar hör-, aber nicht sichtbar die Aufführung beendet.

Die Forderung der Bäume, die Augen während Arthurs Sterbeszene zu schließen, impliziert, dass wir etwas Entscheidendes übersehen, wenn der Tod naturalisiert und auf eine dramatische Funktion festgelegt wird. Tatsächlich werden die beiden hinausgezögerten und sehr theatralischen Tode Robin Arthurs von den Bäumen nachgeahmt, die – als wollten sie sich über den kruden Versuch des Sterbens lustig machen – ebenfalls Spaghetti auf ihren karrikaturartigen Stämmen verteilen. Tod und Spiel werden zusammengebracht, untergraben so den Versuch, den Tod fassbar zu machen, und sprengen jedes Bestreben, die durch den Tod verursachte Angst durch eine formale Auflösung zu dämpfen. Der Tod, wie die maßlose Energie des Spielens, dekonstruiert alles. Es gibt keine endgültigen Antworten, nur die Forderung, dass wir auf die Fragen reagieren, die die Betrachtung des Todes heraufbeschwört.

Nachdem die Bäume das Publikum angewiesen haben, die Augen zu schließen, steigen die Performer aus ihren Kostümen, und einer von ihnen (Terry O'Connor) stellt Robin Arthur eine Reihe von Fragen, die folgendermaßen enden:

Was denke ich?
Was denkst du?
Was denke ich?
Was denkst du?
Was für Geschichten würdest du einem sterbenden Mann erzählen?
Was für Geschichten würdest du einem kleinen Kind erzählen?
Was für Geschichten würdest du einer schwangeren Frau erzählen?
Was für Geschichten würdest du einem Schlafenden erzählen?

Noch einmal werden Spielen und Sterben in diesem Frage-und-Antwort-Spiel zusammengeführt. Die Provokation dieser Fragen wird durch die von Arthur gegebenen Erwiderungen nicht gemildert, da sie eine absolute Antwort nicht zulassen.

Die Behauptung, dass der Tod in Forced Entertainments Arbeiten sich der Darstellung entzieht, mag sonderbar klingen, wenn man die unzähligen Tode in ihren Aufführungen betrachtet. *200% & Bloody Thirsty* wird strukturiert durch das wiederholte Sterben und die Wiedererweckung einer Bühnenfigur durch die „wundersame Macht" ihrer betrunkenen Freunde. In einem Abschnitt von *(Let the Water Run its Course)* führen vier namenlose Figuren mithilfe von Ketchup-Blut

duced by the contemplation of death. After ordering the audience to close their eyes, the trees shed their costumes and one of them (Terry O'Connor) asks Arthur a series of questions that end with:

What am I thinking?
What are you thinking?
What am I thinking?
What are you thinking?
What stories would you tell a dying man?
What stories would you tell a small child?
What stories would you tell a pregnant woman?
What stories would you tell a sleeping person?

Once again, play and dying are brought together in this game of question and answer. The provocations that these questions stir up are not stilled by the replies Arthur makes in the performance, for they do not permit any absolute response.

To make the claim that death somehow escapes representation in the work of Forced Entertainment may appear odd when taking into account the extraordinary number of acts of dying that take place in their performances. *200% & Bloody Thirsty*, for example, is structured around the repeated action of a figure dying in the cold and then being resurrected by the 'miraculous powers' of his/her drunken companions. In one of the sections of *(Let the Water Run its Course) to the Sea that Made the Promise*, the four unnamed figures engage in a game of movie deaths, using bottles of tomato ketchup for blood. As the game gets more frantic and competitive, the fake blood is increasingly splattered across the wooden stage set and over the bodies of the performers. This activity - reaches its climax in a Sam Penkinpah-like slowmotion sequence, ketchup flying out of sombody's mouth as if the player was being whip-lashed by taking a bullet in the head. In the last section of *Some Confusions in the Law about Love*, the figures of the Elvis Presley impersonator and the two showgirls become ghosts, their almost naked bodies whitened by talcum powder. One of the blood-covered narrators (who in previous scenes has been dressed as a skeleton) observes at the closing moments of the performance, "The dead people survey the room and then look out on the city once again". In *Who Can Sing a Song to Unfrighten Me?*, hundreds of deaths are enacted over the twenty-four hours of the performance. Perhaps this surfeit of dying can be explained by the proposition that death and play are inextricably connected. For the ultimate limit of play, as all children know, is playing dead. Death is the impossible limit of play because in the landscape of consciousness, in fantasy, in whatever system of representation that we are able to conjure up, it can only ever be played.

Eye play

As Benjamin subtly observes, play simultaneously binds and unravels those formations which are necessary for the construction of the subject. It is via play that the child learns how to "enter into the life and the often alien rhythm of another human being". Yet, the excessive energies that play creates, its recourse to tireless repetition, its production of shattering experience, also indicate that the terrors generated by 'alienation' are never completely mastered. While play might initiate pursuits through which the child learns how to overcome vulnerability, these very same activities also provoke states of anxiety and loss. If, as Arthur's speech above articulates, certain forms of theatricality promise to make sense of the world, then it should not be surprising that play takes up so many of theatre's trappings (pretending, imitating, role-playing and so on). Of course, once it adopts the traits of

Filmtode vor. Während das Spiel hektischer wird und sich der Wettkampf steigert, wird das falsche Blut immer wilder über das hölzerne Bühnenbild und die Körper der Spieler verteilt. Der Höhepunkt ist dann eine an Sam Penkinpah erinnernde Zeitlupenszene: Ketchup fliegt aus dem Mund eines Spielers wie bei einem Kopfschuss. Im letzten Teil von *Some Confusions in the Law about Love* verwandeln sich der Elvis Presley-Imitator und die Showgirls in Geister, ihre fast nackten Körper geweißt mit Talkumpuder. Wie einer der Blut überströmten Erzähler (der in früheren Szenen als Skelett verkleidet war) gegen Ende feststellt: „Die Toten lassen den Blick durch das Zimmer wandern und wenden sich dann wieder der Stadt zu." In *Who Can Sing a Song to Unfrighten Me?* werden im Lauf der vierundzwanzigstündigen Aufführung gleich Hunderte von Toden dargestellt.

Möglicherweise kann dieses Übermaß des Sterbens mit der untrennbaren Verknüpfung von Tod und Spielen erklärt werden. Denn die äußerste Grenze des Spielens ist es, wie alle Kinder wissen, zu spielen, man sei tot. Tod entpuppt sich als unmögliche Grenze des Spielens, weil er in der Landschaft des Bewusstseins, in der Phantasie, in jeglichem denkbaren Repräsentationssystem immer nur gespielt werden kann.

Augenspiel

Wie Benjamin subtil beobachtet, verbindet und öffnet das Spielen gleichzeitig jene Anordnungen, die für die Konstruktion des Subjekts nötig sind. Durch das Spielen lernt das Kind, wie es „in das Dasein" eintritt und auf „den Rhythmus eines fremden menschlichen Wesens eingeht". Dennoch deutet die übermäßige Energie, die durch das Spielen erzeugt wird, sein Rückgriff auf die unermüdliche Wiederholung und seine Produktion erschütternder Erfahrungen darauf hin, dass der durch ‚Fremdheit' erzeugte Terror niemals gänzlich gemeistert werden kann. Während das Spiel zwar einen Drang erzeugen kann, durch den das Kind lernt, seine Verletzlichkeit zu bewältigen, erzeugen dieselben Handlungen Zustände der Furcht und des Verlustes. Wenn – wie in obiger Rede Arthurs – bestimmte Formen von Theatralität versprechen, der Welt Sinn zu geben, dann kann es uns nicht überraschen, dass sich das Spielen so viel vom Drum und Dran des Theaters aneignet (das Als-ob, die Imitation, das Rollenspiel usw.). Gewiss, sobald es die Charakteristika der Theatralität angenommen hat, untergräbt das Spielen sofort die Autorität der theatralen Repräsentation, wie es die Aufführungen von Forced Entertainment so oft veranschaulichen.

Wenn das Kind immer durch Spielen lernt, dann gehört, wenn man dieser Argumentation folgt, zum Lernen zwangsläufig auch Furcht. Wie Bataille und Benjamin theatricality, as the performance work of Forced Entertainment so often exposes, play immediately begins to undermine the authority of theatre's representational operations.

If the child always learns through play, then, following this argument, learning is inevitably haunted by anxiety. As Bataille and Benjamin indicate, however, the terrors and uncertainties of play can be liberating, rather than constricting. This is, perhaps, forgotten in an adult world that prioritises control, knowledge and security. Yet, we are always caught up in the process of learning, no matter what age we are or how much we presume to know. I am reminded of the debilitating intensity of learning which was the subject of a BBC 2 documentary, *The Man Who Learned to See*,

Who Can Sing a Song to Unfrighten Me?

transmitted in 2002. The documentary explored the partial return of sight to a man who has been made blind in a childhood accident. Despite the fact that he had once been able to see he was forced, years after the accident, to learn how to see again: to focus the eye, to learn how the eye's depth of field works, to ignore the blurring at the edge of the eye and to straighten out the image. Having previously relied on hearing and touch to process information, he found that his newly restored sight was the cause of much disorientation and fear:

Seeing other cars racing by it seemed to me like they were inches away. Today I was waiting for a signal to change, and it turned out I was waiting on the tram tracks. The tram came racing by, and I saw the shadow coming right at me. For a moment I thought I was still on the tracks, and I thought it was all over.

The documentary claimed that this man's methods of negotiating and assimilating visual information were similar, if not identical, to how the child trains itself to see in its formative years; whereby the child repeats the process of turning the blurred image into one that is fully focused with sharp edges: a playing with the mechanisms of the eye. The documentary revealed that touch plays a very important part in this learning process: It is through touch that the problems of distance and the materiality of objects are mastered and stored as memory.

There are many instances in Forced Entertainment's work that signal this return to the first touch, the originary encounter, the play, which we have all experienced as children. In this context, we might ask: Are the most arresting moments in their work not when the performer, like the child struggling with sight, plays with the materiality of experience? For play does not leave us merely hanging in the air, or 'swing-

jedoch zeigen, können der Terror und die Ungewissheiten des Spiels eher befreiend als behindernd sein. Das ist vielleicht vergessen worden in einer Erwachsenenwelt, die Kontrolle, Wissen und Sicherheit bevorzugt, und dennoch sind wir immer in einem Lernprozess gefangen, egal wie alt wir sind oder wie viel wir zu wissen glauben. Ich erinnere mich an die lähmende Intensität des Lernens aus einer BBC-Dokumentation, *The Man Who Learned to See* (26. September, BBC 2), die eine teilweise Rückkehr der Sehkraft eines Mannes untersuchte, der das Augenlicht durch einen Unfall in seiner Kindheit verloren hatte. Obwohl er vor dem Unfall sehen konnte, musste er nun, Jahre später, das Sehen neu lernen. Er musste lernen, das Auge zu fokussieren, lernen, wie die Tiefenschärfe des Auges funktioniert, lernen, die verschwommenen Ränder des Auges zu ignorieren und das Bild zu glätten. Der Mann, der sich zuvor auf Gehör und Tastsinn verlassen hatte, um Informationen zu verarbeiten, erfuhr seine wiederhergestellte Sehkraft als Ursache großer Desorientierung und Angst:

Wenn ich Autos an mir vorbeirasen sah, glaubte ich, sie seien nur wenige Zentimeter von mir entfernt. Heute zum Beispiel wartete ich auf das Umspringen der Fußgängerampel, als ich merkte, dass ich auf den Straßenbahngleisen stand. Die Straßenbahn raste heran und ich sah den Schatten direkt auf mich zukommen. Einen Moment glaubte ich, ich sei noch immer auf den Gleisen, und ich dachte, jetzt ist es vorbei.

Die Dokumentation behauptete, dass seine Methoden, visuelle Informationen auszuwählen und zu integrieren, ähnlich wenn nicht identisch mit denen seien, die das Kind benutzt, um sich das Sehen beizubringen. Das Kind wiederholt den Vorgang, das verschwommene Bild in eines zu verwandeln, das fokussiert und scharf ist: Ein Spiel mit dem Mechanismus des Auges. Berührung, so die Dokumentation, spielt in diesem Lernprozess eine wichtige Rolle, denn durch Berührung werden die Probleme der Distanz und der Materialität von Objekten gemeistert und als Erinnerung abgespeichert.

In der Arbeit von Forced Entertainment gibt es viele Beispiele, die auf diese Rückkehr zu dieser ersten Berührung verweisen, zur ursprünglichen Begegnung, zum Spiel, das wir alle als Kinder erfahren haben. So stellt sich die Frage, ob nicht die atemberaubendsten Momente in ihren Stücken jene sind, in denen der Performer, wie das Kind, das mit seinem Sehvermögen kämpft, mit der Materialität der Erfahrung spielt? Denn das Spielen lässt uns nicht einfach in der Luft hängen oder ,im Wind schwingen', auch wenn das eine Beschäftigung ist, der sich die meisten Kinder und Erwachsenen gerne hingeben. Das Spielen weist in die Zukunft, auf das Aufstellen einer neuen Regel: Einer Regel, die gerechter ist und die selbstverständlich im Zuge eines anderen Spiels wieder gebrochen wird. Das ist die geheime Geste des Spielens – eine Bewegung zwischen Ordnung und Unordnung, Einheit und einer Welt in Scherben, Zusammenhang und Durcheinander, Verlieren und Finden, Leben und Sterben, ,wie die Kinder, wie die Kinder'. Ist das die verdammte Abscheulichkeit des Spielens?

Übersetzt von Kerstin Büschges
und Florian Malzacher

ing in the wind', although swinging is an activity that most children and adults love to indulge in. Play points to the future, to the making of a new rule: one that might be more just, one that will, of course, be broken as a result of an encounter in another game. This is its secret gesture: Play as the movement between order and disorder; unity and the world in bits; coherence and mess; losing and finding; living and dying; "like children, like children". Is this the bloodiness of play?

165

Which is better – nylon or polyester?
Do you have recurring dreams?
Why do all women love weddings?
How can you know something?
Name 6 of the 12 sons of Jacob.
What is memory?
What is history?
What item of cutlery did the dish run away with?
Why does water go down the plug-hole a different
     way on different sides of the equator?
What are Eskimos?
Is photography a proper fine art?
Name three things that you wish for.
Why do young boy children like diggers, trains and guns?
Have you had any serious operations?
Why do you shout so much?
Is swearing bad?
Which wood is plywood mostly made from?
Are you right or left handed?
How much beer can you drink before you are drunk?
Why do people get drunk?
Why do people die?
Why do people like reading books?
Why are you telling all these lies?
Why have you abandoned all your principles?
Why is there a sky?

Quizoola!

12 am: Awake & Looking Down

Performing Games
How to be Cast as a Forced Entertainment Performer – Seven Hypotheses

Performing Games
Sieben Vermutungen über ein erfolgreiches Casting zum Forced Entertainment-Performer

Annemarie Matzke

Stell dir vor, du stehst auf einer Bühne, rechts und links unzählige Schilder:

„RACHEL (BLUTEND); GEIST EINES AM DIENSTAG GETÖTETEN MÄDCHENS; BOXER MIT GERISSENER NETZHAUT; NEUNJÄHRIGER SCHÄFERJUNGE; BILLY MAUDLIN; EIN VON ENTFÜHRERN GROSSGEZOGENES KIND; AUSSERIRDISCHES MÄDCHEN; GUTER BULLE IN EINEM SCHLECHTEN FILM; PRINZESSIN – NICHT SO HELLE; YTS VANDAL TARZANOGRAM; FRANK (BETRUNKEN); MISS TAUBES AMERIKA."

Zu den Schildern kommen auf beiden Seiten Stangen voller Secondhand-Kleider. Laute Musik. Stell dir vor, du musst immer wieder neue aus diesem Pool an Schildern auswählen, immer neue Kleider anziehen und ausziehen, getrieben vom Rhythmus der Musik. Stell dir vor, du musst immer neue Posen einnehmen und zu den Überschriften Bilder stellen. Du rennst auf der Stelle, als ob du nicht vom Fleck kämst. Du musst immer wieder dasselbe tun – auswählen, eine Pose stellen und auflösen. „Charaktere durch Pappschilder dargestellt" ist die Regieanweisung. Das ist deine Aufgabe, mehr nicht. Nicht sprechen, nicht schreien, keine Entwicklung darstellen, keine Haltung zu deinem Tun auf der

Imagine you are on stage, flanked left and right by innumerable signs:

"RACHEL (BLEEDING); THE GHOST OF A CHILD KILLED ON TUESDAY; A BOXER WITH A TORN RETINA; A 9-YEAR-OLD SHEPHERD BOY; BILLY MAUDLIN; A GIRL BROUGHT UP BY KIDNAPPERS; ALIEN GIRL; A GOOD COP IN A BAD FILM; PRINCESS – NOT SO BRIGHT; YTS VANDAL TARZANOGRAM; FRANK (DRUNK); MISS DEAF AMERICA."

Above the signs are racks filled with second-hand clothing. Loud music is booming. Imagine yourself having to constantly choose new signs, changing into and out of clothing, propelled by the incessant rhythm of the music. You have to strike new poses all the time and place images with the signs. You seem to be running on the spot without ever moving, constantly doing the same thing: selecting, striking a pose, and dissolving it. "Characters presented with cardboard signs" is the one instruction you follow – nothing more, nothing less. No speech, no screaming, no progression, no attitude to be exhibited towards one's actions on stage, no enacting or being a character. What you are presenting are the signs, poses

Performing Games / How to be Cast as a Forced Entertainment Performer
Performing Games / ... über ein erfolgreiches Casting zum Forced Entertainment-Performer
Annemarie Matzke

and costumes. However, you have to structure these so that they create ever more images and impressions. You must be fast and decisive, know where your fellow performers are and find your place in front of the audience. You are the container of your own actions; no character, no role to enact. You select and choose; you present and play.

Nothing to hand except what can be found on stage. There are no lines, no written role to use as guidance, except uniform rules for everyone on how the performance is to be structured, aiming to limit the framework for individual expression. On the one hand, the pressure to improvise; on the other, a performance reduced to a few limited actions.

The above scene from *Emmanuelle Enchanted* is typical for the performance style of Forced Entertainment, which is difficult to capture in words. The performers are no role-enactors in the classical sense, even though they are constantly hinting at character fragments. Nor are they performers in Performance Art terms, who present actions on stage, claiming to refer to no other character than their own. They do, however, use all of these elements – enacting characters, relating text and narratives, improvising and playing games, alone and with the others. From the scope of these performance styles arises a special form of delivery, which gives an impression of immediacy. As a seasoned observer, one recognizes the actors and their character traits, believing that one knows them personally. Cathy, Richard, Claire, Terry and Robin – their first names have become engraved in one's memory, but more than that one cannot be sure of. Though the performances may appear autobiographic, no private details of the performers' lives are ever revealed. If it does happen though, those private details are presented in the same way as fictitious material.

Bühne präsentieren, keine Figur sein oder zeigen. Was du zeigst, sind nur die Schilder, Posen und Kostüme. Diese allerdings musst du so organisieren, dass immer neue Bilder und neue Eindrücke entstehen. Du musst schnelle Entscheidungen treffen, überblicken, wo gerade deine Mitspieler sind, dir deinen Platz suchen und den Blick zum Publikum. Du bist die Klammer deiner Handlungen, keine Figur, keine Rolle; du suchst aus, du wählst, du zeigst, du spielst.

In den Händen nichts als das auf der Bühne ausgestellte Material. Es gibt keinen Text, keine Rolle, die Halt geben kann, nur bestimmte für alle gültige Regeln, wie die Darstellung zu organisieren ist, um die individuellen Gestaltungsmöglichkeiten einzuschränken. Auf der einen Seite der Zwang zur Improvisation, auf der anderen die Reduktion der Darstellung auf wenige Handgriffe.

Die beschriebene Szene aus *Emmanuelle Enchanted* ist typisch für den spezifischen Darstellungsstil von Forced Entertainment, der begrifflich schwer zu fassen ist. Denn die Darsteller sind keine rollenspielenden Schauspieler im traditionellen Sinne, obwohl sie immer wieder Rollenfragmente zeigen. Sie sind auch keine Performer im Sinne der Performance Art, die auf der Bühne Aktionen ausführen und behaupten, auf keine andere Figur zu verweisen als auf sich selbst. Gleichwohl greifen sie all diese Elemente auf, stellen auch Figuren dar, erzählen Texte und Geschichten, improvisieren, spielen sich selbst und spielen Spiele mit den Anderen. Aus der Spannbreite dieser verschiedenen Darstellungsformen entsteht eine sehr spezifische Spielweise, die einen Eindruck von Unmittelbarkeit hervorruft. Als jahrelanger Zuschauer erkennt man die Darsteller und ihre Eigenarten wieder, meint sie auf persönliche Weise zu kennen. Cathy, Richard, Claire, Terry und Robin – die privaten Namen haben sich ins Gedächtnis eingeschrieben, aber mehr als ihre Namen kann man nicht sicher wissen. Auch wenn die Darstellungen autobiographisch wirken, so erfährt man keine Fakten aus dem privaten Leben der Performer – oder falls doch, dann werden diese authentischen Geschichten aber auf die gleiche Weise ausgestellt wie die fiktiven.

Es geht – wie in der szenischen Gruppenautobiographie *A Decade of Forced Entertainment* beschrieben – eben nicht um eine authentische Selbstdarstellung: Mal behaupten die Performer sie selbst zu sein, im nächsten Moment jemand anderes. Der Selbstdarstellung wird der gleiche Status zugeschrieben wie der Figurendarstellung.

Dennoch entsteht das Gefühl, die Performer auf der Bühne als sie selbst zu sehen. Was aber zeigen sie, wenn die Selbstdarstellung letztlich nicht anders zu bewerten ist als eine Figurendarstellung? Wie entsteht ‚Authentizität‘, also der Eindruck einer unmittelbaren und spontanen Darstellung? Die Gruppe selbst spricht von bestimmten *performance skills*, die sie über die Jahre erworben hat, bestimmte Qualitäten der Darstellung, die sich aus der langen gemeinsamen Arbeit ergeben, und die zu beschreiben offensichtlich andere, neue Kategorien benötigt. Worin liegen diese *performance skills*? Oder anders gefragt: Wie werde ich ein Forced Entertainment-Performer?

Sieben Vermutungen über ein erfolgreiches Casting zum Forced Entertainment-Performer:

1. Organisiere, arrangiere und teste

Stell dir vor, du bekommst verschiedene Blätter in die Hand, auf denen nichts steht als Geständnisse. Teils banal, teils auf konkrete Situationen bezogen, teils persönlich, als stammten sie von dir selbst. Du bist mit deinen Mitspielern in einem Raum. Es ist hell, du kannst den Zuschauern in die Augen sehen. Du kannst sehen, wie sie auf deine Beichten reagieren, siehst deine Mitspieler. Du wählst ein Blatt aus und beginnst vorzulesen. Dabei versuchst du, möglichst überzeugend,

As outlined in the group autobiography, *A Decade of Forced Entertainment,* they are not concerned with authentic self-representation: One moment, the performers claim to be themselves; a moment later, someone else. Self-representation has the same status as character enactment. However, one does gain the impression that one is seeing the performers on stage as themselves. So what are they showing, if self-representation has the same value as character enactment? How is 'authenticity' (the impression of an immediate and spontaneous act) created? The group speak of certain performance skills they have gained over years of practice, qualities of delivery that have their origins in long-term collaboration. As a consequence, describing them requires a new set of categories. What defines these performance skills? Or to rephrase the question: How can I become a Forced Entertainment performer?

Seven hypotheses on how to be cast as a Forced Entertainment performer:

No.1 Organize, Arrange and Test

Imagine you are handed sheets of paper filled with nothing but confessions. Some banal, some relating to existing situations; others personal, as if they were your own. You are in a space together with your fellow actors. It is bright and you can look the audience in the eyes. You can see how they react to your confessions; you also see the other performers. Choosing a sheet, you begin to read out loud. As you are doing that, you try to look as convincing and as authentic as possible. You try to remember believable confessions or some of your own. You select, you test options, reading out loud.

The foundations of *Speak Bitterness* are admissions and confessions, written in the first person plural. Like the scene from *Emmanuelle Enchanted*, *Speak Bitterness* is reduced to a limited pool of material. Text has a concrete stage presence and is explicitly presented in object and material form. This group trademark allows forms of activity usually confined to rehearsal to be presented on stage. The performers read out lists (*Emmanuelle Enchanted*), confessions and admissions (*Speak Bitterness*), and questions (*Quizoola!*). They are searching for good questions or are selecting seemingly random confessions. Reducing the process to reading and selecting highlights the friction between the text and the performers.

Like a co-performer, text is present on stage, physically held by the actors as a utilitarian object. The pieces of writing Tim Etchells throws into the rehearsal process remain there even during the actual performance. They are left on the floor and on tables, are kicked away or found somewhere by the performers. In reading and assimilating the text, its presence is defined as alien. It is ever-present, even without being spoken. In its materiality, the fixed text becomes a point of contention, a kick-off mark for staging one's voice. Each time an actor reaches for a new sheet of paper, another one of his text choices is revealed. In selecting text, the performer does not claim to be its author; he does however define himself as the one who arranges it. His co-authorship lies not in the text's origin but in the performer's attitude towards it. Consequently, speech is converted into material arrangement, a play with forms of delivery. Based on the material provided on stage, the performers are forced to devise their own style of delivery during the performance itself. The onstage relationship between the actor and his text literally becomes constructive. In the case of *Speak Bitterness*, this means that, because of the show's material breadth and seemingly random nature, its theme is not one of confession. Instead, its

möglichst authentisch zu wirken. Du versuchst, dich an glaubhafte Beichten zu erinnern oder an eigene Geständnisse. Du wählst aus, du testest Möglichkeiten, liest vor.

Grundmaterial von *Speak Bitterness* sind nichts als Beichten und Bekenntnisse, abgefasst in der ersten Person Plural. Wie die Szene aus *Emmanuelle Enchanted* ist auch *Speak Bitterness* auf einen beschränkten Pool von Material reduziert. Der Text ist auf der Bühne als konkreter Gegenstand präsent und als Material explizit ausgestellt – ein Markenzeichen der Gruppe, das Tätigkeiten auf der Bühne ermöglicht, die sonst eher in den Probenprozess gehören. Die Performer lesen Listen (*Emmanuelle Enchanted*), Beichten und Geständnisse (*Speak Bitterness*), Fragen (*Quizoola!*). Sie suchen nach guten Fragen oder wählen scheinbar willkürlich Beichten aus. Die Reduktion auf die Vorgänge des Lesens und Auswählens zeigt die Reibung am Text.

Der Text ist als Spielpartner auf der Bühne präsent, die Performer halten ihn sichtbar als Material in den Händen: ein Gebrauchsgegenstand. Wenn Tim Etchells schreibt, dass er in den Probenprozess Texte hineinwerfe, dann bleiben diese Texte oft in Aufführungen einfach liegen. Sie liegen auf dem Boden, auf den Tischen, sie werden mit den Füßen getreten oder von den Darstellern irgendwo gefunden. Im Prozess des Lesen und Aneignens wird der Status des Textes als Gegenüber, als etwas Fremdes ausgestellt. Er ist immer präsent, auch ohne gesprochen zu werden. In seiner Materialität wird der fixierte Text zum Reibungs- und Abstoßungspunkt für die Inszenierung des eigenen Sprechens. Mit jedem Griff zu einem weiteren Blatt Papier wird eine Entscheidung des Darstellers für einen bestimmten Text offensichtlich. In der Auswahl des Textes markiert der Sprechende sich selbst zwar nicht als Autor des Textes, aber doch als denjenigen, der seinen Text arrangiert. Seine Co-Autorschaft liegt nicht im Ursprung des Textes, sondern in seiner Haltung zum Text, das Sprechen wird zum

Arrangieren von Material und zum Spiel mit Sprechhaltungen. So müssen die Performer ihr Sprechen im Moment der Aufführungssituation anhand des vorgegebenen Materials entwerfen. Konstitutiv wird das situative Verhältnis des Sprechenden zu seinem Text, den er im Moment der Aufführung aus dem ihm zur Verfügung gestellten Material konstruieren muss. Für *Speak Bitterness* heißt das, dass nicht der Inhalt der Geständnisse, der gerade durch die ausgestellte Fülle des Materials der Show beliebig wirkt, sondern das Verhältnis von Sprechendem, Text und Kommunikationsstruktur thematisiert wird. Der Darsteller testet Formen eines aufrichtigen Sprechens vor dem Publikum aus.

2. Handle nach Regeln

Stell dir vor, du sitzt mit deinem Mitspieler auf einer fast leeren Bühne. Als Material gibt es eine Zettelsammlung mit über 2000 Fragen. Du hast einige Spielregeln mitbekommen: Du fragst, dein Mitspieler muss antworten. Willst du die Position wechseln, musst du fragen „Willst du jetzt aufhören?" Weitere mögliche Strategien: „Halte die Dinge im Fluss, indem du die Modalitäten veränderst"; „Die Fassung zu verlieren, ist eine gute Taktik, ebenso wie sehr freundlich und vertrauensselig zu sein." „Auf Fragen zu beharren, ist eine sehr nützliche Strategie" (*Quizoola!*).

Das Spiel bei Forced Entertainment erfordert eine besondere Form von Disziplin; die Disziplin, sich über Stunden an bestimmte Regeln zu halten und nichts anderes zu zeigen. Auch die Darstellungsformen in *Speak Bitterness* oder die Szene aus *Emmanuelle Enchanted* sind durch Regeln strukturiert, die so einfach sind, dass wir sie sofort erfassen. Wie bei einem guten Fußballspiel bewertet man den Umgang der Performer mit den Regeln, vergleicht ihre Strategien, gleicht sie mit den Regeln ab. Die Performer sind nicht mehr gute Schauspieler, die etwas vorspielen, sondern Spieler in ihrem eigenen Spiel, an dem sie scheitern oder in

theme is the relationship between speaker, text and communication structure. Facing the audience, the speaker explores forms of truthful speech.

No.2 Follow Rules

Imagine yourself and another performer sitting on an almost empty stage. The only material present consists of a collection of over 2000 questions. You have been given a set of rules: You pose a question and the other actor answers. If you want to switch roles, you have to ask: "Are you ready to stop?" Other strategy options include: "Keep things fluid by changing modalities"; "Losing your temper completely is a fun tactic, as is being very friendly and intimate"; "Insisting on questions is a very useful strategy" (*Quizoola!*).

In Forced Entertainment, play requires a special form of discipline, which consists of following certain rules for hours at a time without showing anything else. This restriction applies to *Speak Bitterness* just as it does to the scene from *Emmanuelle Enchanted*, both of which are structured according to simple rules that are instantly understood. As in a good football match, performances are understood in terms of how well the players handle the rules, by comparing each of their strategies and through checks against the 'rule book'. The performers are not good actors, but players in their own game, in which they falter or triumph, following the rules only to be able to bend and break them on stage.

No.3 Repeat and Improvise

Imagine you are still on stage, still surrounded by innumerable signs and a huge amount of clothes on racks. What would you select from this mass of material? Suppose you have already used a dozen signs and worn a dozen costumes. How do you keep the performance intriguing, both for yourself and for the audience, despite always presenting the same items?

By revealing and exhibiting the rules that guide the performance, the scope of the performer's stylistic repertoire is severely limited. Surprising plot twists seem impossible. It is precisely through this reduction that a different form of virtuosity comes to the fore, that of experimental freedom within a regulatory framework. At first glance, the performance described above appears monotonous and boring: time and again the same actions are repeated, often through other performers. By its nature, every repetition of a formally identical act differs from the original, without necessarily constituting anything new. This difference is not about change, but rather represents a shift that allows a special staging of the self. The performer's personality inscribes itself into the repetition despite the fact that the performance cannot be linked to an intentional act.

The performer appears to reveal his self precisely through this reductive formal structure. It sparks off an impression of authenticity, of immediate representation, which is differentiated from the visible structure. The impression of immediacy, however, is always linked to a temporal 'in-between'. Through constant repetition, the performances gain a mechanical quality that cannot fully be controlled. Individuality shines through the impossibility of total control, highlighting deviations from the constantly same (which is, of course, by its nature, constantly different).

Similarly, the juxtaposition of both fixed and improvised text creates breathing room. It is the act of reading written text, its friction with the actor, that emphasises the lack of written text in other moments of the performance. In *Quizoola!,* this lack is marked by the missing

dem sie triumphieren, dessen Regeln sie befolgen, um sie dann wiederum auf der Bühne brechen oder biegen zu können.

3. Wiederhole und improvisiere

Stell dir vor, du stehst noch immer vor den unzähligen Schildern, auf den Stangen hängen noch immer unzählige Kleider. Was wählst du aus dieser Überfülle aus? Stell dir vor, du hast bereits ein Dutzend Schilder benutzt, ein Dutzend Kleider angezogen. Wie schaffst du es, die Darstellung für dich und die Zuschauer spannend zu halten, obwohl du doch immer wieder dasselbe zeigst?

Durch die ausgestellten und offen gelegten Regeln ist das Darstellungsspektrum der Performer stark reduziert. Überraschende Wendungen scheinen ausgeschlossen. Doch gerade diese Reduktion öffnet eine andere Form der Virtuosität: den Freiraum der Improvisation im vorgegebenen Regelsystem. Auf den ersten Blick ist das beschriebene szenische Geschehen monoton und langweilig: immer wieder werden die gleichen Aktionen wiederholt, oft durch andere Performer. Jede Wiederholung eines formal Identischen weicht notwendigerweise von der Vorlage ab, ohne zwingend etwas Neues zu konstituieren. Diese Differenz ist weniger eine Veränderung als eine Verschiebung und ermöglicht eine besondere Form der Selbst-Inszenierung. Die Individualität der Performer schreibt sich als persönlicher Gestus in die Wiederholung ein, ohne dass die Darstellung an eine intentionale Handlung gebunden werden könnte.

Der Performer scheint sich selbst gerade durch die formale Struktur und durch die Reduktion zu zeigen. Es ist das Aufblitzen des Eindrucks von Authentizität, also unmittelbarer Darstellung, in der Differenz zur erkennbaren Struktur. Doch der Eindruck von Unmittelbarkeit ist dabei immer auch an ein zeitliches Moment eines Dazwischen gebunden. Durch die Dauer der Wiederholungen werden die Darstellungen mechanisch und

Performing Games / How to be Cast as a Forced Entertainment Performer
Performing Games / ... über ein erfolgreiches Casting zum Forced Entertainment-Performer
Annemarie Matzke

nicht vollständig kontrollierbar. Individualität zeigt sich in dieser Unmöglichkeit vollständiger Kontrolle, die Abweichungen vom Immergleichen (aber doch notwendig Anderen) sichtbar macht.

Auch das Gegenüber von fixiertem und improvisiertem Text eröffnet einen Freiraum. Gerade das Ablesen des aufgeschriebenen Textes, an dem sich der Schauspieler reibt, markiert einen Gegensatz zum fehlenden Text. In *Quizoola!* sind es die fehlenden Antworten. Fixiert sind nur die Fragen, auf die der Darsteller reagieren muss. Diese Zwangslage bestimmt das Verhältnis von Performer und improvisiertem Text. Der aufgeschriebene und offensichtlich abgelesene Text pointiert in dieser Gegenüberstellung auch die Frage nach dem Status der anderen Texte: Entstehen diese wirklich im Spiel oder sind auch sie vorproduziert? Die Markierung des vorgefertigten Textes – sein Vor-Zeigen – definiert genau jenen Bereich, wo das Spielen jenseits des Vor-Spielens beginnen könnte. Denn auch wenn das Spiel seine Beschränkungen und Regeln offen legt, unterliegt es doch der Einschätzung, dass alles auf der Bühne inszeniert sei: Auch die Fehler und Versprecher beim Antworten auf die Fragen in *Quizoola!* könnten ja minutiös in langer Probenarbeit einstudiert sein. Um dieser Skepsis entgegenzuarbeiten sind weitere Authentifizierungsstrategien notwendig.

4. Setz deine Selbst-Inszenierungsstrategien ein

Stell dir vor, du sitzt auf einer Bühne, und dein Mitspieler fragt, wie viele Prominente dunkler Hautfarbe du kennst, die nicht in Sport oder Showbiz berühmt geworden sind. Du denkst nach. Martin Luther King fällt dir ein und Kofi Annan, dann fällt dir niemand mehr ein. Du denkst nach und bist dir bewusst, dass die Zuschauer sehen, wie du nachdenkst, dass sie ebenfalls überlegen. Es ist dir peinlich, und du versuchst diese Peinlichkeit noch zu verstärken und auszuspielen.

answers. Only the questions the actor must respond to are fixed. This quandary defines the relationship between performer and improvised text. The written and obviously read-out text also raises questions about the status of the other texts. Are they really generated in the performance or are they also prefabricated? Defining text as prefabricated, highlighting it, marks the threshold where play beyond enactment could begin. Though play might expose its limitations and rules, it is still subject to the supposition that everything in performance is staged. Of course, this supposition could apply to the mistakes and slips of the tongue made while answering questions in *Quizoola!*, which could have been intricately crafted in intensive rehearsals. To counter this scepticism will require further authentication strategies.

No.4 Use Strategies to Stage Your Presence

Imagine you are on stage and your co-performer asks how many black celebrities you know, excluding those in sport and show business. You think. Martin Luther King comes to mind, as does Kofi Annan, after that you are at a loss. You are thinking, aware that the audience observes you in thought and that they are thinking as well. It is embarrassing, and you try to heighten and project the sense of embarrassment even further. Twenty minutes later, your co-performer asks what you did in your hotel room last night. You quickly bite your lip, trying to remember, you look at the ceiling, wringing your hands. Then, hesitantly you begin to reply, like someone who has been caught out. Or maybe you take the offensive instead and answer directly that you were simply sleeping.

Critiques of Forced Entertainment performers have stated frequently that they are nothing

Performing Games / How to be Cast as a Forced Entertainment Performer
Performing Games / ... über ein erfolgreiches Casting zum Forced Entertainment-Performer
Annemarie Matzke

but themselves on stage, judging them to be authentic. There is a connection here to the idea that common gestures are used by all of us to authenticate the image we wish to project. Every actor consciously employs his own repertoire of such gestures to enact characters on stage. Forced Entertainment performers, however, are neither concerned with characters, nor with presenting their own self on stage. Theirs is an offensive play with established image-projection strategies, i.e. interviews, admissions and confessions, as seen on television. In highlighting the link to broadcasting media, 'theatre' as a framework is duplicated. This mirroring is not intended as a parody or a simple formal reproduction. As the performers stage their presence and speech in a recognizable media format, they are presenting themselves *as* performers. What comes to the fore is not content, but form of speech. Instead of a discourse on the relationship between actor and text, the central concern is the relationship between staging of the self and performance style. In a distinct way, each performer becomes enactor of his own self. Self and performance become inseparable.

No.5 Skilfully Fail and Let Fail

Imagine it is 11 p.m. You have been in the theatre for twenty-three hours straight, which is also true of some members of the audience. Time and again, a storytelling game takes place: "Once upon a time ..." You begin to tell a story, waiting for another actor to interrupt you. Tiredness is clearly visible on your face. Suddenly, you start to laugh while you are talking, unable to stop yourself. Others start to laugh as well, until finally the whole auditorium is laughing. The cause of the laughter is unclear, though the shared experience of tiredness and exhaustion creates a special bond between the performers and their audience: This is a moment where acting strate-

Zwanzig Minuten später – dein Mitspieler fragt, was du gestern Abend in deinem Hotelzimmer gemacht hast. Du beißt dir kurz auf die Lippen um zu überlegen, schaust an die Decke, knetest deine Finger, dann beginnst du stockend zu erzählen, scheinbar verlegen. Vielleicht antwortest du auch gerade heraus und offensiv, dass du einfach geschlafen hast.

In der Kritik heißt es immer wieder, die Darsteller von Forced Entertainment seien sie selbst auf der Bühne oder sie seien authentisch. Offensichtlich ist tatsächlich die Nähe zu einem bestimmten Repertoire alltäglicher Gesten, das jeder von uns nutzt, um seine eigene Selbstdarstellung authentisch wirken zu lassen. Auch jeder Schauspieler wendet dieses eigene Selbstdarstellungsrepertoire bewusst an, um auf der Bühne Figuren darzustellen Die Performer von Forced Entertainment aber zeigen weder Figuren auf der Bühne, noch präsentieren sie Selbstdarstellungen. Vielmehr spielen sie offensiv mit Selbst-Inszenierungsstrategien, die immer bereits medial vermittelt sind: Interviews, Beichten oder Bekenntnisse, ein Sprechen, wie man es aus dem Fernsehen kennt. Der Rahmen ,Theater' wird durch einen zweiten, bewusst ausgestellten Rahmen gedoppelt. Doch handelt es sich weder um eine Parodie noch um eine reine Reproduktion dieser Formen. Indem die Darsteller ihre Selbstdarstellungen und ihr Sprechen in einem wiedererkennbaren medialen Sprechformat inszenieren, präsentieren sie sich in ihrer Funktion als Darsteller. Nicht der Gegenstand, sondern die Form des Sprechens tritt in den Vordergrund. Statt des Verhältnisses von Person und Text wird das Verhältnis von Selbstdarstellung und Darstellungsform thematisiert. Die Performer sind auf besondere Weise zu Schauspielern ihrer Selbst geworden: Selbst und Darstellung sind nicht mehr zu trennen.

5. Scheitere gekonnt und lasse scheitern

Stell dir vor, es ist 23 Uhr abends. Und du bist seit 23 Stunden im Theater und auf den Beinen, einige Zuschauer ebenso. Zum wiederholten

Quizoola!

gies fail and everyone present simply shares in the laughter.

Forced Entertainment frequently play with the duration of their performances. *Quizoola!* and *And on the Thousandth Night...* each lasts six hours and there is also a six-hour version of *Speak Bitterness*. However, the most extreme example is the twenty-four-hour performance *Who Can Sing a Song to Unfrighten Me?*. The length of the performance, combined with the pressure to make decisions on stage, aims to make the performers' acting strategies fail due to loss of control and concentration.

The pressures and overtaxing feel of *Quizoola!* are created through the unequal distribution of power between the questioning and the replying performer. At times, the piece slips into an atmosphere of aggressive interrogation. The title itself – *Quizoola!* – brings to mind familiar television quiz shows. Quiz, however, also means investigation, interrogation or use of power. It tests verbal skills as much as factual knowledge, taxing the candidate's communication skills. *Quizoola!* is a verbal duel and speech contest between the two protagonists, combative in nature and far removed from normal dialogue. Its rules and structures constantly increase the pressure on the performers to improvise, aiming to push them into territory where they might make mistakes. The regulations suggest strategies to throw the contestant off kilter: repeating individual sentences, returning to the same questions time and again, questioning statements ("Why are you telling all these lies?"), or cutting the contestant off with a new question. Since the interrogator is responding to the contestant, as well as to his answers, the quiz gains a momentum of its own, breaking up the performers' staged presence and thus creating authenticity.

Mal findet das Spiel des Geschichten-Erzählens statt: „Es war einmal …". Du beginnst mit einer Geschichte und wartest darauf, dass dich ein Mitspieler unterbricht. Man sieht dir deine Müdigkeit an. Plötzlich beginnst du im Reden zu lachen und kannst nicht mehr aufhören. Andere stimmen ein und schließlich lacht das ganze Auditorium. Es ist nicht mehr klar, worüber gelacht wird – aus der gemeinsamen Erfahrung der Übermüdung, der Überforderung, entsteht ein besonderes Verhältnis zwischen Performern und Zuschauern: ein Moment, in dem die Darstellungsstrategien zusammenbrechen und alle einfach gemeinsam in einem Raum sind und lachen.

Immer wieder spielen die Inszenierungen von Forced Entertainment mit der Dauer ihrer Aufführungen. *Quizoola!* und *And on the Thousandth Night …* haben eine Dauer von sechs Stunden, auch von *Speak Bitterness* gibt es eine Sechs-Stunden-Version. Extremstes Beispiel ist die 24-Stunden-Inszenierung *Who Can Sing a Song to Unfrighten Me?*. Die Länge der Aufführung, gepaart mit dem Zwang, in der Bühnensituation Entscheidungen zu treffen, zielt darauf, die Darstellungsstrategien durch Konzentrations- und Kontrollverlust der Performer zum Scheitern zu bringen.

Bei *Quizoola!* entstehen der Druck und die Überforderung auch durch die Machtdifferenz zwischen Fragesteller und Antwortendem, die das Fragespiel mitunter zu einem Verhör werden lässt. Schon der Stücktitel *Quizoola!* spielt auf die Assoziationen zu ähnlichen Fragespielen im Fernsehen an. Quiz bedeutet aber auch Prüfung, Verhör oder Machttechnik. Ein Quiz ruft neben dem Wissen immer auch verbale Fähigkeiten ab. Der Befragte wird einem Sprachleistungstest unterzogen. *Quizoola!* ist Rededuell und Sprech-Test zwischen beiden Spielpartnern, kein Dialog, sondern ein verbaler Kampf. Die Regeln und Strukturen erhöhen den Improvisationsdruck mit dem Ziel, die Spieler Fehler produzieren zu lassen. Die Spielanweisungen geben Strategien vor, um den befragten Performer ins Schwimmen zu bringen: Die Wiederholung einzelner Sätze, das Zurückkommen auf die gleichen Fragen, das Infragestellen des Gesagten („Warum erzählst du lauter Lügen?"), das Unterbrechen durch eine neue Frage. Weil der Fragende sich nach der Verfassung und den Antworten des Befragten richten kann, gewinnt das Quiz eine Eigendynamik, die die souveräne Selbst-Inszenierung der Performer bricht und damit den Effekt einer authentischen Darstellung erzeugt.

6. Sei ein guter Dramaturg

Stell dir vor, du hast weder eine Rolle noch einen klar umrissenen Text. Wann die Aufführung zu Ende ist, weißt du nur von der Uhr. Du hast keine narrative Struktur, keine *storyline*, sondern nur Textblätter und Regeln. Wie machst du aus diesen wenigen Vorgaben eine Aufführung, wie wirst du interessant? Du jonglierst mit privaten Geschichten und fiktiven Storys, mit ausweichenden Gesten, mit Übersprungshandlungen, mit pointierten Anekdoten und assoziationsreichen Themensprüngen. Du überraschst deine Mitspieler mit Geschichten, die sie nicht kennen, mit unerwarteten und neuen Fragen. Du erkennst den toten Punkt, auf den die Aufführung zuläuft, und versuchst, das Spiel in einen anderen Modus zu bringen. Kurz: Du versuchst, mit dem vorgegebenen Material und den Spielregeln eine spannende und komplexe Aufführung zu konstruieren.

Der Aufbau solcher Inszenierungen erfordert vom Performer ganz besondere Mitarbeit. Er hat nicht nur Verantwortung für seine eigenen Darstellungen, sondern, da der Abend lediglich vorstrukturiert ist und sich immer wieder anders entwickeln kann, auch eine Verantwortung für den Ablauf. Er muss wie ein guter Dramaturg den gesamten Abend im Auge behalten und notwendige Wechsel herbeiführen können. Er muss sich möglichst authentisch und spontan innerhalb des Spielrahmens präsentieren, andererseits seine Darstellung durch verschiedene, gekonnt ein-

No.6 Be a Good Director

Imagine you have neither a role to play nor fixed lines to speak. The only way you can tell when the performance will end is by the clock. There is no narrative structure, no story line, only sheets of text and a set of rules. How do you build a performance from these few given components; how will you make it interesting? You are juggling private stories and fictitious narratives, evasive gestures, nervous habits and poignant anecdotes, changing subjects in free association. You surprise the other players with stories they have never heard before, with new and unexpected questions. You see the dead end the performance is heading towards and try to change the mode of play. To be concise, you are trying to construct a complex and involving performance from given material and using the rules of the game.

Constructing these performances requires special involvement by the performer. Not only responsible for his actions on stage, he is also in charge of progressing the performance, since the evening is only loosely prearranged and subject to constant change. Like a good director, the performer has to constantly keep an eye on the whole event and be ready to make changes if needs be. On the one hand, he has to present himself as authentic and spontaneous as possible within the scope of the performance; on the other hand, he needs to make his performance complex and varied through the skilful use of a diverse range of strategies. There is an interdependence of real play and intentional staging. The performers have to prove their worth as good players. They manage to challenge each other, to surprise and exhaust one another, to elicit unexpected confessions and to make the other lose his temper. The performer is challenged by his combined tasks as player, actor

Performing Games / How to be Cast as a Forced Entertainment Performer
Performing Games / ... über ein erfolgreiches Casting zum Forced Entertainment-Performer
Annemarie Matzke

and director. The failure to live up to these demands is a calculated part of the performance.

No.7 Your Aim: A 'Play-Biography' for the Evening

Imagine again, having to play a game on stage, that you are asking your co-performer questions or replying to those posed by him. Having to tell stories until your fellow actor stops you. Having to play with confessions or with signs. You make decisions, are challenged and in turn, you challenge your counterpart. Throughout the evening, you relate a stream of narratives, returning to specific questions, selecting certain confessions or signs. The items you choose, the kinds of things you are asked and the things you relate, all change from one evening to the next. So who is playing whom, or indeed, what?

Through the structure of play and the engagement with given rules, the performers create a particular onstage presence. It can be described as the duplicity of player and play figure. In board games, each player is given one or more figures to take his place in moving across the board. The play figure represents the player throughout the game. However, apart from those roles assigned by the rules of the game, the figure has no other function. Only during play, by interacting with the other figures, it gains a personal history – a sort of 'play-biography.' This play-biography is a product of chance and of the rules of the game, as much as something originating from the player's projected self.

The *Quizoola!* play-biography is generated through the questions asked and the answers given. Time and again, the questions return to previously visited narratives, giving the audience the impression that their knowledge about the performers is (supposedly) increasing. Brief glimpses of personal stories seem to appear, only to be interrupted by clearly visible role-play or

gesetzte Strategien möglichst komplex und abwechslungsreich gestalten. Reales Spiel und bewusst gesetzte Inszenierung beziehen sich aufeinander. Die Performer müssen sich als gute Spieler erweisen. Es gelingt ihnen tatsächlich, sich herauszufordern, zu überraschen, sich zu ermüden, unerwartete Geständnisse zu entlocken, den anderen aus der Fassung zu bringen. Die Fallhöhe der Aufführung liegt in der Mehrfachanforderung an den Darsteller als Spieler, als Schauspieler und Dramaturg. Das Scheitern an den Anforderungen ist einkalkuliert.

7. Dein Ziel: eine ‚Spiel-Biografie' für den Abend

Stell dir noch einmal vor, du musst auf der Bühne ein Spiel spielen. Musst deinem Mitspieler Fragen stellen oder beantworten. Musst Geschichten erzählen, bis dich dein Mitspieler stoppt. Musst das Spiel mit den Geständnissen oder mit den Schildern spielen. Du triffst Entscheidungen, wirst herausgefordert und forderst dein Gegenüber heraus. Über den Abend erzählst du immer neue Geschichten, kommst auf bestimmte Fragen zurück, wählst bestimmte Geständnisse oder Schilder aus. Was du auswählst, was du gefragt wirst, was du erzählst, ist jeden Abend anders. Wer spielt hier eigentlich wen oder was?

Durch die Spielstruktur und in der Auseinandersetzung mit den vorgegebenen Spielregeln konstituieren sich die Performer auf der Bühne in besonderer Weise. Ihr Status lässt sich mit der Doppelung von Spieler und Spielfigur beschreiben. Bei einem Brettspiel bekommt ein Spieler eine oder mehrere Spielfiguren zugeteilt, die sich an seiner Stelle über das Spielfeld bewegen. Die Spielfigur repräsentiert den Spieler im Spiel, hat aber keine Eigenschaften außer den ihr durch die Regeln zugewiesenen Funktionen. Erst durch den Verlauf des Spiels, die strategischen Entscheidungen des Spielers, den Zufall und die Interaktion mit den anderen Spielfiguren bekommt sie eine eigene Geschichte – eine Art ‚Spiel-Biografie'. Diese Spiel-Biografie entsteht aus dem Selbst-Entwurf im Spiel, ist aber ebenso den Regeln und dem Zufall des Spiel ausgesetzt.

In *Quizoola!* entsteht die Spiel-Biografie durch die gestellten Fragen und die gegebenen Antworten. Immer wieder kommen die Fragen auf bereits angerissene Geschichten zurück, mit den Antworten wächst das (vermeintliche) Wissen des Publikums über den Darsteller. Persönliche Geschichten scheinen aufzublitzen, die allerdings vom offen ausgestellten Rollenspiel oder vom Positionswechsel unterbrochen werden. Die Spiel-Biografie setzt sich aus heterogenen Erzählfragmenten, dem Wechsel der Perspektiven und Positionen zusammen, die nicht in eine einheitliche Bühnenfigur überführt werden können. Jede Form einer festen Subjektzuschreibung löst sich auf. Identifikation findet nicht mehr mit einer Figur oder Rolle statt, sondern mit der Funktion des Spielers und mit der Anforderung sich in vorgegebenen Systemen selbst inszenieren zu müssen.

Stell dir vor, du musst nicht nur ein guter Spieler und Dramaturg sein, nicht nur dir deiner eigenen Selbstdarstellungsstrategien bewusst werden und sie einsetzen können, nicht nur professionell mit dem Scheitern deiner eigenen Darstellung spielen, improvisieren und Entscheidungen treffen können. Stell dir vor, du tust das alles auf einmal. Stell dir vor, du spielst auf der Bühne verschiedene Spiele. Stell dir vor, du spielt ganz bewusst dich selbst und mit dir selbst. Du spielst ein Spiel, das seinen eigenen Regeln folgt. Es ist ein Spiel, das sich in einem wechselseitigen Prozess zwischen Improvisation und Anpassung, Freiraum und Begrenzung im Spiel, zwischen Selbst-Entwurf und fremder Zuschreibung bewegt.

changes of position. The play-biography is composed of dissimilar fragments of narrative, of changing perspectives and positions that cannot merge into a consistent stage persona. The play-biography dissolves any form of subject-assignation. One no longer identifies with a character or role, but instead with the function of the performer and the need of having to stage his self within a given system.

Imagine that you must not only be a good player and a good director, but that you must also be aware of and able to use your strategies for creating an onstage presence. Imagine, furthermore, that you must have more than an ability to exploit your own failure to perform, far more than an ability to improvise and far more than an ability to be decisive. Imagine yourself, doing all of these things simultaneously, playing a range of games on stage. Imagine you are consciously playing yourself and playing with your own self. You are playing a game that follows its own rules. As it progresses, it moves between improvisation and adaptation, free and restricted play, between the process of self-making and that of being defined by others.

Translated by Gero Grundmann

That's the place where you first met someone and that's the place where you fell out of love, and that's the place where your money got stolen and that's the place where you ran for a taxi and it wasn't raining, and there's a building you slept inside, once perhaps, or many times, and isn't this a street you used to lived on, and weren't you always the person staring out the car window, watching the world like the movies, and weren't you always the one who'd travelled a long way, through the day and into the night ...

Nights in this City

Nights in this City
(Pre-production)

Off the Route
Strategies and Approaches to the Appropriation of Space

Jenseits des Weges
Strategien und Aneignungsweisen des Raumes

Anke Schleper

Sie zeichneten eine Karte des Landes und markierten auf ihr die Ereignisse der letzten zehn Jahre – die Schauplätze politischer Konflikte und Arbeitskämpfe, ökologische Katastrophen, die Show-biz-Hochzeiten und die Scheidungen der Stars. Auf derselben Karte markierten sie die Ereignisse ihres eigenen Lebens – die Performances, die sie gezeigt hatten, die Städte und Metropolen, in denen sie gewesen waren, die Orte, an denen sie sich Verletzungen unterschiedlichster Art zugezogen hatten, die Orte, an denen sie ihre Liebe gefunden oder wieder verloren hatten.

A Decade of Forced Entertainment

They drew a map of the country and marked on it the events of the last ten years – the sites of political and industrial conflict, the ecological disasters, the show-biz marriages and celebrity divorces. On the same map, they marked the events of their own lives – the performances they'd given, the towns and cities where they'd stayed, the places where they'd incurred injuries of one kind or another, the places where they'd fallen in or out of love.

A Decade of Forced Entertainment

Liebe und Suff neben Bergarbeiterstreik und Parlamentswahlen, der Moskauer Putsch von 1991, der Tod von Freunden neben der Fatwa gegen Rushdie. Eine Reise nach Polen neben einer Schwarzenegger-Straße. Ein volles Jahrzehnt, die ganze Welt, die Fakten und die Fakes, das Private und das Öffentliche – alles auf einer Karte. *A Decade of Forced Entertainment*, eine *lecture performance* von 1994, war nicht nur der zehnte Geburtstag der Kompanie, sondern auch der explizite Beginn ihrer Auseinandersetzung mit Raumkonzepten und Mappingstrategien.

Love and drunkenness next to the miners' strike and parliamentary elections; the 1991 Moscow coup and the deaths of friends next to the fatwa against Rushdie. A journey to Poland next to an imaginary Schwarzenegger Street. A full decade, a whole world – facts and fakes, the intimate and the public – all on a map. *A Decade of Forced Entertainment* – a 1994 lecture performance – marked not only the company's 10TH birthday, but also the explicit beginning of their examination of spatial concepts and mapping strategies.

186

Off the Route / Strategies and Approaches to the Appropriation of Space
Jenseits des Weges / Strategien und Aneignungsweisen des Raumes
Anke Schleper

Narratives, both told and read aloud, construct the places and the atmosphere around them. Through a collection of shared and personal stories, remembered or invented by the performers, a new space emerges somewhere between documentation and fiction – not the space of an objective political or cultural landscape, but one of "ideas, narratives and bad dreams".

In the work of Forced Entertainment, landscape is a text. Not just the official text of historiography, but a multilayered composition of interpenetrating texts placed next to and on top of each other, texts of diverse origins and reputations, an assemblage of heterogeneous stories, memories, dreams. The emerging map does not claim objectivity, but nonetheless something new emerges from the shards and fragments: a poetic space.

By its nature, poetic space is highly artificial and subject to continuous change. It is constructed by the performers and at the same time, it is clear that it can quickly be done away with. The emerging landscape has but a temporary stability. It consists of loose narratives conjoined into a whole by the performers and the audience. These links, however, are not rigid; they are in permanent flux.

A mixture of strange and paradoxical, the landscape constructed in this way defies any logic. In *A Decade,* the group described a map of the UK, onto which they imposed great events from world history: the 1984 crash of the Challenger taking place in Kent or the 1991 siege of the Russian parliament happening in Liverpool. It is not the factual site of the event, but the subjective site of personal experience that is mapped and at the same time assigned a particular value. A singular memory, a subjective association makes Kent the site of the Challenger crash. The site of the event is thus identified with the site of a singular and subjective mental content. The site of the experience becomes the site of the event.

Erzählte und vorgelesene Geschichten konstituieren die Orte und deren Beschaffenheit. Eine Sammlung von Erzählungen, kollektiven oder persönlichen, die von den Performern erinnert und erfunden werden und in der *performance lecture*, irgendwo zwischen Dokumentation und Fiktion, einen neuen Raum entstehen lassen – keinen der objektiven politischen und kulturellen Landschaft, sondern einen der „Ideen, Narrationen und bösen Träume".

Landschaft bei Forced Entertainment ist Text. Nicht allein der offizielle Text der Geschichtsschreibung, sondern ein vielschichtiges Neben- und Übereinander sich durchdringender Texte verschiedener Herkunft und Reputation, eine Assemblage heterogener Geschichten, Erinnerungen, Träume. Die entstehende Karte beansprucht keine Objektivität, dennoch entsteht aus den Bruchstücken und Fragmenten etwas Neues: ein poetischer Raum.

Der poetische Raum ist seiner Natur nach hoch artifiziell und dauernden Veränderungen ausgesetzt. Er wird von den Performern entworfen; gleichzeitig aber ist offenkundig, wie schnell er auch wieder verworfen werden kann. Die Landschaft, die entsteht, besitzt nur eine temporäre Stabilität. Es sind lose Erzählungen, die von den Performern und den Zuschauern zu einem Ganzen zusammengefügt werden. Zusammenfügungen, die allerdings nicht starr, sondern im ständigen Fluss sind.

In ihrer Mischung fremd und paradox, spottet diese Art der Verortung jeder Logik.

So zeichneten Forced Entertainment in *A Decade* eine Karte von Großbritannien, auf der die großen Ereignisse der Weltgeschichte stattfanden: der Absturz der Challenger 1984 in Kent oder die Belagerung des russischen Parlamentshauses 1991 in Liverpool.

Es ist nicht der faktische Ort des Stattfindens, sondern der subjektive Ort des persönlichen Erfahrens und Erlebens, der hier kartografiert und dem gleichzeitig eine besondere

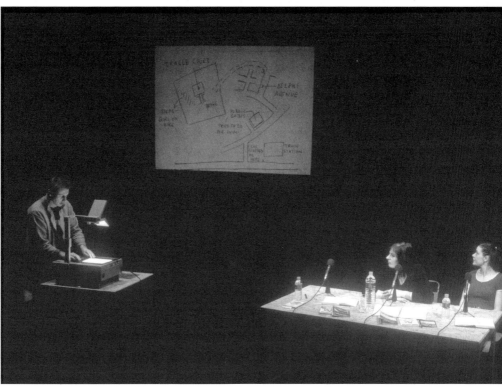

A Decade of Forced Entertainment
The Travels

Off the Route / Strategies and Approaches to the Appropriation of Space
Jenseits des Weges / Strategien und Aneignungsweisen des Raumes
Anke Schleper

The space that emerges in this way is strongly shaped by atmospherics. Besides factual, quantitative aspects, it is endowed with further qualities: an "inner space", not homogenous and empty, but fraught with qualities (Bachelard). A space of passions and dreams, of imaginings and longings, but also of fear and pain and horror.

Places like the ones in *The Travels*: During one summer, the members of Forced Entertainment travelled throughout the country and visited places that contained expectations or whose names in themselves seemed to promise a story: Harmony Street, Cutthroat Alley, Rape Lane … Streets and places that sounded as if the performers/travellers had invented them. Individually, they would seek out numerous streets, parks and places, reading landscapes, people and ground plans with their consciously subjective perspective – akin to reading a book or tea leaves. Hope Street in Liverpool: a desolate pub on one end, a deserted church on the other. Love Lane in Essex: a romantic path lined with roses and lavender. Love Lane in Wakefield: the gulf between two blocks of a high security prison. Fortune Street, supposedly with a dog race track on one end, stops at a brick wall. Memory Lane is brand new, smooth and with no traces of life.

The performance itself takes the form of a lecture. Photographs, videos, recordings of phone conversations and notes – all gathered during the process – have been left in the rehearsal room and transformed into text. We are presented with an interpreted, qualitative landscape. A space full of meanings, characteristically unstable, mediated and accessible only through interpretation. Such a space contrasts strongly with our notion of a neutral space of objective experience. But in fact, such a 'pure space' exists only as a highly abstract concept, a construct that is not found in reality.

Wertigkeit zuerkannt wird. Eine singuläre Erinnerung, eine subjektive Assoziation lässt Kent zu dem Absturzort der Challenger werden. Der Ereignisort wird mit dem Ort eines singulären und subjektiven Bewusstseinsinhalts gleichgesetzt. Der Ort der Erfahrung wird zum Ort des Ereignisses.

Der so entstehende Raum ist stark von Stimmungen geprägt. Neben faktischen, quantitativen Aspekten besitzt er weitere Eigenschaften: ein „Raum des Innen", der nicht homogen und leer, sondern mit Qualitäten aufgeladen ist (Bachelard). Ein Raum unserer Leidenschaften und Träume, der Phantasie und der Sehnsucht, aber auch der Angst, der Qual und des Grauens.

Orte wie in *The Travels*: Einen Sommer lang fuhren die Mitglieder von Forced Entertainment durchs Land und suchten Stätten auf, mit denen sie Erwartungen verknüpften oder deren Namen selbst bereits eine Geschichte versprachen: Harmony Street, Cutthroat Alley, Rape Lane … Straßen und Orte, als wären sie Erfindungen von ihnen selbst. Jeder für sich suchten sie unzählige Wege, Parks und Plätze auf; lasen Landschaft, Leute, Grundrisse mit ihrer bewusst subjektiven Perspektive wie ein Buch oder einen Kaffeesatz. Hope Street in Liverpool: ein verlassener Pub am einen Ende, am anderen eine aufgegebene Kirche. Love Lane in Essex: ein romantischer Weg umsäumt von Rosen und Lavendel. Love Lane in Wakefield: die Schlucht zwischen zwei Blöcken eines Hochsicherheitsgefängnisses. Fortune Street, an deren Ende eine Hunderennbahn verzeichnet ist, endet vor einer Ziegelwand. Nagelneu ist Memory Lane, glatt und ohne irgendeine Spur.

Die Aufführung selbst hat die Form einer Lesung. Fotografien, Videobänder, Telefonaufzeichnungen, Notizen wurden gesammelt, bearbeitet und im Probenraum zurückgelassen: transformiert ist alles eingegangen in die Collage und nun nur noch Text. Eine gedeutete, qualitative Landschaft. Ein Raum voll von Bedeutungen, der seiner Natur nach instabil, vor allem aber vermittelt und nur durch

Interpretation erschließbar ist. Er steht in starkem Kontrast zu unserer Vorstellung eines objektiv erfahrbaren und neutralen Raumes. Tatsächlich aber existiert ein solcher ‚reiner Raum' nur als Konzept äußerster Abstraktion. Ein Konstrukt, das real nie anzutreffen ist.

Im poetischen Raum hingegen sind die Grenzen zwischen Realität und Fiktion derart im Fluss, dass sie ein flimmerndes Ganzes bilden. Kein ‚Raum der Fakten', sondern ein ‚Möglichkeitsraum' tut sich auf. Was als real und fiktiv angesehen wird, ist nur eine Frage des Standpunktes innerhalb eines prozessierenden Feldes der Möglichkeiten. Standpunkte bei Forced Entertainment zeichnen sich dadurch aus, dass sie nicht passiv und rezeptiv, sondern aktiv und projektiv eingenommen werden: Mapping als ein aktiver Prozess des Anordnens – von persönlichen Geschichten des Performers, aber auch des Zuschauers, der im Verlauf des Abends seine Rezeptionshaltung verlässt, um eigene Geschichten zu projizieren. Er fügt neue Orte hinzu, wenn er z. B. überlegt, wo er selbst zu dem Zeitpunkt der Katastrophe war, und überschreibt die Karte mit eigenen, wahren oder falschen Vorstellungen. Das passive Wahrnehmen von externen Ereignissen und Orten weicht einer aktiven Haltung: „Wir haben uns ins Projizieren aufgerichtet. Wir werden erwachsen. Wir wissen, dass wir träumen" (Flusser).

In *Die Kunst des Handelns* (1980) fordert Michel de Certeau dazu auf, sich auf die 110. Etage des World Trade Centers zu begeben und auf Manhattan herabzusehen.

Für einen Moment ist die Bewegung durch den Anblick erstarrt. Die gigantische Masse wird unter den Augen unbeweglich. Sie verwandelt sich in ein Textgewebe, in der die Extreme des Aufwärtsstrebens zusammenfallen, die brutalen Gegensätze von Gebäudegenerationen und Stilen, die Kontraste zwischen gestern geschaffenen buildings, *die bereits zu Mülleimern geworden sind, und den heutigen urbanen Irruptionen, die den Raum versperren.*

In a poetic space, on the other hand, the boundaries between reality and fiction are fluid and the two form a shimmering whole. A space not of facts, but of possibilities opens up. What is seen as real and what as fictitious depends upon one's point of view within a field of possibilities. Points of view in the work of Forced Entertainment are understood not as passive and receptive, but rather as active and projective. Mapping becomes an active process of ordering – of the performers' personal stories as well as those of the audience. Indeed, the performances encourage the viewers to abandon their receptive attitudes in the course of the evening in order to project their own stories. They may – in their minds – add new places to the map, for example when reflecting on where they were at the time of a particular catastrophe or they may overwrite the map with their own true or false notions of narrated events. A passive receptiveness towards external events and places gives way to an active attitude: "We have straightened ourselves up into projecting. We are growing up. We know that we are dreaming" (Flusser).

Michel de Certeau suggests in his 1980 book *The Practice of Everyday Life* that one should ascend to the 110TH floor of the World Trade Center and look down on Manhattan:

For a moment movement freezes through the gaze. The gigantic mass becomes immobile under one's eyes. It is transformed into a textile structure, in which the extremes of an upward strife collapse, the violent juxtapositions between generations of buildings and styles, the contrasts between buildings created yesterday, which have already become trash bins, and today's urban irruptions, which block the space.

The city as a textile web that asks to be deciphered. A perspective from high above the city,

Ground Plans for Paradise

Die Stadt als ein Textgewebe, das zur Entzifferung auffordert. Eine Perspektive, hoch über der Stadt, die es erlaubt, sich ein Bild zu machen; eine Emporhebung, um „diesen maßlosesten aller menschlichen Texte zu ‚überschauen', zu überragen und in Gänze aufzufassen."

Eine Perspektive wie in *Ground Plans for Paradise*: eine Modellstadt aus tausend Balsaholzblöcken, ausgebreitet auf einem Rasterplan und frei schwebend einem Sockel aufgesetzt. Über dem Modell die Gesichter schlafender Menschen. Eine leere und unbewohnte Stadt. Nur die Namen der Straßen und Gebäude zeugen von einer merkwürdigen Bewohntheit. Sie sind benannt nach den Passionen, Ängsten und den narrativen Echos des 20. Jahrhunderts: The Rand Think-Tank on Sex, Dave's Topless Chip Shop, Heartbreak Hotel, The Blood Club … Hinabschauend ist der Betrachter eingeladen zu spekulieren.

Geschichten werden projiziert und erfunden, Erinnerungen wachgerufen. Wir befinden uns fernab, hoch erhoben über der Stadt. Unter uns ein erkennbar wohlorganisiertes Ganzes, als Betrachter sehen wir Grenzen und Verbindungen, Mauern und Straßen.

Die Installation ist allerdings nur das Modell einer Stadt. Sie ist unbestimmbar, gibt keinen Hinweis auf eine konkrete Stadt; eine freie Fläche, die regelrecht dazu auffordert, eigene, private Geschichten, Träume und Erinnerungen hinzuzufügen. Hier sind nur die Namen der Orte Texte, die es zu entziffern gilt, kleine, auf die Oberfläche eingegrabene Spuren, aber weder offizielle noch private Geschichten, die zu finden wären. Nur der eigene Text, der die Stadt, die vor uns liegt, erst erfindet.

Die Stadt erschließt sich aus der Vogelperspektive. Diese Ausschließlichkeit des Blickpunkts, ‚das himmlische Auge', findet sich in *Ground Plans* in seiner reinsten Form. Der Betrachter ist alleiniger und vollständiger Herrscher über die Situation. Er erfindet die Stadt, erschafft diese erst, die vorher nur eine Ansammlung geschichtsloser Holzblöcke war.

enabling one to make an image, an attempt to rise above in order to "gain an overview of this most boundless of all human texts, to overtower it and to grasp it in its entirety."

Such a perspective is found in *Ground Plans for Paradise* – a model city built from a thousand blocks of balsa wood, arranged on a grid and floating on a pedestal. Above the model, the faces of sleeping people. An empty, desolate city. Only the names of streets and buildings speak of a strange kind of inhabitation. The streets and buildings bear the names of various passions, fears and echoes of narratives from the 20TH century: The Rand Think-Tank on Sex, Dave's Topless Chip Shop, Heartbreak Hotel, The Blood Club … Looking down, the observer is invited to speculate.

Stories are projected and invented; memories kindled. We are far away, lifted high above the city. Beneath us, a visibly well organised whole. As observers, we recognise the boundaries and connections, walls and streets.

The installation is, however, only the model of a city. It is indeterminable, not a portrait of any single existing city, but rather an open space, an invitation to infuse it with one's own private stories, dreams and memories. The names of places are the only text to be deciphered, the only traces carved onto their surface: Neither official nor private stories are to be found here. Only one's own text, inventing the city down below.

The key to reading the city is in adopting a bird's-eye view. The exclusivity of this viewpoint, the divine eye in its purest form, is found in *Ground Plans*. The viewer is the sole and exclusive ruler of the situation. He invents and creates the city, which before had been only a collection of ahistorical wooden blocks.

In the case of an actual city, such a point of view, such a gaze from above, which promises transparency and complete legibility, is nothing but an illusion. It is a gaze that unifies the numerous texts and traces carved into the city into a single and legible one; it abstracts from details, bestows a systematic order. It is a gaze that creates a homogenous narrative from the plurality and the multiplicity of text layers that comprise the city. This panoramic city is a theoretical construct, an image that comes about only through a process of forgetting and misrecognition of various singular processes.

As is the case with the maps of spatial planners, geographers and cartographers, representation of the city produces a certain distance. It abstracts from details and misrecognizes numerous events and actions that have taken and are still taking place there. That city down there actually consists of numerous multilayered texts, which here remain out of grasp.

The motif of looking down from a distance resurfaces in various forms in several of the works of Forced Entertainment. For *Hidden J*, for example, a photograph by Hugo Glendinning became an early point of departure for the piece: Richard Lowdon lying on the crest of a hill in early dusk, with the lights of the city of Sheffield behind him. The motif of looking down on the city is also present in *Emanuelle Enchanted (or a Description of this World as if it were a Beautiful Place)*, where Terry O'Connor delivers her monologue: "And on the wild night that the rain stopped we looked down at the city for a while and said: Why such a big city, why such a big world?" O'Connor describes a restless city whose hustle and bustle had been left behind and which can now be seen from a distance. It is night, as it so often is in the work of Forced Entertainment – in this time, shapes blur, objects and places lose their hard contours. While night is often the refuge for dreams and possibilities, here it is inhospitable, cold and sad. Terry's monologue links to the strand of 'curtain texts'

Im Falle einer tatsächlichen Stadt ist solch ein Blickpunkt, der Transparenz und eine vollständige Lesbarkeit verheißt, jedoch nur Illusion. Es ist ein Blick, der die Unzahl der dort eingegrabenen Spuren vereinheitlicht und die Unmenge von Texten zu einem einzigen, lesbaren zusammenfasst: der von Details und Einzelheiten abstrahiert, ordnet und systematisiert. Ein Blick, der eine homogene Erzählung aus der Vielzahl und Vielschichtigkeit der Texte, die diese Stadt sind, schafft. Diese Panorama-Stadt ist ein theoretisches Konstrukt, ein Bild, das nur durch ein Vergessen und Verkennen der vielen singulären Vorgänge zustandekommt.

Ebenso wie für die Karten der Raumplaner, Geographen und Kartographen wird eine Abbildung erzeugt, die eine gewisse Distanz herstellt. Sie abstrahiert von Einzelheiten und verkennt die zahllosen dort stattfindenden und stattgefundenen Ereignisse und Handlungen. Tatsächlich besteht diese Stadt dort unten aus einer Unmenge vielschichtiger Texte, deren Zugriff man sich hier entzieht.

Dieses Motiv des Hinabschauens aus Distanz taucht in verschiedener Gestalt in zahlreichen Arbeiten Forced Entertainments auf. Für *Hidden J* beispielsweise wurde eine Fotografie von Hugo Glendinning zum Ausgangspunkt für die Entwicklung des Stückes: Richard Lowdon, hingestreckt auf einem Hügelkamm, im frühen Abendlicht, hinter ihm die Lichter der Stadt Sheffield. Oder *Emanuelle Enchanted (or a Description of this World as if it were a Beautiful Place)*, wo Terry O' Connor ihren Monolog auf die Stadt herabspricht: „Und in der wilden Nacht, in der der Regen aufhörte, sahen wir eine Weile lang auf die Stadt hinab und sagten: Warum so eine große Stadt, warum so eine große Welt?" Eine ruhelose Stadt, deren Treiben man sich entzogen hat, die man wie von Ferne betrachtet. Wie so oft ist es Nacht, Konturen verwischen, die Dinge und Orte verlieren ihre harten Umgrenzungen; Nacht ist die Herberge von Träumen und Möglichkeiten. Doch hier ist sie unwirtlich,

Off the Route / Strategies and Approaches to the Appropriation of Space
Jenseits des Weges / Strategien und Aneignungsweisen des Raumes
Anke Schleper

kalt und traurig. Der Monolog stammt aus einem der narrativen Fragmente aus den ‚Vorhang-Texten', allesamt Betrachtungen über die Stadt: einer der Performer spricht, meist allein, vor einem halbdurchsichtigen Vorhang stehend, über die nächtliche Stadt dort draußen. Die Szenen ‚dahinter' durchspielen verschiedene Typen von Raumsituationen: ein hektischer und chaotischer TV-Nachrichtenraum, angedeutet durch ein Mikrofon auf einem Tisch mit einer gegenübergestellten Kamera; der private Raum, sehr schlicht durch Arrangieren der vorhandenen Sperrholzwände des Bühnensets erzeugt; und ein sehr weiter, offener Raum, in dem die Gruppe, durch den Gebrauch von Pappschildern, den Blick auf eine Unzahl von Charakteren freigibt. Sichtbar bleiben auch die Wände des öffentlichen Theaterraums und die Rückwand als der Himmel über uns: ein Sternenhimmelvorhang. Alle Räume befinden sich im Fluss: sie werden sichtbar arrangiert und wieder eingerissen, Vorhänge auf- und zugezogen, Wände werden lebendig und beginnen in wilden Choreographien zu tanzen, die Räume überlagern sich, verschwinden plötzlich oder dringen ineinander ein. Eine verrückte Welt, die sich der kalten dort draußen entgegenzustemmen versucht.

In dieser merkwürdigen Nacht, als der Regen aufhörte, begannen wir ein paar Zaubertricks, um die Kälte fernzuhalten. Es war alles BEÄNGSTIGEND MAGISCH und erschien und verschwand, und es war OFFENBARUNG UND VERLUST für uns damals. Alles FALTETE SICH und VERBARG SICH und entschlüpfte.

Emanuelle Enchanted bewirkt eine Verunsicherung unserer Raumerfahrung durch Bühnenmittel; in *Nightwalks*, eine Zusammenarbeit mit Hugo Glendinning, wird diese Verstörung mit anderen Strategien und Mitteln erreicht. Das CD-ROM Projekt ist eine Sammlung von navigierbaren Panorama-Landschaften, die auf realen Orten –

that run through *Emanuelle,* in which the performers speak directly to the audience, mostly alone, stood in front of a semi-transparent curtain at the front of the stage. Each of these texts are reflections on the city. The scenes revealed 'behind' the curtain act out various kinds of spatial situations: a frantic and chaotic TV newsroom, indicated by a microphone on a desk and a camera facing it; a domestic room, produced by a particular arrangement of the plywood screens which make up the set; and a wider, open space, in which the group enact characters using cardboard signs. The walls of the actual theatre space also remain visible, as does the back wall of the stage which represents the sky above us: a curtain with electric stars. All spaces are in flux: They are visibly being arranged and taken down again. Curtains are drawn open and shut, walls become alive and begin to dance in wild choreographies, rooms run into each other, disappear suddenly or enter into each other. A crazy world that tries to resist the cold one outside.

That strange night when the rain stopped we started on some magic acts to keep away the cold. It was all FRIGHTENING MAGIC and appearing and disappearing and REVELATION and LOSS for us then. It was all FOLDING and HIDING and slipping away.

While *Emanuelle Enchanted* unsettles our spatial experience through stage practice, in *Nightwalks* this unsettling is achieved by other strategies and means. The CD-ROM project – made in collaboration with Hugo Glendinning – is a collection of navigable panoramic landscapes based on real locations – forgotten places somewhere in England. By means of a navigation bar, the viewer can move through the frozen landscapes, zoom in and out, and by clicking on the key points and figures (hot spots), leave one scene and enter a new one. The way places are connected to other places follows not a geographical, but a poetic logic. The atmosphere is cold; it is night. The immobile scenes are open to unobstructed viewing with no possibility for interaction. In spite of the liberties that arise through associative navigation, the viewer is compelled and able to turn, but fixed in a static position. It is a panoptical gaze (in the sense of an optical system): like the gaze of the king in the menagerie of Le Vaux in Versailles described by Foucault. There, a first-floor pavilion in the palace contained only one room, the king's salon. On all sides of the room, wide windows opened onto a walled-in enclosure, in which there were animals, continuously subjected to his observation.

In *Nightwalks*, the viewer is the king, choosing objects and persons according to his interest, but unable to break the existing distance between himself and the place he is exploring. A feeling of "unrealness" arises, as if angel beings roamed those untouchable spaces. At the same time, the viewer's gaze discovers an indifferent and ambiguous spatial situation: most scenes are open spaces, squares, crossroads, streets that lead nowhere. The openness is only deceptive, however, since each place is actually

vergessenen Orten in einem Irgendwo in England – basieren. Der Betrachter kann sich mit einer Navigierleiste durch die eingefrorenen Landschaften bewegen, hinein- und hinauszoomen und die Szene über Schlüsselpunkte und -figuren *(hot spots)* wieder verlassen, um in eine neue einzutauchen. Die Verbindung der Orte gehorcht dabei keiner geographischen, sondern einer poetischen Logik. Es herrscht eine kalte Atmosphäre, es ist Nacht. Die unbeweglichen Szenen geben sich ungehindert der Betrachtung preis, ohne dass eine Interaktion möglich wäre. Trotz der Freiheiten, die sich durch die assoziative Navigation ergeben, ist der Betrachter gebunden, er kann sich zwar drehen, sein Standpunkt aber ist fixiert. Es ist ein panoptischer Blick (gemeint als optisches System): wie der Blick des Königs in der von Foucault beschriebenen Menagerie von Le Vaux in Versailles. Ein Pavillon, der im 1. Geschoss nur einen Raum enthielt, den Salon des Königs. Alle Seiten öffneten sich durch breite Fenster auf ein ummauertes Gehege, in denen die Tiere uneingeschränkt seiner Beobachtung ausgesetzt waren.

In *Nightwalks* ist der Betrachter König; er wählt die Objekte und Personen allein nach seinem Interesse aus, kann aber die vorhan-

Nightwalks

dene Distanz niemals durchbrechen. Es entsteht ein Gefühl von Unwirklichkeit, als streife man als Engelswesen durch Orte, die man aber nicht anfassen kann. Gleichzeitig konstituiert der Blick eine indifferente Raumsituation: Die Szenerien sind meist offene Räume, Plätze, Kreuzungen, Straßen, die ins Nirgendwo führen. Die Offenheit ist allerdings nur eine vorgebliche, tatsächlich ist der jeweilige Ort durch die Fixierung begrenzt. Der Raum ist das, was ich sehe. Alles hinter dem optischen Horizont existiert nicht. Der Betrachter kann nicht die Entscheidung treffen, loszulaufen und nachzusehen, was sich wohl hinter der Mauer verbirgt, oder zur Straßenkreuzung zu gehen, um dann dort in eine andere Richtung abzubiegen. Der als vorerst dreidimensional erfahrene Raum ist planar – ein Bild – und verwehrt den Zugang. Zu dieser räumlichen Verunsicherung kommt eine weitere: Verlässt der Betrachter die Szene über einen der gewählten Schlüsselpunkte, landet er unmittelbar in einer anderen städtischen Szene. Diese Orte besitzen keinen räumlichen Zusammenhang, obwohl sie, da sie Fotostills ‚echter‘ urbaner Szenerien sind, dies vorerst suggerieren. Der Versuch einen Raumzusammenhang zu erstellen scheitert. Es sind räumliche Fragmente, gebildet aus den

limited and fixed. Space is what one sees. Whatever is behind the optical horizon does not exist. The spectator cannot decide to go ahead and see what lies hidden behind this wall or that wall or to walk to this corner or that crossroad and take a different turn. The space that is at first experienced as three-dimensional is actually planar – a flat image – and as such, it resists access. This spatially unsettling experience is accompanied by another one: When the observer leaves the scene through one of the key points, he immediately arrives in another city scene. The two places have no spatial connection, even though – being still photographs of 'real' urban scenery – they suggest one at first. The attempt to arrive at a spatial connection fails; these are spatial fragments, shaped by the stories that the observer makes up on the basis of the traces he finds and the routes he chooses.

The perspective in *Nightwalks* differs from that in *Ground Plans for Paradise* in one crucial point. While here perspective is equally distanced and panoptical, it by no means represents a 'divine gaze'. The viewer moves at the usual eye level, that of a pedestrian. He is down below and, in that sense, 'in the city'. As part of it, he

cannot view it abstractly from above and arrive at a coherent narrative. Instead, he moves below a threshold of visibility. He must drift and go with the flow; he is a *flâneur* to whom only shards and fragments are offered. The *flâneur*, as described by Walter Benjamin, is a freely mobile spectator engulfed by the city of Paris and its frantic hustle and bustle. Immersed in his environment, he is free to roam about, to consume and enjoy the pleasures of the city. He is not able to grasp the city as a whole, to create an homogenous whole in his mind. His sense of the city's cohesion is afforded by the routes he takes. A *flâneur* whose walking creates connections, a subjective narrative that did not exist before. As in *Nightwalks,* he roams about, finding traces here and there which he may read and put together in his mind or which he may not notice or ignore. In this way, he creates his own space, stumbling through his own "play of steps" (de Certeau).

The perspective of the pedestrian with his way of processing and appropriating space can also be found in the performance-installation

Geschichten, die der Betrachter sich aus den gefundenen Spuren zusammengereimt hat.

Die Perspektive in *Nightwalks* unterscheidet sich in einem wesentlichen Punkt von der in *Ground Plans for Paradise*. Erstere ist zwar ebenfalls distanziert und panoptisch, keineswegs aber ein ‚göttlicher Blick‘. Der Betrachter bewegt sich auf der ihm gewohnten Augenhöhe: der Blickwinkel eines Fußgängers. Er ist unten, in diesem Sinne ‚in der Stadt‘. Als Teil von ihr kann er nicht mehr abstrakt von oben betrachten und eine homogene Geschichte bilden, sondern er bewegt sich unterhalb einer Sichtbarkeitsschwelle. Er muss sich treiben und mitziehen lassen, er ist ein Flaneur, dem sich nur Bruchstücke und Fragmente bieten. Ein *flâneur*, wie er von Walter Benjamin beschrieben wird, als ein von der Stadt umschlungener, frei beweglicher Betrachter im hektischen Treiben von Paris. Eingetaucht in seine Umgebung ist er frei herumzustreunen, zu konsumieren und die Freuden der Stadt zu genießen. Ihm ist es nicht möglich, die Stadt als Ganzes zu erfassen, ein homogenes Ganzes zu schaffen. Sein Zusammenhang sind die Wegfiguren, die er schafft. Ein Spaziergänger, dessen Gehen Zusam-

Nightwalks

menhänge bildet, seine subjektive Erzählung, die vorher nicht existierte. Wie in *Nightwalks* streunt er umher, findet hier und dort Spuren, die er liest und zusammenfügt oder auch unbeachtet liegen lässt. Auf diese Weise gestaltet er sich einen eigenen Raum, taumelnd durch sein eigenes „Spiel der Schritte" (de Certeau).

Die Perspektive des Fußgängers mit seiner Art und Weise, wie ein Raum von ihm erfasst und in Anspruch genommen wird, findet man auch in der Installations-Performance *Red Room*, einer Kollaboration von Forced Entertainment mit dem Fotografen Hugo Glendinning und dem Performer Will Waghorn 1993 in der Londoner Showroom Gallery. Als Besucher der Arbeit wird man mit einer Taschenlampe ausgestattet und in einem dunklen Raum sich selbst überlassen. Dort streift man umher, sucht sich in der Fülle des Materials – Fotos und Texte, die aus einem drittklassigen Krimi zu stammen scheinen – seinen Weg und aus den vielen Bruchstücken seinen eigenen Zusammenhang.

Der Blick ist explizit begrenzt; auch wenn der Besucher seine Lampe beliebig herumfahren lassen kann, zeigt sich ihm doch immer nur ein kleiner Ausschnitt aus der Gänze des

Red Room, a collaboration between Forced Entertainment, the photographer Hugo Glendinning and the performer Will Waghorn, presented in London's Showroom Gallery in 1993. The visitor to the gallery is provided with a flashlight and left to his own devices in a dark room. There one is invited to roam about, make one's way through a wealth of material – pictures and texts that seem to be taken from a third-rate crime story – and piece together one's own connections from the fragments encountered.

On this journey, the visitor's gaze is explicitly limited – even though he can move about freely with his torch, only a small part of the available material will be visible to him at any given time. As the beam of light creates a focus, a linear order is imposed onto the disjointed fragments, even though that order is determined by the viewer himself and the way he lingers or rushes through the installation. A subjective and temporal narrative. The texts and photos assembled here as a lose ensemble present themselves in a sequence created by the viewer, and are thus read and interpreted by him

in that sequence – his interpretation infused with the knowledge that what is being experienced is a created narrative that did not exist before, without his own gaze.

At the back wall of the gallery, the viewer can discover a passageway that leads to a second room. Inside, Will Waghorn sits in the faint red glow of a light bulb, developing photos and writing texts.

The material for the performance is created here during the exhibition: The few objects that one might have assumed to be fixed and stable are now revealed to be just as temporary and exchangeable as the stories one had imagined around them.

Those who venture to this point in the installation may suddenly recognise themselves as discoverers of an internal site of production, a recognition that makes apparent the constructed nature of all the experiences and all the narratives created in the first room.

In another CD-ROM project, *Frozen Palaces*, which utilises the same technical means as *Nightwalks*, we witness grotesque scenes taking place in the rooms of a house. Time seems to stand

Materials. Ihm wird durch den Lichtkegel ein Fokus aufgezwungen, der die unverbundenen Fragmente durch seine Betrachterzeit in eine lineare Ordnung zwingt, auch wenn diese nur durch ihn selbst bestimmt ist. Eine subjektive und temporäre Narration. Die Texte und Fotos, die als loses Ensemble angeordnet sind, bieten sich in einer vom Betrachter erzeugten Reihenfolge dar, in der sie von ihm gelesen und verstanden werden – allerdings in dem Bewusstsein, dass es sich um eine geschaffene Erzählung handelt, die zuvor, ohne sein Betrachten, nicht existierte.

An der Rückwand der Galerie lässt sich ein Durchgang zu einem Korridor entdecken, der zu einem zweiten Galerieraum führt. Dort sitzt, Fotos entwickelnd und Texte schreibend, im schwachen Licht einer roten Glühbirne, Will Waghorn.

Während der gesamten Dauer der Ausstellung wird hier das Material für die Performance erstellt; die wenigen Objekte, die man als fix und stabil wahrgenommen hat, entpuppen sich als ebenso temporär und austauschbar wie die Geschichten, die man ihnen angedichtet hat.

Wer bis hierher vorzudringen vermag, erkennt sich plötzlich als Entdecker einer internen Produktionsstätte, die das Konstruierte

Nightwalks

aller im ersten Raum gemachten Erfahrungen und Narrationen offensichtlich werden lässt.

In einem weiteren CD-ROM-Projekt, *Frozen Palaces*, das technisch mit den gleichen Mitteln arbeitet wie *Nightwalks*, wird man Zeuge grotesker Szenen in den Zimmern eines Hauses. Die Zeit scheint stillzustehen. Partys, ein Liebespaar, ein Mord … alle Szenen wirken wie konserviert. Eingefrorene Momente aus der Geschichte dieses Hauses. Das Haus als ein Archiv der dort stattgefundenen Ereignisse.

Kaum ein Zimmer lässt sich durch Türen oder Fenster verlassen, die Schlüsselpunkte sind symbolisch aufgeladene Objekte oder Personen: ein blutbeschmiertes Messer, Luftballons, eine Leiche oder ein Bild an der Wand. Das Haus verliert seinen architektonischen Zusammenhang, der zusätzlich durch eine Faltung der Zeit verloren geht: Gerät man unversehens in ein bereits besuchtes Zimmer, kann man auf eine vollkommen andere Szene stoßen: ein Zimmer, das man gerade erst durch eine Party verwüstet fand, sieht man wenig später als Stätte des bereits vergangen geglaubten, rauschenden Festes. Eine in sich gekrümmte Raum-Zeit. Als Betrachter ist man sich seines Blickes mehr noch als in *Nightwalks*

still. Parties, a couple of lovers, a murder … All scenes seem to have been preserved. Frozen moments from the history of a house. The house as an archive of the events that may have taken place there.

There is hardly a room one can leave through doors or windows; instead, key points that serve as entrances and exits are symbolically charged objects or people: a knife smeared in blood, air balloons, a corpse, or a picture on the wall. Moreover, the house loses its architectural coherence: If one stumbles into a room for the second time, one might find a completely different scene than before. A room that one encountered completely wrecked in the aftermath of a party might on the second encounter become the site of that very celebration which one had believed to be long past. Space-time folds back onto itself. As viewer, one becomes conscious of one's own gaze, even more so than in *Nightwalks*. As these are private rooms one is roaming, one inevitably feels like an undesired witness, a voyeur peeping in on most private scenes.

Nights in this City, a guided bus tour through Sheffield at night, and a second version through Rotterdam (1995 and 1997 respectively),

Off the Route / Strategies and Approaches to the Appropriation of Space
Jenseits des Weges / Strategien und Aneignungsweisen des Raumes
Anke Schleper

stages an even more complex play with space and perspective.

Performers and audience travel on a bus through the city's centre and peripheries, through main and secondary roads, past public places and through the marginalised 'non-places' of the city.

These tours offer an excessive play with the stories inscribed into the urban body of the city. Not so much searching for some existing truth, but rather creating new versions of it, Forced Entertainment venture out to inscribe the city with their own stories. "Writing onto the city", Etchells calls this process. Take a city and project your stories onto it: invented, dreamed, associative. In *Nights in this City*, the resulting text hardly contains any hard facts. The tour in Sheffield begins with "Ladies and Gentlemen, welcome to Paris …", and moments later, we find ourselves in Dresden, Pisa, Rome or Delhi. An adventurous tour begins, narrated by a travel guide who poses as many questions as he gives wrong answers, who tells his private stories about where he lives and where the next good pub can be found, and who not only tells numerous rumours, speculations, official versions, lies and fairy tales in one breath, but who also adds to this wealth of information his own countless embellishments. This is a journey that will take the tour participant further and further away from the city that he thought he knew.

Cities are great places for the beginning of a story, and they are good places for the end but for the middle you usually have to go somewhere a bit more out of the way, somewhere a bit more, you know, remote …

A magical city far removed from any everyday experience is described during the tour, which develops into a multilayered, poetic web of texts. This web consists not only of the performers'

bewusst: Es sind private Räume, durch die man hier streift; sofort stellt sich das Gefühl ein, ungebetener Zeuge zu sein: ein Voyeur, der Einblicke ins Privateste bekommt.

Ein noch komplexeres Spiel mit Raum und Perspektive ist *Nights in this City* (1995 und 1997), eine geführte Bustour durch die nächtliche Stadt Sheffield und in einer zweiten Version durch Rotterdam.

Performer und Zuschauer an Bord, fährt der Bus durch das Zentrum und die Peripherien der Stadt, über Haupt- und Nebenstraßen, an öffentlichen Plätzen vorbei und durch die Neben- und Unorte der Stadt hindurch.

Diese Touren sind ein exzessives Spiel mit den Geschichten, die in den urbanen Stadtkörper eingeschrieben sind. Weniger auf der Suche nach der einen Wahrheit, sondern eher unterwegs, neue Versionen zu schaffen, ziehen sie hinaus, der Stadt ihre eigenen Geschichten einzuschreiben. „Auf die Stadt schreiben" nennt Etchells diesen Prozess; man nehme sich eine Stadt und projiziere seine Geschichten auf sie drauf. Erfundenes, Geträumtes, Assoziatives. Der Text, der entsteht, enthält kaum noch harte Fakten. Die Tour in Sheffield beginnt gerade noch mit: „Meine Damen und Herren, willkommen in Paris …", schon findet man sich in Dresden, Pisa, Rom oder Delhi wieder. Eine abenteuerliche Reise, gecoacht von einem Reiseführer, der ebenso viele Fragen stellt, wie er falsche Antworten gibt, der seine privaten Geschichten erzählt, wo er wohnt und wo man den nächsten guten Pub findet, und der in einem Atemzug nicht nur eine Unmenge von Gerüchten, Vermutungen, offiziellen Versionen, Lügen und Märchen zu nennen vermag, sondern diesen noch zahlreiche eigene Vorschläge hinzugesellt. Eine Reise, die sich von der Stadt, wie man sie zu kennen glaubt, immer weiter entfernt.

Städte sind gute Orte für den Anfang einer Geschichte, und sie sind gute Orte für das Ende, aber für die Mitte muss man normalerweise etwas weiter weggehen, an einen Ort, der etwas, sagen wir mal, fernab liegt …

Eine magische Stadt, fernab aller Alltagserfahrungen, die man während der Tour beschrieben findet und die sich zu einem vielschichtigen, poetischen Textgewebe entwickelt, das sich nicht nur aus den Texten der Performer, sondern auch aus denen der Zuschauer und, nicht zu vergessen, den Benutzern und Bewohnern der Stadt zusammensetzt. Für den mitreisenden Zuschauer öffnet sich die Stadt zu einem komplexen Gebilde. Er ist Rezipient der vorgetragenen Erzählungen, und zugleich fügt er dem Stadttext seine eigenen Erinnerungen und Assoziationen hinzu. Auch seine Erkenntnisposition, seine Perspektive, ist eine eigenartige Mischform. Als Teil der Stadt, mitten in ihr, ist er umschlungen, und als solcher wird er von den Details, die sich ihm bieten, mitgezogen. Gleichzeitig ist er der Stadt aber auch enthoben, er kann sich distanzieren und seinen eigenen Text finden und erfinden. Er kann sich aus ‚göttlicher Perspektive' als auch aus der Perspektive des Flaneurs auf die Stadt beziehen. Aktiv ist er am Prozess des Überschreibens beteiligt und vermag der Situation des Gegebenen seine eigenen Varianten hinzuzufügen.

Es ist eine Reise als Versuch, einigen Dingen das Durchschaubare, das Offensichtliche zu nehmen, um eine schwebende und pulsierende Welt zu erschaffen, die sich, fern von der Realität, immer wieder neu bestimmt.

,Wir sind ab vom Weg ...' Ist das nicht die Definition von Lebendigkeit? Wenn die Sache, die lediglich als ein theatralischer Akt begonnen hatte, zu einem Ereignis wird? Wenn der Pförtner nervös zuckt und die Führer anscheinend den Weg nicht mehr wissen? Wo der sichere Weg zurück in den Alltag nicht mehr garantiert ist? (Tim Etchells)

In anderen Stücken von Forced Entertainment ist die Perspektive des Betrachters nicht mehr durch seinen physikalischen Ort bestimmbar, allerdings bleibt das Spiel mit der Art und Weise, wie der Raum von ihm erfasst und erfahren wird, erhalten. In The Travels

texts but also those of the audience and, not to be forgotten, those of the users and inhabitants of the city. For the audience on board the bus, the city opens up to form a complex shape. They become recipients of the narratives told by the performers and at the same time, they add their own memories and associations to the text of the city. Their own viewing position, their own perspective becomes a strange mixture of the information they receive and the material they project, remember or imagine. Immersed and engulfed by the city, the audience are drawn into the details offered to them. At the same time, they are removed from the city, able to distance themselves from it, able to find and invent their own texts. They can relate to the city from a 'divine perspective' as well as from the perspective of the *flâneur*. They are actively involved in the process of overwriting and are able to add their own variations to the existing situation.

This journey is an attempt to strip things of their transparency, their obviousness and create a hovering, pulsating world that keeps reinventing itself, far removed from any reality.

,We're off the route ...' Isn't that the definition of liveness? When the thing which began as nothing more than a theatrical act has turned into an event? When the gatekeepers twitch nervously and the guides appear lost? Where safe passage back to the everyday is no longer assured? (Tim Etchells)

In other pieces by Forced Entertainment, the perspective of the spectator cannot be determined by his physical location, although these pieces still play with the way in which space is processed and experienced. In the landscapes described by *The Travels,* the spectator cannot experience his own physical presence, as he is not able to turn around, move or direct his gaze according to his interests. Instead, the performers read to him the cities, places, locations and

Off the Route / Strategies and Approaches to the Appropriation of Space
Jenseits des Weges / Strategien und Aneignungsweisen des Raumes
Anke Scheper

streets they experienced in the past. The experience of these places is mediated, processed and filtered through the subjective lens of the performers. Each of them reconstructs and reads about their journeys, making *The Travels* a subjective map of emotional topographies.

The spectator sees things from diverse perspectives and witnesses subjective and private observations. The boundary between documentation, biography and invention can hardly be discerned; moreover, such a distinction is apparently of little interest here. Instead, the places described and the narratives associated with them are immediately recognisable as personal and imagined.

In *The Travels*, as in the other works described in this essay, the worlds shown differ from the world of hard facts: These works offer versions of that what we usually call reality, which is defined by the criteria of 'true' and 'false', and which we understand in everyday life as something homogeneous and singular. A rich reservoir of true stories that complement, overlap or contradict each other, and not one of them can be removed by Ockham's razor. It is a space that opens up into all directions – providing refuge for the magical, the dreamy and the factual at the same time, a space that grants the same claim to reality to all places, locations, landscapes and worlds that buzz around in our heads: "Ladies and Gentlemen, a story in the city should end with a long road running down into town. There should be people and shadows, there should be ghosts in it".

Translated by Benjamin Marius Schmidt

erfährt sich der Zuschauer nicht mehr als körperlich im Raum agierend, als Person, die sich drehen und wenden, nach eigenem Interesse hin- oder wegschauen kann, sondern ihm werden die von den Performern zuvor erfahrenen Städte, Orte, Plätze und Straßen vorgelesen. Die Orte sind mittelbar gegeben, über den Umweg der subjektiven Erfahrung der Performer. Jeder für sich rekonstruiert, erzählt und liest von seinen Reisen zu den vielen kleinen Plätzen. *The Travels* ist eine subjektive Landkarte emotionaler Topografie.

Als Zuschauer teilt man die verschiedenen Perspektiven und wird Zeuge sehr subjektiver und privater Betrachtungen. An kaum einer Stelle lässt sich die Grenze zwischen Dokumentation, Biografie und Erfundenem ausmachen, und tatsächlich ist das eine Unterscheidung, die hier von keinem Interesse mehr ist. Vielmehr sind die erzählten Orte und die mit ihnen assoziierten Erzählungen als persönliche und erzeugte Geschichten direkt erkennbar.

Hier und in den anderen beschriebenen Arbeiten zeigt sich eine Welt, die von der *hard fact world* bewusst verschieden ist: Sie sind Versionen von dem, was mit den Kriterien von ‚richtig' und ‚falsch' als ‚wirklich' bezeichnet und meist als etwas Homogenes und Singuläres verstanden wird. Ein reicher Fundus an wahren Geschichten, die sich ergänzen, überschneiden, ja sogar widersprechen können, ohne dass man eine von ihnen mit einem Ockham'schen Messer entfernen könnte. Es ist ein Raum, der sich in alle Richtungen öffnet – der Magisches, Geträumtes und Faktisches zugleich beherbergt, ein Raum, der all den Orten, Räumen, Landschaften und Welten, die in unseren Köpfen herumschwirren, den gleichen Anspruch an Wirklichkeit zuerkennt: „Meine Damen und Herren, eine Geschichte in der Stadt sollte mit einer langen Straße enden, die in die Stadt hinabführt, dort sollte es Menschen und Schatten, dort sollte es Gespenster geben."

Nights in this City

In the summer, when the earth changed, it rained for five months and in the silence that followed the end of the rain we GAVE UP WITH THE MESSAGES ALREADY. No answers came.

On leaving our room we became lost and were looking for each other, calling out in the dark streets.

I LOVE YOU MORE THAN ALL THE TELEGRAPH POLES IN THE WORLD we shouted.

VOICE OF HOPE we yelled and BIG WALL OF REASON.

That was a night of losing and of finding again, of losing and of finding, of losing and then of finding once again.

Emanuelle Enchanted

Emanuelle Enchanted

The Dusk of Language
The Violet Hour in the Theatre
of Forced Entertainment

Die Abenddämmerung der Sprache
Die blaue Stunde im Theater
von Forced Entertainment

Gerald Siegmund

Im dritten Teil von T.S. Eliots epochalem Gedicht *Das wüste Land* aus dem Jahr 1922, *Die Brandparole*, verhüllen Nebelschwaden die Stadt. Merkwürdige Gestalten, wie der Händler von Smyrna, von dem niemand weiß, ob er nicht schon längst tot ist, tauchen plötzlich wieder im Zwielicht auf, nur um sich kurz darauf im undurchdringlichen Dickicht den Blicken zu entziehen. Eine andere Zeit wird aufgerufen: die blaue Stunde, eine merkwürdige Zwischenzeit, in der die Dinge einen ganz besonderen Glanz bekommen. Es ist dies die Zeit, in der in Eliots Kabinett aus mythologischen Fragmenten eine eigentümliche Gestalt auftritt, die ungewöhnliche Fähigkeiten besitzt.

Zur lila Stunde, da sich Blick und Nacken
Vom Schreibtisch abwinkeln, da der
> *menschliche Motor im Leerlauf*
Pulst, so wie ein Taximotor ausgekuppelt
> *läuft und wartet,*
Seh ich, Teiresias, flatternd im Puls zwischen
> *zwei Leben,*
Greis, mit eines Weibes Zottelzitzen, wiewohl
> *blind,*
Zur lila Stunde das Zwielicht, das den Sinn
> *Heimwendet*

Wie Teiresias, der Seher, pulsieren auch die Stücke Forced Entertainments zwischen zwei

In the third part of T.S. Eliot's monumental poem *The Waste Land* of 1922, *The Fire Sermon*, fog covers up the city. Strange figures, such as the Smyrna Merchant, who is rumoured to be already dead, reappear in the twilight only to disappear shortly thereafter into an impenetrable thicket of text. A different kind of time is evoked: the violet hour, a strange zone of in-between, in which everything gains a particular brilliance. In this in-between period, a unique character with unusual capacities appears from Eliot's cabinet of mythological fragments.

At the violet hour, when the eyes and back
Turn upward from the desk, when the human
> *engine waits*
Like a taxi throbbing waiting,
I Tiresias, though blind, throbbing between two lives,
Old man with wrinkled female breasts, can see
At the violet hour, the evening hour that strives
Homeward

The works by the British group Forced Entertainment, much like Tiresias, the seer, hover between two lives. In their pieces, there are remarkably numerous violet hours – times in which the world appears in a particular state of

The Dusk of Language / The Violet Hour in the Theatre of Forced Entertainment
Die Abenddämmerung der Sprache / Die blaue Stunde im Theater von Forced Entertainment
Gerald Siegmund

arousal, temporarily suspending the usual course of events. This time is often crammed – as it is in Eliot's poem, in which an office clerk gets up from his desk, – with trivial and banal things, which now appear in a different light.

The time of the violet hour is a time of transition, in which awareness of the moment that has just passed slowly slides away, opening itself towards the future that has not yet arrived. In the moment of suspension, of hesitation, perception changes. Since the present crumbles away, certain things suddenly appear more clearly, while others gain additional dimensions. The habitual contours of the world lose definition and forgotten things become present again. In the violet hour, all aspects of time enter a strange union. Simultaneously present and absent, the past and the future perforate the present and make one feel something of the loss inherent in it.

As in *Emanuelle Enchanted*, this experience of altered perception and sensitivity to time might very well happen after nightfall. The performance narrates the story of a nocturnal car ride to the top of a hill. From this place, the performers look down on the lights of the city. They, too, inhabit a kind of twilight state at this point, half escaped from the city, yet continually tied to it; away from the nightlife, yet watching its goings-on from afar. Or perhaps, this uncertain in-between time occurs after a night of excess, as in *Pleasure*, when even light becomes torturous. In *Speak Bitterness*, the stage backdrop itself is literally blue. What at first seems to be a simple blue screen of a television studio, in which people feel compelled to make public confessions – as we know it from hundreds of talk shows – soon becomes an elegy for life in general. And yet other times, as in *And on the Thousandth Night …*, night already forms part of the title of the piece.

The violet hour is a time not alien to theatre in general. Theatre, after all, generates

Leben. Hier gibt es auffallend viele solcher blauen Stunden, in denen die Welt sich in einem besonderen Erregungszustand befindet, der den Gang der Dinge vorübergehend aussetzt. Oft ist diese Zeit auch wie in Eliots Gedicht, in dem sich ein Angestellter im Büro von seinem Schreibtisch aufrichtet, bei Forced Entertainment angefüllt mit banalen, alltäglichen Dingen, die in ein anderes Licht gerückt werden.

Die Zeit der blauen Stunde ist eine Zeit des Übergangs, in dem das Bewusstsein von dem, was eben noch war, langsam weggleitet, um sich für die Zukunft, die noch nicht da ist, zu öffnen. Im Moment des Innehaltens, des Zögerns, verändert sich die Wahrnehmung. Weil die Gegenwart wegbröselt, erscheinen manche Dinge mit einem Mal viel klarer. Andere gewinnen zusätzliche Aspekte, weil die gewohnten Konturen der Welt sich auflösen und vergessene Dinge plötzlich wieder präsent werden. In der blauen Stunde gehen alle Zeitaspekte eine merkwürdige Verquickung ein. Zugleich anwesend und abwesend, durchlöchern sie die Gegenwart und machen etwas von dem Verlust spürbar, der ihr unweigerlich innewohnt.

Dabei kann, wie in *Emanuelle Enchanted*, auch schon mal die Nacht bereits hereingebrochen sein. Immer wieder wird die Geschichte von einer nächtlichen Autofahrt hinauf auf eine Anhöhe erzählt, von wo aus die Performer hinunterschauen auf die Lichter der Stadt. Auch sie befinden sich in diesem Moment in einer Art Dämmerzustand, der Stadt halb entflohen, doch ihr immer noch verbunden, zum Nachtleben auf Distanz gerückt, ihr Treiben aus der Ferne beobachtend. Es kann wie in *Pleasure* die unbestimmte Zeit nach einer Nacht voller Ausschweifungen sein, in der selbst die Lust zur Qual wird. In *Speak Bitterness* ist der Bühnenhintergrund tatsächlich blau. Was zunächst als Blue Box eines Fernsehstudios gedacht ist, in dem sich Menschen einem merkwürdigen öffentlichen Geständniszwang unterwerfen, wie wir ihn aus Hunderten von

Talkshows kennen, wird jedoch bald zum Schwanengesang auf das Leben. Und manchmal, wie in *And on the Thousandth Night…*, ist die Nacht auch schon Teil des Titels.

Die blaue Stunde ist ein Zustand, der dem Theater generell nicht ganz fremd ist. Erzeugt es doch ein erhöhtes Bewusstsein von der Gegenwart, in der es unweigerlich spielen muss, ohne sich in bloßer Gegenwärtigkeit zu erschöpfen. Denn immer verweist es auf etwas, das nicht gegenwärtig ist, auf etwas, das hinter der Bühne und ihrem gegenwärtigen Leben liegt. Irgendwie ist es mitsamt den Menschen, von denen es handelt, immer auch aus der Zeit gefallen, die Bilanzierung eines Verlusts ebenso wie die Freude am Moment. Nicht zuletzt deshalb hat Teiresias seinen großen Auftritt ausgerechnet in der Dämmerung. Man könnte ihn mit gutem Gewissen zum Schutzheiligen aller Schauspieler machen. Wie sie ist er ein androgynes Zwitterwesen, vom dem eine große Faszination ausgeht, ein Seher, der blind ist und dessen Sehen im Gedicht und auf der Bühne vor allem ein Sprechen ist, das Vorstellungen hervorruft; ein Wiedergänger aus alten Zeiten, der bei den Mauern von Theben saß, als Ödipus die schreckliche Wahrheit über sich entdeckte und der Odysseus an jenem „Ort des Entsetzens", wie es im elften Buch von Homers *Odyssee* heißt, einem Spalt zwischen Erde und Totenreich, die Zukunft weissagte. Auch im Theater entsetzt sich die Welt. Sie setzt sich mit sich auseinander, indem die Toten von den lebenden Schauspielern Besitz ergreifen. Teiresias steht aber auch für ein Theater neben dem Theater. Er ist gerade nicht Ödipus, der tragische Held *par excellence*, dessen Drama auf der Bühne ausagiert wird. Er steht vielmehr für das Prinzip des Theaters: das des andauernden Verschwindens. Wo Teiresias gerade wieder herkommt, wohin er geht, weiß niemand. Sein Erscheinen ist stets gepaart mit einem Wiederaufleben der Geschichte, die er wiederholend zitiert, um ihr die Möglichkeit einer Veränderung in Aussicht zu stellen. Er steht für den performativen Aspekt des Theaters.

a heightened awareness of the present, of the 'here' and 'now' in which it must inevitably take place. On the other hand, it does not exhaust itself in the 'here' and 'now', because it always points to something that is not here and not 'now', something that lies beyond the stage and its life in the present. Somehow, the theatre and all the people it deals with seem to have fallen out of time. It is a medium which is at the same time the sum of its losses and the joy of its present moments. It is no coincidence that Tiresias's grand appearance happens precisely in twilight. With some justification, one might see him as a patron saint of actors. Like them, he is a fascinating androgynous hybrid creature, a revenant from old times, who sat by the walls of Thebes when Oedipus discovered the horrible truth about himself and who correctly predicted the future to Odysseus, while being in the "space of terror" – as the eleventh book of Homer's *Odyssey* calls it – a gap between the world and the realm of the dead. In the theatre, too, the world becomes terrified, dealing with itself by letting the dead take over the living actors. Yet Tiresias also represents a theatre beyond theatre. He is, however, not Oedipus, the tragic hero *par excellence*, whose drama is enacted on stage. Instead, he represents the principle of theatre itself: that of incessant disappearance. No one knows where Tiresias materialises from or where he goes after he's vanished. His appearance is tied to a re-enactment or re-living of history itself, which he repeats and quotes at the same time, thus opening it up to a possible change in the future. In this sense, Tiresias represents the performative aspects of theatre.

Performance, in certain Forced Entertainment pieces, primarily means talking, as those pieces are often composed largely of speech acts. Through various strategies, the performances constantly direct the viewers' attention towards the act of speaking itself. These strategies

Gerald Siegmund

The Dusk of Language / The Violet Hour in the Theatre of Forced Entertainment
Die Abenddämmerung der Sprache / Die blaue Stunde im Theater von Forced Entertainment

include reading out texts, addressing the audience from the front of the stage and avoiding all kinds of theatrical illusion. In *The Travels* and *Instructions for Forgetting*, for instance, the performers simply read stories from sheets of paper. The performers are seated at tables, inviting – and returning – the audience's gaze. Somewhere on the stage, there is a TV set, a screen, or an old blackboard on which words are occasionally written. Naked, without unnecessary adorning props or sets, the principle of speech itself becomes the real theme of the work. Tim Etchells trusts the power of language to conjure up imaginary worlds in the heads of the audience. The reality on stage is created through speaking alone, producing 'facts', or statements – images that become the basis for the performers' playful interaction.

Yet I wish to concentrate on a particular kind of speech. Forced Entertainment's work pushes to the fore a dimension of language which for whatever pragmatic reasons we cannot utilize or focus on in everyday life. In the speeches of the performers, language gains a corona or an additional echo chamber, which makes audible both the language's own disappearance and the disappearance of the world which that language has only just conjured up. It is a language of loss. This sense of loss becomes most evident in Forced Entertainment's six-hour performance *And on the Thousandth Night* …. The subject of the piece is storytelling itself and the time that passes while doing it. Four men and four women are seated on simple wooden chairs in a neat row at the front of the stage, framed by red velvet curtains. They stare into the audience. Barefoot and wrapped in red robes, wearing simple cardboard crowns on their heads, they are kings and queens for one night, telling stories to one another and to the audience. Each story starts with the ritual formula of fairy tales, "Once upon a time", and continues unfolding,

Performance, das heißt in den Stücken von Forced Entertainment vor allem Sprechen. Jedes ihrer Stücke besteht einzig und allein aus Sprechakten. Durch verschiedene Verfahren lenken sie Aufmerksamkeit stets auf den Akt des Sprechens selbst. Dazu gehören das Lesen vom Texten und das frontale Spiel an der Rampe, bei dem die Darsteller direkt ins Publikum sprechen, ebenso wie der Verzicht auf jedweden szenischen Illusionismus. So werden in *The Travels* und *Instructions for Forgetting* Geschichten einfach vom Blatt abgelesen. Die Darsteller sitzen an Tischen, auf die sich die Blicke der Zuschauer richten. Irgendwo im Raum steht ein Fernsehgerät, eine Leinwand oder eine alte Schultafel, auf die Worte geschrieben werden. Nackt, ohne schmückende Requisiten oder Kulissen und auf sich alleine gestellt, wird das Prinzip Sprechen zum eigentlichen Thema erhoben. Tim Etchells vertraut auf die Fähigkeit der Sprache, imaginäre Welten in den Köpfen der Zuschauer entstehen zu lassen. Nur durch das Sprechen wird die Realität der Bühne geschaffen, entstehen die Tatsachen, mit denen die Darsteller spielend umgehen müssen.

Doch es ist ein besonderes Sprechen, auf das ich hier meine Aufmerksamkeit richten will. In den Stücken von Forced Entertainment kommt eine Dimension der Sprache zum Vorschein, der wir aus pragmatischen Gründen im Alltag keine Beachtung schenken können. Im Sprechen der Performer bekommt die Sprache Höfe, die ihr eigenes Verschwinden und mit ihr das Verschwinden der Welt, die sie gerade noch heraufbeschworen hat, hörbar machen. Es ist eine Sprache des Verlusts. Am eindringlichsten macht das wohl ihre Sechs-Stunden-Performance *And on the Thousandth Night* … deutlich. Der Inhalt der Performance ist das Geschichtenerzählen selbst und die Zeit, die dabei verstreicht. Vier Männer und vier Frauen sitzen auf einfachen Holzstühlen in Reih' und Glied an der Rampe der mit roten Theatersamtvorhängen verhängten Bühne und blicken ins Publikum. Barfuß und in rote Umhänge gehüllt, einfache

Pappkronen auf dem Kopf tragend, sind sie Könige und Königinnen für eine Nacht, die sich und dem Publikum Geschichten erzählen. Jede beginnt mit der rituellen Formel „Es war einmal" des Märchens und dauert so lange, bis ein anderer sie mit einem „Stopp" unterbricht.

Nach einiger Zeit glaubt man in ihrem Wortwechsel mehrere Regeln ausmachen zu können. So wird immer dann unterbrochen, wenn jemand nicht weiter weiß, sich jemand langweilt, die Geschichte zu weit geht oder man den anderen mit seiner eigenen Version überbieten will. Der oder die Nächste muss ein Element der Geschichte aufgreifen, um sie fortzuspinnen. Keine Geschichte darf zweimal erzählt werden, was zu aberwitzigen Anknüpfungen und Perspektivwechseln führt. Märchenhaftes und Filmisches mischt sich mit Biblischem und Literarischem, Obszönes mit Zotigem, Absurdes mit Makabrem. Hinter dem Erzählen werden rasch individuelle Haltungen und persönliche Obsessionen deutlich, die für zusätzliche Spannung sorgen. Wer beleidigt ist, dass ihm eine Geschichte abgenommen wurde, oder wer einfach eine Pause braucht, nimmt seinen Stuhl und zieht sich in den Bühnenhintergrund zurück. Trotz zum Teil vorbereiteter Geschichten lebt *And on the Thousandth Night …* ganz aus dem jeweiligen Moment heraus. Wie sich die Darsteller gegenseitig die Geschichten abjagen, sie umdrehen und weiterspinnen, bevor sie erneut unterbrochen werden und der Gegner sich das Wort zurückerobert, das sind kleine dramatische Konflikte in Reinform. Keine der Geschichten wird zu Ende erzählt, bis ein ganzes Universum aus Geschichten entstanden ist, ein gewebter Teppich aus Erfahrungen und Phantasien, auf dem man sicher durch die Nacht fliegen kann. Denn hörten die Performer einmal auf zu erzählen, risse der Erzählfluss einmal ab, ereilte sie wie in der Geschichte von *Tausend und einer Nacht*, auf die der Titel anspielt, der sichere Bühnentod.

Forced Entertainment hat von der cleveren Scheherazade gelernt. Als die Wahl auf

improvised in real time, until another actor interrupts it by saying "Stop".

After some time, one notices what seem to be some of the rules behind this game. Interruptions seem to take place when someone loses the thread, when someone gets bored, when someone's story goes too far, or when someone tries to outdo the current story with a different version. The subsequent narrator may take up any element from the preceding story and continue from there, or else, start an entirely new narrative. Some stories come back in different versions, which creates absurd connections and wild changes of perspective. Fairy tale and film elements are mixed with Biblical and literary material, obscene and lewd stuff, absurd and macabre ingredients. Behind the storytelling, individual perspectives and obsessions of the performers soon become visible, creating additional tension. Any player who gets annoyed at having a story interrupted, or who needs a break, simply takes his or her chair and retires to the back of the stage, where a table laden with food and drinks provides refreshment. Despite its retelling of sometimes familiar tales, *And on the Thousandth Night … * thrives on moment-to-moment interaction. The way the actors fight over stories, turn them around, embellish and change them, produces interactions which are small dramatic conflicts in their purest form. No story is ever completed and the game continues until an entire universe of unfinished stories has materialised, a woven carpet of experiences and fantasies on which one can surely fly through the night. One might suspect that a certain stage death would await the performers if they suddenly ceased telling tales, if they allowed the flow of narrative to end – just as death threatens Scheherazade in the *Tales from a Thousand and One Nights*, to which the title of the performance refers.

Forced Entertainment have learned from the clever Scheherazade. When she is chosen to

Emanuelle Enchanted

become the next wife of the sultan, she decides to seduce him not only with her physical charms, but also with her words. The sultan, who is notorious for having his wives killed after the wedding night, is prevented from doing so by the very act of storytelling. For Scheherazade never completes any of her tales. When morning comes, she begins a new story to escape her death. Scheherazade's endless narration and the eroticism of her speech produce a language designed to prevent the extinction of her world and of the world in general, a speech wrested from death and designed to keep it at bay, because it delays presence, while making it felt with each word. Forced Entertainment's *And on the*

sie fällt, die nächste Ehefrau des Sultans zu sein, entschließt sie sich, ihn nicht nur erotisch zu umgarnen, sondern auch verbal. Der Sultan, der dafür berüchtigt ist, seine Ehefrauen nach der Hochzeitsnacht zu töten, wird durch das Geschichtenerzählen davon abgehalten, sie hinzurichten. Denn Scheherazade vollendet keine ihrer Geschichten. Am Morgen beginnt sie eine neue, um dem Tod zu entgehen. Das endlose Erzählen, die Erotik des Erzählens, ist ein Sprechen, das das Verlöschen ihrer Welt und der Welt verhindern soll, ein Sprechen, das dem Tod abgerungen ist und ihn in Schach hält, weil es die Abwesenheit hinauszögert, und sie doch mit jedem Wort spürbar macht. *And on the Thousandth Night …* ist ein Hochseilakt, dessen Faszination sich aus dem Absturz herleitet, der sich jede Sekunde ereignen könnte.

Die Sprache und das Sprechen sollen das Nichts, die Abwesenheit, die Leere der Welt, die sie ausfüllen, im Zaum halten. Darin, dass Sprache immer mit dem und gegen das Nichts spricht, liegt die melancholische Dimension des Sprechens, die man bei Forced Entertainment hören kann. Im Zentrum des melancholischen Komplexes macht Freud den Verlust eines Objekts oder eines Details am Objekt aus, von dem das melancholische Subjekt nicht weiß, wer oder was es ist. Im Gegensatz zum Trauernden kennt der Melancholiker den Gegenstand nicht, um den er trauert. Für Freud hat eine Identifikation mit dem verlorenen Objekt stattgefunden, das nun das Ich entleert. Im Anschluss an Freuds Theorie betonen zahlreiche Forscher den oralen Charakter der Melancholie. Melancholiker reden viel, sagen aber wenig, um mit ihren Worten die Leere zu füllen und zugleich auf sie hinzuweisen.

Die Lust des Melancholikers wächst während des Redens, sie wohnt der endlosen Bewegung der Sprache inne, die die Grenzen des Subjekts abläuft. Dadurch zerstreut sie einerseits das verlorene Objekt, das in der Sprache weggeschlossen bleibt wie in einer Krypta. Andererseits diffundiert sie damit auch das Subjekt selbst, das sich im Sprechen verliert. Die Sprache des Melancholikers, die schon Aristoteles in die Nähe der Sprache der Kunst und des Künstlers gerückt hat, ist die ursprüngliche symbolische Ersetzung eines imaginären Objekts, das, weil es in der Entwicklungsgeschichte des Kindes schon vor dem Spracherwerb verloren war, nur als Phantasma existiert hat. Die Wände des Subjekts bestehen demnach aus der Sprache, die das Subjekt spricht. Sprache errichtet einen Schutz gegen die Leere und erinnert zugleich an sie. Bricht der Schutzwall ein, fällt das Ich der Melancholie anheim. Dann verliert die Sprache ihren kommunikativen Charakter und bezieht sich nur noch auf sich selbst als Instanz, die, wie in den Stücken von Forced

Thousandth Night … is a similar kind of trapeze act whose fascination derives from the potential fall that could happen at any moment.

Language and speech are meant to reign in the nothingness, the absence, the void within the world which they fill. In the fact, that language always speaks in and against a void, lies the melancholy dimension of speech, which becomes audible in Forced Entertainment's pieces. For Freud, at the core of the melancholic complex is the loss of an object or of some aspect of an object which the melancholic subject does not and cannot know. In contrast to the mourner, the melancholic does not know the object for which he or she mourns. According to Freud, the melancholic suffers an identification with the lost object, a condition which now depletes the subject's sense of self. Following Freud's theory, many scholars emphasise the oral character of melancholy. Melancholics tend to talk a lot, supposedly in order to fill the void with their words – a process which, of course, also points to their loss.

The pleasure the melancholic gains while speaking, resides in this endless movement of language that marks the limits of the subject. In doing so, on the one hand, speech dissolves the lost object, which remains locked away in language as in a crypt. On the other hand, the excessive language also diffuses the subject itself, who loses him or herself in speaking. The language of the melancholic – compared by Aristotle to the language of art and the artist – can be seen as the original symbolic substitution for an imaginary object, an object which – since it was lost in the developmental history of the child even before its mastery of speech – only exists as a phantasm. The limits of the subject consist of the language spoken by the subject. Language erects a barrier against the void and at the same time reminds us of this void. If the barrier collapses, the self falls victim

to melancholy. In this instance, language loses its communicative character and only refers to itself as the force which – as in the pieces by Forced Entertainment – creates an imaginary world. In this state of self-referentiality, language makes audible the absence of the real world and of the subject at its edges. Forced Entertainment's work stages these very edges. On the edge, the extinction of language and of the world it has conjured up becomes audible. While disappearing, however, language glows and gains clarity as if each sentence in itself were already a small violet hour.

The principle of melancholy also takes over the actors. In Forced Entertainment's six-hour performance *12 am: Awake & Looking Down*, they use a large number of cardboard signs, each

Entertainment, diese Welt als das Imaginäre aller erst hervorbringt. In diesem Zustand der Selbstreferentialität macht sie an ihren Rändern die Abwesenheit der Welt und des Subjekts hörbar. Forced Entertainment inszenieren diese Ränder. An ihnen wird das Verlöschen der Sprache und der Welt, die sie heraufbeschworen hat, hörbar. Doch im Verschwinden glüht sie noch einmal auf und gewinnt an Klarheit und Leuchtkraft, gerade so, als wäre jeder Satz für sich schon eine kleine blaue Stunde.

Das Prinzip der Melancholie ergreift auch die Darsteller. In der Sechs-Stunden-Performance *12 am: Awake & Looking Down* agieren die Darsteller mit einer Reihe von Pappschildern, die sie sich gegenseitig vorhalten. Kostüme werden ebenso rasch gewechselt wie Haltungen und Positionen. Dabei erstarren

Dirty Work

216

The Dusk of Language / The Violet Hour in the Theatre of Forced Entertainment
Die Abenddämmerung der Sprache / Die blaue Stunde im Theater von Forced Entertainment

Gerald Siegmund

bearing a name or a description of a character, which they display to the audience, thus naming themselves. Costumes are switched as rapidly as postures and positions. Holding cardboard signs with names on them, the performers freeze into living pictures, and a combination of visual image and text lends them an emblematic quality. Who or what the performers represent in each instance depends entirely on the act of naming, performed by themselves or their colleagues on stage. Through the emblematic connection between language and image, the act of naming becomes a theatrical act. The meaning of these visual images is, however, without foundation. As quickly as it has appeared through the combination of language, costume and gesture, it disappears and flees again – just as the performers quickly move on to a new enactment after enactment. There is nothing to which one can attach oneself. In the endless rearrangement of the three elements – language, costume, and gesture – no performer really embodies any character. Which of the characters are played at any time seems simply to be the effect of a constant shifting and reshuffling of signs. The arbitrary nature of signification is most noticeable in the figures who are resting in the chair centre stage. Without expression, they slouch in the chair, as another performer repeatedly names them with a series of signs. Even though this process of being named and renamed has no apparent effect on their posture or demeanour, different characters with different stories emerge before our eyes. In these moments, the economy of transformation, however, does not reside in the figures themselves. The transformation is performed on them by another performer who momentarily changes them into something that he or she sees in, or projects onto, them. Under the gaze of the emblematic, as Walter Benjamin has described, anything can mean anything. Only by positing linguistic signs over and over

die Darsteller immer wieder zu lebenden Bildern, denen wie bei einem Emblem durch das Schild ein Motto beigefügt ist. Wer oder was die Darsteller gerade sind, hängt von ihrer jeweiligen Benennung ab, die vollkommen willkürlich durch die anderen Darsteller vorgenommen wird. In dieser Verbindung von Sprache und Bild zu einem Emblem wird der Akt der Bezeichnung durch Sprache zum theatralen Akt. Doch die Bedeutung der Bildfiguren gründet in nichts. Ebenso rasch wie sie durch die Kombination von Sprache, Kostüm und Geste entstanden ist, flieht sie im nächsten Moment wieder dahin. Es gibt nichts, an dem man sich festhalten kann. In den ständig wechselnden Kombinationen der drei Elemente verkörpert niemand irgendetwas. Welche Rollen die Figuren gerade einnehmen, erscheint lediglich als Effekt einer permanenten Verschiebung und Kombination von Zeichen. Besonders deutlich wird das bei den Figuren, die auf dem Sessel in der Bühnenmitte Platz genommen haben. Ausdruckslos lümmeln sie sich in verschiedenen Haltungen darauf herum, während ein anderer in rascher Folge irgendwelche Schilder vor sie hält. Obwohl sich an ihrer Haltung nichts ändert, entstehen vor unsrem geistigen Auge ganz andere Figuren mit einer ganz anderen Geschichte. Doch die Logik der Verschiebung liegt nicht in den Dingen selbst. Sie wird von einem anderen von außen an sie herangetragen, der sie für einen Moment zu dem macht, als was er sie sieht oder liest. Unter dem Blick des Emblematikers, wie ihn Walter Benjamin beschrieben hat, kann alles alles bedeuten. Nur wenn er immer wieder sprachliche Zeichen setzt, vermag er die Dinge vor dem Vergessen zu bewahren.

Im Prinzip ist daher jede Theateraufführung für sich genommen eine blaue Stunde, egal zu welcher Uhrzeit sie stattfindet. Theater ist immer ein Zwischenreich, in dem sich zwei Welten überlagern, die unsere und die fremde Welt der Bühne, in der Menschen, Zuschauer und Akteure zugleich sie selbst und andere sind, in der unsere Zeit und zugleich eine andere Zeit herrscht. Stellen Sie sich vor: *Dirty Work*. Eine wacklige Bretterbude, gerahmt von verblichenen roten Theatervorhängen, an der Rampe ein paar putzige Scheinwerfer gen Himmel gerichtet, bedeuten die Welt. Ein Mann und eine Frau sitzen auf zwei Stühlen, den Blick ins Publikum gerichtet, und reden. Eine zweite Frau hört zu. Sie bedient rechts hinten einen alten Plattenspieler, aus dem leise ein paar melancholische Klavieretüden zu hören sind. Charakterisiert sind sie alle nicht. Lediglich violettfarbene Kleider (für die Frauen) und ein grünes, ein wenig zu stark glänzendes Hemd (für den Mann) geben sie als Theaterfiguren zu erkennen. Tim Etchells hat zusammen mit den Schauspielern aus Floskeln, Redewendungen, Theaterkonventionen und altbekannten Bildern einen Theaterabend in vier Akten gebaut, der den ganzen Kosmos umspannt. Das Welt-Theater, das es an diesem Abend zu sehen gibt, findet einzig in unserem Kopf statt. Akt Eins beginnt mit einer Reihe von Atomexplosionen, Akt Zwei mit einem Kampf. Die Katastrophen des Jahrhunderts werden aufgerufen, Kennedy in seiner Limousine, das Massaker vom Tiananmen Platz, der Blutige Sonntag in Irland, eine vierte Wand wird gebaut, kritisiert und wieder eingerissen, Zeitgeschichte vermischt sich mit Alltäglichem. Wo Pathos droht, ist das Lächerliche nicht fern. Robin Arthur und Cathy Naden sprechen stets in klaren Hauptsätzen, neugierig auf das, was der andere sich ausgedacht hat, ehrgeizig angestachelt, die Ideen des anderen zu überbieten. Auch hier werden die Geschichten nur kurz angerissen. Im permanenten Wechsel der Szenarien, die von Satz zu Satz andere sind, heben sie sich nur kurz hervor, bevor sie wieder im Dickicht der Bilder verschwinden.

Die Katastrophen, von denen die beiden erzählen, kann man auf der Bühne nicht darstellen. Sie sind zu groß, zu unvorstellbar und 'einmalig', um sie zu repräsentieren. Man kann sie sich vorstellen, um mit diesen Vorstellungen die Leere zu füllen. Stellen Sie sich vor: Die Aufführungen von Forced Entertainment

again the emblematic is capable of preserving things from oblivion.

In principle thus, every theatrical performance is a violet hour, no matter when it takes place. Theatre is always an in-between realm, in which two worlds overlap – ours and the strange world of the stage; in which human beings – spectators and actors – are simultaneously themselves and others; in which our time rules, but simultaneously encounters another one. Imagine: *Dirty Work*. The whole world is signified by a ramshackle wooden stage, framed by faded red theatre curtains and a few ridiculous spots directed at the ceiling from the front of the stage. A man and a woman are seated on chairs, talking, their gazes directed towards the audience. A second woman listens. She fumbles with an old record player in the right back corner of the stage and from time to time, quietly plays some melancholy piano pieces. None of the three performers has a character. Violet dresses (for the women) and a green, rather too shiny shirt (for the man) are the only things that mark them as theatrical characters. Together with the actors, Tim Etchells has constructed a four-act performance made up of chance remarks, figures of speech, theatrical conventions and well-known images that somehow, nonetheless, encompasses the entire universe. The world-theatre that is shown, however, exists only in our heads. Act One starts with a series of nuclear explosions; Act Two with a fight. The catastrophes of the last century are called up: Kennedy in his limousine, the Tian An Men massacre, Bloody Sunday in Northern Ireland. A fourth wall is created, criticised, and torn down again. History is mixed with the quotidian. Wherever pathos is threatening to take over, the ridiculous is not far away. Robin Arthur and Cathy Naden always talk in straightforward sentences, curious about each other's inventions, ambitiously aiming to outdo each other. Here too,

The Dusk of Language / The Violet Hour in the Theatre of Forced Entertainment
Die Abenddämmerung der Sprache / Die blaue Stunde im Theater von Forced Entertainment
Gerald Siegmund

as in *12 am* and *And on the Thousandth Night …*, stories are only mentioned in passing. In the constant shifting between different scenarios, narratives only emerge briefly before dissolving again in the thicket of images.

The many catastrophic events that the two performers narrate cannot be represented on stage. They are too vast, too incredible and too "unique" to be shown. One can imagine them in order to fill the void with these ideas. Imagine: The performances by Forced Entertainment are allegories of the theatre, not because they tell us of the melancholy that affects the spectator when watching our catastrophic world, but because they stage the melancholy of performance itself: its permanent dwindling and disappearance in the twilight of time.

The lights go down on stage. Slowly, the violet hour in *Speak Bitterness* shades over into night, while from somewhere, a piano, once again, plays a melancholy tune. Slowly, lost and tired, the eight performers are swallowed by darkness. One after the other, they disappear from our field of vision, as if slowly fading away, entering a different sphere, a world to which we have no access. They disappear into the in-between world of the actors and the backstage, where they are not yet themselves again, but no longer the stage personae they invoked in text throughout the performance. "We had hopes, dreams and fears", Sue Marshall recalls her childhood and a youth that seems gone forever. "When we cried, we cried. That's all there is to say". Once the last harsh and discomfiting word has been spoken, speech is extinguished and silence enters. In this condition of silence, pain and loss echo on, though we do not know where they have come from and what has triggered them. What remains are the sheets of paper covering the tables: promised language, language read out, language cast aside, abject language. Dead letters not spoken or used by anyone any

sind Allegorien des Theaters, nicht etwa weil sie von der Melancholie erzählen, die den Zuschauer beim Betrachten unserer katastrophischen Welt befallen kann, sondern weil sie die Melancholie der Performance, ihr permanentes Dahinstürzen und Verschwinden im Dämmerlicht der Zeit, in Szene setzen.

Das Licht senkt sich über der Bühne. Langsam neigt sich die blaue Stunde in *Speak Bitterness* der Nacht entgegen, während irgendwo ein Klavier eine melancholische Weise spielt. Langsam, verloren und ermüdet werden die Darsteller von der Dunkelheit verschluckt. Einer nach dem anderen verschwindet aus unserem Gesichtsfeld, als blende er sich unmerklich vor unseren Augen aus und trete ein in eine andere, für uns nicht zugängliche Sphäre. Sie tauchen ein in die Zwischenwelt der Schauspieler, die Hinterbühne, wo sie noch nicht wieder sie selbst und schon nicht mehr der Andere sind, von dem sie zu uns gesprochen haben. „Wir hatten Hoffnung, Träume, Ängste", erinnert sich Sue Marshall an die Kindheit und die Jugend, die unwiederbringlich vorbei scheinen. „Wenn wir weinten, weinten wir. Mehr gibt es dazu nicht zu sagen." Nachdem das letzte, ebenso harte wie trostlose Wort verklungen ist, erlischt die Sprache, und Stille kehrt ein. In ihr klingt die Vorstellung von Schmerz und Verlust nach, von dem wir nicht wissen, woher er kommt und was ihn ausgelöst hat. Zurück bleiben die vollgeschriebenen Blätter auf den Tischen: versprochene Sprache, abgelesene Sprache und abgelegte Sprache. Tote Buchstaben, die von niemandem mehr gesprochen und verwendet werden und von denen daher zunächst alle Bedeutung abgefallen ist. Sprache in ihrem Status als Objekt, das nur darauf wartet, wie es Walter Benjamin wollte, von einem vorbeiflanierenden Melancholiker aufgegriffen, verwendet und mit Bedeutung belegt zu werden.

Komm, wir gehen, du und ich,
Wenn der Abend ausgestreckt ist am
                    Himmelsstrich
Wie ein Kranker äthertaub auf einem Tisch

Der Patient, um im Bild zu bleiben, das T. S. Eliot in seinem Gedicht *J. Alfred Prufrocks Liebesgesang* verwendet hat, ist die Sprache, die am Ende von *Speak Bitterness* tatsächlich auf dem Tisch liegt wie ein betäubter Patient. Es ist die Sprache, die wie die blaue Stunde zwischen zwei Leben pulsiert, zwischen Abwesenheit und Präsenz, ein Zwitterwesen wie Teiresias, von dem wir nicht wissen, was er sieht, nur dass er sieht. Eine solche Sprache ist eine permanente Aufforderung. Doch das Sehen bedeutet sowohl bei T. S. Eliot wie bei Forced Entertainment vor allem Sprechen. So können wir sicher sein, dass ein anderer Melancholiker in einer anderen blauen Stunde aus dem reichen Fundus von Forced Entertainment demnächst vorbeikommen wird, um die Sprache erneut aufzusammeln, um mit ihr die Leere, auf der sie gründet, und uns zu zerstreuen.

more and thus temporarily devoid of all meaning. Language in its status as object, only waiting, as Walter Benjamin had it, to be picked up again and invested with meaning by a passing melancholic.

Let us go then, you and I,
When the evening is spread out against the sky
Like a patient etherised upon a table.

The patient – to remain within the image that T.S. Eliot employed in his poem *The Love Song of J. Alfred Prufrock* – is language itself, which at the end of *Speak Bitterness* indeed lies on the table like a sedated patient. It is language that, like the violet hour, is throbbing between two lives, between absence and presence, a hybrid creature like Tiresias, of whom we do not know what he sees, only that he sees. Such a language is a permanent call to action. Yet seeing, in Eliot as well as in Forced Entertainment, primarily means speaking. Thus we can be sure that soon another melancholic figure will emerge from Forced Entertainment's rich storehouse during another violet hour, to collect language once again in order to fill the void on which it rests and, by doing so, divert us.

Translated by Gerald Siegmund

He wakes up at 3 am with the TV on, playing static and he thinks it's talking to him. It goes, "Shhhhhhhhh" and, like, he says, "What? What? What do you want?"

Disco Relax

Spin

No Mere Interlude
On Some Digital Works by Forced Entertainment

Mehr als nur ein Zwischenspiel
Zu einigen digitalen Werken Forced Entertainments

Astrid Sommer

Das Leben ist zu zeitgenössisch.

Don de Lillo, *Cosmopolis*

Life is too contemporary.

Don de Lillo, *Cosmopolis*

Theater, will es nicht gänzlich aus der Zeit fallen und jegliche Relevanz verlieren, kann sich der – zärtlichen, leidenschaftlichen oder kritischen – „Neigung auf die Maschinen hin" (Martina Leeker), die unseren Alltag bereits so fundamental transformiert haben, nicht verschließen. Da Theater per se eine hybride, intermediale Kunstform ist, wird es sich weiter verändern und doch seinen Kern bewahren: ein Schauspieler/Performer vor einem Publikum. Auch wenn Präsenz, der damit verbundene Begriff, kompliziert und vielschichtig geworden ist. Es ist im zurückliegenden Jahrzehnt deutlich geworden, dass die darstellenden Künste auf der Suche sind, dass sie etwas Anderes, Neues entstehen lassen müssen – zwischen Leib und Medien, wie Hans-Thies Lehmann feststellt – und nicht bloß die von der Medien- oder Filmkunst (und natürlich der Industrie) entwickelten Konzepte, Apparate und Interfaces auf die Bühne transferieren können oder wollen: Es geht eher um „Abweichung vom medialen Dispositiv" (Lehmann), auch um Reduktion, um Verlangsamung, um die hartnäckige, immer wieder neu zu formulierende Frage leiblicher Präsenz und Ko-Präsenz.

Tim Etchells schrieb 1995, dass man „über Technologie nachdenken, sie benutzen muss, denn am Ende ist sie im Blut. Techno-

If theatre is not to fall behind the times and lose all relevance, then it obviously has to heed that affectionate, passionate or critical "inclination towards the machines" (Martina Leeker) which have already brought about so radical a transformation of our daily lives. Being *per se* a hybrid, intermedia art form, theatre will continue to change. Yet its core – an actor/performer in front of an audience – will remain the same, even if the associated notion of presence has become complex and multilayered. The past decade has shown that the performing arts are seeking an alternative route, are having to develop something new and different – something *between* body and media, as Hans-Thies Lehmann says – instead of simply transferring to the stage the concepts, machines and interfaces developed in the fields of film and media art (and, of course, by commercial ventures). For the performing arts, it is more a question of "divergence from the technical apparatus of the media" (Lehmann), of reduction, of deceleration, of addressing and repeatedly reformulating the stubborn question of physical presence and co-presence.

Back in 1995, Tim Etchells stated that "you have to think about technology, you have to use it, because in the end, it is in your blood.

Technology will move in and speak through you, like it or not. Best not to ignore". At the same time, however, he made it clear that Forced Entertainment have no interest whatsoever in putting technology on the stage purely in order to play with special effects and hi-tech equipment. On the contrary: Forced Entertainment have in their work for the theatre increasingly returned to the essential – one might also say traditional – conditions of the stage, to theatre degree zero: the self-revealing actor, live, with nothing other than body and voice vis-à-vis the audience. Confessing, as in *Speak Bitterness* (1994); telling stories to get through the night, as in *Who Can Sing a Song to Unfrighten Me?* (1999); or even inventing the whole theatre/the whole world, as in *Dirty Work* (1998). In general, the sets look rough, thrown together, with lighting, props and action kept to a minimum. Nevertheless, the ensemble's work for the theatre is anything but backward-looking. It always addresses, no matter how implicitly, the fact that "technology (from the phone and the walkman upwards) has re-written and is rewriting bodies, changing our understanding of narratives and places, changing our relationship to culture, changing our understanding of presence" (Etchells), as well as the way these changes are taking effect. This position appears as an aspect of something one

logie wird uns durchdringen und durch uns sprechen, ob wir das wollen oder nicht. Besser, sie nicht zu ignorieren." Im selben Text wird allerdings klargestellt, dass es Forced Entertainment keineswegs darum geht, Technologie auf die Bühne zu bringen. High-Tech-Experimente und -Effekte wird man bei ihnen vergeblich suchen. Im Gegenteil: In ihrer Theaterarbeit sind sie mehr und mehr zurückgegangen zu den wesentlichen – man könnte auch sagen: traditionellen – Bedingungen von Theater, zu seinem Nullpunkt: der sich entblößende Schauspieler, live, mit nichts als Körper und Stimme als Gegenüber des Publikums, bekennend wie in *Speak Bitterness* (1994), mit Geschichten erzählen die Nacht herumbringend wie in *Who Can Sing a Song to Unfrighten Me?* (1999) oder auch das ganze Theater (die ganze Welt) im Erzählen erfindend wie in *Dirty Work* (1998). Das Bühnenbild wirkt meist roh zusammengeschustert, Licht, Requisiten, Aktion sind auf ein Minimum reduziert. Und trotzdem ist auch die Theaterarbeit von Forced Entertainment alles andere als rückwärtsgewandt. Dass und auf welche Weise, wie Tim Etchells schreibt, „Technologie (angefangen bei Telefon und Walkman) dabei ist, unseren Körper neu zu schreiben, unser Verständnis von Erzählung und Ort, unser Verhältnis zur Kultur, unser Verständnis von Präsenz zu verändern", wird, wie implizit auch immer, thematisiert. Es ist Teil dessen, was man

Down Time

als Programm von Forced Entertainment ausmachen könnte, was all ihren Arbeiten letztendlich zugrunde liegt, ihr Ethos, ihr immer wieder verfolgtes, zuweilen verfehltes, aber nie aufgegebenes Ziel: „Gleichzeitig die Schönheit und den Horror des modernen Lebens zu zeigen, offen über diese Welt zu sprechen ohne die Komplexität, die die Bedingung für Wahrhaftigkeit ist, auch nur für einen Moment auszulöschen" (Etchells).

Seit etwa Mitte der 90er Jahre verfolgen Tim Etchells und Forced Entertainment die Auseinandersetzung mit anderen Medien allerdings auch ganz explizit: durch die Realisierung von Projekten außerhalb des Theaterkontextes, besonders in gemeinsamen Arbeiten mit dem Fotografen Hugo Glendinning. Forced Entertainment war nie sonderlich interessiert an einer puristischen Sichtweise, was Genre, Grenzen und vorgegebene Kontexte betrifft – für sie bedeutet die Arbeit mit Video, Fotografie oder digitalen Medien keinen Bruch, sondern das konsequente Weiterverfolgen ihrer Themen und Obsessionen mit anderen Mitteln, aber mit der gleichen Leidenschaft und Virtuosität wie in ihren Bühnenstücken. Und das macht sie zu einer Ausnahmeerscheinung.

Dem Meisterwerk *Nightwalks* (1998, CD-ROM) gingen intensive Vorarbeiten und ein erstes Projekt für CD-ROM, *Frozen Palaces* (veröffentlicht 1999) voraus. Beide Arbeiten benutzen als Ausgangsmaterial inszenierte Fotografien, die mit Hilfe des Programms Quick-Time VR zu navigierbaren und miteinander verbundenen Panoramen zusammengefügt sind. Beide spielen mit der unheimlichen Erfahrung der stehen gebliebenen Zeit in den Stillfotografien – nur die Betrachterin ist frei, sich per Mausbewegung durch die eingefrorenen Szenen zu bewegen. Während das Szenario von *Frozen Palaces* aus den Innenräumen eines einzigen Hauses besteht und die Anzahl der Szenen damit begrenzt und überschaubar ist, ist *Nightwalks* ein Spaziergang durch unwirtlich-unwirkliche Stadtlandschaften mit einer Vielzahl von Orten, in denen man sich unweigerlich verirrt und verliert.

might see as the programme of Forced Entertainment, as something ultimately underlying all their works, as their ethic, as a goal relentlessly pursued – not always attained, but never abandoned: "To present the beauty and the horror of modern life at the same time; to speak of this world frankly without for one moment erasing the complexity that makes it true" (Etchells).

Since the mid-1990s, however, Tim Etchells and Forced Entertainment have also made their investigation of other media entirely explicit by realizing projects outside the context of theatre, especially in collaborative works with the photographer Hugo Glendinning. Forced Entertainment were never particularly interested in a purist perspective on genre, boundaries, and predefined contexts. For them, work with video, photography or digital media does not represent a rupture; instead, it is a logical pursuit of their topics and obsessions – using different means, but retaining the passion and virtuosity of their theatre pieces. And that is what makes them exceptional.

The masterpiece *Nightwalks* (1998, CD-ROM) was preceded by intensive research and development as well as by the initial CD-ROM project *Frozen Palaces* (published 1999). Both works use as basic material staged photographs which, with the aid of QuickTime VR software, are linked up into navigable, interconnected panoramas. The two CD-ROMs play with the disquieting sensation that the still images convey: that of time being halted – and only the viewer, by moving the mouse, has the freedom to travel through the frozen scenes. Whereas the scenario of *Frozen Palaces* is based on the rooms inside a single house, thus limiting the number of possible scenes, the walk through the inhospitable, unreal cityscapes of *Nightwalks* abounds with locations, inevitably leading you astray.

All the photographs in *Nightwalks* were taken in London and Sheffield between midnight and dawn. And that is also the best time to experience the CD-ROM. "Night is the text to a secret history, night is a key to the past" (Luc Sante). The streets are deserted and dark, the light eerily unreal. There is the occasional encounter with individual members of Forced Entertainment – strangely forlorn figures, sometimes in a straw skirt, sometimes in a wedding dress, now as a horse or an angel, then as a gangster, or a pair of lovers, or a sleepwalker, and at times in guises familiar from stage productions such as *Pleasure*. These personae simultaneously function as hot spots, connecting points, which enable the viewer to travel to different locations and scenes. The scenes are linked by the logic of poetry, not geography. Like in so many other works by Forced Entertainment, stories are merely alluded to. It is left up to the viewer to weave them further, to invent them on the basis of the key figures and hints – something that the images almost force you to do.

Quotations from a Ruined City

As I borrow the title of a piece by Reza Abdoh, I think of how the city and its conditions provide the framework for so many works by Forced Entertainment. The city – the former manufacturing city of Sheffield as the physical environment of the company and equally, a more general notion of the city – serves as a backdrop for commenting upon present-day life. Tim Etchells describes the importance of urban life and "the joy of living in fractious, debatable space, living subject to contradictory needs, desires and rules". If one agrees with Ulrich Beck that "the city symbolizes the laboratory of civilization", it is only logical that a company that sees their work as relevant to modern life, and their role as seismographers of the present, would use as source of inspiration, as metaphor and as subject, this space – their own environment, post-industrial,

Alle Aufnahmen entstanden in London und Sheffield, zwischen Mitternacht und Morgengrauen. Und das ist auch die beste Zeit, sich *Nightwalks* anzuschauen. „Die Nacht ist der Text für eine verborgene Geschichte, die Nacht ist der Schlüssel zur Vergangenheit." (Luc Sante) Die Straßen sind ausgestorben, das Licht unwirklich-unheimlich. Ab und zu begegnet man dem Personal von Forced Entertainment – merkwürdig verlorene Gestalten, mal im Baströckchen, mal im Hochzeitskleid, als Pferd oder Engel, mal Gangster, mal Liebespaar oder Schlafwandler, bisweilen vertraut aus den Bühnenstücken. Die Personen sind gleichzeitig *hot spots*, Verbindungspunkte, durch die man zu anderen Orten und Szenen gelangen kann. Die Verbindungen zwischen den Szenen gehorchen keiner geografischen, sondern einer poetischen Logik. Geschichten sind hier, wie in so vielen anderen Arbeiten von Forced Entertainment, lediglich angedeutet und es bleibt dem Betrachter überlassen, sie mithilfe der Schlüsselfiguren und Hinweise weiterzuspinnen, zu erfinden – die Bilder zwingen förmlich dazu.

Quotations from a Ruined City

Indem ich diesen Titel eines Stücks von Reza Abdoh entleihe, denke ich darüber nach, wie sehr die Arbeiten von Forced Entertainment durch den städtischen Kontext geprägt sind. Die Stadt – die Ex-Industriestadt Sheffield als konkreter Lebensraum der Truppe ebenso wie Stadt als allgemeinere Idee – dient als Folie für die Kommentierung unserer Gegenwart. Tim Etchells beschreibt das, wenn man so will, ‚städtische Lebensgefühl', um das es ihnen geht, mit „der Freude am Leben in reizbaren, strittigen Räumen, widersprüchlichen Bedürfnissen, Wünschen und Regeln." Geht man mit Ulrich Beck davon aus, dass „die Stadt das zivilisatorische Laboratorium symbolisiert", so ist es nur konsequent, dass ein Ensemble, das sich zuallererst als Zeitgenossen, als Seismografen des Gegenwärtigen versteht, vor allem anderen diesen ihren Lebensraum –

Frozen Palaces

run-down, conflict-ridden, devoid of all romanticism, but indubitably alive.

Terry: Remember we used to draw cities in the mud on the ground? Well now we're almost living in the places that we drew.

(Emanuelle Enchanted)

And so it is scarcely surprising that in another project Forced Entertainment, together with Hugo Glendinning, chose to devise an entire city. The installation (or, perhaps more aptly, sculpture) *Ground Plans for Paradise* was created in 1994 as a model city consisting of one thousand balsa-wood tower blocks, on which the only details are roughly cut-out holes for windows. These uniform wooden buildings vary merely in height, but each one of them and the surrounding streets bears a name – ranging from The Big World Building to Helium House, Silent Hotel and Voodoo Tower, from Aluminium Square to Daydream, Delirium and Love Street. The distinction between the buildings, their individuality, is fictional rather than visual. As in many other works by the ensemble, the stories are not told. The "speaking" names are only clues for invention, for imagination – an invitation to speculate. Looking down at the model, I would love to be small enough to dive into this city, to wander along the streets, from house to house, name to name, from one possible story to the next. Who lives in Blue Screen House, whom might I meet on Iron Street, and what happens in Post-Babel Tower? However, this beautifully lit model, seemingly so inviting, remains hermetic and impenetrable, refuses to accommodate me.

In 1998, in a further development of *Ground Plans*, Forced Entertainment implemented their model city as a net project entitled *Paradise* (http://www.lovebytes.org.uk/paradise/). On the web you can zoom into this imaginary city,

postindustriell, verkommen, konfliktreich, fragmentarisch, offen, jenseits aller Romantik, aber ohne Zweifel lebendig – als Inspirationsquelle, als Metapher, als Thema benutzt.

Terry: Erinnerst du dich, dass wir Städte in den Matsch gezeichnet haben? Jetzt leben wir fast schon in den Räumen, die wir zeichneten.

(Emanuelle Enchanted)

Und so verwundert es kaum, dass Forced Entertainment zusammen mit Hugo Glendinning gleich eine ganze Stadt entworfen haben: *Ground Plans for Paradise* entstand 1994 zunächst als Installation, oder, besser vielleicht, Skulptur: Modell einer Stadt, bestehend aus 1000 Balsaholztürmen, aus denen lediglich grob Fensterlöcher ausgeschnitten sind. Diese 1000 Holzhochhäuser sind unterschiedlich hoch, sehen ansonsten aber alle gleich aus. Doch jedes von ihnen hat einen Namen, ebenso wie jede der umgebenden Straßen benannt ist: von The Big World Building zu Helium House, Silent Hotel und Voodoo Tower, von Aluminium Square zu Daydream-, Delirium- und Love Street. Die Unterscheidbarkeit der Häuser und Straßen, ihre Individualität, ist also weniger visuell als fiktional. Auch hier werden keine Geschichten erzählt – die sprechenden Namen sind lediglich Einladungen an die Betrachterinnen zur Spekulation, zum Erfinden der vielen möglichen Geschichten. Wenn ich das Modell betrachte, wünschte ich mir, ich wäre klein genug um in diese Stadt eintauchen, durch ihre Straßen laufen zu können, von Haus zu Haus, von Name zu Name, von einer möglichen Geschichte zur nächsten. Wer wohnt im Blue Screen House, wem könnte ich in der Iron Street begegnen und was passiert im Post-Babel Tower? Doch das wunderbar beleuchtete Modell verschließt sich diesem Wunsch, nimmt mich nicht auf – es bleibt hermetisch und undurchdringlich.

Forced Entertainment entwickelte *Ground Plans* weiter: 1998 wurde das Stadtmodell als Internet-Projekt mit dem Titel *Paradise* realisiert (http://www.lovebytes.org.uk/paradise/):

Hier, im Netz, ist es möglich, sich hineinzu-zoomen in die imaginäre Stadt, sie Haus für Haus, Straße für Straße zu erkunden. Man kann per Mausklick durch die verschiedenen Viertel flanieren, man kann die Häuser ‚bewohnen' – mit Texten – und kann die Geschichten anderer Bewohner entdecken, indem man die jeweiligen Häuser besucht. Als das Projekt vorgestellt wurde, waren alle Häuser leer; eine offene Einladung, die Assoziationen und Ge-schichten manifest werden zu lassen durch in-dividuelle Textbeiträge. „Eine Utopie braucht einen unbewohnten oder unbewohnbaren Ort und gleichzeitig Menschen und Material, um sich zu entfalten" (Boris Groys). In die-sem Sinne ist *Paradise* durchaus ein utopischer Ort, eine Gemeinschaft, die von vielen verschie-denen Stimmen gebildet wird. Jedoch gibt es keine direkte Kommunikationsmöglichkeit zwischen den Besuchern – die Texte sind lediglich Spuren einer imaginären Präsenz.

Die Stadt war von Anfang an als Meta-pher und Mythos mit der Entwicklung des Internet verbunden. Zahlreiche Künstler- und andere Gruppen entwickelten virtuelle Städte im Netz, wobei überwiegend die positiven, die utopischen, die demokratischen, die kommu-nikativen Elemente – oft überaus naiv – im Vordergrund standen. Im Gegensatz zu Wer-ken der Netzkunst, die die behaupteten posi-tiven kommunikativen Strukturen des Netzes vor allem durch „Dysfunktionalisierungen der Software" (Hans-Peter Schwarz) kritisch kom-mentieren und unterlaufen, nutzt *Paradise* die technischen Möglichkeiten optimal für einen poetischen Kommentar, der über die Fragwür-digkeit der Netzutopien keineswegs hinweggeht. Die Häuser, aus denen *Paradise* besteht, sind keine virtuellen, ‚begehbaren' 3D-Konstruk-tionen, sondern fotografische Ausschnitte – bestenfalls Metaphern, eher aber Erinnerungen, nicht frei von Melancholie. Die Abbildungen variieren nur zwei verschiedene Hausansichten, der schräge Anschnitt evoziert den Eindruck des Untergehens. Wie schon im Modell geht es nicht um Repräsentation oder Simulation von Realität, sondern um Freiräume für

explore it building by building, street by street. With a click of the mouse, you can move through the various districts, even 'move into' a house by contributing a text for it, and discover the stories of other contributors by visiting the houses they have 'moved into'. The buildings were all vacant when the project was launched, inviting visitors to "join the community" and through individual texts make manifest their fantasies and stories. "In order to develop, a utopia needs an uninhabited or uninhabitable place and also people and material" (Boris Groys). In that sense, *Paradise* is a utopian place, a community, inhabited by many individual voices. Yet no direct communication is possible among the contributors. Instead, the texts and buildings resonate the imaginary presence of their visitor-occupants.

People associated the city with the inter-net from the very start – as both a metaphor and a myth. Any number of (artists') groups developed virtual cities on the net, and tended to emphasize – sometimes naively – its positive, utopian, democratic and communicative aspects. Unlike works of net art that primarily use "dys-functionalizing software" (Hans-Peter Schwarz) to undermine the purportedly positive commu-nication structures of the internet, *Paradise* makes optimum use of current technical possibilities to produce a poetic comment that by no means ignores the questionable nature of utopian net visions. The buildings in the net version of *Paradise* are not virtual 3-D constructions the visitor can 'enter', but photographic cut-outs – metaphors at best, memories tinged with melan-choly. Only four different views are offered, in-cluding a slanting angle evoking a sinking, slight-ly apocalyptic feeling. As with the physical model of *Ground Plans*, the piece doesn't aim to rep-resent or simulate reality, but to offer space for fiction, for fantasies about things not, or per-haps no longer, existing in a certain form.

Draw a map for me. Go on draw. Show me which roads are safe, which places I may sleep in without fear for my life. Tell me which of these cities still function and who lives in them. Does the phone system operate round here? Show me the places where I can still fall in love, show me the places where I can still believe in something. Would this be a good place to raise a kid? Would this be a good place for a party? (Hidden J)

Paradise, like *Ground Plans* and *Nightwalks*, is reminiscent more of (anti-)utopian "ruined cities" from *Blade Runner* to Reza Abdoh, of a sphere in which the body still matters as something which can (be) hurt and even die, than of the antiseptic and safe web spaces in which, apparently, there is neither ageing nor death, in which even trash doesn't stink, and everyone and everything pretends to be accessible at any time. *Paradise* forces us to rethink the shape of this strange parallel world with its invitation to become immersed, to leave the body behind, to assume any desired identity and change it at random; this world where the Other can be identical with a 'real life' person, with a fictional figure, or even a bot – or a mixture of all three. It is a world where conversation with a stranger can be so surprisingly and deceptively intimate, and where we are confronted with a constant shift between the feeling of being very close and very far apart. *Paradise* reminds us that we mistakenly associate the concept of permanent (electronic) availability with interpersonal communication. A 'genuine' encounter inevitably involves risk and responsibility, and does in fact require co-presence – an insight that echoes the experience imparted throughout the performances of Forced Entertainment and constituting their strength, their sorrowing, their solace.

Fiktionen, für Fantasien über das so nicht oder vielleicht nicht mehr existierende.

Zeichne mir eine Karte. Mach weiter. Zeig mir, welche Straßen sicher sind, wo ich schlafen kann ohne um mein Leben zu fürchten. Sag mir, welche der Städte noch intakt sind und wer dort lebt. Funktioniert das Telefonsystem hier noch? Zeig mir die Orte, an denen ich mich noch verlieben kann, zeig mir die Stellen, wo ich noch an etwas glauben kann. Wäre das ein guter Ort, ein Kind großzuziehen? Wäre das ein guter Ort für eine Party? (Hidden J)

Paradise, wie auch *Ground Plans* und *Nightwalks*, erinnert eher an die (Anti-) Utopien der *ruined cities* von *Blade Runner* bis Rezah Abdoh, an eine Sphäre, in der der Körper – verletzlich, sterblich – noch eine Rolle spielt, als an die antiseptischen und gefahrlosen Räume des *World Wide Web*, in denen es weder Altern noch Tod zu geben scheint, in denen selbst Müll nicht stinkt und jeder und alles zugänglich zu sein vorgibt. *Paradise* legt uns nahe, die Form dieser merkwürdigen Parallelwelt zu überdenken, dieser Welt, die uns einlädt, einzutauchen, den Körper zurückzulassen, jedwede Identität anzunehmen oder beliebig zu wechseln. Diese Welt, in der der Andere identisch mit einer Person des ,wirklichen Lebens' sein kann, oder ein fiktionaler Charakter, oder ein *bot* – oder eine Mischung aus all dem. In der wir ständig das Gefühl extremer Nähe vorgegaukelt bekommen und doch mit größter Ferne, Fremdheit und Verlorenheit konfrontiert sind. *Paradise* erinnert uns daran, dass das Konzept ständiger Verfügbarkeit nur fälschlicherweise mit zwischenmenschlicher Kommunikation in Verbindung gebracht wird, dass der ,wahren' Begegnung immer auch Risiko und Verantwortung innewohnt und sie tatsächliche Ko-Präsenz voraussetzt. Mit dieser Erkenntnis knüpft *Paradise* an Erfahrungen an, die der Zuschauer in den Performance-Projekten von Forced Entertainment immer wieder macht und die ihre Stärke sind, ihre Trauer, ihr Trost.

Ich habe etwas verloren, dadurch habe ich Sehnsucht. Das setzt den lebendigen Menschen in Gang. Das Leben ist in dieser Hinsicht indirekt und sucht etwas, das verloren ging. Wie man weiß, wiederholen sich die 37 Grad der Urmeere, aus denen wir kommen, verblüffender Weise in unseren Körpern. Auch der Salzgehalt der Urmeere entspricht genau dem Salzgehalt unserer Nieren. Es scheinen in der Entwicklung, in einer enormen Erinnerungsfähigkeit, Glücksmomente verborgen zu sein, die Millionen Jahre zurückliegen, nach denen sich die Zellen zurücksehnen, ohne dass wir davon wissen.

(Alexander Kluge, *Die Sehnsucht der Zellen*)

Warum ist es so anrührend und so unvergesslich, wenn Cathy Naden sich (zum Sterben) in der Mitte der Bühne niederlegt (wie ein verwundetes Tier) und dem Publikum erzählt, dass wir durch die Art und Weise, wie sie sich niederlegt, zu Tränen gerührt sein werden, und zwar so sehr, dass wir noch weinen werden, wenn die Vorstellung zu Ende geht, dass wir noch Weinen werden, wenn wir zu Hause ankommen, wenn wir einschlafen, wenn wir aufwachen, dass wir auch am darauf folgenden Tag, in der nächsten Woche, ja, dass wir bis an unser Lebensende weinen werden? Weil sie die Sehnsucht benennt, dass der Theaterabend über sich hinausweist, ja, unser Leben verändern könnte? Weil diese Szene so klein, leise und bescheiden und gleichzeitig so allumfassend ist? Weil es so grotesk und so offensichtlich unzutreffend ist? Weil es eingebettet ist in das Chaos und die Hässlichkeit der Show, ihre Radikalität und Ehrlichkeit? Weil es konterkariert wird durch Terry O'Connors übersteigerten Aktionismus, ihr Schreien, ihr immer verzweifelteres sich mit Wasser überschütten und sich in zu kurze, zu enge, zu geschmacklose Kleider zwängen während des gesamten Abends (*Work-in-Progress/Bloody Mess*, 2003)?

Diese Szene, ihre prekäre Balance von Lebendigkeit und Todesahnung, führt zurück

I have lost something, and this loss makes me yearn. That sets in action the living person. In this regard, life is indirect and seeks something that was lost. As we know, the 37 degrees of the primeval seas from which we originate is – astonishingly – reproduced in the temperature of our bodies. The salt content of these seas is likewise exactly duplicated by that of our kidneys. Evolution, with its vast capacity for recollection, apparently conceals moments of happiness stretching back millions of years and for which the cells yearn without us knowing anything about it.

(Alexander Kluge, *Die Sehnsucht der Zellen*)

Why is it so touching and unforgettable when Cathy lays herself down (to die) in the middle of the stage (like a wounded animal), and tells the audience that we will be moved to tears by the way she lies down, and in fact to such an extent that we will still be weeping when the show is over, still be weeping when we get home, when we fall asleep, wake up, that we will still be crying the next day, the next week, and indeed for the rest of our lives? Because this scene names our yearning for an evening at the theatre to have a lasting impact, one that might even change our lives? Because the scene is so small, quiet and modest yet so all-embracing? Because it is so grotesque and so obviously inappropriate? Because it is embedded in the chaos and the ugliness of the show, in its radicalism and honesty? Because it is counteracted by Terry's exaggerated actions, her wailing, her dowsing herself in water, her getting increasingly more desperate in the course of the evening, her forcing herself into dresses that are too short, too tight, too tasteless (*Work in Progress/Bloody Mess*, 2003)?

This scene, fundamentally live yet so very bound up with death, leads us back to Heiner

Müller, who did not tire of repeating that the transformation of death is what is essential about theatre. That "not the presence of the living actor or living spectator, but the presence of the potentially dying one" is specific to the theatre. Peggy Phelan demonstrated that, astonishingly, Forced Entertainment make it possible to experience this fundamental propensity of the theatre even in the CD-ROM project *Frozen Palaces*: "Hugo Glendinning, the photographer, exposes the *tableaux vivants* of an oddly familiar theatre of death. The spectator's silent scrolling through virtual space carries the aroma of the belated and the posthumous."

Renate Klett called this inherent balance in the work of Forced Entertainment "sprightly mourning, desolate beauty, a dance of the soul on the blade of the knife"; Ron Vawter described it – in an interview with Tim Etchells – as "connecting to the past with an eye to the future". Even in the video works (produced by Forced Entertainment and sometimes made in collaboration with Hugo Glendinning, or other artists and performers), Tim Etchells casually and effortlessly achieves this necessary degree of presence and authenticity, this mixture of mourning and tenderness, of frankness and inconsistency. In *Down Time* (performance / video, 2001), Tim Etchells films himself, looking into the camera, silent, thinking. His voiceover commentary tries to describe what he was thinking from moment to moment. His thoughts revolve around farewells he has experienced – cheerful, sad or moving – or more broadly, around people's attempts to use cameras and other gadgets to negate the necessity of parting. Shortly before the end of the video, this face, this human being looks especially vulnerable. And then comes his final thought: That the preceding ten minutes are about to come to an end, and that this too is a goodbye. That realization applies to the figure in the video, to the moment

zu Heiner Müller, der nicht müde wurde zu wiederholen, dass das Wesentliche von Theater die Verwandlung, das Sterben sei. Dass das Spezifische des Theaters „nicht die Präsenz des lebenden Schauspielers oder des lebenden Zuschauers (ist), sondern die Präsenz des potentiell sterbenden." Peggy Phelan hat gezeigt, dass es Forced Entertainment erstaunlicherweise gelingt, diese Grunddisposition des Theaters auch im CD-ROM-Projekt *Frozen Palaces* erfahrbar werden zu lassen: „Hugo Glendinning, der Fotograf, enthüllt die *tableaux vivants* eines eigenartig vertrauten Theater des Todes. Die stummen Bewegungen der Betrachterin, die sich durch den virtuellen Raum scrollt, erhalten ein Aroma des Verspäteten, Posthumen."

„Heitere Trauer, wüste Schönheit; ein Seelentanz auf Messers Schneide", nannte Renate Klett diese Balance, die die Arbeiten von Forced Entertainment prägt. Als „sich mit der Vergangenheit verbinden mit einem Blick auf die Zukunft" beschrieb es Ron Vawter in einem Interview mit Tim Etchells. Selbst in den Videoarbeiten (die z. T. in Zusammenarbeit mit Hugo Glendinning, z. T. mit anderen Künstlern entstehen) gelingt es Tim Etchells, dieses notwendige Maß an Präsenz und Authentizität, diese Mixtur aus Trauer und Zartheit, Offenheit und Widersprüchlichkeit zu erreichen, ganz nebenbei und ohne jeden Aufwand. *Down Time* (Performance/ Video, 2001): Tim Etchells filmt sich selbst, an einem Tisch sitzend, in die Kamera schauend, stumm, nachdenkend. Als *voice over* kommentiert er, was er dort von Augenblick zu Augenblick gerade dachte. Die Gedanken drehen sich um erlebte Abschiede – fröhliche, traurige, bewegende – oder allgemeiner um das Phänomen, dass man mithilfe von Kameras und anderen Apparaten versucht, die Notwendigkeit des Abschiednehmens zu negieren. Kurz vor Ende des Videos wirkt dieses Gesicht, dieser Mensch plötzlich ganz besonders verletzlich. Und dann kommt der Schlussgedanke: dass die zuvor festgelegten 10 Minuten nun gleich zu Ende gehen, und dass

» *Continued on page 240*

» *Fortsetzung auf Seite 240*

Pleasure

Showtime

Showtime

Who Can Sing a Song to Unfrighten Me?

Who Can Sing a Song to Unfrighten Me?

in which the video was shot, and equally to the viewer's 'here and now', to the moment in which this video, a recording from a different time, comes to an end. This finding is obviously trivial, yet in Tim Etchells' descriptions of the partings he has experienced, in his attempts to comment upon – or rather interpret – expressions of his own face as he recollects, there is very often a hint of the thought of the last parting of all: "It's funny (no, not really) when I wrote about her going behind that wall in departures at the airport, the only thing like it I could think of was the point where a coffin goes slowly through the curtains in a crematorium. Disappearing through a barrier, over a line."

Down Time takes up the thread of *Looking Forwards* (1996), a photo project by Hugo Glendinning and Forced Entertainment, even if the earlier work follows the opposite temporal direction. The photo series portrayed people "from the street" – "real-life counterparts to the fictional figures who have often haunted Forced Entertainment's work" (Etchells) – and asked them to think about the future. The explanatory text accompanying each photograph merely provides the person's name and occupation, as well as the label of 'optimist' (all the people portrayed were optimists, or at least wished to be described as such). It is therefore up to the viewer to glean the thoughts about the future from the bodies, faces, and postures of people depicted in the photographs and to speculate upon them, to invent their stories, or even to place oneself in another's shoes.

What is it that makes the works of Forced Entertainment so inescapable, compelling and plausible – regardless of whether we are viewing a performance that lasts two, six or twenty-four hours, an open structure for the internet, or a ten-minute video? One aspect is the extent of participation demanded from and conceded to the viewer who is by turns accomplice or

auch dies ein Abschied ist. Dies ist gültig für die Person im Video, für den Moment, in dem das Video aufgenommen wurde, und ebenso für das Jetzt des Betrachters, für den Moment, in dem dieses zu irgendeiner früheren Zeit aufgenommene Video endet. Natürlich eine banale Feststellung, doch in der Art und Weise, in der Tim Etchells von den Abschieden, die er erlebt hat, erzählt, sich selbst in der Erinnerung kommentierend oder vielmehr interpretierend, schwingt oftmals auch der Gedanke an den letzten aller Abschiede mit: „Es ist lustig (nein, nicht wirklich) – als ich über sie schrieb, wie sie am Flughafen beim Abflug hinter der Wand verschwand, war das einzig Vergleichbare, an das ich denken konnte, der Moment, in dem ein Sarg langsam durch die Vorhänge in einem Krematorium verschwindet. Durch eine Barriere verschwinden, eine Grenze überschreiten."

Down Time knüpft an eine Fotodokumentation von Hugo Glendinning und Forced Entertainment von 1996 an, auch wenn die zeitliche Richtung hier genau entgegengesetzt war: *Looking Forwards*. In einer Fotoserie wurden Leute ‚von der Straße' – „Gegenstücke aus dem realen Leben zu den fiktionalen Figuren, die so oft in den Arbeiten von Forced Entertainment herumgegeistert sind" (Etchells) – porträtiert und gebeten, dabei über die Zukunft nachzudenken. Als erläuternden Text enthält jedes Foto lediglich Name und Beruf der Person sowie die Bezeichnung ‚Optimist'. (Alle Porträtierten waren Optimisten oder wollten jedenfalls als solche bezeichnet werden.) Der Betrachterin bleibt es also überlassen, die Gedanken über die Zukunft aus den Körpern, den Gesichtern, der Haltung der Personen zu filtern, darüber zu spekulieren, die Geschichten zu erfinden oder sich selbst an die Stelle der jeweiligen Person zu setzen.

Was ist es, das die Arbeiten von Forced Entertainment so unausweichlich, mitreißend und überzeugend macht – egal, ob zwei, sechs oder 24 Stunden dauernde Performance, offene Internetstruktur oder zehnminütiges Video? Das große Maß an Teilhabe, Komplizen- oder

Zeugenschaft, die den Zuschauern abverlangt und zugestanden wird, ist ein Aspekt. „Namenlose Intimität." (Etchells) Ein dunkles Zimmer, der Monitor scheint wie ein Lagerfeuer, an dem ich sitze, um Tim Etchells Geschichten zuzuhören und seine Notizen zu lesen, um Ausschnitte aus Forced Entertainment-Projekten zu sehen, kurze Episoden aus vergangenen Aufführungen, Proben, *home movies*. Um mich im Forced Entertainment-Kosmos aus Schweigen und Privatheit, Magie, Schlaf und Tod, den Grenzen der Sprache, der Strukturierung des Chaos, Denken, Versagen, Leere zu bewegen. *Imaginary Evidence* (CD-ROM, 2003) ist ein radikal subjektives Archiv der künstlerischen Arbeit von Tim Etchells und Forced Entertainment. Pragmatisch-simpel im Aufbau und damit in der Handhabung, dennoch poetisch und warmherzig, so unzeitgemäß dies im Zusammenhang mit einem ‚multimedialen Datenträger' auch klingen mag: Ein Netz der Begriffe, die für die Arbeit der Compagnie prägend, wichtig, bestimmend waren und sind („Catalogues", „Magic", „Interruptions", „Silence", „Death" …) bildet das Interface. Wählt man einen der Begriffe aus, erscheinen auf dem Bildschirm Videostills als *thumbnails*, die per Mausklick im nebenstehenden polaroidgroßen Videofenster ablaufen. Zu jedem der Videoausschnitte gibt es einen gesprochenen Kommentar von Tim Etchells sowie weitere Kommentare auf einem ‚Notizzettel'. Viele der Notizen und Kommentare beginnen mit „My Love …", „Dear X …", oder auch „Dear No One …". Vielleicht ist eben dies das Wesentliche: die Generosität und Radikalität, mit der Tim Etchells und Forced Entertainment ihre Welt, ihren Kosmos mit uns, den Zuschauern, Zeuginnen und leidenschaftlichen Fans zu teilen bereit und bestrebt sind. Ohne Tricks, ohne falsche Geheimnisse, immer in einer unauflösbaren Schwebe und Spannung zwischen Privatheit und Darstellung, die mit dem Begriff *live art* nur unzureichend beschrieben ist.

witness: "Intimacy that doesn't have a name" (Etchells).

In a dark room lit up by the camp-fire glow of the monitor, I am listening to Tim Etchells' stories and reading his notes, exploring the CD-ROM *Imaginary Evidence* – watching excerpts from Forced Entertainment projects, short episodes from bygone performances, rehearsals, home movies; navigating through the Forced Entertainment cosmos of silence and privacy, magic, sleep and death, of the borders of language, of structuring chaos, of thinking, failure, blankness. *Imaginary Evidence* (CD-ROM, 2003) is a radically subjective archive of the artistic work of Tim Etchells and Forced Entertainment – pragmatically simple in its structure and therefore its use, yet lyrical and warm-hearted, however old-fashioned this may sound in connection with a 'multimedia data carrier'. The interface is composed of a network of concepts that have been, and continue to be, important for the work of the company ("catalogues", "magic", "interruptions", "silence", "death" …). Upon choosing one of these terms, video stills appear on the screen in the form of thumbnails, which can be clicked on and played in an adjacent snapshot-sized window. Every video clip is accompanied by a spoken commentary by Tim Etchells, as well as by further notes. Many of the notes and commentaries begin with the words, "My Love …", "Dear X …" or even, "Dear No One …". Perhaps the important thing is precisely this: the generosity and radicalism with which Tim Etchells and Forced Entertainment are willing and striving to share their world, their cosmos, with us, the viewers, witnesses and ardent fans. Without any tricks, without false secrets, always hovering in a space filled with the irresolvable tension between privacy and presentation, which is inadequately described by the term *live art*.

Translated by Thomas Morrison

Aeroplanes leave vapour trails in the sky, writing amusing messages as they loop beneath the clouds.

I Love Love, writes the first plane.
Happy Birthday, writes the second.
I Seem To Be Having Some Difficulties. May Day. May Day. May Day, writes the third, but it's too late and the plane crashes. A tragic waste of human life.

More mistakes are presented. Acrobats stumble. Tightrope walkers miss their footing. Trapeze artists miss their catches. The knife thrower's assistant is helped, bleeding from the podium.

Dirty Work

Club of No Regrets
(Rehearsal / Probe)

Peculiar Detonation
The Incomplete History and Impermanent Manifesto of The Institute of Failure

Sonderbare Detonation
Die unvollständige Geschichte und das vergängliche Manifest des Institute of Failure

Matthew Goulish

1.	Einfach Teil 1
2.	Wal-Detonation Teil 1
3.	Tesafilm
4.	Wal-Detonation Teil 2
5.	Einladung
6.	Manifest Teil 1: Unfälle gibt es nicht
7.	Wal-Detonation Teil 3
8.	Manifest Teil 2: Das Scheitern breitet sich aus
9.	Dem Irrtum folgen
10.	Institut für Scheitern und Fehlschläge
11.	Einfach Teil 2: Manifest Teil 3: Wir suchen das ungesuchte Unglück

1.	Simply part 1
2	Whale detonation part 1
3.	Scotch tape
4.	Whale detonation part 2
5.	Invitation
6.	Manifesto part 1: There is no such thing as accident.
7.	Whale detonation part 3
8.	Manifesto part 2: Failure proliferates
9.	Following the error
10	Institute of Failure
11.	Simply part 2: Manifesto part 3: We seek the unsought misfortune

1. Einfach Teil 1 – von Tim Etchells

Ich werde dir hierbei nicht helfen.

Du musst ‚zurechtkommen'. Das heißt klarkommen, mit Un-Bedeutung. Oder mit der Möglichkeit von Un-Bedeutung. Oder klarkommen, dass ich nicht nicht klarkomme. Oder damit, dass ich nicht bedeute. Das Zittern dieses Augenblicks.

Um es einfach zu sagen, noch einfacher. Um es sehr einfach zu sagen: Du gehst dort rauf (du kommst hier hoch) und du scheiterst.

1. Simply part 1 – by Tim Etchells

I will not help you with this.

You have to 'deal'. Which means cope with un-meaning. Or with the possibility of un-meaning. Or cope with me not not coping. Or with me not meaning. The trembling of this moment.

To put it simply, more simply. To put it very simply: You get up there (you come up here) and you fail. And in that failing is your heartbeat …

As part of The Center for Land Use Interpretation's on-going *Event Marker Project*, commemorating unusual and exemplary forms of land use, a monument was placed at the site where a car was crushed by a piece of whale blubber following a 1970 attempt to "disintegrate" a beached whale. The monument was the second instalment in the *Peculiar Detonations*-series of the *Event Marker Project*.

The story of the failed disposal incident, recounted in the CLUI monument, goes as follows:

On November 12, 1970, the Oregon State Highway Department performed the detonation, in an attempt to remove a beached whale, discovered dead on the shore five days earlier, upwind from the coastal town of Florence. The decision was made to disintegrate the whale with explosives, with the belief that it would break into small fragments which would then be picked up by gulls, crabs and other scavengers. Twenty 50-lb. cases of dynamite were placed under the 45-foot Pacific Gray whale, and a quarter mile radius was cleared of spectators for safety. The explosion, captured on film by a news team, was more vigorous than anticipated, and many in attendance were hit by whale debris. Much of the whale carcass remained unexploded on the beach, and was buried where it had lain.

Nobody was injured, though everyone in attendance was coated in a "sticky film" by the ensuing cloud of rotting whale vapour. The most damage was suffered by a car parked 450 yards from the blast site. A 1970 Oldsmobile, owned by Walter Umenhofer, was struck by a large blubber fragment, which entirely flattened the roof, effectively totalling the car. The car had been purchased two days earlier from Dunham Olds in Eugene, a dealership then advertising "A Whale of a Deal."

Und in diesem Scheitern ist dein Herzschlag …

2.   Wal-Detonation Teil 1

Als Teil des laufenden *Ereignismarkierungsprojektes* des Center for Land Use Interpretation (Zentrum zur Interpretation von Landnutzung) – eines Projektes zum Gedenken an ungewöhnliche und beispielhafte Formen von Landnutzung – wurde ein Monument an der Stelle errichtet, an der 1970 bei dem Versuch, einen gestrandeten Wal zu ‚entsorgen', ein Auto von einem Stück Walfischspeck zerquetscht. Das Monument war der zweite Teil der Serie *Sonderbare Detonationen* des *Ereignismarkierungsprojektes*.

Das CLUI-Monument erzählt die Geschichte dieser gescheiterten Entsorgung folgendermaßen:

Am 12. November 1970 führte das Oregon State Highway Department eine Detonation aus, um einen gestrandeten Wal zu entfernen, der fünf Tage zuvor oberhalb der Küstenstadt Florence tot am Ufer aufgefunden worden war. Es wurde entschieden, den Wal mit Sprengstoff zu entsorgen, in der Annahme, dass er in kleine Stücke zerfallen würde, die dann von Seemöwen, Krabben und anderen Aasfressern aufgeklaubt würden. Zwanzig halbzentnerschwere Kästen mit Dynamit wurden unter dem 15 Meter langen pazifischen Grauwal platziert und ein Sicherheitsabstand von 400 Metern für die Zuschauer festgelegt. Die Explosion, die von einem Nachrichtenteam gefilmt wurde, war heftiger als erwartet, und viele der Anwesenden wurden von Waltrümmern getroffen. Ein großer Teil des Walkadavers blieb ungesprengt auf dem Strand liegen und wurde an Ort und Stelle begraben.

Niemand wurde verletzt, aber die Wolke der vom verrottenden Walfleisch aufsteigenden Schwaden legte sich als ‚klebriger Film' auf alle Anwesenden. Den größten Schaden erlitt ein Auto, das 400 Meter vom Ort der Explosion entfernt geparkt war. Ein Oldsmobile Jahrgang 1970 im Besitz von Walter Umenhofer wurde von

Peculiar Detonation
Sonderbare Detonation
Matthew Goulish

einem großen Stück Walspeck getroffen, das das Dach gänzlich eindellte. Das Auto erlitt effektiv einen Totalschaden. Es war zwei Tage zuvor bei Dunham Olds in Eugene gekauft worden, einem Händler, der zu dem Zeitpunkt mit dem Slogan „Ein Wal von einem Schnäppchen" warb.

Das wetterfeste Gedenkmonument aus Plexiglas und Holz, das diese Ereignisse beschreibt, wurde im April 1995 von Mitgliedern des CLUI errichtet. Auf der Basis der Erinnerungen von Mr. Umenhofer und anderen, von CLUI-Personal interviewten Zeugen der Wal-Detonation wurde es genau an der Stelle errichtet, an der Mr. Umenhofers Auto parkte, als es getroffen wurde.

3. Tesafilm

Die Geschichte der Wal-Detonation hatte ich zu einem Bestandteil meines Seminars *Ethik und Ästhetik des Scheiterns* gemacht, das ich mehrere Jahre an der School of the Art Institute Chicago in der Abteilung für Schöne Künste gab. Die Idee für das Seminar war mir in den frühen Neunzigerjahren gekommen, als ich Jack Smiths *Notes for the Ford Foundation Application Program in the Humanities* las. Smith, der Regisseur des berüchtigten Films *Flaming Creatures* von 1963, der den New Yorker Theaterregisseuren Richard Foreman und Elizabeth LeCompte eine große Inspiration gewesen ist, war als wichtige Figur wiederentdeckt worden. Ron Vawter, Schauspieler der Wooster Group, hatte Smith in der zweiten Hälfte seines Solo-Performance-Stücks *Roy Cohn/Jack Smith* wiederauferstehen lassen. Anthologien von Smiths Fotografien und Schriften waren veröffentlicht worden. In *Film Culture* erschien ein Wiederabdruck der Notizen für seine Bewerbung bei der Ford Foundation aus den frühen Sechzigerjahren.

Nachdem ich zwei Jahre lang als Schauspieler und Assistent mit Ken Jacobs an seinem Film Star Spangled to Death *gearbeitet hatte, beschloss ich, einen eigenen Film zu drehen.*

The Center's weather-resistant Plexiglas and wood commemorative monument describing the events was installed by CLUI members in April 1995. The monument was placed at the exact spot where Mr. Umenhofer's car was parked when it was struck, based on the recollections of Mr. Umenhofer and other attendees of the whale detonation event that were interviewed by CLUI personnel.

3. Scotch tape

I included the story of the whale detonation in the course packet of my seminar *The Ethics and Aesthetics of Failure*. I had been teaching the course for several years in the Liberal Arts Department of The School of the Art Institute of Chicago. The idea for the class had presented itself to me in the early nineties while reading *Notes for the Ford Foundation Application Program in the Humanities* by the late Jack Smith. Smith, the director of the infamous 1963 film *Flaming Creatures*, which had been so inspirational to New York theatre directors Richard Foreman and Elizabeth LeCompte, had re-emerged as a figure of significance. Ron Vawter, the Wooster Group actor, had re-created Smith in the second half of his solo performance piece *Roy Cohn/Jack Smith*. Anthologies of Smith's photographs and writings had been published. *Film Culture* reprinted the application notes, which dated from the early sixties.

After I had worked for two years with Ken Jacobs as an actor and assistant on his film Star Spangled to Death, *I decided to shoot a film of my own. Jacobs lent me his camera and a roll of colour film after we had finished a day's shooting on his film in a New Jersey junkyard. While some of the actors were doing an improvised dance around a green lotus, I shot them at various distances and in various positions on the screen. My framing within* a shot and the rhythm of the relative shot lengths were meant to create delirium …

Unknown to us, a little piece of scotch tape had been lodged in the camera gate all day, and when the film came back from the developing laboratory, we saw the imprint of the transparent tape halfway up the left hand side of the screen throughout the footage. The effect was a strange one: the tape remained in the same place in every shot but the dancers moved from extreme close-ups to long shots and from the centre of the screen to its furthest edges. The combination of the static and moving images gave me more than I had ever expected from the shots of the dancers, and I realized at once that all I needed was a soundtrack to have a finished film. Although I loathe imperfections in the execution of a visual image ordinarily, this incident taught me that the creative distance between a projected idea and a realized piece of film can be to a filmmaker's advantage. In my present film-in-progress, Normal Love, I have tried to take maximum advantage of what would ordinarily be errors. For instance, early in the film all the scenes of wigs falling off, props falling apart, and actors staring blankly into the camera will be intercut. In this way normally 'ruined' footage, manipulated with a beautiful rhythm, will add to the aesthetic delirium I seek in all my films.

Yet I do not mean that my films have been made by chance occurrences. Every shot I have taken since the making of Scotch Tape has regarded formal composition, placing of actors, and lighting. I have tried to execute visual fantasies with the maximum amount of professionalism accessible to the 16mm filmmaker, especially in Normal Love. Nevertheless I know that there is a plethora of possibilities for transformation between the conception and the developed filmstrip. The shooting of Scotch Tape and the subsequent experiences in Flaming Creatures and Normal Love have taught me that the 'obvious

Nachdem wir den Dreh für seinen Film auf einem Schrottplatz in New Jersey für den Tag abgeschlossen hatten, lieh Jacobs mir seine Kamera und eine Rolle Farbfilm. Ich filmte einige der Schauspieler aus unterschiedlichen Entfernungen und in unterschiedlichen Bildpositionen, während sie einen Tanz um eine grüne Lotusblume improvisierten. Meine Absicht war es, mit der Rahmung innerhalb einer Aufnahme und dem Rhythmus der relativen Aufnahmelängen ein Delirium zu erzeugen …

Ohne unser Wissen blieb ein kleines Stück Tesafilm den ganzen Tag über im Bildfenster der Kamera hängen. Als der Film aus dem Kopierwerk zurückkam, sahen wir auf dem gesamten Material das Abbild des halbtransparenten Klebebands auf halber Höhe am linken Bildrand. Es war ein merkwürdiger Effekt: Das Klebeband blieb in jeder Aufnahme an derselben Stelle, aber die Tänzer bewegten sich von extremen Nahaufnahmen zur Totalen und von der Bildmitte an die äußersten Ränder. Diese Kombination statischer und dynamischer Bilder gab mir mehr, als ich je von den Aufnahmen der Tänzer erwartet hätte, und ich begriff sofort, dass ich für einen fertigen Film nur noch einen Soundtrack brauchte. Obwohl ich normalerweise Unvollkommenheiten in der Ausführung eines visuellen Bildes verabscheue, lernte ich durch diesen Zwischenfall, dass der kreative Abstand zwischen einer Projektidee und einem verwirklichten Stück Film durchaus zum Vorteil des Filmemachers gereichen kann. In meinem gegenwärtigen film-in-progress Normal Love habe ich versucht, aus dem, was normalerweise Fehler wären, größtmöglichen Vorteil zu ziehen. So werden beispielsweise zu Anfang des Films alle Szenen zwischengeschnitten, in denen Perücken verrutschen, Kulissen zusammenbrechen oder Schauspieler verdutzt in die Kamera starren. Auf diese Weise wird das, was normalerweise ‚verlorenes' Material wäre, in schönem Rhythmus manipuliert, zu dem ästhetischen Delirium beitragen, das ich in all meinen Filmen suche.

Ich will damit aber nicht sagen, dass meine Filme durch Zufallsereignisse zustande gekommen sind. *Jede Aufnahme, die ich seit* Scotch Tape *gemacht habe, legt Wert auf formale Komposition, Schauspielerplatzierung und Lichtführung. Ich habe versucht, visuelle Phantasien mit dem Maximum an Professionalität, die einem 16mm-Filmemacher zur Verfügung steht, auszuführen, insbesondere in* Normal Love. *Doch ich weiß, dass es zwischen dem Entwurf und dem entwickelten Filmstreifen eine Fülle an Transformationsmöglichkeiten gibt. Das Drehen von* Scotch Tape *und die folgenden Erfahrungen mit* Flaming Creatures *und* Normal Love *haben mich gelehrt, dass die oben erwähnten ‚offensichtlichen Fehler‘ zum Prozess des Filmemachens gehören, und dass sie, richtig genutzt, ein Segen sein können.*

Die Abteilung für Schöne Künste lud mich ein, ein Seminar zu einem Thema meiner Wahl zu halten. Der Satz „die oben erwähnten ‚offensichtlichen Fehler‘ sind ein inhärenter Bestandteil des Prozesses" aus Jack Smiths Bewerbung bei der Ford Foundation spukte seit mehreren Monaten in meinem Kopf herum, und ich fing an zu bemerken, wie häufig in allen kreativen Prozessen Zufälle eine wesentliche Rolle spielen. Der berühmte spinnenartige Sprung in Marcel Duchamps *Large Glass*, der wie eine perfekte Duchamps-Linie aussieht, war das Ergebnis eines Transportunfalls. Ich kam zu der Ansicht, dass der Hauptunterschied zwischen wichtigen und unwichtigen Künstlern in der Fähigkeit liegt, das Zufällige nicht nur zu akzeptieren, sondern es in den Vordergrund zu stellen. Jack Smith gab seinem ersten Film den Titel *Scotch Tape* offensichtlich erst, nachdem er den Fehler mit dem Klebeband bemerkt hatte, und behauptete so rückwirkend eine Absicht. In diesen Prozessfehlern präsentiert sich eine Tiefenschicht kreativer Intentionalität.

Ich recherchierte über Fehleranalyse in den Schlüsselwerken des Ingenieurwesens wie etwa Petroskis *To Engineer is Human* und Levi und Salvadoris *Why Buildings Fall Down*. In der Regel vertreten Ingenieure die Ansicht, dass unvorhergesehene, katastrophenartige

errors' mentioned above are inherent in the process of film-making and can be turned into blessings when properly used.

The Liberal Arts Department invited me to teach a seminar on the topic of my choice. The phrase "… the 'obvious errors' mentioned above are inherent in the process …" from Jack Smith's Ford Foundation application had echoed in my head for several months, and I had begun to notice how frequently accidents played an essential role in all creative processes. The famous spidery crack in Marcel Duchamp's *Large Glass*, which looks like a perfect Duchampian line, resulted from a shipping accident. I began to think that the key difference between major artists and minor artists lay in the ability not only to accept the accidental, but even to foreground it. Jack Smith had apparently titled his first film *Scotch Tape* only after observing the error of the tape, thus retroactively claiming it as intentional. A substratum of creative intentionality presented itself in these process errors.

I researched failure analysis in key engineering works such as Petroski's *To Engineer is Human*, and Levi and Salvadori's *Why Buildings Fall Down*. The unforeseen catastrophic collapse, engineers routinely propose, inspires technological advance with the intention of avoiding such collapses in the future. While this approach seems clearly important in preventing tragedy, it also reminded me of psychologist Gregory Bateson's comment about how the response to the problem institutionalises both the problem and the response – while in Zen philosophy, the response to a rupture is another rupture. This distinction offered a stark contrast between the processes of the artist and those of the engineer. Could the two fields hybridise? Could creative engineering and/or mechanical creativity exist? Could failure propose the meeting place of engineering and art?

The famous leaning tower of Pisa, unknown to most people, had begun leaning even while under construction, prompting the builders to correct the angle of the cupola. This produced a somewhat impossible building, since, were the body of the tower ever to be straightened, the straightening would cause the top to lean. On the other hand, part of the tower, under either foreseeable circumstance, would remain at the correct inclination: rupture as response to rupture.

While much of the engineering discourse seemed starkly limiting, I liked the term: 'failure'. It seemed to allow for a number of categories of distinction, between mistake (the scotch tape in the camera), accident (the crack in the glass), incorrect methodology (the tower on a foundation of clay above an aquifer, with construction that compensates for the lean), and certainly other categories which investigation might reveal. The topic's definition would go something like this: "Any system is best understood by an investigation of its failure."

The notion of building a seminar on this ill-defined topic seemed quixotic at best, but I had to face the facts: It was at the moment my only idea. In any case, I had Jack Smith's essay as a foundation. I proposed a course on the study of failure. The Liberal Arts Department approved the proposal.

Shortly thereafter, I discovered an essay in a later issue of *Film Culture* titled *Writing Jack Smith's Ford Foundation Application* by P. Adams Sitney, which began with the following paragraph.

When I saw Jack Smith's Ford Foundation application published in Film Culture #76 *(June 1992, pp. 24-26) I realized from a new perspective how an archival document could be misconstrued as history. In the past I had taken the role of the historian studying the sense and implications of documents. But now I worried about how the document would be read by others; for Jack Smith*

Zusammenbrüche als Inspiration für technologischen Fortschritt dienen, um solche Zusammenbrüche in Zukunft zu vermeiden. Diese Herangehensweise ist für die Prävention von Tragödien bestimmt sehr wichtig, erinnert mich aber auch an eine Bemerkung des Psychologen Gregory Bateson, dass die Reaktion auf ein Problem sowohl das Problem wie auch die Reaktion darauf institutionalisiert – während in der Philosophie des Zen die Antwort auf einen Bruch ein weiterer Bruch ist. Diese Unterscheidung deutet auf einen scharfen Kontrast zwischen den Prozessen des Künstlers und denen des Ingenieurs hin. Ist eine Hybridisierung dieser beiden Bereiche möglich? Sind kreatives Ingenieurwesen und/oder mechanische Kreativität möglich? Kann Scheitern den Punkt des Zusammentreffens von Ingenieurwesen und Kunst markieren?

Die wenigsten Leute wissen, dass der berühmte schiefe Turm von Pisa schon während des Baus in Schieflage geraten war, was die Erbauer dazu veranlasste, den Winkel der Kuppel zu korrigieren. Das Ergebnis war ein in gewisser Weise unmögliches Gebäude, da diese Korrektur, sollte der Turm jemals aufgerichtet werden, eine Schieflage der Kuppel verursachen würde. Andererseits aber würde ein Teil des Turmes unter beiden vorhersehbaren Umständen immer im richtigen Winkel bleiben: Bruch als Reaktion auf Bruch.

Während mir ein Großteil des Diskurses im Ingenieurwesen sehr einschränkend vorkam, gefiel mir der Begriff: ‚Scheitern'. Er schien mir eine Reihe von Unterscheidungskategorien zuzulassen: zwischen Fehler (dem Tesafilm in der Kamera), Unfall (dem Sprung im Glas), falscher Methode (der Turm auf Lehmfundament über einer Wasserader, mit einer Konstruktionsweise, die die Schieflage kompensiert) und gewiss noch anderen Kategorien, die eine weitere Untersuchung offen legen würde. Die Definition des Themas würde etwa folgendermaßen lauten können: „Jegliches System wird am besten verstanden durch eine Untersuchung seines Scheiterns."

Die Idee, ein Seminar um dieses unklar definierte Thema herum zu bauen, schien bestenfalls exzentrisch. Aber ich musste den Tatsachen ins Gesicht sehen: Es war momentan meine einzige Idee. Auf jeden Fall hatte ich Jack Smiths Essay als Grundlage. Ich schlug einen Kurs über das Studium des Scheiterns vor, und die Abteilung für Schöne Künste nahm den Vorschlag an.

Wenig später entdeckte ich in einer späteren Ausgabe von *Film Culture* einen Essay von P. Adams Sitney mit dem Titel *Wie ich Jack Smiths Bewerbung bei der Ford Foundation schrieb*, der mit dem folgenden Absatz begann:

Als ich Jack Smiths Antrag bei der Ford Foundation in Film Culture *#76 (Juni 1992, S.24 – 26) veröffentlicht sah, begriff ich aus einer neuen Perspektive, wie ein Archivdokument als Historie missdeutet werden kann. Ich hatte schon früher die Rolle eines Historikers eingenommen und als solcher die Bedeutungen und Implikationen von Dokumenten studiert. Was mich jetzt beschäftigte, war die Frage, wie dieses Dokument von anderen gelesen würde; denn Jack Smith hat diesen Antrag nicht ,geschrieben'. Ich habe ihn geschrieben. Ich fühle mich daher verpflichtet, die Geschichte seiner Entstehung zu veröffentlichen, nicht aus Stolz, denn es handelt sich weder um einen guten Text noch um eine aufschlussreiche Kritik oder auch nur um einen geschickten Antrag – Smith wurde von der Ford Foundation abgelehnt. Vielmehr schreibe ich hier, um den Ruf von Jack Smith zu schützen. Damit kein zukünftiger Gelehrter, in der Annahme, mein Text sei seiner, zu dem Schluss kommt, er sei ein falsch spielender Blender gewesen, der all der prächtigen Exzentrizitäten, für die er bekannt war, und zugleich trockener, akademischer Stipendienanträge fähig war. Dass diese Aufgabe mir, dem damals 19-jährigen ,Herausgeber' von* Film Culture *zufiel, lag daran, dass er sich genau auf diese Ebene eben nicht herablassen konnte oder vielmehr: wollte.*

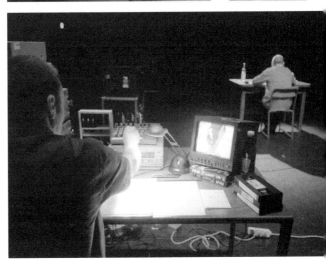

Kent Beeson Is a Classic & an Absolutely New Thing

did not 'write' that proposal, I did. Thus I feel compelled to print the story of its creation not out of pride; for it is not good writing, insightful criticism, or even skilful grantsmanship – Smith was rejected by the Ford Foundation. Actually, I write now to protect the reputation of Jack Smith, lest some future scholar, taking my text for his, should conclude that he was a duplicitous poseur, capable of all of the gorgeous eccentricities for which he is known while at the same time able to write trite, academic grant applications. It was because he could not, or more accurately, would not stoop to that level that the task somehow fell to me, then a nineteen-year-old 'editor' of Film Culture.

The Leaning Tower of Pisa had provided me with a more perfect example than I had realised. I had built my own tower of thought on a false foundation. Yet because of this, my own profound process error, my failure creation had escaped my laboratory. Still in its infancy, it ran wild in the landscape, displaying its uncanny paranoiac superpower: to absorb any unforeseen eventuality with the triumphant cry, "But that just proves my point!" This elusive topic seemed to me all at once to be everywhere, proliferating in every process of thought, creativity, or action. Failure ruled the universe.

Still, I might have been a little more sceptical of the Ford Foundation application in *Film*

Der schiefe Turm von Pisa war als Beispiel perfekter, als ich gedacht hatte. Ich hatte meinen eigenen Gedankenturm auf einer falschen Grundlage errichtet. Doch durch diesen fundamentalen Prozessirrtum war die Kreatur meines Scheiterns dem Labor entflohen. Noch in den Kinderschuhen steckend rannte sie in der Gegend umher und brüstete sich ihrer unheimlichen, paranoiden Superkräfte, jegliche unvorhergesehene Eventualität mit dem Triumphschrei zu absorbieren: „Aber das beweist ja gerade, dass ich Recht habe!" Dieses schwer zu bestimmende Thema schien mir auf einmal überall aufzutauchen und in jedem Prozess des Denkens, der Kreativität oder der Handlung zu wuchern. Scheitern beherrschte das Universum.

Dennoch hätte ich gegenüber der Bewerbung bei der Ford Foundation in *Film Culture #76* etwas skeptischer sein können. Selbst ein flüchtiger Vergleich dieser Erzählung mit dem unmittelbar davor abgedruckten Artikel *Astrology of a Movie Scorpio* hätte ein Problem nahe legen sollen. Ich hätte bemerken können, wie sehr der Stil sich von einem unzweifelhaft von Jack Smith verfassten Prosastück unterschied, dessen letzte Zeilen unmittelbar oberhalb der Bewerbung auf derselben Seite erschienen:

Um Ihnen jetzt zu beweisen, dass ich weiß, worüber ich nachdenke, und dass ich jedes Recht der Welt habe, einen Film mit dem Titel Normal

Love *zu machen, werde ich Ihnen etwas über normale Liebe erzählen.*

Menschen sollten in der Lage sein, einander während ihrer Streitereien zu liebkosen. Dann könnten ihre Streitereien wirklich leidenschaftlich sein. Skorpione: Seid eifersüchtig und streitet weiter, das liegt in eurer Natur. Wir müssen humorvoll, fair und liebevoll sein, selbst während wir streiten … der zarte Teil des Lebens hängt davon ab. Wir können diese Balance erreichen, weil wir unglaublich sind.

4. Wal-Detonation Teil 2

„Hey, Matthew, die Sache mit dem Wal kommt im Fernsehen.“

Stephen Fiehn war damals einer meiner Studenten. Heute ist er Mitglied des Performance-Duos Cupola Bobber. Er hatte den Scharfblick, die Episode in *Die erstaunlichsten Videos der Welt* zu entdecken, wo sie beworben wurde als Original-Fernsehmaterial von der Detonation eines gestrandeten Wals 1970 an der Küste von Oregon. Ich hatte am ersten Tag des Kurses einen kurzen Vortrag über die Detonation gehalten. Da ich nicht wusste, wann genau in der Show das Video ausgestrahlt würde, war ich gezwungen, die gesamte Stunde aufzuzeichnen. Das führte dazu, dass ich zufällig auch Luftaufnahmen einer Polizeiverfolgungsjagd im Stau aufnahm, die zur Basis für einen Teil der Choreographie in Goat Islands *It's an Earthquake in My Heart* wurde. Aber das ist eine andere Geschichte. Das Video der Wal-Detonation kam gegen Ende der Stunde, und es erzählte eine etwas andere Geschichte als die vom Center for Land Use Interpretation aufgezeichnete. Hier wurde betont, dass das Highway Department in der Absicht, den Wal ins Meer zu sprengen, die landseitige Hälfte des Kadavers mit Dynamit überladen hatte. Das Filmmaterial zeigte spektakuläre Aufnahmen der Explosion, wenige Augenblicke später gefolgt von dem prasselnden Klang und nebligen Bildern eines roten Regens von Walstücken. Der interviewte Mann erzählte, wie die Kleider aller Anwesenden sich rosa färbten

Culture #76. Even a cursory comparison of the narrative to the article printed directly before it, *Astrology of a Movie Scorpio*, should have suggested a problem. I might have noticed how the style differed from that of an undisputed piece of Jack Smith prose, the final lines of which appeared above the application on the very same page:

Now to prove to you that I know what I am thinking about and that I have every right in the world to make a movie called Normal Love, *I'll tell you something about normal love.*

People should be able to caress each other during their quarrels. Then their quarrels can really be passionate. Scorpios: be jealous and quarrel on, that is your nature. We must be humorous, fair and affectionate even while we quarrel … the tender part of life depends on it. We can achieve this balance because we are incredible.

4. Whale detonation part 2

"Hey Matthew, that whale thing is going to be on television."

Stephen Fiehn was one of my students at the time. Now he is a member of the performance duo Cupola Bobber. He had the sharp eye to spot the episode of *World's Most Amazing Video*, publicised as televising original footage of the detonation of a beached whale on the Oregon coast in 1970. I had given a short lecture about the detonation on the first day of class. Since I did not know when in the program the video would air, I was forced to record the entire hour. As a result, I accidentally captured aerial footage of police car chases through traffic jams, which became the basis for some of the choreography in Goat Island's *It's an Earthquake in My Heart*. But that is another story. The whale detonation video concluded the hour. It told a slightly different story than the one reported by the Center for Land Use Interpretation, emphasising that the Highway Department, intending to blast the whale out to sea, had overloaded the inland side of the carcass with dynamite. The footage spectacularly captured the blast, followed a moment later by the pelting sounds and misty image of a red rain of whale chunks. The man interviewed related how everyone's clothing turned pink, permeated with stench of whale cloud. We revisited the event in the seminar, this time with the visual aid of the video.

"How would you classify this particular failure, and how does it elucidate the system under scrutiny?"

A conversation ensued with the following conclusions.

Failure #1: whale dies on beach – accident
Failure #2: Highway Department decides to use dynamite to dispose of carcass, miscalculating effect – incorrect methodology
Failure #3: Highway Department uses too much dynamite and atomises much of carcass – mistake
Failure #4: whale blubber flattens car – catastrophe

5.   Invitation

The invitation came from Tim Etchells. He asked for fragments of writing or video. "Stories," he called them, as I recall. The material collected eventually produced the performance *Instructions for Forgetting*. Coincidentally, he came to Chicago around this time, visiting classes in the Performance Department, and screening his video work. We wanted to meet for lunch.

I said, "I can meet you after my Failure seminar."

Tim said, "You're teaching a Failure seminar?"

und von dem Gestank der Walwolke durchdrungen waren. Wir kamen im Seminar erneut auf dieses Ereignis zu sprechen, diesmal mit der visuellen Hilfe des Videos.

„Wie würdet ihr dieses spezifische Scheitern klassifizieren, und was erklärt es über das zu untersuchende System?"

Die sich daraus ergebende Diskussion führte zu den folgenden Ergebnissen:

Scheitern #1: Wal stirbt am Strand – Unfall
Scheitern #2: Das Highway Department entscheidet, für die Entsorgung des Kadavers Dynamit zu verwenden und schätzt die Auswirkungen falsch ein – falsche Methode
Scheitern #3: Das Highway Department verwendet zu viel Dynamit und atomisiert einen Grossteil des Kadavers – Fehler
Scheitern #4: Walspeck zerquetscht das Auto – Katastrophe

5.   Einladung

Die Einladung kam von Tim Etchells. Er bat mich um Fragmente von Texten oder Videos. Soweit ich mich erinnern kann, sprach er von ‚Geschichten'. Das gesammelte Material wurde schließlich zu der Performance *Instructions for Forgetting*. Um diese Zeit herum kam er zufällig nach Chicago, wo er Kurse im Performance Department besuchte und seine Videoarbeiten zeigte. Wir trafen uns zum Mittagessen.

Ich sagte: „Ich kann dich nach meinem Scheitern-Seminar treffen."

Tim sagte: „Du unterrichtest ein Scheitern-Seminar?"

Bei einer Pizza erzählte ich ihm von dem Seminar, und er erzählte mir von seinem Kent Beeson-Video. Er hatte einen fünfminütigen Monolog für einen Performer in Seattle geschrieben. Der Monolog beschreibt detailliert ein Phantasieleben voll Reichtum und Dekadenz und muss in halsbrecherischer Geschwindigkeit aus dem Gedächtnis vorgetragen werden. Am Morgen vor den Filmaufnahmen wurde Tim bei der Fahrt an den Drehort klar,

Tim Etchells & Matthew Goulish (2003)

dass Kent das Skript noch nicht auswendig gelernt hatte. Vor laufender Kamera konnte Kent nicht mehr als ein oder zwei Zeilen rezitieren, bevor er in frustrierte Flüche ausbrach. Tim zeigte mir das fertige Video: zusammengeschnittene Stücke, in denen Kent die Zeilen mehr oder weniger richtig hinkriegt, bevor er wieder in sich zusammensackt, das Skript zu Rate zieht, wieder zurückgeht, von Neuem beginnt. Nach zwölf quälenden Minuten gelingt es ihm, den wunscherfüllenden Monolog zu beenden. Zum Schluss fixiert er die Kamera mit dem starren Blick eines zähen Gladiators.

Später am selben Nachmittag fertigte ich als Antwort auf Tims Einladung eine Kopie des Wal-Detonation-Videos an.

Over pizza, I told him about the class, and he told me about his Kent Beeson video. He had written a five-minute monologue for a performer in Seattle. The monologue described a fantasy life of wealth and decadence in great detail, to be recited at breakneck pace from memory. On the morning of the filming, while driving to the location, it became clear to Tim that Kent had not yet memorised the script. As the camera rolled, Kent could recite one or two lines maximum before collapsing into frustrated curses. Tim showed me the completed video: edited together bits of Kent getting the lines more or less right before falling apart, checking the script, backing up, starting again. After twelve agonising minutes, he manages to complete the wish-fulfilment monologue. He ends by fixing the camera with the intense glare of a dogged gladiator.

Later that afternoon, I duplicated a copy of the whale detonation video in response to Tim's invitation.

6. Manifesto part 1: There is no such thing as accident.

"Ever tried, ever failed. Try again, fail again. Fail better."

Those are the words of Samuel Beckett, exactly, I think. As the study of failure progressed, quotations appeared, foundations like Jack Smith's scotch tape, suggesting, like guideposts in uncharted territory, precisely how the wrong direction becomes the right one. A pattern began to emerge, and an unlikely philosophy to take shape.

The Ise Shrine, an ancient temple in Japan dating from the 3RD century AD, always occupies only half of a double site. Built with materials gathered from the surrounding forests, the temple decomposes after twenty years. Monks construct an identical temple on the empty half of the site. In a nocturnal ceremony, they transfer the relics, consecrate the new temple, and demolish the old. The oldest temple in the country never gets older than twenty years. Impermanence lasts forever.

In his book *The Soul's Code – In Search of Character and Calling*, psychologist James Hillman writes:

Hitler's own greatest passion was neither the German Reich, nor war, nor victory, nor even his own person. It was architectural construction. Megalomaniac emperors, from Nebuchadnezzar and the Egyptian pharaohs through the Roman rulers to Napoleon and Hitler, construct in concrete … For this reason, megalomania haunts the

6. Manifest Teil 1: Unfälle gibt es nicht

„Immer versucht. Immer gescheitert. Wieder versuchen. Wieder scheitern. Besser scheitern."

Dies sind die Worte Samuel Becketts, die genauen Worte, glaube ich. In dem Maße, in dem das Studium des Scheiterns fortschritt, tauchten Zitate auf, Grundlagen wie Jack Smiths Tesafilm, die wie Wegweiser in unbekanntem Terrain anzeigten, auf welche Weise die falsche zur richtigen Richtung wird. Ein Muster begann sich abzuzeichnen und eine unwahrscheinliche Philosophie zu entstehen.

Der Ise-Schrein, ein alter japanischer Tempel aus dem dritten Jahrhundert, nimmt immer nur die Hälfte seines Baugrundstücks ein. Aus Materialien der umgebenden Wälder errichtet, zerfällt der Tempel nach zwanzig Jahren. Mönche errichten einen identischen Tempel auf der leeren Hälfte der Fläche. In einer nächtlichen Zeremonie überführen sie die Reliquien, weihen den neuen Tempel ein und zerstören den alten. Der älteste Tempel des Landes wird nie älter als zwanzig Jahre. Vergänglichkeit währt ewig.

In seinem Buch *The Soul's Code – In Search of Character and Calling*, schreibt der Psychologe James Hillman:

Hitlers größte Leidenschaft war weder das Deutsche Reich, noch Krieg und Sieg, noch seine eigene Person. Seine größte Leidenschaft war die Architektur. Megalomane Herrscher, von Nebukadnezar und den ägyptischen Pharaonen über die römischen Herrscher bis hin zu Napoleon und Hitler bauen mit Stein und Beton … Aus diesem Grund wird der tatsächliche Architekt von Megalomanie heimgesucht – wie die Bibel mit der Geschichte vom Turmbau zu Babel warnt, die nicht nur vom Ursprung der Sprache handelt, sondern auch von der Megalomanie, die allen Versuchen innewohnt, Glanz und Erhabenheit der Phantasie (in Beton) konkret werden zu lassen.

Könnte das Scheitern, in seinem Gegensatz zum Streben nach Dauerhaftigkeit, für das der

Ise-Schrein ein Beispiel ist, eine Ethik (vielleicht eine Anti-Ethik) hervorbringen? Diese Möglichkeit gab den Werken der ikonographischen Denker des Scheiterns einen neuen Fokus: Franz Kafka, Paul Virilio, John Cage; und der Geschichte irrer Erfindungen eine neue Relevanz, von Daedalus' tödlichen Flügeln für seinen Sohn Ikarus bis hin zu Arthur Pedricks Plan, die Kraft des Nordlichts zu nutzen und Schneebälle aus der Antarktis per Pipeline zur Bewässerung in die australische Wüste zu transportieren. Aber die prägnanteste und effektivste *ars poetica* erfüllt die Werke der französisch-algerischen Schriftstellerin und Philosophin Hélène Cixous, die sagt: „Unfälle gibt es nicht. Deshalb sind wir alle für das Unglück der Welt verantwortlich."

Um eine solche Aussage zu verstehen, kann man sich vor Augen führen, dass es vor der Erfindung des Automobils keine Auto-‚unfälle' gab. Man betrachtet ‚Unfälle' als inhärenten Bestandteil der Technologie. Jede neue Technologie produziert ein unendliches neues Subset an ‚Unfällen'. Belege für die Omnipräsenz des Glaubens an die Rolle von ‚Unfällen' bei der Erschaffung menschlicher Existenz finden wir weltweit in der religiösen Mythologie. Im Judentum finden wir beispielsweise den Glauben, dass Gott das Universum in Form von Lichtgefäßen erschaffen habe. Die Gefäße aber, zu schwach, die Macht der Schöpfung zu enthalten, brachen, und aus diesem Riss entstand die Welt des Menschlichen. Jede freundliche menschliche Handlung setzt ein Bruchstück der Gefäße wieder an seinen richtigen Ort. In diesem Schema wird Gefälligkeit ein Akt der Selbstauflösung, denn die vollständige Wiederherstellung der Gefäße würde die menschliche Schöpfung rückgängig machen. Das Ergebnis bleibt ein Geheimnis. Viele ziehen es daher vor, an ‚Unfälle' zu glauben, die von menschlichen Ursachen unabhängig sind. Die Alternative, dass es keine ‚Unfälle' gibt und wir daher alle für das Unglück dieser Welt verantwortlich sind, ist schlichtweg zu traurig.

actual architect – as the Bible warns with the story of the Tower of Babel, which is not only about the origin of language but also about the megalomania inherent in all attempts to make concrete the grandeurs of fantasy.

Could failure produce an ethics (an anti-ethics, perhaps) in its opposition to the pursuit of permanence, for which the Ise Shrine provides the example? The possibility brought a new focus to the works of the iconographic thinkers of failure: Franz Kafka, Paul Virilio, John Cage; a new relevance to the history of lunatic inventions from Deadalus' fatal wings for his son Icarus, to Arthur Pedrick's plan to harness the Coriolis force and pipe snow balls from Antarctica to irrigate the Australian desert. But the most concise and effecting *ars poetica* infused the works of French-Algerian writer and philosopher Hélène Cixous, who said, "There is no such thing as *accident*. For this reason we are all responsible for the misfortunes of the world."

To comprehend such a statement, one may consider that before the invention of the automobile there was no automobile 'accident'. One sees 'accident' as inherent to and embedded in technology. Each new technology produces an infinite new subset of 'accident'. For evidence of the ubiquity of the belief in 'accident' as generative to human existence, one need only look to religious mythology the world over. In Judaism, for example, we find the belief that God created the universe in vessels of light. The vessels, too weak to contain the force of creation, shattered, and from this fracture emerged the world of the human. Each act of human kindness now restores a fragment of the vessels to its rightful place. In this scheme, kindness becomes a self-undoing act, as a complete restoration of the vessels would reverse human creation. The result of this reversal remains a mystery. Many thus prefer to believe in 'accident' as independent of human cause. The alternative, that there is no such thing as 'accident', and for this reason we are all responsible for the misfortunes of the world, is just too sad.

7.   Whale detonation part 3

Instructions for Forgetting premiered in Vienna in June 2001. By chance, Goat Island performed in the same festival, and I had the opportunity to see Tim's performance. We talked afterwards, and he proposed an idea. The whale detonation video had started off the third and last part of his performance, a section, he explained, with a loose motif of the fragmentation that follows an explosive event. Tim felt that certain issues arose around this theme, and a small museum of material had begun to collect: the whale detonation video, the Kent Beeson video we had watched in Chicago, the ideas of my seminar (which he mentioned in *Instructions for Forgetting*). He felt that we needed to start a forum for a more thorough investigation of this material, a forum not primarily performative, but rather pedagogical, semi-intellectual, a kind of institute. He said that if I was willing, he could apply for funding and administrate the project. We did not know it at the time, but that was the birth of The Institute of Failure.

8.   Manifesto part 2: Failure proliferates

Proliferation defies analysis, growing exponentially, independent of theory or philosophy. Like crabgrass, rhizomatic and unstoppable, the failure collection postulates and delineates a finite terrain, then demonstrates that terrain as infinite. This could be part two of the manifesto, whose part one stated, in the non-existence of accident, the permanence of the impermanent. Now we see that impermanence is everywhere, reproducing according to its own logic.

7.   Wal-Detonation Teil 3

Die Premiere von *Instructions for Forgetting* fand im Juni 2001 in Wien statt. Zufällig trat Goat Island beim selben Festival auf, und so hatte ich Gelegenheit, Tims Performance zu sehen. Anschließend redeten wir miteinander, und er hatte eine Idee. Das Video mit der Wal-Detonation hatte den dritten und letzten Teil seiner Performance eröffnet, welcher, wie er erklärte, dem losen Motiv der Fragmentierung, die auf ein explosives Ereignis folgt, nachgeht. Tim hatte das Gefühl, dass um dieses Thema herum bestimmte Fragestellungen auftauchen, und Material für ein kleines Museum begann sich anzusammeln: das Video der Wal-Detonation, das Kent Beeson-Video, das wir uns in Chicago angesehen hatten, die Ideen aus meinem Seminar (das er in *Instructions for Forgetting* erwähnt hatte). Er meinte, dass wir für eine gründlichere Untersuchung dieses Materials ein Forum gründen müssten, das nicht in erster Linie auf Performance, sondern eher pädagogisch ausgerichtet sein sollte, halb-intellektuell, eine Art Institut. Er sagte, dass er Gelder beantragen und die Verwaltung des Projektes übernehmen könnte, wenn ich einverstanden sei. Damals wussten wir es nicht, aber das war die Geburt des Institute of Failure, des Instituts für Scheitern und Fehlschläge.

8.   Manifest Teil 2:
Das Scheitern breitet sich aus

Ausbreitung und Wucherung trotzt jeder Analyse; es ist ein exponentielles Wachstum unabhängig von Theorie oder Philosophie. Rhizomatisch und unaufhaltsam wuchernd wie Quecken, postuliert und umreißt die Sammlung von Fehlschlägen ein endliches Terrain, nur um zu zeigen, dass dieses Terrain unendlich ist. Dies könnte Teil Zwei des Manifests bilden, dessen erster Teil in der Nicht-Existenz von Unfällen die Ewigkeit des Vergänglichen behauptete. Jetzt sehen wir, dass Vergänglichkeit überall ist und sich gemäß der ihr eigenen Logik ausbreitet.

Der große zeitgenössische Dichter und Chronist des Scheiterns, Kenneth Goldsmith, hat eine Reihe solcher Wucherungen zusammengestellt. In seiner Eigenschaft als Radio-Persönlichkeit hat er unter dem Titel *Head Citations (Aus dem Kopf zitiert)* einen Band mit (absichtlich oder versehentlich) missverstandenen Texten von Popsongs herausgegeben. Die bloße Aneinanderreihung dieser Texte deutet ihre eigene sonderbare Detonation an, als ob jeder korrekte Liedtext zehn fehlerhafte, und jeder Fehler potentiell seinen eigenen neuen Song hervorbrächte. Die folgenden Beispiele geben einen kurzen Einblick in diese erstaunliche Maschinerie des Scheiterns:

Kenneth Goldsmith, the great contemporary poet and chronicler of failure, has compiled a number of such proliferations. In his capacity as a radio personality, he collected a volume of (deliberately or accidentally) misheard pop song lyrics titled *Head Citations*. The simple listing of these lyrics suggests its own peculiar detonation: as if each correct lyric produces ten mistaken lyrics, and each mistake produces its own new potential song. The following brief sample provides a glimpse of this awesome failure engine:

Das Zeitalter der Malaria bricht an.
Ein schwules Paar von Jungs hat einen Parkplatz aufgemacht.

This is the dawning of the age of malaria.
A gay pair of guys put up a parking lot.

Es schmeckt sehr gut, das Parkplatzessen.
Eins kann ich dir sagen: Du musst Käse essen.
Sie war ein schwuler Stripper.
Hey, komm runter von meiner Kuh!
Wir sagen nur: Kinder brauchen einen Vater.
Wir sagen nur: ein gutes Stück Käse.
Oh, wir segeln, ja, gib Jesus Hosen!
Der Papst arbeitet nicht, weil die Vandalen die Kerzen gestohlen haben.
Deine Liebe ist wie schlechtes Hirschsteak.
Es passiert etwas, aber du weißt nicht was.
Hast du den Witz verpasst?
Michelle, meine Glocke, die Sonntagsaffen sagen, das Ende ist geschehen, das Ende ist geschehen.
Michelle, meine Glocke, Sonntag, Montag, Dienstag, Mittwochtag, Mittwochtag.
Michelle, ma belle, einige Leute sagen, dass Affen gut Klavier spielen, gut Klavier spielen.
Die besten Liebeslieder werden mit einem gebrochenen Arm geschrieben.
Ich steh' auf und brat' ein Ei.
Wer wird mich rasieren?
Du kannst meine Leber in einem alten Marmeladeglas trockenlegen.
Tritt nicht auf meine Bruce Wayne-Schuhe!

It tastes very nice, food of the parking lot.
One thing I can tell you is you got to eat cheese.
She was a gay stripper.
Hey you, get off of my cow.
All we are saying is kids need a dad.
All we are saying is good piece of cheese.
Oh, we are sailing, yes, give Jesus pants.
The Pope don't work cause the vandals took the candles.
Your love is like bad venison.
Something is happening but you don't know what it is, did you miss the joke.
Michelle, my bell, Sunday monkeys say the end is done, the end is done.
Michelle, my bell, Sunday, Monday, Tuesday, Wednesday day, Wednesday day.
Michelle, ma belle, some say monkeys play piano well, piano well.
The best love songs are written with a broken arm.
I'll get up and fry an egg.
Who's gonna shave me?
You can drain my liver in an old fruit jar.

Don't step on my Bruce Wayne shoes.

She wore blue, Melvin.

Waking up is hard to do.

You lead your life like a canary in a coma.

I can't, I can't, I can't stand music.

Come together, right now, wolverine.

Will you still feed me when I'm six-feet-four?

Don't let your son go down on me.

Well I'd like to know where you got the nose from.

Since you put me down, I've got owls spinning in my head.

Little blue scoop.

And she'll have fun fun fun 'til her daddy takes the teabag away.

Hit me with your pet shark.

Ground control to Mao Tse-Tung.

Become-a come-a come-a come-a come-a comedian.

There's a frog at your back step, you must drown him in the drain.

Four hundred children and a clock in the field.

Four hundred children and the turnips won't peel.

Four hundred children and a dog with no wheels.

Four hundred children and a cop in the field.

What's love but a sticky body lotion?

Lucy's getting high with Linus.

Lucy knew this guy with diamonds.

Lucy in disguise with lions.

Lucy and this guy are dying.

Lucy in disguise with diamonds.

The girl with colitis goes by.

Super salad bar.

Jesus is just a rat with beads.

Burning all the shoes off Avalon.

Saturday night's all right for fighting, even in election year.

Sie trug blau, Melvin.

Aufwachen ist schwierig.

Du führst ein Leben wie ein Kanarienvogel im Koma.

Ich kann, ich kann Musik nicht ausstehen.

Lass uns zusammenkommen, sofort, Vielfrass.

Wirst du mir noch zu Essen geben, wenn ich zwei Meter groß bin?

Lass nicht zu, dass dein Sohn mir einen bläst!

Nun, ich würde gerne wissen wo du die Nase her hast.

Seit du mich fallen gelassen hast, drehen sich Eulen in meinem Kopf.

Kleine blaue Schaufel.

Sie hat Spaß, Spaß, Spaß, bis ihr Vater den Teebeutel wegnimmt.

Schlag mich mit deinem Haustier-Hai.

Flugsicherungskontrolldienst an Mao Tse-Tung.

Werd' ein, werd' ein, werd' ein Komödiant!

Auf deiner Hintertreppe sitzt ein Frosch. Du musst ihn im Abflussrohr ertränken.

Vierhundert Kinder und eine Standuhr auf dem Acker.

Vierhundert Kinder, und die Steckrüben lassen sich nicht schälen.

Vierhundert Kinder und ein Hund ohne Räder.

Vierhundert Kinder und ein Polizist auf dem Feld.

Was ist Liebe als eine klebrige Hautcreme?

Lucy bekifft sich mit Linus.

Lucy kennt diesen Typ mit den Diamanten.

Lucy verkleidet mit Löwen.

Lucy und dieser Typ liegen im Sterben.

Lucy verkleidet mit Diamanten.

Das Mädchen mit Dickdarmentzündung geht vorbei.

Super Salatbar.

Jesus ist nur eine Ratte mit Perlen.

Alle Schuhe von Avalon wegbrennen.

Selbst im Wahljahr ist Samstagnacht okay zum Kämpfen.

Halt mich näher bei dir, Tony Danza.
Zähl die Kopfläuse auf der Autobahn.
Leg mich nieder in Käse und Lenin.
Wie eine Ken-Puppe im Wind.

9. Dem Irrtum folgen – aus *Stigmata* von Hélène Cixous

Vorläufig folgen wir dem Irrtum, ohne Furcht, mit Respekt.

Wie sehr wir den Irrtum brauchen, der das Versprechen von Wahrheit ist, wie sehr wir ohne die silberhelle Explosion des Irrtums, der das Zeichen ist, nicht auskommen, alle, die mit dem Stift reisen, staunen darüber auf ähnliche Weise, von Jahrhundert zu Jahrhundert.

„*Felix culpa*" nannte ihn der Heilige Augustin, „*portal of discovery*" sagt James Joyce, „*subimssão ao processo*", sagt Clarice Lispecter, der Prozess besteht aus Irrtümern ... Und zuvor schon sagte unser wandernder Großvater Montaigne: „naive und essentielle Unterordnung".

Notwendiger Irrtum, Lehrerin, strauchelnde, essentielle Gefährtin, wir lieben sie, weil wir nur durch sie auf dieser Erde die Wahrheit spüren können, die immer etwas weiter ist, die immer etwas weiter weg existiert.

Und Reue? Keine Reue.

Unsere Fehler sind unsere Sprünge in der Nacht.

Irrtum ist keine Lüge: Er ist Annäherung.

Zeichen, dass wir auf der Spur sind.

Und: sich nicht bedrücken lassen vom nicht ‚Erreichen'. Wir verlieren nichts durch den Irrtum, im Gegenteil: Unglücklich wäre es zu glauben, wir hätten gefunden.

Solange wir suchen, sind wir unschuldig. Wir befinden uns in naiver Unterordnung.

Mit jedem Irrtum schreiten wir fort, mit irrenden Schritten, mit der Kraft des Irrtums. Es ist Leiden, es ist Freude.

Wir suchen Wahrheit, wir finden Irrtum. Er ist offensichtlich wie die Wahrheit.

Hold me closer, Tony Danza.
Count the head lice on the highway.
Lay me down in cheese and Lenin.
Like a Ken doll in the wind.

9. Following the error – from *Stigmata* by Hélène Cixous

For the moment, we are following the error, without fear, with respect.

To what extent we need error which is the promise of truth, to what extent we can't do without the silvery burst of error, which is the sign, all those who go by pen don't cease to marvel at this in a similar way, from century to century.

"*Felix culpa*", Saint Augustine calls it, and then "portal of discovery", says James Joyce, "*submissão ao processo*", says Clarice Lispecter, the process is made up of errors ... And before that, "naïve and essential submission," said our wandering grandfather Montaigne.

Necessary error, school mistress, faltering essential companion, we love her, because she is the only way we have on this earth to feel the truth, which is always a little farther, exists, a little farther away.

And repentance? No repentance.

Our mistakes are our leaps in the night.

Error is not lie: It is approximation.

Sign that we are on track.

And: to not become gloomy from not 'attaining.' We don't lose anything by erring, to the contrary. The unhappy thing would be to believe we had found.

As long as we are seeking we are innocent. We are in naïve submission.

We advance error by error, with erring steps, by the force of error. It is suffering, but it is joy.

We seek truth, we encounter error. It is obvious, like truth.

Tim's proposal received funding. Neither Tim nor I could attend the Institute of Failure inaugural lecture. We had stand-ins read our parts. The Institute then began as a webpage. We invited submissions – writing, art, theory, philosophy, architecture, economics. We collected relevant links. We presented more live lectures. We refined the categories, taking many of the suggestions of my seminar students. The list, still incomplete, now stands at 26:

Types of Failure

1. Accident
2. Mistake
3. Weakness
4. Inability
5. Incorrect Method
6. Uselessness
7. Incompatibility
8. Embarrassment
9. Confusion
10. Redundancy
11. Obsolescence
12. Incoherence
13. Unrecognizability
14. Absurdity
15. Invisibility
16. Impermanence
17. Decay
18. Instability
19. Forgetability
20. Tardiness
21. Disappearance
22. Catastrophe
23. Uncertainty
24. Doubt
25. Fear
26. Distractibility

Tims Antrag wurde angenommen. Weder Tim noch ich konnten den Eröffnungsvortrag des Institute of Failure besuchen. Ersatzdarsteller mussten unsere Beiträge verlesen. Das Institut begann als Webseite. Wir baten um Einsendungen – Texte, Kunst, Theorie, Philosophie, Architektur, Wirtschaft. Wir sammelten relevante Links. Wir hielten weitere Vorträge. Wir verfeinerten die Kategorien und nahmen viele der Vorschläge, die Studenten meines Seminars gemacht hatten, auf. Die immer noch unvollständige Liste hat inzwischen 26 Punkte.

Typologie des Scheiterns

1.   Unfall
2.   Fehler
3.   Schwäche
4.   Unfähigkeit
5.   Falsche Methode
6.   Nutzlosigkeit
7.   Mangelnde Kompatibilität
8.   Peinlichkeit
9.   Verwirrung
10.   Redundanz
11.   Veralten und Verschleiß
12.   Inkohärenz
13.   Mangelnde Erkennbarkeit
14.   Absurdität
15.   Unsichtbarkeit
16.   Vergänglichkeit
17.   Verfall
18.   Instabilität
19.   Vergessbarkeit
20.   Säumnis
21.   Verschwinden
22.   Katastrophe
23.   Ungewissheit
24.   Zweifel
25.   Furcht
26.   Ablenkbarkeit

Das Institut hat sein Eigenleben. Es hat einen eigenartigen Treffpunkt der Ästhetiken von Forced Entertainment und Goat Island

Peculiar Detonation
Sonderbare Detonation
Matthew Goulish

definiert, betrachtet durch die Linse des Scheiterns. Wir haben die Verbindung zwischen dem Institut und der Arbeit der beiden Gruppen nie forciert. Aber man kann nahezu jeden beliebigen Zugangspunkt wählen und wird eine Verbindung finden – die Bewegungssequenzen von Goat Island mit dem ihnen eigenen Gefühl, dass die Performer nie in der Lage sind, den Tanz zu beherrschen; die Inszenierung der Zurückgewiesenen bei Forced Entertainment, wie unfähige Kinder, die im Schultheater eine Rolle im Chor der Pappbäume zugewiesen bekommen. Wie in Jack Smiths *Scotch Tape* rücken beide Gruppen auf sehr unterschiedliche, doch verwandte Weise diese unbequemen Hintergründe in den Vordergrund.

Am wichtigsten ist vielleicht, dass das Institut begonnen hat, einen Hafen und Rahmen für diejenigen unangepassten Denker und Künstler zu bieten, die eine genaue Chronik der Arten und Weisen zusammenstellen, wie im 21. Jahrhundert Leben ins Ungewollte erodiert. Eine Brücke bricht ein, ein Gebäude zerfällt, ein Computerschirm friert ein, ein Wasserglas fällt in einem ewigen Augenblick aus der Hand eines Kindes. Das Institut betrachte solche Ereignisse, wieder und wieder. Respekt vor dem Scheitern. Es ist so offensichtlich wie die Wahrheit.

Wir können die Zukunft des Instituts nicht vorhersagen, da wir nicht exakt vorhersagen können, welche Fehlschläge geschehen werden. Wir können nur exakt vorhersagen, dass Fehlschläge geschehen werden. Auf diese Weise können wir nur sagen, dass das Institut eine Zukunft hat. Definitionsgemäß ist und bleibt die Katastrophe gewiss und unvorhersehbar.

Anfang 2003 hatte ich die Gelegenheit, einen Vortrag von Tim bei der Live Culture-Konferenz in der Tate Modern in London zu hören. In *A six thousand one hundred and twenty seven word manifesto on liveness in three parts with three interludes* sprach er über die Ästhetik, den Prozess und den Präsentationsstil von Forced Entertainment. Während ich ihm zuhörte, merkte ich, wie sich meine

The Institute has a life of its own. It has defined a strange meeting place of the aesthetics of Forced Entertainment and Goat Island, as seen through the failure lens. We have never forced a connection between the Institute and the work of either company. But one could select almost any access point and find a connection – Goat Island's movement sequences, with their sense of the performers' constant inability to master the dance; Forced Entertainment's staging of the rejected, like the incompetent kids of the school play relegated to the role of a chorus of cardboard trees. Like Jack Smith's *Scotch Tape*, both companies, in very different yet kindred ways, foreground these uncomfortable backgrounds.

Perhaps most importantly, the Institute has begun to frame a haven for those misfit thinkers and artists who so astutely chronicle the exact ways life in the 21ST century degrades into the unintentional. A bridge collapses, a building disintegrates, a computer screen freezes, a water glass drops from the hand of a child in a picnoleptic instant. The Institute looks at this, and looks again. Respect the failure. It is obvious, like truth.

We cannot predict the Institute's future, since we cannot accurately predict what failure will occur. We can only accurately predict that failure will occur. In this way we can only say that the Institute has a future. Catastrophe, by definition, remains both certain and unforeseeable.

In early 2003, I had the opportunity to hear Tim give a lecture at the Live Culture conference at the Tate Modern in London. In *A six thousand one hundred and twenty seven word manifesto on liveness in three parts with three interludes*, he spoke of the genesis of Forced Entertainment's aesthetic, process, and presentation style. As I listened to his talk, I found myself thinking of the great mystic Catholic saints of Spain,

Teresa of Avila and John of the Cross. They shared the singular belief that one attains grace only through the advent of unsought misfortune. I had never before considered the arrival of a beached Pacific Gray whale on the Oregon coast in 1970 as a metaphor for enlightenment, yet as I listened to Tim, the logic made sense. No dynamite will dispose of the divine, or of the folly of our response to it. It seemed to me that Forced Entertainment had refined the art of seeking the unseekable, like setting a snare for misfortune itself. While our failures remain quotidian and theatrical, not profound like those of the Spanish saints, they are ours nonetheless. These ruptures compose the fabric of our existence. We respond to each with another rupture. Tim's conclusion, it seemed to me on that afternoon, could have been the third and last part of an Institute of Failure manifesto, were we to compose one. It stated an objective: to observe a method for seeking the unsought misfortune, to repeat that method, and to trust in the result. It went like this.

11.   Simply part 2: Manifesto part 3:
      **We seek the unsought misfortune –
      by Tim Etchells**

I am in love with you.
I want you to see me.
I want you to see me without filters, without frames, borders, deceits.
I want us to meet in this time. In this moment
To abandon expectations. Defences. Limits.
     To breathe.

And I want you to be wary.
     To be aware that your gaze judges and prescribes me.
And that my gaze is also judgmental.
That I do not love or trust you. How could I?
I do not know who you are.

Gedanken den großen katholischen Mystikern und Heiligen aus Spanien, Teresa von Avila und Johann vom Kreuz, zuwandten. Sie hatten beide den eigenartigen Glauben, dass man Gnade nur durch die Ankunft eines ungesuchten Unglücks erfährt. Der Gedanke war mir zuvor nie gekommen, dass die Ankunft eines gestrandeten Pazifischen Grauwals an der Küste von Oregon im Jahr 1970 eine Metapher für Erleuchtung sein könnte. Aber während ich Tim zuhörte, leuchtete mir diese Logik ein. Kein Dynamit wird das Göttliche entsorgen können oder die Torheit unserer Reaktionen darauf. Mir schien, dass Forced Entertainment die Kunst, das nicht Suchbare zu suchen, verfeinert hatte, als wollte es dem Unglück selbst eine Falle stellen. Während unsere Fehlschläge alltäglich und theatralisch sind und bleiben, kein tiefgründiges Scheitern wie das der spanischen Heiligen – sind es doch *unsere* Fehlschläge. Diese Brüche machen das Gewebe unserer Existenz aus. Wir reagieren auf jeden Bruch mit einem weiteren Bruch. Tims Schlussfolgerung hätte, so schien mir an jenem Nachmittag, der dritte und letzte Teil eines Manifests für das Institute of Failure sein können, wenn wir eines schreiben würden. Er formulierte ein Ziel: eine Methode zu verfolgen, um das ungesuchte Unglück zu suchen, diese Methode zu wiederholen und sich auf die Ergebnisse zu verlassen. Sie geht folgendermaßen.

11.   Einfach Teil 2: Manifest Teil 3:
      **Wir suchen das ungesuchte Unglück –
      von Tim Etchells**

Ich bin verliebt in dich.
Ich will, dass du mich siehst.
Ich will, dass du mich siehst ohne Filter, ohne Rahmen, Grenzen, Täuschungen.
Ich will, dass wir uns in dieser Zeit treffen. In diesem Augenblick
Erwartungen aufzugeben. Verteidigungen. Einschränkungen.

     Zu atmen.

Und ich will, dass du auf der Hut bist.

Dass du gewahr bist, dass dein Blick mich beurteilt und mir Vorschriften macht.

Und dass mein Blick auch urteilt.

Dass ich dich nicht liebe und dir nicht vertraue. Wie könnte ich? Ich weiß nicht, wer du bist.

Gegenwart.
Der Augenblick.
Das Jetzt.

Auf dich selbst zurückgeworfen. Ich werde dir hierbei nicht helfen. Du musst ‚zurecht-kommen'. Das heißt klarkommen, mit Un-Bedeutung. Oder mit der Möglichkeit von Un-Bedeutung. Oder klarkommen, dass ich nicht nicht klarkomme. Oder damit, dass ich nicht bedeute. Das Zittern dieses Augenblicks.

Um es einfach zu sagen, noch einfacher. Um es sehr einfach zu sagen: du gehst dort rauf (du kommst hier hoch) und du scheiterst. Und in diesem Scheitern ist dein Herzschlag, und in dem Scheitern bist du, verbunden mit allem und jedem.

www.institute-of-failure.com

Übersetzt von Benjamin Marius Schmidt

Presence.
The moment.
The now.
Thrown back on your own devices. I will not help you with this.

You have to 'deal'. Which means cope with un-meaning. Or with the possibility of un-meaning. Or cope with me not not coping. Or with me not meaning. The trembling of this moment.

To put it simply, more simply. To put it very simply: You get up there (you come up here) and you fail. And in that failing is your heart-beat, and in that failing is you connected to everything and to everyone.

www.institute-of-failure.com

R: These things that you're planning or rehearsing right now, there seems to be a change, a kind of change in tone, is that right?

CL: Yes.

R: Mike?

F: It's a kind of image change.

R: Why do you think it's changed?

F: Yeah. It's hard to explain.

R: We'd be interested to know.

F: We did a thing quite a while ago now, it was a love show and everyone on the stage drank down a love potion and then the love potion sent them all to sleep.

R: What happened then?

F: The potion sent them all off to sleep and when they all woke up again they were all in love and no one felt sad.

R: Uh-huh.

F: Well, that's not the kind of work we want to do anymore.

Some Confusions in the Law about Love

Bloody Mess

A Text on 20 Years with 66 Footnotes

Ein Text über 20 Jahre mit 66 Fußnoten

Tim Etchells

Es beginnt irgendwo[1] und entfaltet sich schnell in verschiedene Richtungen.[2]

Erste Proben zu *Bloody Mess.* Jerry Killick tritt an die Rampe[3] und ‚erklärt' dem Publikum[4],

---

1   Weil es muss.

2   Ich habe diese Geschichte schon so viele viele Male erzählt, dass es schwierig ist, sich ihr von neuem zu nähern. Wenn ich jetzt darüber schreibe oder spreche, kommt es mir manchmal so vor, als erzählte ich weniger das, was passiert ist, als das, was ich bereits darüber gesagt habe – so wie das Foto eines Ereignisses die Erinnerung daran überlagern kann, oder wie (umgekehrt?) ein Foto selbst zu einer Erinnerung werden kann. Es gibt ein Foto von Hugo Glendinning, das uns in Danzig (Polen) am Strand zeigt – wir tourten dort 1989 mit der Theaterperformance *200% & Bloody Thirsty*. Ich habe keine wirkliche Erinnerung an den Tag, an dem wir am Strand waren, aber manchmal rufe ich mir dieses Bild ins Gedächtnis – im Glauben, es wäre eine Erinnerung.

3   Wir sind im Lyceum-Theater, Sheffield, mit seinem grandiosen Goldproszenium und dem rot-samtenen Zuschauerraum und zwängen diese Probe zwischen das, was wir eigentlich tun sollten, nämlich das Monolog-Projekt *The Voices* zu proben. Es ist ein (der) Nachmittag, irgendwann, 2003.

4   Tatsächlich besteht das Publikum nur aus mir, Tobias Lange (einem deutscher Performer, mit dem wir bei vielen Gelegenheiten zusammengearbeitet haben), Helen Gould (einer der Darstellerinnen aus *The Voices*) und Sara Stenström, eine schwedische Dramaturgie-Studentin, die unsere Proben beobachtete.

It starts somewhere[1] and rapidly unfolds in many directions.[2]

During very early rehearsals for *Bloody Mess,* Jerry Killick comes to the front of the stage[3] and 'explains' to the audience[4] why the atmosphere

---

1   As it must do.

2   I have told this story, spoken of this history so many many times that it is hard to approach it afresh. When I do write or speak about it now it can seem to me that I am not telling what happened as much as telling what I have told before – the way a photograph of an event can come to stand in place of a memory of it, or the way that (conversely?) a photograph itself can become a memory. There is a photograph by Hugo Glendinning that shows us on the beach in Gdansk in Poland – we were touring there in 1989 with the theatre performance *200% & Bloody Thirsty*. I have no real memory of the day we visited the beach, but sometimes call to mind the picture, believing it to be a memory.

3   We are in the grand gold-proscenium and red-velvet auditorium of Sheffield's Lyceum Theatre, squeezing this rehearsal in between what we should actually be doing, which is rehearsing the monologues project *The Voices*. It is (the) afternoon, sometime in 2003.

4   In fact, the audience is only me, Tobias Lange (a German performer with whom we've worked on many occasions), Helen Gould (one of the performers in *The Voices*) and Sara Stenström, a Swedish dramaturgy student who is following rehearsals.

A Text on 20 Years with 66 Footnotes
Ein Text über 20 Jahre mit 66 Fußnoten
Tim Etchells

is completely wrong. As far as the text goes, in fact, Jerry is improvising a version of what he has just heard John Rowley improvising in a previous run-through. And John – when he was onstage about fifteen minutes earlier – was simply improvising around what I'd explained to him of what I could vaguely remember of Cathy's first, original, improvisation of a text for this part of the performance, which she had done about a month beforehand, back in our rehearsal studio.[5] This kind of swapping around of material from one performer to another sometimes takes place at the start of rehearsal processes – either for logistical reasons (such as Cathy is busy in London working on a film script today, or someone is sick, or …) or for 'artistic' reasons (such as we think that it would be interesting to change the gender of the performer doing a particular thing, or that it would be 'useful' to switch who's doing something because of how it will connect (or disconnect) to some

warum die Atmosphäre völlig falsch ist. Was den Text angeht, so improvisiert Jerry eine Version dessen, was John Rowley in einem vorangegangenen Durchlauf improvisiert hatte. Und John – als er eine Viertelstunde vorher auf der Bühne war – hatte über etwas improvisiert, was ich ihm erklärt hatte; eine vage Erinnerung an Cathys erste, ursprüngliche Improvisation des Textes für diesen Teil der Performance von vor etwa einem Monat, damals noch im Probenstudio.[5] Dieses Weitergeben von Material von einem Performer zum nächsten passiert bisweilen zu Beginn des Probenprozesses – entweder aus logistischen Gründen (weil Cathy heute vielleicht in London an einem Drehbuch arbeitet, oder jemand krank ist, oder …) oder aus ‚künstlerischen' Erwägungen (weil wir etwa meinen, es wäre interessant, einen bestimmten Moment von einem männlichen statt einem weiblichen Darsteller probieren zu lassen, oder weil es ‚nützlich' scheint, es von jemand anderem machen zu lassen, weil es sich dann mit irgendetwas anderem an

---

5   We have this initial improvisation (and all subsequent ones) on video tape for reference, but at this point in the rehearsals, I am too lazy to find it or we are too short of time in the Lyceum to spend time on watching it. In any case, for the moment at least, the fact that John and Jerry will come up with something in the same broad area as Cathy's original version but different in emphasis and detail is probably a useful thing. When the text 'returns' to Cathy a month or so hence, she may borrow from the material that John and Jerry have created. 'The John version' and 'the Jerry version' of this scene (and of the persona at the centre of it) will be useful models in discussions through the process, points of comparison and conjecture against which the unfolding work will be measured and changed.

5   Wir haben diese erste Improvisation (und alle folgenden) zum Vergleich auf Video, aber in diesem Moment der Proben bin ich einfach zu faul, die Stelle rauszusuchen, oder wir haben im Lyceum zu wenig Zeit, es uns anzusehen. In jedem Fall, zumindest für diesen Augenblick, ist die Tatsache, das John und Jerry etwas im Kontext von Cathys ursprünglicher Version entwickeln, das sich aber in Betonung und Details davon unterscheidet, wahrscheinlich nützlich. Wenn der Text in vielleicht einem Monat zu Cathy ‚zurückkommen' wird, kann sie Material, das John und Jerry entwickelt haben, benutzen. ‚Die John-Version' und ‚die Jerry-Version' dieser Szene (und des Charakters in ihrem Zentrum) werden nützliche Modelle in den Diskussionen während des Prozesses sein, Momente des Vergleichs und der Mutmaßung, an denen die entstehende Arbeit gemessen und durch sie sich verändern wird.

irgendeiner anderen Stelle des Stücks anders verbindet (oder trennt).[6]

Es springt[7] und macht einen Schnitt, rückwärts in der Zeit[8].

---

6   Trotz alledem, und nicht um absichtlich zu verwirren: sobald wir uns jenseits dieser allerersten Probenphase befinden – sobald Material einem bestimmten Darsteller oder einer Darstellerin zugeordnet ist – bleibt es normalerweise auch dabei. Die erste Entscheidung, wer was macht, kann willkürlich oder pragmatisch sein, aber hat es sich erst einmal in Aktionen konkretisiert, bleibt es gewöhnlich dabei. Die besondere Art und Weise, in der eine Person etwas Bestimmtes tut, die spezielle Energie, die sie mit einer bestimmten Aktion oder einem Text verbindet, wird zu einer kompositorischen Setzung – eine wichtige Bedingung für ihren Platz im Stück.

7   Wozu es, sehr häufig, neigt.

8   Ich denke an Robin in einem Moment in *Showtime*, in dem er von Cathy schikaniert wird, die in einem Hundekostüm auf Händen und Knien krabbelt und ihn anbellt. Soweit ich mich erinnere, ist Robin nackt, abgesehen von einer Strumpfmaske, wie sie Bilderbuch-Bankräuber tragen. Er hält einen roten Luftballon, mit dem er versucht, seine Genitalien zu bedecken. Zwangsläufig interessiert sich der ‚Hund‘ besonders für den Luftballon. Robin sagt: „Ich habe viel über Zeit nachgedacht. Sie verläuft nur in eine Richtung. Sie geht nur vorwärts. Also kann man nicht zurückgehen. Sie sollte eigentlich auch immer mit der gleichen Geschwindigkeit ablaufen, aber das stimmt nicht, oder, denn manchmal geht sie langsamer als zu anderen Zeiten … Was ich sagen will ist, dass die Zeit … Zeit ist ein wichtiges Thema. Es ist eins der wichtigsten, oder? Es ist ein wichtiges Thema. Man sollte sie nicht trivialisieren, sie sollte nicht Gegenstand eines billigen Witzes sein. Zeit ist ein großes Thema. Zeit – wie Raum, Krieg oder Liebe – ist ein großes Thema, mit wichtigen Konsequenzen für jedermann.“

other activity they have at some other point in the piece).[6]

It jumps[7] and cuts backwards in time.[8]

Years before, Richard is stood at the long metal table we use for *Speak Bitterness*, and he is

---

271

6   Despite all this, and not to be deliberately confusing, once we're out of the very early stages of making a piece – once some material is attached to a performer in rehearsal – it generally tends to stay with them. Initial decisions about who does what can be arbitrary or pragmatic, but once concretised in action these decisions tend to stick. The particular way that a person does a certain thing, the particular energy they bring to an action or a text becomes a compositional given – an important part of its place in the piece.

7   As it tends, very often, to do.

8   I think of Robin in one section of *Showtime*, being harassed by Cathy crawling on her hands and knees dressed in a dog costume, barking at him. The way I remember him, Robin is naked, except for a stocking mask like those that picture-book bank robbers wear. He holds a red balloon with which he tries to hide his genitals. Inevitably the 'dog' is very interested in the balloon. Robin speaks: "I've been thinking a lot about time. It only goes in one direction. It just goes forwards. So you can't go back. It's also supposed to go at the same speed all the time, but that is not true, is it, because sometimes it goes more slowly than other times … I mean the thing about time is that … Time is an important subject. It's one of the fundamentals, isn't it? It's an important subject. It's not meant to be trivialized, its not meant to be the subject of a cheap joke … Time is a big subject. Time – like space, war, love – is a big topic, with important consequences for everybody."

dealing the texts out along its length. Setting up for the performance, he is isolating special parts of the text that need to be in particular places on the table for particular people at particular times and placing them accordingly, and simply scattering the rest of the papers on the table here and there, covering it completely. The texts are lists of confessions. The piece, we say, is an attempt to confess to everything – a vast catalogue of wrong-doings that includes murder, fraud, genocide, eating the last biscuit in the tin, not washing up properly, hiding the TV remote control, and buggery.[9]

It slides around, becomes non-specific.

We are in a van[10], in a theatre, in a dressing room, in a bar late at night, in a taxi to an airport. We are walking in a strange city looking for somewhere to eat, we are repeatedly drawing diagrams of the structure of a show on paper napkins[11] in the corner of a bar, with furrowed brows and shaking heads, or in a restaurant, rearranging elements, passing paper down the table to get a comment or a raised eyebrow from

Einige Jahre vorher: Richard steht an dem langen Metalltisch, den wir in *Speak Bitterness* benutzen; er verteilt Texte über dessen gesamte Länge. In Vorbereitung für die Performance separiert er bestimmte Teile der Texte, die zu einer bestimmten Zeit an bestimmten Stellen des Tisches für bestimmte Leute da sein müssen, und legt sie an ihren Platz; die übrigen Papiere verteilt er über den Tisch, hier und da, bis er vollständig bedeckt ist. Die Texte sind Listen mit Bekenntnissen. Das Stück, so sagen wir, ist der Versuch, alles zu bekennen – ein gewaltiger Katalog von Missetaten, der Mord, Betrug und Genozid ebenso beinhaltet wie das Essen des letzten Keks aus der Dose, den Abwasch schlecht machen, die Fernbedienung verstecken oder Sodomie.[9]

Es entgleitet, wird unbestimmt.

Wir befinden uns in einem Transporter[10], in einem Theater, in einem Umkleideraum, in einer Kneipe spätabends, in einem Taxi zum Flughafen. Wir laufen durch eine merkwürdige Stadt, auf der Suche nach etwas zu Essen, wir zeichnen in der Ecke einer Kneipe wiederholt Diagramme der Stückstruktur auf Papierservietten[11], mit Kopfschütteln und gerunzelter Stirn, oder in einem Restaurant, ord-

---

9   If *Speak Bitterness* is a catalogue of (all?) possible confessions, then *Quizoola!* is a catalogue of all possible questions, *And on the Thousandth Night…* a catalogue of all possible stories, *12am: Awake & Looking Down* a catalogue of all possible characters and costumes, etc. It's not so much the content of any particular confession, story, question, etc. that's of interest, but the way that the nature of the catalogue itself – its boundaries, its built-in agendas, its formal extremities, its *concerns* – is revealed.

10   Soundtrack: Tom Waits' *Rain Dogs* or Al Green.

11   Or on beer mats or in a notebook.

9   Ist *Speak Bitterness* ein Katalog (aller?) möglichen Bekenntnisse, dann ist *Quizoola!* ein Katalog aller möglichen Fragen, *And on the Thousandth Night …* ein Katalog aller möglichen Geschichten, *12 am: Awake & Looking Down* ein Katalog aller möglichen Charaktere und Kostüme usw. Es geht nicht so sehr um den Inhalt eines bestimmten Bekenntnisses, einer Geschichte, einer Frage usw., sondern darum, auf welche Weise das Wesen des Katalogs – das zentrale Anliegen, seine Grenzen, eingebauten Regeln und formalen Extreme – enthüllt wird.

10   Soundtrack: Tom Waits' *Rain Dogs* oder Al Green.

11   Oder auf Bierdeckeln oder in ein Notizbuch.

nen Elemente neu, reichen Papiere über den Tisch in Erwartung eines Kommentars oder einer hochgezogenen Augenbraue von einem der anderen, wir trinken mit zehn oder mehr Leuten, eingezwängt in einem Einzelzimmer irgendeines Hotels.[12]

Es lässt sich wieder nieder, an einem anderen Punkt.

Jetzt sind es Terry und Cathy, im mit Kreide bekritzelten Bühnenbild von *Club of No Regrets* in Berlin, die vor der Aufführung Texte und Requisiten auf der Bühne platzieren. Ich beobachte sie vom Zuschauerraum aus.[13] Während ich ihnen zuschaue, denke ich, dass ihr Tun auf der Bühne wie ein schematisches Durchspielen des Stücks wirkt – seine Orte aufsuchen, seine Positionen, eine nach der anderen, aber in umgekehrter Reihenfolge.[14]

someone else, we are drinking with ten or more people crammed into a single hotel room.[12]

It settles again, at some other point.

Now Terry and Cathy are on the chalk-scrawled set of *Club of No Regrets* in Berlin, placing texts and props on the stage in the right places prior to the performance. I'm watching them from the auditorium.[13] As I watch, I am thinking that their activity on stage looks as if they were doing the piece in schematic form – visiting its places, its positions, each in turn, only in reverse.[14] On the stage, Terry and Cathy are putting the bucket of water at the back, so that later, in the performance, it can be moved to the front by the shoddy wooden house that sits on the stage. When she leaves the stage, job completed, Terry passes Robin on the stairs. Later, for years and years, she will tell the story that Robin looked completely crazy on the stairs[15] and that his eyes

---

12   Exemplarische Erinnerungen – so viele Variationen der gleichen Szene sind übereinander geschichtet, dass sie mittlerweile fast ununterscheidbar geworden sind. Verschwommene Dichte.
13   Ich weiß nicht, um welches Jahr es sich handelt. Ich habe viel Zeit damit verbracht, Leute auf der Bühne bei Dingen zu beobachten, die nicht als Performance im engeren Sinn zu bezeichnen sind – Sachen vorbereiten, das Bühnenbild aufbauen, Unsinn machen, Licht hängen.
14   Mehrmals versuchten wir, Durchläufe in die tatsächliche Performance einzubauen, ohne Erfolg. Etwas an der Energie dieser Probenaktivität ist faszinierend – die hohe Geschwindigkeit, die Lässigkeit der Energie des ‚Markierens' von Positionen und Texten, die Kurzfassung, die kommentierte Zusammenfassung, gelegentlich unterbrochen durch ein Detail eines Moments oder einer Interaktion, das jemand ‚richtig' durchspielen muss.

12   Generic memories – so many variations of the same scene layered one on top of the other that they are by now almost impossible to distinguish. A density blur.
13   I don't know what year this is. I spent a lot of time watching people on stage doing things that are not strictly speaking performance – setting up for things, building sets, fooling around, hanging lights.
14   Several times we tried to include walkthroughs of performances as part of performances themselves, but never succeeded. Something fascinating about the energy of these rehearsal activities – the high-speed, casual energy 'marking' of positions and lines, the précis, the annotated summary disrupted by the occasional detail of a moment or interaction that someone needs to practice 'for real'.
15   Whenever it was, this week in Berlin involved quite a lot of parties.

A Text on 20 Years with 66 Footnotes
Ein Text über 20 Jahre mit 66 Fußnoten
Tim Etchells

were in a very strange state and that he was muttering to himself and that she thought, "Oh God. What's he going to be like in the performance …"

It speeds up.

We are in a rehearsal room. We are loading a van. We are checking into a shitty English bed and breakfast. The stench of fifty years worth of cooked full breakfasts has been fried into the brown paint walls. The building shrieks and groans when the taps run, the floorboards creak in incomprehensible ways – unbearable burden of the lives that passed through here, the lights dim whenever anyone takes a shower.

Robin crawls, stripped to the waist, his head in the fun-fur mask of the pantomime horse,[16] and he swigs from the whisky bottle through the eye hole of the horse – more like brutal IV drug use than drinking. As Robin pushes the bottle in through the eye, the horse head is bent grotesquely out of shape – driven crazy by drinking[17], wracked in bewildered cartoon agonies.

---

16   This is a pantomime horse costume we borrowed from a local theatre when we did a kids' project for them. A spectacularly crappy and comical horse with a goofy expression and teeth too big for its mouth.

17   Normally it would be water in the whisky bottle, not actual whisky, although in shows where there is beer drunk onstage (and there are quite a few of these), people tend to drink beer for real, even in rehearsals. It's an interesting thing that people sometimes manoeuvre a little, 'speculate' while improvising so that their role might involve having a beer or two, or smoking the odd cigarette, or having a nice sit-down from time to time.

Auf der Bühne bringen Terry und Cathy den Wassereimer nach hinten, so dass er später, während der Aufführung, nach vorne, zu dem schäbigen Holzhäuschen, das auf der Bühne steht, gebracht werden kann. Als Terry – Arbeit erledigt – die Bühne verlässt, trifft sie Robin auf der Treppe. Später, jahrelang, wird sie die Geschichte erzählen, dass Robin auf der Treppe völlig verrückt ausgesehen habe[15], dass seine Augen in einem seltsamen Zustand waren, dass er etwas vor sich hinmurmelte und dass sie dachte: „Oh Gott. Wie wird er bloß nachher in der Performance sein …"

Es beschleunigt sich.

Wir sind im Probenraum. Wir beladen einen Transporter. Wir checken in ein beschissenes englisches Bed-and-Breakfast-Hotel ein. Der Gestank von 50 Jahren Frühstückszubereitung hat sich in die braun gestrichenen Wände eingebrannt. Das Gebäude jammert und ächzt wenn ein Wasserhahn läuft, die Flurdielen knarren auf unbegreifliche Weise – unerträgliche Last der Schicksale, die hier durchgekommen sind; das Licht wird schwächer, wenn geduscht wird.

Robin kriecht auf dem Boden, bis zur Hüfte ausgezogen, sein Kopf in der Kunstpelzmaske eines Pferdekostüms[16]; er nimmt durch die Augenöffnung der Pferdemaske einen Schluck aus der Whiskyflasche – eher brutaler intravenöser Drogengebrauch als Trinken. Wenn Robin die Flasche durch das Auge führt, gerät der Pferdekopf jedes Mal grotesk aus der Form

---

15   Wann immer das war, in dieser Woche in Berlin gab es jede Menge Partys.
16   Ein Pferdekostüm, das wir von einem Sheffielder Theater ausgeliehen hatten, als wir dort ein Kinderprojekt machten. Ein auf spektakuläre Weise beschissenes und komisches Pferd mit blödem Gesichtsausdruck und Zähnen, die zu groß sind für sein Maul.

– wie verrückt geworden durchs Trinken[17], abgefüllt in verwirrter Cartoon-Agonie.

Terry wechselt das Kostüm.[18]
Cathy spricht zum Publikum.[19]
John schüttelt ungläubig den Kopf.[20]
Jerry lacht, sein Gesicht zerschmettert von einem Fahrradunfall.[21]
Terry schreit auf italienisch.[22]
Richard verbindet sich die Augen und steht da, als warte er darauf, erschossen zu werden.[23]

---

17 Normalerweise ist kein echter Whisky in der Flasche, sondern Wasser, obwohl in Shows, in denen Bier auf der Bühne getrunken wird (und davon gibt es einige), die Leute dazu neigen, tatsächlich Bier zu trinken, sogar in den Proben. Es ist ein interessantes Phänomen, dass die Leute manchmal ein bisschen manipulieren, während der Improvisation darauf ‚spekulieren‘, dass ihre Rolle die Möglichkeit beinhalten könnte, ein oder zwei Bier zu trinken, zwischendurch eine Zigarette zu rauchen oder sich von Zeit zu Zeit gemütlich hinzusetzen.
18 *Emanuelle Enchanted.*
19 *Disco Relax.*
20 Proben zu *First Night.*
21 Aufführung von *And on the Thousandth Night…*, Münster, 2003.
22 Aufführung von *Club of No Regrets* in Italien, Volterra(?)-Festival, 1993 (?). Alle hatten den größten Teil ihrer Texte auf italienisch gelernt, plapperten ihn nach wie Papageien. Die Performance fand draußen statt, auf dem Gelände eines alten Klosters. Noch Jahre danach erzählten die Leute davon, wie der Rauch aus dem Stück (in die Luft geschleudertes Talkumpuder) zu den Bäumen aufstieg und während der Aufführung im Mondlicht vom Wind weggeweht wurde. Ich war nicht dabei, aber manchmal scheint es mir, ich würde davon sprechen, als hätte ich es selbst erlebt.
23 *Hidden J.*

Terry changes costume.[18]
Cathy addresses the audience.[19]
John shakes his head in disbelief.[20]
Jerry laughs, his face all smashed up from a bicycle accident.[21]
Terry yells in Italian.[22]
Richard puts on a blindfold and stands as if waiting to be shot.[23]
Robin parts the curtains slightly and peers through them at the arriving audience.[24]

It slides in time[25].

Claire dances in her bra and knickers, midriff wrapped in skimpy, improvised fake feather tutu, a knife in her hands. There is slowed down

---

18 *Emanuelle Enchanted.*
19 *Disco Relax.*
20 *First Night* rehearsals.
21 Performance of *And on the Thousandth Night…*, Munster 2003.
22 Performance of *Club of No Regrets* in Italian for Volterra (?) Festival, 1993 (?). Everyone learned most of their texts in Italian, parrotfashion. The performance took place outdoors, in the grounds of an old monastery. For years afterwards, people would talk about the way the smoke from the performance (talcum powder hurled into the air) rose and drifted up towards the trees, blown on the wind in the moonlight during the show. I was not there but sometimes I find that I talk about it as if I had been.
23 *Hidden J.*
24 A generic memory and one which, in any case, I wouldn't have witnessed. Robin likes to see the audience before they see him … checking them out … weighing the possibilities of how the gig will go. Other performers prefer not to see the public till they get on the stage.
25 As it tends to do.

music from the record player[26] and to go with it, Claire dances kind of suicidal and ultra slow-motion.[27] She does not know that this dance will be in the final performance, but already, perhaps, suspects. She knows that 'something' is happening, that somewhere in the confluence of what she and the others on stage are doing (improvising) there is a 'scene', or that this is some particular nuanced articulation of what we have been doing for a month or more.[28]

276

A Text on 20 Years with 66 Footnotes
Ein Text über 20 Jahre mit 66 Fußnoten
Tim Etchells

26   We used the same battered record player in a whole string of shows from *Showtime* to *Disco Relax*. In the first of these it played a number of old 45rpm records that Richard had found at his parents' house. We liked the record player because it meant that the means of producing music and the operation of it were visible on and controlled from the stage. Prior to this, music slammed or drifted in as if controlled by some unseen hand ("from God" we used to say, joking), and we became suspicious of this … preferring that all of the signification (except the lights) remain in control of the performers onstage. Using the record player (and with it 'found' songs or music on vinyl) meant that the music was (literally) an object held up for use and scrutiny much like a found text, or a second-hand costume. It meant an end, more or less, to our theatre work with composer John Avery who'd done soundtracks for almost all of the performances prior to the arrival of the record player.

27   This is *Pleasure* rehearsals.

28   It is a big joke in rehearsals and afterwards that the stupidest, most painful or random improvisational move can end up being your fate for a whole show and for a whole year of touring. As in "If I'd have known I was going to end up doing *that* for a year, I wouldn't have done it in the first place".

Robin zieht den Vorhang ein wenig zur Seite, um einen Blick auf das hereinkommende Publikum zu werfen.[24]

Es verschiebt sich in der Zeit.[25]

Claire tanzt in BH und Schlüpfer, um die Taille ein spärlicher, improvisierter Tutu aus falschen Federn, in der Hand ein Messer. Verlangsamte Musik von einem Plattenspieler[26], und Claire tanzt dazu auf suizidale Weise in Ultra-Zeit-

24   Eine exemplarische Erinnerung und in jedem Fall ein Moment, dessen Zeuge ich nicht gewesen sein kann. Robin möchte immer gerne das Publikum sehen, bevor es ihn sieht … die Leute abchecken … abwägen, wie die Aufführung werden wird. Andere Schauspieler ziehen es vor, das Publikum nicht zu sehen, bis sie auf der Bühne sind.

25   Wozu es neigt.

26   Wir haben denselben batteriebetriebenen Plattenspieler in einer ganzen Reihe von Stücken benutzt – von *Showtime* bis *Disco Relax*. Im ersten dieser Stücke spielte er einige alte 45er-Platten ab, die Richard im Haus seiner Eltern gefunden hatte. Wir mochten den Plattenspieler, weil durch ihn die Mittel, Musik hervorzubringen und zu benutzen, auf der Bühne sichtbar wurden. Davor war die Musik immer wie von unsichtbarer Hand gesteuert hereingebrochen oder -geschwebt („von Gott", wie wir – scherzhaft – zu sagen pflegten), und das sahen wir irgendwann mit Skepsis … es war uns lieber, dass alles Bedeutende (außer dem Licht) von den Performern auf der Bühne gesteuert werden konnte. Der Plattenspieler (und mit ihm ‚gefundene' Songs oder Musik auf Vinyl) bedeutete, dass die Musik (im wörtlichen Sinn) ein Objekt wurde, das genauso benutzt und untersucht werden konnte wie ein gefundener Text oder ein gebrauchtes Kostüm. Es bedeutete aber auch mehr oder weniger das Ende unserer Zusammenarbeit mit dem Komponisten John Avery, der den Soundtrack für nahezu alle Stücke vor dem Auftauchen des Plattenspielers gemacht hatte.

lupe.[27] Sie weiß noch nicht, dass dieser Tanz wirklich im Stück sein wird, vermutet es aber – vielleicht – bereits. Sie weiß, dass ‚etwas‘ passiert, dass irgendwo im Zusammenspiel dessen, was sie und die anderen auf der Bühne machen (improvisieren), die ‚Szene‘ entsteht, oder dass es zumindest ein bestimmter nuancierter Ausdruck dessen ist, woran wir seit einem Monat oder länger gearbeitet haben.[28] Claire tanzt und Cathy schreibt Obszönitäten auf eine Tafel: Fotze. Bumsen. Einen blasen.[29] Die Musik ist *Last Mile Home*, aber so stark verlangsamt, wie sie abgespielt wird, kann man den Text kaum verstehen.[30]

Während sie tanzt, weiß Claire noch nicht, dass sie Jahre später auf der Bank im Probenraum sitzen wird – etwa dort, von wo aus ich ihr in diesem Moment zuschaue – und Wendy Houston beobachten wird, wie sie diesen Tanz macht. Claire wird ihn ihr beibringen, denn sie wird schwanger sein, und Wendy wird sie während eines Teils der *Pleasure*-Tour ersetzen. Und Claire weiß noch nicht, dass sie zu Wendy sagen wird: „Nein. Schwerer. Mach es schwerfälliger. Es muss schlechter sein …“, und dass Richard während der ganzen Zeit

---

27   Es sind Proben zu *Pleasure*.

28   Es ist ein ständiger Witz in Proben und danach, dass die blödeste, schmerzhafteste oder zufälligste improvisierte Bewegung schließlich zum Schicksal in der Show und während der gesamten Tour wird: „Wenn ich gewusst hätte, dass ich *das* schließlich das ganze Jahr über machen werde, ich hätte es gar nicht erst ausprobiert.“

29   Aus einer Liste schmutziger Wörter und Redewendungen, die ich aus dem Intenet heruntergeladen hatte.

30   Als der Performancekünstler Michael Atavar einmal die Proben besuchte, erinnerte er sich, wie er und seine Schwester alle Platten ihrer Eltern verlangsamt abgespielt haben und sich dabei mit den Nachrichten vom Teufel, die sie darin hörten, gegenseitig Angst einjagten.

Claire dances and Cathy writes obscenities on the blackboard: Cunt. Get Your Rocks Off. Blow Job.[29] The music is *The Last Mile Home* but because it's slowed down so much you can hardly hear the words.[30]

As she dances, Claire does not know that years later she will sit on the seating bank in the rehearsal room – close to where I am watching her from now – and she will watch as Wendy Houston does this dance. Claire will be teaching it to her because Claire will be pregnant and Wendy will be replacing her in some part of the *Pleasure* touring. And Claire does not know that she will be saying to Wendy, "No. Heavier. Make it clumsier. It needs to be worse …" and that Richard will be sat at the front of the stage the

---

29   This is a list of dirty words and phrases I have downloaded from the Internet.

30   When performance artist Michael Atavar comes to see a rehearsal one day, he remembers how he and his sister used to play all their parents' records slowed down and scare each other with the messages from the Devil they could hear in there.

whole time[31] loading the gun[32] with his blindfold on, and Claire does not know that she will watch Wendy and that as she does so, her hands will be clasped over her belly inside of which will be Ruby May – of whom, at this point in

vorne am Bühnenrand sitzen wird[31], mit verbundenen Augen die Waffe ladend[32], und Claire weiß noch nicht, dass sie Wendy

---

31   There is a whole strand of the work where someone (often Richard) 'comes to the front' or 'takes centre' to frame or MC the pieces. Occupying this place appears something of a structural necessity but is rarely weighted with the kind of actual authority that a narrator/MC might be expected to project. We took to calling the role/position 'frame' and then, as it decayed further, etiolated or 'weak frame'. The storyteller is weak, prone to distraction (like me, here), disorganised, crazed, uncertain. We understood this MC position as a structural tactic – about one (or more) people coming forwards so that others might have the space to live/exist/work in the back. The front provides covering fire (deals with the audience, acknowledges them, speaks to them directly) so that the rest can get on with what they need to do.

32   In rehearsal, any action with the gun has a real tension about it since many of the performers like to fire the bloody thing. The bangs from the gun (which fires real blanks) are horribly horribly loud in the studio, ripping through the atmosphere of the work and prompting people to nervously keep their fingers near their ears whenever it is in play. Often in these days, I think about Burroughs in *The Place of the Dead Roads* where he talks about gunshots blowing a hole in the fabric of space and time. I remember in *Marina & Lee* we used audio from movies (gunfights, brawls, kung-fu fights) to interrupt the action on stage – throwing the performers into chaotic and clumsy fight sequences, jump cutting the piece to a new place.

31   Es gibt eine ganze Reihe von Arbeiten, in denen jemand (oftmals Richard) ,an die Rampe tritt' oder ,sich in den Mittelpunkt stellt', um dem Stück einen Rahmen zu geben oder als Showmaster zu agieren. Die Besetzung dieser Position erscheint wie eine strukturelle Notwendigkeit, hat aber selten das Gewicht tatsächlicher Autorität, die man von einem Erzähler/Showmaster erwarten würde. Wir nannten die Rolle/Position ,Rahmen', und dann, als sie noch mehr verfiel, ,ausgebleichter' oder ,schwacher Rahmen'. Der Geschichtenerzähler ist schwach, neigt zu Abschweifungen (wie ich, hier), ist schlecht organisiert, verrückt, unsicher. Wir verstanden die Showmaster-Position als strukturelle Taktik – eine (oder mehrere) Person(en) kommen nach vorne, um den anderen Raum zu geben, im Hintergrund zu leben/zu existieren/zu arbeiten. Im vorderen Bereich sein, bedeutet Feuerschutz geben (sich mit dem Publikum befassen, es wahrnehmen, es direkt ansprechen), damit die anderen tun können, was sie tun müssen.

32   In den Proben ist jede Aktion mit der Waffe spannungsgeladen, da viele der Performer das verdammte Ding gerne abfeuern. Der Knall des Schusses (die Waffe feuert echte Platzpatronen ab) ist im Studio entsetzlich, entsetzlich laut, zerreißt die Atmosphäre des Stücks und veranlasst die Leute, ihre Hände nervös in der Nähe der Ohren zu halten, wann immer sie im Spiel ist. An solchen Tagen denke ich oft an Burroughs in *The Place of the Dead Roads*, wo er davon spricht, dass Schüsse ein Loch in das Raum-Zeit-Gefüge reißen. Ich erinnere mich daran, dass wir in *Marina & Lee* den Ton von Filmen verwendeten (Schießereien, Schlägereien, Kung-Fu-Kämpfe), um die Handlung auf der Bühne zu unterbrechen – es warf die Performer mitten hinein in chaotische und plumpe Kampfsequenzen, ein Jump-Cut zu einem anderen Ort.

A Text on 20 Years with 66 Footnotes
Ein Text über 20 Jahre mit 66 Fußnoten
Tim Etchells

zuschauen und dass sie, während sie das tut, ihre Hände über dem Bauch gefaltet haben wird, in dem sich Ruby May befindet – von der man, an diesem Punkt der Geschichte (Claires erster Improvisation des Tanzes), nicht die geringste Ahnung hat.[33]

Es springt weiter.

the story of Claire first improvising the dance, there will not even be the tiniest idea.[33]

It continues to jump.

We are in a hotel room. The technician Andy Clarke is drinking whisky from a toothpaste mug whilst various people add to the uncharacteristic makeup and pink-wig outfit that he is sporting. It is 5 in the morning. I am filming.[34]

---

33   Und nochmals einige Jahre später spielen Ruby May und einige andere Kinder aus dem allgemeinen Forced-Entertainment-Gefolge – Miles, Seth, Megan, Jacon, Leon, Izzy – im Probenstudio mit einem Kleiderschrank, der mit einer primitiven ‚Geheimtür' für imitierte Zaubertricks in der Rückwand ausgestattet ist. Der Schrank wurde in Proben zu *First Night* gebraucht, während einer Phase, in der wir dachten, dass in der Show verschiedene Zauberkunststücke oder -tricks vorkommen würden. Zuvor waren Richard, mein Sohn und ich – zu Forschungszwecken – nach Blackpool an der englischen Nordostküste zu einer Magier-Konferenz in irgendeinem Strandhotel gefahren. Auf der Konferenz erstehen wir die Pläne verschiedener Bühnentricks – fotokopierte Beschreibungen, die in verschlossenen Umschlägen verkauft werden. Die Vorderseite des Umschlags zeigt die Beschreibung des Tricks, aber um herauszufinden, wie er konstruiert ist, muss man die Pläne kaufen. An einem Abend auf dieser Konferenz sehen wir einen sehr einfachen Zaubertrick, vorgeführt von irgendeinem deutschen Typ, und wir sind alle begeistert. Es ist ein Trick mit einen Schuh, der wie durch ein Wunder in der Hand des Zauberers auftaucht. Sechs oder sieben Monate nach der Magier-Konferenz wird Richard versuchen, den Schuh-Trick des Deutschen nachzustellen – wir sind in Wien, betrunken, in einer Kneipe, nach einer Aufführung von *Instructions for Forgetting* – ein Versuch, der mit einem vorhersehbaren Gemengsel aus Zerstörung und zerbrochenem Glas enden wird.

33   Years later than this even, Ruby May and a bunch of other kids in the general Forced Entertainment entourage – Miles, Seth, Megan, Jacob, Leon, Izzy – play in the rehearsal studio, using a wardrobe which has been crudely fitted with a 'secret' door in the back to perform imitation magic tricks. The wardrobe has been used in *First Night* rehearsals during a phase where we think the show will have various solo magic acts or tricks in it. At one point prior to this – for research purposes – Richard, my son Miles and I go to a Magicians' Convention at some seafront hotel in Blackpool on the northeast coast of England. At the convention, we purchase the plans for a number of stage illusions – photocopied plans which are sold in sealed envelopes. The fronts of the envelopes bear a description of the illusion, but to find out how it is constructed, you have to buy the plans. One night at the same Convention, we watch a very simple close-up magic trick performed by some German guy, and we all think it's great. The trick involves a shoe magically appearing in the hands of the conjuror. Six or seven months after the Magicians' Convention, Richard will try to recreate the German guy's shoe trick – we are now in Vienna, drunk, in a bar, following a performance of *Instructions for Forgetting* – a recreation that will end with a predictable melee of destruction and broken glass.

34   The tape is lost.

We are in Columbus, Ohio. Outside there is snow.

We are somewhere between Berlin and Warsaw in a three-and-half ton truck, overtaking in swirling dense fog on narrow roads. Whoever is in the passenger seat has to spot for oncoming headlamps appearing out of the gloom.[35] It's a nerve-wracking business. You feel close to your death every time we pull out to overtake.

We are in Sheffield, rehearsing in a church hall.[36]

We are in Sheffield, rehearsing in an abandoned school with smashed windows and industrial gas heaters.[37]

We are in Sheffield, rehearsing in an old factory above which is a boxing gym. When the guys upstairs are training, their skipping sends showers of plaster falling from the decaying ceiling. The dust and plaster settling like a strange rain over everything. When you look from the set of (Let the Water Run its Course) to the Sea that Made the Promise to this ice-cold, smashed up old factory that we call home for five years, you can hardly tell one from the other.

We are making Some Confusions in the Law about Love. We seem to change it every time we do a performance. One of those shows that never ever gets finished. Years later, we find texts and video tapes relating to the show and can't figure out

35   This story gets told in The Travels (2002).
36   Soundtrack: The Fall, Hex Enduction Hour.
37   When the guys come to deliver gas canisters, they are wary of Mark Randle and Robin because they are wearing cowboy hats and dresses, and wary of Claire because she has a fake-penis and a beard drawn on her face (costumes for Marina & Lee).

Wir sind in einem Hotelzimmer. Der Techniker Andy Clarke trinkt Whisky aus einem Zahnputzbecher, während verschiedene Leute sein ungewöhnliches Make-up und rosa Perücken-Outfit ergänzen. Es ist fünf Uhr morgens. Ich filme.[34] Wir sind in Columbus, Ohio. Draußen liegt Schnee.

Wir sind irgendwo zwischen Berlin und Warschau unterwegs in einem Dreieinhalbtonner, überholen im wogenden dichten Nebel auf schmalen Straßen. Wer immer auf dem Beifahrersitz sitzt, muss nach aus dem Dunkel auftauchenden Vorderlichtern Ausschau halten.[35] Ein nervenaufreibendes Geschäft. Jedes Mal, wenn wir zum Überholen ausscheren, fühlt man sich dem Tode nahe.

Wir sind in Sheffield, proben in einem Gemeindesaal.[36]

Wir sind in Sheffield, proben in einer verlassenen Schule mit eingeschlagenen Fenstern und Industriegasofen.[37]

Wir sind in Sheffield, proben in einer alten Fabrik, über uns eine Boxhalle. Wenn die Typen oben trainieren, lösen ihre Sprünge Schauer von Putz von der verfallenen Decke aus. Der Staub und Putz legt sich wie ein seltsamer Regen über alles und jedes. Wenn man das Bühnenbild von (Let the Water Run its Course) to the Sea that Made the Promise mit dieser eiskalten, verfallenen Fabrik, die wir für fünf

34   Das Videoband ist verloren gegangen.
35   Diese Geschichte wird in The Travels (2002) erzählt.
36   Soundtrack: The Fall, Hex Enduction Hour.
37   Als die Männer die Gasflaschen liefern, schauen sie argwöhnisch auf Mark Randle und Robin, die beide Cowboyhüte und -kostüme tragen, und auf Claire, die einen falschen Penis umgebunden und einen Bart ins Gesicht gemalt hat (Kostüme für Marina & Lee).

Jahre unsere Heimat nannten, vergleicht, kann man eins vom anderen kaum unterscheiden.

Wir arbeiten an *Some Confusions in the Law about Love*. Wir scheinen es bei jeder Aufführung zu verändern – eines dieser Stücke, die nie fertig werden. Jahre später finden wir Texte und Videobänder von diesem Stück und können nicht mehr herausfinden, zu welcher Version sie gehören. War das Nottingham? War das die ICA-Version? Wer weiß.[38]

Wir sind in München. Terry lässt während der Proben zu *Bloody Mess*[39] eine Glasflasche fallen und das Glas zerbricht – Scherben und

what versions they represent. Was this Nottingham? Was this the ICA version? Who knows.[38]

We are in Munich. Terry drops a glass bottle during *Bloody Mess* rehearsals,[39] and the glass shatters everywhere – shards and fragments[40] all over the floor. The rest of the run-through is

---

38   Irgendwann 1999 bringen wir sämtliche Probenvideos zum Tonarchiv der British Library in London. Darunter sind Videos von nahezu jeder Probe seit *Emanuelle Enchanted* und einige Bänder von früheren Sachen. Kisten über Kisten – die meisten von ihnen lediglich auf rudimentärste Weise katalogisiert – die Bänder mit dem Datum beschriftet oder manchmal einfach nur mit einer Nummer oder einem Buchstaben. Sicher aber ist, dass einige der Bänder, die wir zur Probendokumentation benutzt haben, auch noch andere, privatere Sachen enthalten. Es ist eine seltsame Vorstellung, dass sich irgendwo in den Tiefen der British Library ein Hi-8-Band befindet, beschriftet mit „Dirty Work 9", auf dem sich auch Aufnahmen von Seth und Deb befinden, die im Garten herumrennen, oder der Blick aus dem Fenster eines Hauses von vor Jahren.

39   Sie benutzte das Wasser aus der Flasche, um auszusehen als habe sie geweint.

---

38   Sometime in 1999, we lodge all of our rehearsal video tapes at the National Sound Archive of the British Library in London. This includes videos of almost every rehearsal hour of everything we made since *Emanuelle Enchanted*, plus some occasional tapes of earlier stuff. Boxes and boxes of it – most of it uncatalogued in anything but the most rudimentary way – tapes labelled by date or in some cases simply by number or letter. What's for sure is that some of the tapes used to document rehearsals also have other more personal stuff on them. It's weird to think that somewhere in the depths of the British Library there is a Hi-8 tape marked "Dirty Work 9" that also has some footage of Seth and Deb running around in the garden or some footage of the view from a window in a house from years ago.

39   She has been using the water in the bottle to make it look like she has been crying.

40   I am thinking about fragments but in an absolutely different sense. Disconnected from its 'original' place, lacking context, lacking 'beginning' or 'end', lacking place in an argument lacking 'reason' – the fragment is both statement and question. We cannot know (and can therefore only guess) what the fragment is, what purpose it has, what intention is behind its production or presentation. In this sense and for our purposes (here and elsewhere), the fragment remains an ideal compositional unit.

A Text on 20 Years with 66 Footnotes
Ein Text über 20 Jahre mit 66 Fußnoten
Tim Etchells

peppered with attempts to clean the mess up, which becomes part of the action.[41]

We are in Beirut. The city is covered in posters for an election – huge portraits, hand painted, almost all of which show these fine-looking Arabic guys with extravagant well-groomed moustaches. We are here to do the durational performance *And on the Thousandth Night …* – six hours of improvised stories – from fairy tales to personal stories and movie plots – each story interrupting its predecessor and none of them allowed to finish. Beirut seems a perfect location for this performance. That night when we do it, there are many stories in response to the posters we have seen on the streets, all the stories fanciful, playful, absurd: a story about a city in which several men are in love with one woman, the various suitors covering the streets with their portraits in an attempt to seduce her; another story about a city in which the king organises a moustache competition, and so on. People are delighted – seeing the reality of the

41   There is an audience at this rehearsal comprising some people from the Big Art Group (who are performing in the same festival, but who won't be able to see an actual performance) and a couple of Russian guys who we think are also part of the festival, but we aren't sure.

Bruchstücke[40] überall auf dem Boden. Der Rest des Durchlaufs ist geprägt von dem Versuch, das Chaos zu beseitigen, was Teil der Handlung wird.[41]

Wir sind in Beirut. Die Stadt ist gepflastert mit Wahlplakaten – riesige Porträts, handgemalt, und fast alle zeigen diese eleganten arabischen Männer mit extravaganten, gepflegten Schnurrbärten. Wir sind hier, um die lange Performance *And on the Thousandth Night …* zu zeigen – sechs Stunden improvisierter Geschichten – von Märchen über private Anekdoten bis zu Filmhandlungen – wobei jede Geschichte die vorangegangene unterbricht und keine zu Ende erzählt werden darf. Beirut erscheint als der perfekte Ort für diese Performance. In der Aufführung hier reagieren viele Geschichten auf die Plakate, die wir in den Straßen gesehen haben; alle unrealistisch, spielerisch, absurd: Eine Geschichte über eine Stadt, in der mehrere Männer dieselbe Frau lieben und – um sie zu verführen – die Straßen mit ihren Porträts bedecken. Eine andere Geschichte über eine Stadt, in der der König einen Schnurrbart-Wettbewerb organisiert,

40   Ich denke an Bruchstücke, Fragmente, aber in einem völlig anderen Sinn. Abgeschnitten von seinem ‚ursprünglichen‘ Ort, ohne Kontext, ohne ‚Anfang‘ oder ‚Ende‘, hat es keinen Platz in einer These, fehlt ihm der ‚Grund‘ – das Fragment ist Aussage und Frage zugleich. Wir können nicht wissen (und deshalb nur mutmaßen) was das Fragment ist, welchen Zweck es hat, welche Intention hinter seiner Herstellung oder Vorstellung steht. In diesem Sinn und für unsere Zwecke (hier und anderswo) bleibt das Fragment ein ideales kompositorisches Element.

41   Es gibt bei dieser Probe Publikum, bestehend aus einigen Leuten der Big Art Group (die auf demselben Festival spielen, aber keine Vorstellung von uns sehen können) und einigen Russen, die wohl auch zum Festival gehören, aber wir sind uns nicht ganz sicher.

usw. Die Leute sind begeistert – sie sehen, wie die Realität der Stadt direkt aufgenommen und im verzerrenden Spiegel der Performance reflektiert wird.[42]

Wir sind in New York.[43] Richard befindet sich in einem Hotelzimmer und gibt einer selbst gebastelten Bombe den letzten Schliff. Die Bombe besteht aus mit rotem Klebeband umwickelten Besenstielen, einem Wecker und dem Rest eines alten Schaltbretts. Das ganze wird von einem behelfsmäßigem Klettergurt, der um den Körper geht, zusammengehalten. Es ist eine Art perfekte Cartoon-Zeitbombe. Wir machen im Hotel[44] eine Menge Fotos von Leuten, die die Bombe halten und gehen dann nach draußen in den Central Park, um noch mehr Aufnahmen zu machen.[45] Über-

---

42   Und die Performance wird, später, wieder zurückkehren in die Realität. Einige Monate nach unserem Beirut-Aufenthalt treffe ich Walid Ra'ad, einen Künstler von dort. Er erzählt, dass sechs Wochen nach unserer Beiruter Aufführung von *And on the Thousandth Night …* Vico – der Techniker des dortigen Festivals – verhaftet wurde. Ich frage warum, und Walid antwortet „was Politisches", und lacht dann – „nein, nichts Politisches, nichts von Bedeutung, nur betrunken und eine Ordnungswidrigkeit". Er sagt, dass Vico drei Tage im Gefängnis war, in einer kleinen Zelle zusammen mit acht anderen Gefangenen. Und er sagt, dass dort, im Hauptgefängnis von Beirut, Vico diesen Typen das improvisierte Spiel, aus dem das Stück besteht, beigebracht habe. Sie verbrachten die Tage und Nächte in der Zelle auf diese Weise – Geschichten erzählend, Berichte vermischend …

43   Viele Jahre früher.

44   Hotel 17.

45   Hugo macht die Fotos, wie er es seit 1986 gemacht hat. Über Hugos Aufnahmen aus der Mitte der Probenphasen pflegten wir zu sagen, dass wir, wenn wir die Bilder in den Händen hielten, zum ersten Mal sehen konnten, was wir da eigentlich machten.

---

city outside pass straight into the distorting mirror of the work.[42]

We are in New York.[43] Richard is in a hotel room putting the finishing touches to a home-made bomb. The bomb is made of broom handles covered in red tape, an alarm clock, and a bit of old circuit board. The whole lot held together on a makeshift harness that goes around the body. It's a kind of perfect 'cartoon ticking bomb'. We shoot a load of pictures of people holding the bomb in the hotel[44] and then go out to Central Park and shoot some more.[45] There is snow everywhere. Super-beautiful. Various people pose amongst the snowbound trees with the bomb. The suggestion of an explosion from the toy bomb seems so perfect and delicate next to

---

42   And the work, later, will pass right back into the world. After we've been back from Beirut for a couple of months, I bump into Walid Ra'ad, an artist who's from the city. He says that six weeks after we'd done *And on the Thousandth Night …* performance in Beirut, Vico – who's the technician of the festival there – had been arrested. I asked why, and Walid said 'something political', then laughed – 'oh, not political, nothing important, just drunk and disorderly'. He said that Vico had spent three days in jail, in a small cell shared with 8 other prisoners. He said that there, in the central jail of Beirut, Vico had taught these guys to play the improvised game that makes up the show. They'd passed the days and nights in the cell together that way, telling stories, interweaving tales.

43   This is years before.

44   Hotel 17.

45   Hugo is doing the photographs as he has since 86. When it comes to mid-rehearsal shoots with Hugo, we liked to say that getting the pictures back was a way to see for the first time what you were really doing.

A Text on 20 Years with 66 Footnotes
Ein Text über 20 Jahre mit 66 Fußnoten
Tim Etchells

the tree branches which look like they will shed their snow at the slightest knock. People are walking their dogs and snowballing in the park. They see us – a group of people standing around and a bomb being passed around – and they just smile and go about their business.[46] Lewis Nicholson is with us and we talk about the beautiful publicity objects he used to make for us – wonderful, oblique and amazing things that were somehow completely at odds with their supposed function as advertising.[47] Later in the early morning, when we have done the gig and have been drinking a lot in the East Village, we step out of the Ukrainian National Home or the Telephone Bar,[48] and Cathy and Claire walk across 1ST Ave (?) having looked right and not left or something and they come very close (i.e. as close as I have ever seen) to being killed by an oncoming car which squeals and slides to a halt just in front of their drunken lurch, the driver looking with a mixture of anger, disbelief and distress like he will be tortured by remembering this near-terrible moment for the rest of his

all liegt Schnee. Superschön. Verschiedene Leute posieren mit der Bombe zwischen den schneebedeckten Bäumen. Die Anspielung auf die Explosion dieser Spielzeugbombe wirkt so perfekt, so heikel vor dem Hintergrund der Zweige, die aussehen, als würden sie schon bei der leichtesten Berührung all ihren Schnee abwerfen. Leute führen ihre Hunde im Park spazieren oder machen Schneeballschlachten. Sie sehen uns – eine Gruppe von Leuten, die herumstehen und eine Bombe herumreichen – und lächeln nur, ohne sich stören zu lassen.[46] Lewis Nicholson ist dabei und wir sprechen über die schönen Werbeobjekte, die er für uns zu machen pflegte – wundervolle, verborgene und erstaunliche Dinge, die in gewisser Weise völlig verfehlt waren im Hinblick auf ihre Funktion als Werbung.[47] Später, am frühen Morgen, nach der Aufführung und nachdem wir in East Village ziemlich viel getrunken haben, kommen wir aus dem ukrainischen Volksheim oder aus der Telephone Bar,[48] und Cathy und Claire gehen über die First Ave (?), wobei sie nach rechts, aber nicht nach links geschaut haben oder so ähnlich, und sie kommen dem Tod sehr nahe (d. h. näher, als ich es je gesehen habe), indem sie fast von einem herankommenden Auto überfahren werden, das quietscht und schlingert und genau vor dem betrunkenen Torkeln der beiden zum Stehen kommt. Der Fahrer schaut mit einer Mischung aus Wut, Unglauben und Sorge, als ob er für den Rest seines Lebens von der Erinnerung an diesen beinahe-schrecklichen Moment gequält werden würde, wäh-

---

46   This is 1998.

47   A book of burnt matches for *Club of No Regrets*, a note inserted behind the matches bearing supposed directions to the Club itself. A set of price lists for brutal and banal objects and acts for *Hidden J*. A limited edition of handmade maps of an imaginary country for *Emanuelle Enchanted*.

48   Or somewhere else.

---

46   Das war 1998.

47   Ein Heftchen abgebrannter Streichhölzer für *Club of No Regrets*, zwischen denen sich eine Notiz mit mutmaßlichen Adressen des Clubs verbirgt. Preislisten brutaler und banaler Objekte und Taten für *Hidden J*. Eine limitierte Auflage handgezeichneter Karten eines imaginären Landes für *Emanuelle Enchanted*.

48   Oder von woanders.

rend sie (Cathy und Claire) es – tatsächlich – vollkommen vergessen werden.[49]

Ich erinnere mich, dass E. M. Forster den Rat gab: „Auf jeden Fall Verbindungen herstellen". Aber in dieser Geschichte (meiner) (wie in jeder anderen) (z. B. deiner) kann alles mit jedem verbunden werden. Oder andersherum: alles beinhaltet bereits alles andere. Jede Geschichte ist eine chinesische Schachtel, oder eine Tür, die zu jeder weiteren führt.[50] ‚Verbinden'. „Auf jeden Fall Verbindungen herstellen." Merkwürdig – wir haben in unseren Arbeitsprozessen so viel Zeit damit verbracht, das Material nicht zu verbinden, sondern es getrennt zu halten. Versuchten, das Material einfach bei sich selbst zu belassen, ‚als Objekte', wie wir zu sagen pflegten. ‚Das Ding ist das Ding ist das Ding'. Einmal zugestanden, dass alles von Bedeutung sein kann – alles sich verbinden kann, alles das, woran man gerade arbeitet, produktiv beeinflussen kann, wollten wir Materialspuren, Zeitblöcke, die manchmal kollidierten oder sich zu treffen schienen,

life and they (Cathy and Claire), in fact, will forget all of it.[49]

I remember that E. M. Forster had the advice *only connect*. But in this history (mine) (like any other) (i.e. yours) anything can be connected to anything else. Or else: Everything already contains everything else. Every story is a Chinese box, or a doorway that leads to every other one.[50] *Only connect. Only connect.* Strange – we spent so much of our time in the process not connecting material, but rather trying to keep it separate. Trying to let stuff just sit there as itself, 'as objects', as we liked to say. 'The thing is the thing is the thing'. Having admitted that anything might be relevant – anything might be connectable, anything might have a productive bearing on what you are currently doing – we wanted tracks of material, blocks of time that sometimes collided or appeared to meet, but which always,

---

49   Diese Beinahe-Tode sind ein fester Bestandteil der Geschichte. Einmal, nach der letzten Vorstellung von *Some Confusions in the Law about Love* in Sheffield, am Leadmill-Theater, beobachte ich den Lichtdesigner Nigel Edwards, wie er auf einer Traverse hoch oben in der Beleuchtungsanlage sitzt und ruhig (ohne es zu bemerken) die letzten Klemmen, die die Stange an der Anlage halten, abschraubt. Es war purer Comic – der Typ sägt an dem Brett, auf dem er steht. Ich bat Nigel aufzuhören.

50   Vielleicht ist es wirklich genau das, worum es uns in der langen improvisierten Performance *And on the Thousandth Night…* ging – eine Art verrückter Unzucht von Geschichten, Verbindungen, Jump-Cuts, Umkehrungen.

---

49   These near-deaths are a constant part of the story. Once, after we had done the final performances of *Some Confusions in the Law about Love*, in Sheffield, at the Leadmill, I watched the lighting designer Nigel Edwards sitting on a scaffolding pole high up in the lighting rig and calmly (without realising it) undoing the only clamps which were attaching the pole itself to the rig. It was pure cartoon – the guy sawing at the plank on which he himself is standing. I asked Nigel to stop.

50   Maybe this is in fact what we tried to deal with in the improvised durational performance *And on the Thousandth Night…* – a mad fornication of stories, connections, jump cuts, reversals.

in fact, stayed resolutely separate.[51] We wanted something that would not ever homogenise down into a single narrative, a single statement. "Oh," we would say, as an insult in rehearsals if the structure ever collapsed into unwanted clarity. "Oh, it's become a play now."[52]

We did not, it seems, want 'a play', which, for us, became a by-word for the homogenised, the pre-packaged, the performance which somehow wanted to deny presence and performance and liveness and insist instead on writing, closure, absence and fixity. We wanted the unstable. The trembling. The thrill of live decisions. The colli-

---

51   I think about something that Ron Vawter told me once when I did an interview with him in Belgium. Sitting in a café, Ron said: "What we tend to do in the Wooster Group, and in my own work, is to appropriate from several different sources at the same time. That way we can juggle all these separate things until the weights are familiar and then a new kind of theatre text is created between these different places …"

52   Notebook fragment (dream). "She has hypermedia and hypertextual links embedded in her body – when you kiss her hands or her elbows or her eyelids, she opens up to streams of data, opening like a doorway to a hidden kingdom. X could never work out if this hypertextual woman was meant as metaphor or not, and never having met her couldn't be sure … I mean wasn't sex itself always a kind of hypertext … the body blossoming in memory and enactment of other loves, other beds, previous embraces … the texts of the past inscribing themselves into the present to create possibilities, impossibilities, structures, doorways …"

---

tatsächlich aber immer strikt getrennt blieben.[51] Wir wollten etwas, das sich unter keinen Umständen in eine einzige Erzählung, in eine einzige Aussage zusammenführen ließe. „Oh", würden wir sagen, als Beleidigung während der Proben, wenn die Struktur ungewollt klar ausgefallen wäre: „Oh, da ist ja ein richtiges Theaterstück draus geworden."[52]

Wir wollten, wie es scheint, kein ‚Stück', das – für uns – zum Inbegriff des Homogenisierten, Abgepackten geworden war; wollten keine Aufführung, die Präsenz und Performance und Live-Erlebnis irgendwie verneint und statt dessen auf Text, Abgeschlossenheit, Abwesenheit und Fixiertheit besteht. Wir wollten das Ungewisse. Das Beben. Den Kick

---

51   Mir fällt ein, was Ron Vawter mir einmal während eines Interviews, das ich in Belgien mit ihm machte, erzählt hat. Ron sagte, in einem Café sitzend: „Was wir mit der Wooster Group versuchten – und ich in meiner eigenen Arbeit – ist, sich Dinge gleichzeitig aus verschiedenen Quellen anzueignen. So dass wir mit all diesen unverbundenen Dingen jonglieren können, bis das Gewicht vertraut ist und eine neue Art von Theatertext zwischen diesen verschiedenen Orten entsteht …"

52   Notizbuch-Fragment (Traum): „In ihren Körper sind Hypermedia- und Hypertext-Links eingebaut – küsst man ihre Hände oder Ellbogen oder Augenlider, öffnet sie sich Datenströmen, öffnet sich wie eine Tür zu einem verborgenen Königreich. X konnte nicht herausfinden, ob diese Hypertext-Frau als Metapher gemeint war oder nicht, und da er sie nie getroffen hatte, konnte er sich nicht sicher sein … Ich meine, war Sex nicht immer eine Art Hypertext … der Körper erblüht in der Erinnerung und im Durchleben früherer Lieben, anderer Betten, vergangener Umarmungen – die Texte der Vergangenheit schreiben sich in die Gegenwart ein und lassen Möglichkeiten entstehen, Unmöglichkeiten, Strukturen, Durchgänge …"

286

A Text on 20 Years with 66 Footnotes
Ein Text über 20 Jahre mit 66 Fußnoten
Tim Etchells

der spontanen Entscheidungen. Die Kollision unterschiedlicher Materialien, verschiedener Erzählweisen.[53] Ein Theater, das dich einer Welt aussetzte statt dir eine zu beschreiben. Oder das dich einer Situation aussetzte statt sie nur zu beschreiben. Ein Theater, in dem von Anfang an deine Eigenschaft als Betrachter ein anerkannter und vorausgesetzter Teil der Aufführung war. Ein Theater, das eher wie ein Ereignis wirkte. Ein Theater, das Forderungen stellte. Ein Theater, das hässlich und unangenehm war. Ein Theater, das seine Zweideutigkeiten, seine Unentschiedenheiten, seine Unverbundenheiten mochte. Ein Theater, das sehr sehr komisch war, lächerlich, absurd. Ein Theater, bei dem die Komödie sich nie ganz als Komödie bestätigte.[54] Ein Theater, das keinen Hehl daraus machte, dass es hier, vor dir, einen Haufen Leute gab, die etwas machten. Ein Theater, das seiner eigenen Sprache misstraute, obwohl es sie benutzte. Ein Theater, dass das Publikum spaltete. Ein Theater, das das Publikum auch 'einen' konnte, obwohl es diesem Wort misstraute. Ein Theater, das

53 Wir sprachen an einem bestimmten Punkt viel über das nicht-narrative Theater. Wir stellten fest, dass wir nichts gegen das Erzählen einzuwenden hatten – wir wollten bloß jede Menge davon. Das beste Beispiel dafür ist vielleicht die lange Performance *12 am: Awake & Looking Down*, in der das Zirkulieren der Pappschilder, die die Namen von Charakteren zeigen, wie eine Art erzählerisches Kaleidoskop funktionierte. Als ich die Performance einmal zusammen mit Miles ansah (irgendwann in Paris), erkannte ich, wie sehr die Arbeit darauf vertraut, dass das Publikum bestimmtes kulturelles Wissen besitzt. Für Miles war das meiste unverständlich (er war damals acht oder neun), weil er die Quellen nicht kannte (tatsächliche oder exemplarische), aus denen die Charaktere/Figuren stammten.
54 Eine Art Paraphrase von etwas, das der britische Performance-Künstler Gary Stevens mal zu mir gesagt hat.

sion of different materials, different narratives.[53] A theatre that placed you in a world rather than describing one to you. Or which placed you in a situation rather than describing one to you. A theatre in which your agency as a watcher was an acknowledged and known part of the performance from the out-set. A theatre that felt more like event. A theatre that made demands. A theatre that was ugly, awkward. A theatre that liked its ambiguities, its undecidednesses, its disconnections. A theatre that was very very funny, ridiculous, absurd. A theatre where the comedy did not ever, quite, confirm itself as comedy.[54] A theatre that did not hide the fact that here, in front of you, were a bunch of people doing something. A theatre that critiqued its own language even as it was using it. A theatre that divided audiences. A theatre that could also bring audiences 'together' even as it critiqued that word. A theatre constantly looking to breach its own edges, to duck into performance, into installation, into event, into blankness. A vulnerability.

53   There was a lot of talk at some point about non-narrative theatre. We said we had nothing against narrative at all – in fact, we just wanted lots of it. The best example of this might be the durational performance *12 am: Awake & Looking Down* where the circulation and re-circulation of the cardboard signs bearing the names of characters functions as a kind of narrative kaleidoscope. Watching this performance with Miles (in Paris sometime) I realised how very much the work relies on the watcher having certain kinds of cultural knowledge. Most of it was lost on Miles (he was maybe 8 or 9 at the time) because he didn't know the sources (actual or generic) from which the characters/figures were drawn.
54   This is something of a paraphrase of what the UK performance artist Gary Stevens once said to me.

A Text on 20 Years with 66 Footnotes
Ein Text über 20 Jahre mit 66 Fußnoten
Tim Etchells

A frailty. A provisionality. Home-made. Human-scale. A slipperiness. An air of anti-art. A work-man-like attitude. A rawness. A bleakness. A melancholy. A hilarity. An anger. A lack of compromise. A theatre that insisted on its own time, brought you into collision with its own temporality. A theatre that had no beginning and no end.

And finally it[55] ends, as it must.[56]
The sound of taped gunshots blows a hole in the fabric of space and time.

Robin closes the curtain and leaves off staring at the audience.

Terry changes costume again.[57]

Cathy screams and yells in gibberish language inside the house centre stage in *Hidden J*, the curtains drawn across the window so she cannot be seen. The other performers listen, and wait, wait until she is done.

Claire watches her own face on video, expression blank.[58]

Huw Chadbourn smears dirt across his face.[59]

Hugo checks the screen on his camcorder as various people from Forced Entertainment and from Richard Maxwell's company sing together *Goodnight Eileen*.[60]

---

55   This text, or the rhizome of memories it constructs and contains.
56   In fact nothing actually ends.
57   *Bloody Mess*, 2003.
58   *Some Confusions in the Law about Love.*
59   *The Day that Serenity Returned to the Ground*, 1986.
60   In a bar, very late at night, Theatre Mousonturm, Frankfurt, Friday 28TH November 2003.

immer darauf aus war, seine Grenzen zu überschreiten, in der Performance zu verschwinden, in Installationen, im Ereignis, in der Leere. Verletzlichkeit. Zerbrechlichkeit. Vorläufigkeit. Hausgemacht. Nach menschlichem Maß. Flüchtigkeit. Etwas von Anti-Kunst. Arbeiterhaltung. Rauheit. Kargheit. Melancholie. Ausgelassenheit. Wut. Kompromisslosigkeit. Ein Theater, das auf seine eigene Zeit bestand, dich in Konflikt brachte mit seiner eigenen Zeitlichkeit. Ein Theater ohne Anfang und ohne Ende.

Es[55] endet schließlich, weil es muss.[56]
Das Geräusch aufgenommener Schüsse reißt ein Loch in das Raum-Zeit-Gefüge.

Robin schließt den Vorhang und geht ins Publikum starrend ab.

Terry wechselt nochmals das Kostüm.[57]

Cathy heult und schreit in einer unverständlichen Sprache im Haus, das in *Hidden J* in der Bühnenmitte steht, die Vorhänge vor den Fenstern zugezogen, so dass sie nicht gesehen werden kann. Die übrigen Performer hören zu, warten, warten, bis sie fertig ist.

Claire beobachtet ihr eigenes Gesicht im Video, ausdruckslos.[58]

Huw Chadbourn schmiert sich Dreck ins Gesicht.[59]

Hugo überprüft den Bildschirm seines Camcorders, während einige Leute von Forced

---

55   Dieser Text, oder das Rhizom der Erinnerungen, die er konstruiert und enthält.
56   Tatsächlich endet nichts.
57   *Bloody Mess*, 2003.
58   *Some Confusions in the Law about Love.*
59   *The Day that Serenity Returned to the Ground*, 1986.

Entertainment mit Richard Maxwells Kompanie *Goodnight Eileen* singen.[60]

Will Waghorn beobachtet, wie ein Foto im Entwicklerbad entsteht, den Vorgang mit seinem eigenen Pulsschlag timend.[61]

Vlatka Horvat lernt die Technik für *Instructions for Forgetting*.[62]

Robins Brille wird wieder und wieder zerschmettert.[63]

Susie Williams schmeißt 1984[64] in Sheffield einen Stuhl hin, der in Brüssel auf den Boden kracht, im Mai 2004.[65]

Richard (in Wien, 2000) zieht sich einen Schuh von seinem Fuß, um einen Zaubertrick, den wir damals während der Magier-Konferenz in Blackpool gesehen hatten, nachzustellen – der Trick mit dem Schuh, der wundersamer Weise in der Hand auftaucht. Es ist laut in der Wiener Kneipe. Es gibt dafür kaum Platz. Der Trick mit dem Trick ist, auf einem Bein zu stehen, verdeckt den Schuh von dem angewinkelten Bein in die linke Hand zu nehmen, um ihn dann nach plötzlichem Herumschleudern mit der hochgestreckten rechten Hand aufzufangen, genau vor dem unglück-

Will Waghorn watches a photographic print emerge from the fluid in a developing tray, timing the procedure by taking his own pulse.[61]

Vlatka Horvat learns the tech for *Instructions for Forgetting*.[62]

Robin's spectacles are smashed and smashed again.[63]

Susie Williams throws a chair in Sheffield, 1984[64] and it crashes to the ground in Brussels, May 2004.[65]

Richard (in Vienna in 2000) takes the shoe from his foot, intending a recreation of the Magic trick we saw back at the Magicians' Convention back in Blackpool – the trick with the shoe that miraculously appears in your hand. The bar in Vienna is noisy. There is hardly space for this. The trick with the trick is to stand on one leg, secretly slip the shoe off the raised foot into your left hand, and then to bring the shoe slamming round suddenly and into the palm of your raised right hand, right in front of the hapless spectator. Richard moves. And the trick begins, except in this case, at four in the morning and a

---

60   In einer Kneipe, spät nachts, Mousonturm, Frankfurt, 28. November 2003.
61   *Red Room*, Showroom Gallery, 1988.
62   Gent, Belgien, 2003.
63   *The Set-up*, 1985.
64   Proben zu *Jessica in the Room of Lights*.
65   Ich stelle es mir vor, denn ich schreibe im Januar 2004.

61   *Red Room*, Showroom Gallery, 1988.
62   Gent, Belgium, 2003.
63   *The Set-up*, 1985.
64   *Jessica in the Room of Lights* rehearsal.
65   I am imagining this, since I am writing in January 04.

lot of Caipirinhas under the bridge, the shoe comes slamming round and misses the hand. It becomes a size 8 torpedo – a shoe flying across the bar. It crashes into a table that is all mountained up with drinks, and the glass goes bursting everywhere.

"Oh. You know …," the barmaid says. "It happens all the time."[66]

seligen Zuschauer. Richard bewegt sich. Der Trick beginnt, nur dass, in diesem Fall um vier Uhr morgens und mit einer ganzen Menge Caipirinhas intus, der Schuh herumgeschleudert wird und die Hand verfehlt. Er wird zu einem Torpedo Größe 43 – ein durch die Kneipe fliegender Schuh. Er kracht in einen Tisch, auf dem sich Getränke türmen. Das Glas splittert und fliegt nach allen Seiten.
„Ach, weißt du …", sagt die Kellnerin. „Das passiert andauernd."[66]

Übersetzt von Astrid Sommer

A Text on 20 Years with 66 Footnotes
Ein Text über 20 Jahre mit 66 Fußnoten
Tim Etchells

---

66   And keeps on happening. The glass shards flying out from there in every direction, backwards and forwards in time. Connections spin and multiply. The screen shimmers, cuts to black and then kicks into life again.

66   Und geht noch weiter. Die Glassplitter fliegen von dort in alle Richtungen, vorwärts und rückwärts in der Zeit. Verbindungen kreisen und multiplizieren sich. Der Bildschirm flimmert, wird schwarz, um erneut zum Leben erweckt zu werden.

This is the last thing you see.
You see me sat in the light, in the last of the light.
I'm sitting on a table.
You see my face. You see my lips. You see my eyes.
And you can see that I'm thinking.
It's the last thing you see.
You see my face. You see my eyes and you can't tell what I'm thinking.
My face is completely blank.
The eyes don't really give anything away.
The expression is somewhere between nothing and everything.
You don't know me. You think you know me. It's not important.
What's important is that you see me breathing. You see the rise and fall
of my breathing.
You hear the traffic outside, or drunks in the street, or the sound of rain
on the roof of the theatre, or the sounds of the others sat around you
in the auditorium. Or you hear none of these things. It's not important.
What's important is that you see me. You see me sat alone on a table in
the last of the light and then, suddenly, perhaps much more suddenly
than you had expected, it's over and I'm gone, and this time, I'm gone
forever and I never come back.

Bloody Mess

Pleasure
(Pre-production)

Chronology of Works
Chronologisches Werkverzeichnis

P: Performer/Spieler; **V:** Voiceover; **D:** Direction/Regie; **C:** Concept/ Konzept; **T:** Text;
S: Set Design/Bühnenbild; **L:** Lighting Design/Licht Design; **ST:** Soundtrack; **PH:** Photographs;
Fotografien; **V:** Video; **CO:** Commissioners/Auftraggeber; **CP:** Co-Producers/Koproduzenten.

The credits of the cast follow the first performances.
Die Besetzungslisten richten sich nach den Uraufführungen.

Works for Theatre Spaces and Durational Performances
Theaterarbeiten und durational performances

Jessica in the Room of Lights
P: Robin Arthur, Huw Chadbourn, Cathy Naden, Susie Williams. D: Tim Etchells,
Richard Lowdon. T: Tim Etchells. S/L: Richard Lowdon. ST: John Avery.
14. 12. 1984, Yorkshire Arts Space Society, Sheffield (GB).

Using dialogue, taped voiceover, soundtrack and choreographed action, the performance explores
a blurred storyline about a cinema usherette whose real life becomes mixed with films she's absorbed
at work. Moving from the suburbs to the city, Jessica's story – a failed romance – is retold in contradictory versions as a form of incomplete memory.
Mit Dialogen, Bandeinspielungen, Musik und choreographierten Aktionen folgt die Performance der ver-
worrenen Geschichte einer Kinoanweiserin, deren Leben sich vermischt mit den Filmen, die sie bei der
Arbeit sieht. In einer Bewegung von den Vororten hinein in die Stadt wird diese Geschichte einer gescheiter-
ten Liebe wieder und wieder in den widersprüchlichen Versionen unvollständiger Erinnerung geschildert.

The Set-up
P: Robin Arthur, Huw Chadbourn, Susie Williams. D: Tim Etchells, Richard Lowdon.
T: Tim Etchells. S: Richard Lowdon, Huw Chadbourn. L: Richard Lowdon. ST: John
Avery. CO: National Review of Live Art (GB).
12. 10. 1985, Midland Group, Nottingham (GB).

Three performers use choreographed gestures and narrative moments from gangland interrogation
scenes. The piece draws on TV and film genre clichés to explore ideas of guilt, confession and sexual
identity. The style explores a kind of minimalist choreography in which the shapes and gestures of a
story are worked in repetition and phase to reveal their musical and narrative possibilities.
Drei Performer bedienen sich choreographierter Gesten und narrativer Momente aus Verhörszenen im
Gangster-Milieu. Das Stück untersucht mit Hilfe von Genre-Klischees aus Film und Fernsehen Vorstel-
lungen von Schuld, Beichte und sexueller Identität. Die minimalistische Choreographie wiederholt und
synchronisiert Formen und Gesten einer Geschichte, um ihre musikalischen und narrativen Möglichkeiten
aufzuzeigen.

Nighthawks
P: Huw Chadbourn, Tim Etchells, Richard Lowdon, Susie Williams. VO: Tim Etchells, Cathy Naden.
D: Robin Arthur, Cathy Naden. T: Tim Etchells. S: Richard Lowdon, Huw Chadbourn. L: Richard
Lowdon. ST: John Avery.
23. 10. 1985, North Riding College, Scarborough (GB).

The near-mythical world of American bars, inspired by the paintings of Edward Hopper, American
film and literature. The text, again, is pre-recorded; the choreography poetical and repetitive.
Die nahezu mythische Welt der American Bars, inspiriert von den Gemälden Edward Hoppers, ameri-
kanischen Filmen und Büchern. Wieder kommt der Text vom Band und die poetische Choreographie
arbeitet mit Wiederholungsstrukturen.

The Day that Serenity Returned to the Ground
P: Robin Arthur, Huw Chadbourn, Tim Etchells, Cathy Naden. D: Susie Williams,
Tim Etchells, Richard Lowdon. T: Tim Etchells. S: Richard Lowdon, Huw Chadbourn.
L: Richard Lowdon. ST: John Avery. CO: The Zap Club, Brighton (GB).
6. 2. 1986, The Zap Club, Brighton (GB).

The setting is a white polythene isolation chamber, in which the performers are divided from the audi-
ence by a wall of metal grilles. At the centre of the piece is a science fiction story about the return of a
group of cosmonauts to Earth. Presenting the shapes or outlines of the narrative rather than its details,
The Day that Serenity moves through the initial genre material towards other strands of content.
In einer weißen Kunststoff-Isolationszelle sind die Performer durch ein Drahtgitter vom Publikum getrennt.
Ausgehend vom Genrematerial einer Science-Fiction-Geschichte über die Rückkehr einer Kosmonauten-
gruppe zur Erde, entwickelt die Erzählung andere Handlungsstränge, wobei das Interesse mehr deren
Gestalt und Umrissen als ihren Details gilt.

(Let the Water Run its Course) to the Sea that Made the Promise
P: Robin Arthur, Richard Lowdon, Cathy Naden, Susie Williams. VO: Tim Etchells,
Sarah Singleton. D: Huw Chadbourn, Tim Etchells, Richard Lowdon, Terry O'Connor.
T: Tim Etchells. S: Huw Chadbourn, Richard Lowdon. ST: John Avery.
6. 10. 1986, Trent Polytechnic, Nottingham (GB).

A pair of recorded voices speak, in a rough poetic tone, about life in a post-apocalyptic city. Whim-
pering, shouting and whispering, two parallel Bonnie & Clyde couples play a game-cum-ritual of
scene fragments which could be about their lives and possible deaths.
Zwei Stimmen vom Band berichten in rauer, poetischer Sprache vom Leben in einer Stadt nach der Apo-
kalypse. Wimmernd, schreiend und flüsternd spielen zwei sich spiegelnde Bonnie & Clyde-Paare ein ritu-
alisiertes Spiel mit Szenenfragmenten, die von ihrem Leben oder ihrem möglichen Tod handeln könnten.

200% & Bloody Thirsty
P: Robin Arthur, Richard Lowdon, Cathy Naden. Video performer: Mark Etchells,
Sarah Singleton. D: Tim Etchells, Terry O'Connor. V: Jo Cammack, Terry O'Connor.
T: Tim Etchells. S/L: Richard Lowdon. ST: John Avery.
10. 10. 1988, Trent Polytechnic, Nottingham (GB).

Three drunks in bad wigs and jumble-sale clothes enact endlessly the events surrounding the supposed or imagined death of one of their friends, as if by replaying the events, their truth might be revealed. In a stage set reminiscent of a homemade kitsch snow shaker, the piece repeats a chaotic nativity
play in various versions, including one done blindfolded and at breakneck speed. The onstage action
is framed by a poetic narration/dialogue from a pair of angels on video monitors.

Drei Betrunkene mit schlechten Perücken und Flohmarkt-Klamotten spielen schier endlos die Ereignisse rund um den vermuteten oder erfundenen Tod eines Freundes durch – als könnten sie dadurch deren wahre Bedeutung aufdecken. Ein chaotisches Krippenspiel im an eine selbstgemachte kitschige Schneekugel erinnernden Bühnenbild wird in verschiedenen Varianten wiederholt (z. B. mit verbundenen Augen oder in halsbrecherischem Tempo). Gerahmt wird die Handlung durch eine poetische, dialogische Erzählung von zwei Engeln auf Videomonitoren.

Some Confusions in the Law about Love

P: Robin Arthur, Terry O'Connor, Claire Marshall, Cathy Naden, Mark Randle. D: Tim Etchells, Richard Lowdon. T: Tim Etchells. S/L: Richard Lowdon, Nigel Edwards. ST: John Avery.

30. 10. 1989, Trent Polytechnic, Nottingham (GB).

A rather unlikely Elvis Presley impersonator in Birmingham, England performs his act on a tacky nightclub stage. As the evening progresses, he is joined by two jaded showgirls, a pair of forlorn skeletons who perform an archaic Japanese love-suicide story and special guests, Mike and Dolores, "sex act escapologists", interviewed "live by satellite from Hawaii" on two monitors at the edges of the stage.

Ein ziemlich unähnlicher Elvis-Presley-Imitator aus Birmingham, England, auf einer billigen Nachtclub-bühne. Im Laufe des Abends gesellen sich zwei abgewrackte Showgirls, zwei einsame Skelette (die eine altertümliche japanische Geschichte von Liebe und Selbstmord aufführen) und weitere special guests dazu: Mike und Dolores, „Sex-Flüchtlinge", die auf zwei Monitoren am Rand der Bühne „live via Satellit aus Hawaii" interviewt werden.

Marina & Lee

P: Robin Arthur, Terry O'Connor, Claire Marshall, Cathy Naden, Mark Randle. Video performer: Richard Lowdon. D: Tim Etchells, Richard Lowdon. T: Tim Etchells. S/L: Richard Lowdon, Nigel Edwards. ST: John Avery.

18. 3. 1991, Nuffield Studio, Lancaster (GB).

The piece begins with a dysfunctional physics lecture from a woman in a shop-girl's overalls. Through-out the show, the central figure, Marina, describes her journey through a bizarre contradictory land-scape – part desert, part city and part paradise – whilst the rest of the performance collides around her. There are kung-fu fights and raucous operas that seem to turn into adverts, cowboys, barking dogs and hysterical women with guns. At other times, the performers play a set of confessions directly to the audience.

Mit der fehlplatzierten Physikvorlesung einer Frau im Verkäuferinnenkittel nimmt das Stück seinen Anfang, im weiteren Verlauf dann beschreibt Marina, die zentrale Figur des Abends, ihre Reise durch eine bizarre, widersprüchliche Landschaft – teils Wüste, teils Stadt, teils Paradies – während der Rest der Performance um sie herum kollidiert: Kung-Fu-Kämpfe und lärmende Opern scheinen sich in Werbespots zu verwandeln, Cowboys, bellende Hunde und hysterische Frauen mit Pistolen treten auf. Zwischendurch wenden sich die Performer mit einer Reihe von Geständnissen direkt an das Publikum.

Welcome to Dreamland

Cast/Besetzung: as above/wie oben.

15. 7. 1991, The Leadmill, Sheffield (GB).

Retrospective trilogy consisting of *(Let the Water Run its Course) to the Sea that Made the Promise, 200% & Bloody Thirsty* and *Some Confusions in the Law about Love.*

Retrospektive Trilogie aus (Let the Water Run its Course) to the Sea that Made the Promise, 200% & Bloody Thirsty *und* Some Confusions in the Law about Love.

Emanuelle Enchanted
(or a Description of this World as if it Were a Beautiful Place)
P: Robin Arthur, Richard Lowdon, Claire Marshall, Cathy Naden, Terry O'Connor.
D/T: Tim Etchells. Assistant director/Regiesassistent: Nick Crowe. S: Richard
Lowdon. L: Nigel Edwards. ST: John Avery.
6. 10. 1992, Nuffield Studio, Lancaster (GB).

On a crude wooden stage, a group of five performers use a semi-translucent curtain, whisked backwards and forwards to reveal the fragmentary traces of a single apocalyptic night. Read narratively, the piece shows a night of crisis which is perhaps both personal and global. The invoked 'scenes' include a chaotic, almost nonsensical TV newsroom, a domestic space in which the walls themselves are always in motion, and a panoramic glimpse of many characters presented via cardboard signs that bear names, such "A TELEPATH (AGE 12)", "A SEXUALLY FRUSTRATED WOMAN LIVING IN A DREAM WORLD" or "A 9-YEAR-OLD SHEPHERD BOY".

Auf einer simplen Holzbühne ziehen fünf Perfomer einen halbdurchsichtigen Vorhang abrupt auf und zu und enthüllen so die fragmentarischen Spuren einer apokalyptischen Nacht der womöglich gleichermaßen persönlichen wie globalen Krise. Die heraufbeschworenen 'Szenarien' umfassen ein chaotisches, nahezu unsinniges Fernseh-Nachrichtenstudio, ein Haus, dessen Wände andauernd in Bewegung sind, und einen Panoramablick auf Charaktere, die mittels Pappschildern vorgestellt werden: „EIN TELEPATH (12 JAHRE)", „EINE SEXUELL FRUSTRIERTE FRAU, DIE IN EINER TRAUMWELT LEBT" oder „EIN NEUNJÄHRIGER SCHÄFERJUNGE".

Club of No Regrets
P: Robin Arthur, Richard Lowdon, Claire Marshall, Cathy Naden, Terry O'Connor.
D/T: Tim Etchells. Assistant director/Regieassistent: Ju Row Farr. S: Richard
Lowdon. L: Nigel Edwards. ST: John Avery.
5. 10. 1993, Nuffield Studio, Lancaster (GB).

Forced by the tyrannical director Helen X, two performers in a flimsy box-set centre stage are forced to act out the same fragmentary TV movie scenes again and again. Helped and hindered by two brutal stage hands with toy guns, this process becomes increasingly violent, the scenes intercut and overlayed in a poetic collision of narratives; the stage covered with talcum powder, fake blood, water and dead leaves.

Gezwungen von der tyrannischen Regisseurin Helen X, wiederholen die zwei Performer in einem wackeligen Bühnenbild immer wieder die gleichen Szenenfetzen aus TV-Filmen. Unterstützt und behindert von zwei brutalen Bühnenarbeitern mit Spielzeugpistolen, wird dieser Vorgang immer gewalttätiger. Die Szenen werden unterbrochen und überlagert durch einen poetischen Zusammenprall der Geschichten; die Bühne übersät mit Talkumpuder, falschem Blut, Wasser und toten Blättern.

12 am: Awake & Looking Down
(6-11 h/Std., durational performance)
P: Robin Arthur, Cathy Naden, Claire Marshall, Terry O'Connor, Richard Lowdon.
D: Tim Etchells. S: Richard Lowdon.
22. 10. 1993, National Review of Live Art, ICA, London (GB).

From "LOST LISA" to "ELVIS PRESLEY (THE DEAD SINGER)": Five mute performers, using secondhand clothes as costumes and a series of cardboard signs which bear the names of characters, present role after role in rapid succession. Based on a section of *Emanuelle Enchanted*, this is the group's first durational work. Over the long duration, exhaustion sets in on stage whilst those watching form innumerable possible connections and interpretations of the presented images. The piece lasts anywhere between 6 and 11 hours and – as in other durational works by the company – the public are free to arrive, depart and return at any point.

Von „VERLORENE LISA" bis „ELVIS PRESLEY (DER TOTE SÄNGER)": Fünf stumme Performer etablieren im Schnelldurchlauf mit Hilfe von Kostümen und Pappschildern, auf denen Figurennamen stehen, immer neue Rollen. Basierend auf einem Abschnitt aus Emanuelle Enchanted*, ist dies die erste durational performance der Gruppe. Die lange Spieldauer führt zur Erschöpfung auf der Bühne, während die Zuschauer die gezeigten Bilder auf unzählige Weisen verbinden und interpretieren. Das Stück dauert zwischen sechs bis elf Stunden und – wie in den folgenden durational performances – das Publikum kann beliebig kommen und gehen.*

Dreams' Winter
(Site-specific work / Ortsspezifische Arbeit)
P: Robin Arthur, Richard Lowdon, Claire Marshall, Sue Marshall, Cathy Naden, Terry O'Connor. Guests: Nicky Beaumont, Nicola Bertram, Alex Bliss, Paulette Terry Brian, Kath Cooke, Susie Dick, Ian Greenall, Tim Hall, Steve Jackson, Alex Kelly, Jamie McAffer, Kit McCudden, Ellen Mills, Susan Scott, Juliet Sebley, Fleur Soper, Michelle Stanbridge, Liz Tomlin, Rachel Walton. D: Tim Etchells. T: Tim Etchells, Forced Entertainment. S/L: Richard Lowdon. ST: John Avery. CO: Manchester Central Library (GB).
15. 7. 1994, Central Library, Manchester (GB).

297

The group's first site-specific performance, inspired by the Manchester Central Library with an audience seated at tables in the main dome-ceilinged hall of the building. Approximately thirty performers, both Forced Entertainment and guests, wander as if sleepwalking, barefoot in pyjamas, amongst the endless bookshelves.

Diese erste site-specific performance *der Gruppe ist inspiriert vom Gebäude der Manchester Central Library. Das Publikum sitzt an Tischen in der großen Kuppelhalle, während die dreißig Performer, Forced Entertainment und Gäste, wie im Schlaf barfuß in Pyjamas an den schier endlosen Bücherregalen entlang wandeln.*

Hidden J
P: Robin Arthur, Cathy Naden, Terry O'Connor, Richard Lowdon, Claire Marshall.
D/T: Tim Etchells. Assistant director/Regieassistent: Nick Crowe. S: Richard Lowdon. L: Nigel Edwards. ST: John Avery.
10. 10. 1994, Nuffield Studio, Lancaster (GB).

On a stage that looks like a construction site, this distorted portrait of England centres on a drunk bloke in the process of messing up a wedding speech. Around this hapless figure, the group present diverse fragments of apparently unrelated material – scenes of some unnamed East European war zone, a botched hospital operation, the narration of an angel and a devil, and accounts of a massacre in what could possibly be Africa.

Aus der vermasselten Hochzeitsrede eines Besoffenen entwickelt sich ein entstelltes Porträt Englands. Um diese unglückselige Figur auf einer Großbaustellenbühne werden Bruchstücke scheinbar unzusammenhängenden Materials präsentiert: Szenen aus einem unbestimmten osteuropäischen Kriegsgebiet, eine verpfuschte Krankenhausoperation, die Erzählung eines Engels und eines Teufels und Berichte von einem Massaker in einem Land, das möglicherweise in Afrika liegt.

Speak Bitterness

(Durational performance)

P: Robin Arthur, Tim Etchells, Tim Hall, Richard Lowdon, Claire Marshall, Sue Marshall, Cathy Naden, Terry O'Connor. D: Tim Etchells. T: Tim Etchells, Forced Entertainment. S: Richard Lowdon. L: Nigel Edwards. CO: National Review of Live Art (GB).

23. 10. 1994, National Review of Live Art, Glasgow (GB).

A line of people take turns to read confessions from behind a long table in a brightly lit space. The litany of wrongdoing to which they confess ranges from the big time of forgery, murder or genocide to nasty little details, such as reading each other's diaries and refusing to take the dogs out for a walk. Dressed in suits, the performers compete to confess the most horrific, amusing or convincing things. The viewers are free to enter and leave as they please.

Eine Reihe von Leuten hinter einem langen Tisch liest auf der hell erleuchteten Bühne abwechselnd Beichten vor, eine Litanei des Fehlverhaltens, von Fälschungen im großen Stil, Mord oder Genozid bis zu kleinen Gemeinheiten, wie dem Lesen in fremden Tagebüchern oder versäumtem Gassi-Gehen. Gekleidet in Anzügen und Kostümen treten die Performer in einen Wettstreit der schrecklichsten, lustigsten oder überzeugendsten Beichten. Die Zuschauer können beliebig kommen und gehen.

A Decade of Forced Entertainment

(Performance-lecture)

P: Robin Arthur, Tim Etchells, Richard Lowdon, Claire Marshall, Cathy Naden, Terry O'Connor. T: Tim Etchells, Forced Entertainment. S: Richard Lowdon. L: Nigel Edwards. ST: John Avery.

3. 12. 1994, ICA Theatre, London (GB).

A fictitious, as well as truthful remembered map of the years from 1984 to 1994, made on occasion of the tenth anniversary of Forced Entertainment. Combining documentary and autobiographical material in a performance/lecture, the piece links introspection on their own work with the group's reflection on historical and world events and the changing fabric of urban England.

Eine ebenso erfundene wie wahrhaftig erinnerte Landkarte der Jahre 1984 bis 1994 zum zehnten Geburtstag von Forced Entertainment. Dokumentarisches und autobiografisches Material wird zu einer Mischung aus Performance und Vortrag kombiniert und verbindet so die Innensicht der eigenen Arbeit mit Reflexionen über historische Ereignisse und die veränderte urbane Landschaft Englands.

Nights in this City

(Site-specific bus tour and installation / Ortsspezifische Bustour und Installation)

P: Robin Arthur, Richard Lowdon, Claire Marshall, Cathy Naden, Terry O'Connor. Coach driver/Busfahrer: Martin Tether. T: Tim Etchells, Forced Entertainment. ST: John Avery.

16. 5. 1995, Sheffield (GB).

Performers and viewers on a nocturnal bus tour through the centre of Sheffield. The commentary on the city outside mixes the fictitious, the official, and the purely personal to create a poetical exploration of urban life. Twice, the tour is interrupted by small scenes, which are performed in the street. The work ends with an installation in which the entire street index for the city is written out in chalk on the floor of a found space.

Performer und Zuschauer auf einer nächtlichen Bustour durch das Zentrum Sheffields. Die Kommentare über die Stadt vermischen Erfundenes, Offizielles und rein Persönliches zu einer poetischen Erkundung städtischen Lebens. Zweimal wird die Tour durch kleine gespielte Szenen auf der Straße unterbrochen. Die Arbeit endet mit einer Installation, für die der gesamte Straßenindex der Stadt mit Kreide auf den Boden eines vorgefundenen Ortes geschrieben wurde.

Speak Bitterness
(Theatre version / Theaterfassung)
P: Robin Arthur, Tim Hall, Richard Lowdon, Claire Marshall, Sue Marshall, Cathy Naden, Terry
O'Connor. D: Tim Etchells. T: Tim Etchells, Forced Entertainment. S: Richard Lowdon.
L: Nigel Edwards. ST: John Avery.
26. 9. 1995, Alsager Arts Centre, Stoke-on-Trent (GB).
Short version of the durational performance.
Kurze Version der durational performance.

Break In!
(Project for children / Projekt für Kinder)
P: Robin Arthur, Tim Hall, Richard Lowdon, Claire Marshall, Terry O'Connor. D: Tim Etchells. T: Tim
Etchells, Forced Entertainment.
30. 1. 1996, Crucible Theatre, Sheffield (GB).

A misguided tour of the Crucible Theatre in Sheffield for audiences of children. Borrowing the strategies of *Nights in this City*, the tour features a lost tour guide and fictional characters adrift in the
backstage spaces of the theatre.
Eine irreführende Tour durch das Crucible Theatre in Sheffield für Kinder. Ähnlichen Strategien wie
Nights in this City *folgend, irrt die Tour mit einem verlorenen Führer und fiktionalen Charakteren*
hinter der Bühne umher.

Showtime
P: Robin Arthur, Richard Lowdon, Claire Marshall, Cathy Naden, Terry O'Connor.
D: Tim Etchells. T: Tim Etchells, Forced Entertainment. S: Richard Lowdon. L: Nigel
Edwards. ST: John Avery.
25. 9. 1996, Alsager Arts Centre, Stoke-on-Trent (GB).

Narrated by a man with a fake dynamite bomb strapped to his chest, the piece begins with a naïve text
describing just what a good piece of theatre should be. From this amateurish advice about simple
scenery, good casting and dress rehearsals, *Showtime* soon decays into a chaos of cardboard pantomime trees, a dog that talks about suicide and a series of insistent questions asked of a dying thug
as he lies bleeding outside a Wendy house.
Das Stück beginnt mit der naiven Beschreibung eines guten Theaterstücks, vorgetragen von einem Mann
mit einer selbstgebastelten Bombe um den Bauch. Doch schon während seiner laienhaften Ratschläge
bezüglich einfacher Bühnenbilder, guter Besetzungen und Kostümproben versinkt Showtime *in einem*
Chaos aus Pappkostüm-Bäumen, einem Hund, der über Selbstmord spricht, und einer Reihe von beharr-
lichen Fragen an einen Sterbenden, der blutend vor einem Spielzeughaus liegt.

Quizoola!
(6 h/Std., durational performance)
P: Tim Etchells, Tim Hall, Sue Marshall. T: Tim Etchells. S: Richard Lowdon.
CO: ICA Live Arts, National Review Of Live Art (GB).
29. 10. 1996, National Review of Live Art, Glasgow (GB).

A team of three actors in smeared clown makeup take turns choosing from a text of 2000 questions
and making up answers on stage. The shape and content of each *Quizoola!* performance hangs in
the balance, negotiated live between players and the public. As new questions are chosen and new
answers made up, the mood shifts from low comedy to personal scrutiny to harsh interrogation
and intellectual hairsplitting. The piece lasts six hours and the public are free to arrive, depart and
return at any point.

Drei Performer mit schlecht geschminkten Clownsgesichtern (davon immer zwei auf der Bühne) stellen sich abwechselnd Fragen von einer Liste mit zweitausend Möglichkeiten, der andere gibt improvisierte Antworten. Form und Inhalt werden in jeder Aufführung durch Spieler und Publikum neu austariert. Während immer andere Fragen ausgewählt und Antworten erdacht werden, schwankt die Stimmung zwischen billiger Komödie, sehr persönlicher Befragung, barschem Verhör und intellektueller Haarspalterei. Das Stück dauert sechs Stunden, das Publikum kann jederzeit kommen und gehen.

Nights in this City

(Site-specific bus tour and installation / Ortsspezifische Bustour und Installation)
P: Robin Arthur, Richard Lowdon, Claire Marshall, Cathy Naden, Terry O'Connor. T: Tim Etchells, Forced Entertainment. ST: John Avery. CO: R Festival/Rotterdamse Schouwburg (NL).
23. 9. 1997, R Festival/Rotterdamse Schouwburg, Rotterdam (NL).
Rotterdam version.
Rotterdamer Fassung.

Pleasure

P: Robin Arthur, Richard Lowdon, Claire Marshall, Cathy Naden, Terry O'Connor.
D/T: Tim Etchells. S: Richard Lowdon. L: Nigel Edwards. ST: John Avery, found sources/ Fundstücke.
2. 11. 1997, Nieuwpoorttheater, Gent (B).

A bizarre night club, in the early hours of the morning, complete with slowed down music from a battered record player. A place of surreal melancholy with bad Hawaiian dancers, a horny pantomime horse, a cynical disc jockey/MC and failed William Tell routines. A catalogue of obscene words and phrases is scrawled on a blackboard at the back of the stage.

Ein bizarrer, frühmorgendlicher Nachtclub – vom schäbigen Plattenspieler wabert stark verlangsamte Musik. Ein Ort surrealer Melancholie mit schlechten Hawaii-Tänzerinnen, einer aufgegeilten Pferdefigur, einem zynischen DJ-Conferencier und missglückten Wilhelm-Tell-Übungen. Im Bühnenhintergrund wird ein Katalog obszöner Wörter und Redewendungen auf eine Tafel geschrieben.

Dirty Work

P: Robin Arthur, Claire Marshall, Cathy Naden. D/T: Tim Etchells, Forced Entertainment. S: Richard Lowdon. L: Nigel Edwards. M: John Avery, found sources/Fundstücke.
12. 11. 1998, Phoenix Arts, Leicester (GB).

Set on a tiny wooden stage with ragged curtains, *Dirty Work* involves two performers who alternately compete and work together to imagine and describe an impossible performance that ranges from mechanical dogs, scenes from Shakespeare, great battles from world history and the banalities of daily life. Summoned in text alone, accompanied by the sound of piano on a battered record player, the performance explores a world in which real life is so often presented as spectacle.

Auf einer kleinen, hölzernen Bühne mit zerschlissenen Vorhängen konkurrieren und kollaborieren zwei Performer bei der Schilderung einer unmöglichen Aufführung, die von mechanischen Hunden, Shakespeare-Szenen, großen Schlachten der Weltgeschichte bis zu den Banalitäten des Alltags reicht. Nur durch den Text heraufbeschworen und begleitet durch Klaviermusik von einem ramponierten Plattenspieler, erkundet die Performance eine Welt, in der das wahre Leben so häufig als Spektakel präsentiert wird.

Who Can Sing a Song to Unfrighten Me?
(24 h/Std., durational performance)
P: Robin Arthur, Tim Hall, Richard Lowdon, Claire Marshall, Sue Marshall, Cathy
Naden, Terry O'Connor. Guests/Gäste: Mark Etchells, Ruth Geiersberger, Gisela
Jürcke, Tobias Lange, Thomas Peters, Susanne Plassmann, Sanne van Rijn. D: Tim
Etchells. S: Richard Lowdon. L: Nigel Edwards. CO: London International Festival of Theatre,
London (GB), Royal Festival Hall, London (GB), SpielArt Festival, Munich/München (D).
18. 6. 1999, LIFT/Queen Elizabeth Hall, London (GB).

Stretching from midnight to midnight the show takes the public and its fourteen performers on a
long journey from night to day and back again. Combining a firm frame with an endless demand
for improvisation and 'liveness', the performance cycles and mutates a collection of scenes, performance structures and costumes. Dressed as kings, they tell stories without endings; dressed as
skeletons, they speculate on their cause of death. There are lists of fears, language lessons and alpha-
bets chalked on a blackboard. There are disappearing routines, dances and sleazy cabaret demon-
strations of the difference between life and death.

*Von Mitternacht bis Mitternacht nimmt diese Show ihr Publikum und die vierzehn Performer mit auf
eine lange Reise durch die Nacht, den Tag und wieder in die Nacht. Mit festgelegtem Rahmen und zugleich permanenter Aufforderung an die Performer, zu improvisieren und ,da zu sein', dreht sich der
Abend um eine Anzahl immer variierter Szenen, Performancestrukturen und Kostüme. Verkleidet als
Könige erzählen die Performer Geschichten ohne Ende, als Skelette spekulieren sie über ihre Todes-
ursachen. Listen von Ängsten, Sprachkurse und Alphabete werden mit Kreide auf eine Schultafel geschrieben, Routinen des Verschwindens und Tänze werden vorgeführt, billige Kabarettnummern sinnieren
über den Unterschied von Leben und Tod.*

Disco Relax
P: Robin Arthur, Tim Hall, Richard Lowdon, Sue Marshall, Cathy Naden. D/T: Tim
Etchells. S: Richard Lowdon. L: Nigel Edwards. ST: Tim Hall, found
sources/Fundstücke.
19. 10. 1999, Forced Entertainment Studio, Sheffield (GB).

A surreal examination of Britain at the end of the '90s, the piece centres on a fragmented, foul-
mouthed, word-association-driven, disconnected dialogue between two women. Set in the back
room of a pub, after a long night of drinking the protagonists are joined by three men who function as much as scenery as they do as characters – a VJ/DJ, a guitar player/pub singer and a third
man disguised with a plastic Halloween mask and labelled with a sign: DRUNKEN TWAT. Alongside
the live action, scraps of video present fragmentary scenes of soap operas, films, home movies, bed-
time stories and magic tricks.

*Als surreale Untersuchung Großbritanniens Ende der Neunzigerjahre dreht sich das Stück um einen
fragmentierten, unflätigen, wortspielerischen, unzusammenhängenden Dialog zwischen zwei Frauen
nach einer durchsoffenen Nacht im Hinterzimmer einer Kneipe. Drei Männer kommen dazu, die gleichzeitig Kulisse und Figuren sind – ein VJ/DJ, ein singender Gitarrenspieler und ein dritter Mann mit
einer Halloween-Maske aus Plastik und einem Schild um den Hals: BESOFFENER TROTTEL. Dazu
werden auf Video Schnipsel von Seifenopern, Filmen, home movies, Gutenachtgeschichten und Zaubertricks gezeigt.*

Scar Stories
(Performance version)
P: Richard Lowdon, Terry O'Connor. D: Tim Etchells. C: Tim Etchells, Hugo
Glendinning, Forced Entertainment. S: Richard Lowdon. L: Nigel Edwards.
CO: KunstenFESTIVALdesArts, Brussels/Brüssel (B).
16. 5. 2000, KunstenFESTIVALdesArts, Brussels/Brüssel (B).

Interviews conducted in Brussels, on the theme of scars as physical reminders with an emotional echo, provided the base material for an installation and the beginnings of this theatre performance. In a steeply raked auditorium designed to reference a demonstration operating theatre, a man and a woman develop a vast catalogue of accidents, operations, fights and mishaps as they describe the scars they have allegedly accrued.

Material der Installation und Ausgangspunkt der Theateraufführung sind in Brüssel geführte Interviews über Narben als physische Erinnerung mit emotionalem Echo. Die steil ansteigende Zuschauertribüne erinnert an einen Lehr-Operationssaal, auf der Bühne entwickeln ein Mann und eine Frau eine gewaltige Liste von Unfällen, Operationen, Schlägereien und Missgeschicken, von denen sie angeblich ihre Narben haben.

And on the Thousandth Night ...
(6 h/Std., durational performance)
P: Robin Arthur, Tim Etchells, Tamzin Griffin, Jerry Killick, Richard Lowdon, Claire
Marshall, Cathy Naden, Terry O'Connor. D: Tim Etchells. C: Forced Entertainment.
L: Richard Lowdon.
3. 9. 2000, Festival Ayloul, Beirut (LIB).

Eight kings and queens in red robes and cardboard crowns line up along the edge of the stage to tell stories, in a structure first developed for *Who Can Sing a Song to Unfrighten Me?*. Each speaker can, at any time, be interrupted with a simple "Stop" and then a new narrative must begin. This simple rule creates a spontaneous, though complex performance with frequent changes in pace and tone. Moving from the extraordinary to the banal, it mixes everything from film plots, religious stories, children's stories, traditional tales, jokes and modern myths, to scary stories, love stories and sex stories. Viewers are free to enter and leave as they please.

Acht Könige und Königinnen in roten Umhängen und mit Papp-Kronen sitzen am Bühnenrand und erzählen Geschichten. Die Struktur wurde erstmals für Who Can Sing a Song to Unfrighten Me? *entwickelt: Jeder Sprechende kann zu jeder Zeit mit einem einfachen „Stopp" unterbrochen werden und eine neue Geschichte beginnt. Diese einfache Regel provoziert eine spontane, jedoch komplexe Performance mit ständigem Tempo- und Tonfallwechsel. Immer irgendwo zwischen dem Außergewöhnlichem und dem Banalem wechseln sich Filmplots, religiöse Erzählungen, Kindergeschichten, Sagen, Witze, moderne Mythen, Grusel-, Liebes- und Sexgeschichten ab. Die Zuschauer können kommen und gehen, wie sie wollen.*

Instructions for Forgetting
P/D/T: Tim Etchells. S: Richard Lowdon. V: Hugo Glendinning. CO: Wiener
Festwochen.
31. 5. 2001, Wiener Festwochen, Vienna/Wien (A).

Following Etchells' invitation, friends from all over the world sent true stories and videos for the project. Seated at a table, with three monitors and Lowdon as a technician in the background, Etchells begins a journey through documents, fiction and memory, creating an 'intimate documentary'.

Von Etchells aufgefordert schickten Freunde aus aller Welt wahre Geschichten und Videos. An einem Tisch sitzend, mit drei Monitoren und Lowdon als Techniker im Hintergrund, beginnt Etchells eine Reise durch Dokumente, Fiktionen, Erinnerungen und schafft so eine ‚intime Dokumentation'.

Down Time

(Video and live performance / Video und Liveperformance)
P/D/T: Tim Etchells.
29. 6. 2001, Monologfestival, Schauspielhaus Zurich/Zürich (CH).

A short solo work from Tim Etchells, which exists in live and video versions. In the former a silent recorded image of Tim Etchells' thinking face is accompanied by a live commentary, in which he attempts to describe the unfolding narrative of his thoughts on the chosen topic of 'goodbyes'.
Eine kurze Soloarbeit Tim Etchells', die es als Live- und als Videoversion gibt. In der Live-Version kommentiert Etchells eine Aufnahme seines in Gedanken versunkenen Gesichts und versucht, seine damaligen Überlegungen zum Thema „Abschiede" zu rekonstruieren.

Starfucker

(Video and live performance / Video und Liveperformance)
P/D/T: Tim Etchells.
29. 6. 2001, Monologfestival, Schauspielhaus Zurich/Zürich (CH).

Another short solo project from Tim Etchells existing in live and video versions. He stands alone on stage, performing a text comprising endless images of Hollywood celebrities caught in bizarre, violent or sexually graphic acts. The images, like those in *Dirty Work*, unfold only in the mind of those watching.
Ein weiteres Solostück von Tim Etchells, das als Live- wie als Videofassung existiert. Etchells steht allein auf der Bühne und evoziert – wie in Dirty Work *nur durch Text – in den Köpfen der Zuschauer eine endlose Reihe von Bildern, in denen Hollywood-Stars bei bizarren, brutalen oder sexuellen Handlungen ertappt werden.*

First Night

P: Robin Arthur, Jerry Killick, Richard Lowdon, Claire Marshall, Cathy Naden, Terry O'Connor, John Rowley, K. Michael Weaver. D: Tim Etchells. T: Tim Etchells, Forced Entertainment. S: Richard Lowdon. L: Nigel Edwards. CP: Rotterdamse Schouwburg, Rotterdam (NL), SpielArt Festival, Munich/München (D), Festival Theaterformen, Hannover (D) and Wiener Festwochen, Vienna/Wien (A).
15. 9. 2001, Rotterdamse Schouwburg, Rotterdam (NL).

Eight performers with broad, frozen smiles are desperately trying to save a doomed night of strange bitter vaudeville. *First Night* begins with a grand welcome, but soon disintegrates into dark predictions of the future, psychotic escapology acts, playful attacks on the audience, unexpected dances and unhinged show-biz anecdotes.
Acht Performer mit eingefrorenem, breiten Lächeln versuchen verzweifelt einen ziemlich schrägen und ziemlich bitteren Varietéabend zu retten, der nicht zu retten ist. Was mit einer groß angelegten Begrüßung beginnt, zerfällt bald in eine Aneinanderreihung dunkler Prophezeiungen, psychotischer Entfesslungskunststücke, spielerischer Attacken gegen das Publikum, unerwarteter Tänze und unzusammenhängender Show-biz-Anekdoten.

The Travels

P: Jerry Killick, Richard Lowdon, Claire Marshall, Cathy Naden, Terry O'Connor, John Rowley. D: Tim Etchells. T: Tim Etchells, Forced Entertainment. S: Richard Lowdon. L: Andy Clarke. CP: Künstlerhaus Mousonturm, Frankfurt (D).

27. 9. 2002, Künstlerhaus Mousonturm, Frankfurt (D).

For one summer, the Forced Entertainment performers travelled through England, separately: taking notes and photographs in a search for streets with promising names. Seated at a table, they relate the results in an intimate documentary essay-performance: Paradise Road – a Neighbourhood Watch Area; Effort and Recovery Streets – just behind a hospital. Fortune Street ends at a brick wall.

Einen Sommer lang reisten die Performer von Forced Entertainment jeder für sich durch England und machten Aufzeichnungen und Fotografien auf der Suche nach Straßen mit verheißungsvollen Namen. An einem Tisch sitzend verlesen sie die Ergebnisse als intime, dokumentarische Essay-Performance: Paradise Road – eine neighbourhood watch area; Effort und Recovery Street – direkt hinter einem Krankenhaus. Fortune Street endet vor einer Ziegelwand.

The Voices

(Berlin version / Berliner Fassung)

P: Robin Arthur, Sonja Augart, Katie Ewald, Tobias Lange, Richard Lowdon, Claire Marshall, Terry O'Connor, John Rowley. S: Bert Neumann. D/T: Tim Etchells.

L: Nigel Edwards. CP: Volksbühne Berlin (D), Warwick Arts Centre (GB), Sheffield Theatres (GB), Tramway Glasgow (GB).

24. 1. 2003, Prater der Volksbühne am Rosa-Luxemburg-Platz, Berlin (D).

Eight performers are seated on the bare steps behind the lighting desk in Prater, whilst the audience are seated in the rooms of Bert Neumann's living room stage in this prototype version of *The Voices*. One by one, the actors come to stand on a chair in the centre of the floor area and, on this provisional stage, perform a monologue concerning personal aspirations for the future. Etchells' stream of consciousness texts – depicting fantasies of perfect death, great wealth and success, love and disappearance – are banal at times, inventive and spectacular at others.

In der Muster-Version von The Voices *sitzen acht Performer auf den Stufen hinter dem Lichtpult im Prater, während das Publikum in den Räumen von Bert Neumanns Wohnzimmerbühne Platz genommen hat. Ein Spieler nach dem anderen stellt sich auf einen Stuhl in der Mitte des freien Raumes und präsentiert einen Monolog über persönliche Zukunftshoffnungen. Etchells' innere Monologe – Fantasien über den perfekten Tod, großen Reichtum und Erfolg, Liebe und Verschwinden – sind mal banal, mal originell, mal spektakulär.*

The Voices

(Full version / Vollständige Fassung)

D: Robin Arthur, Jerry Killick, Richard Lowdon, Claire Marshall, Terry O'Connor, John Rowley. Guests/Gäste: Helen Gould, Mary Agnes Krell, Tobias Lange. Local performers/lokale Darsteller: Julie Carson, Nicholas Cooke, Simon Day, John O'Hanlon, Kate Kordel, Newrouz Mawlood, Ben Neale, Sabreen Pervaiz, Jon Tipton, Alison Ward. D/T: Tim Etchells. S: Richard Lowdon. L: Nigel Edwards. CP: Volksbühne Berlin (GB), Warwick Arts Centre (GB), Sheffield Theatres (GB), Tramway, Glasgow (GB).

5. 3. 2003, Warwick Arts Centre, Warwick (GB).

A fully developed version of *The Voices*, following the smaller version in Berlin, performed by Forced Entertainment and guests alongside a group of amateur performers recruited through workshops in each of the UK cities that played host to the project. Nineteen performers are seated on a bare stage.

One by one, they step into centre stage to present a monologue concerning personal aspirations for the future. Etchells' stream of consciousness texts – depicting fantasies of perfect death, great wealth and success, love and disappearance – are banal at times; inventive and spectacular at others.

Die ausgereifte Version von The Voices *(die auf die kleinere Berliner Fassung folgte) wird gespielt von Forced Entertainment, Gastperformern und einer Gruppe Laiendarsteller aus Workshops, die in verschiedenen am Projekt beteiligten britischen Städten stattgefunden hatten. Auf einer kahlen Bühne sitzen neunzehn Performer. Einer nach dem anderen tritt vor in die Mitte der Bühne und präsentiert einen Monolog über persönliche Zukunftshoffnungen. Etchells' innere Monologe – Fantasien über den perfekten Tod, großen Reichtum und Erfolg, Liebe und Verschwinden – sind mal banal, mal originell, mal spektakulär.*

Bloody Mess
(Work in progress)
P: Robin Arthur, Davis Freeman, Wendy Houstoun, Jerry Killick, Richard Lowdon, Claire Marshall, Cathy Naden, Terry O'Connor, Bruno Roubicek, John Rowley.
D: Tim Etchells. T: Tim Etchells, Forced Entertainment. S: Richard Lowdon. L: Nigel Edwards. CP: Festival Theaterformen Hannover (D), KunstenFESTIVALdesArts Brussels/Brüssel (B), Rotterdamse Schouwburg (NL), Les Spectacles Vivants/Centre Pompidou Paris (F), SpielArt Festival Munich/München (D), Wiener Festwochen, Vienna/Wien (D).
1. 11. 2003, SpielArt Festival, Munich/München (D).

From the outset – at which each actor confides in the audience about how he or she would like to be seen during the show – trouble seems inevitable; rivalries, contradictions and complete incompatibility seem to rule the day. *Bloody Mess* is highly structured, energetic chaos. A cheerleader dances while another performer weeps and wails in operatic grief. Rock-gig roadies creep across the stage – bringing disco lights, new speakers and a microphone that no one really wants. A woman in a gorilla suit chucks popcorn at anything that moves like a demented refugee from a pantomime.

Von Beginn an – zu dem jeder Schauspieler dem Publikum anvertraut, wie er während der Show gerne wirken würde – scheinen Schwierigkeiten unvermeidbar. Rivalitäten, Widersprüchlichkeiten und völlige Unvereinbarkeit herrschen vor. Bloody Mess *ist streng durchkonstruiertes, Energie geladenes Chaos. Ein Cheerleader tanzt, während ein anderer Performer in opernhaftem Trübsinn weint und klagt. Rockshow-Roadies kriechen über die Bühne und bringen Disco-Beleuchtung, neue Lautsprecher und Mikrofone, die eigentlich niemand haben wollte. Eine Frau im Gorilla-Kostüm schmeißt mit Popcorn nach allem, was sich bewegt – wie eine aus einer Pantomime entflohene Verrückte.*

Marathon Lexicon
(12 h/Std., lecture performance)
P: Robin Arthur, Jerry Killick, Claire Marshall, Terry O'Connor. Curated by/Kuratiert von: Tim Etchells, Adrian Heathfield. T: Sara Jane Bailes, Simon Bayly, Steven Connor, Franko B, Hugo Glendinning, Matthew Goulish, Rinne Groff, Ant Hampton, Lin Hixson, Vlatka Horvat, Joe Kelleher, Jeremy Killick, Thomas Lehman, Andre Lepecki, Deborah Levy, Kate McIntosh, Peggy Phelan, Andrew Quick, Alan Read, Nick Ridout, Oscar Sahlieh, Elyce Semenec, Grant Smith, Willy Thomas, Allen Weiss, Lisa Wesley, David Williams.
29. 11. 2003, Künstlerhaus Mousonturm, Frankfurt (D).

From "audience", "breath", "blood", and "charisma" though "crying", "laughter", "silence", "shivering" to "spirits", and "voyeurism". Videos, imagery and text by contemporary thinkers, academics and artists – all based on the term 'performance' – form an impossible lecture, a lexicon, read and viewed live. The audience can arrive, depart and return whenever they please.

Von „Atem“, „Blut“, „Charisma“ über „Geister“, „Gelächter“, „Stille“ bis zu „Voyeurismus“, „Weinen“ und „Zittern“. Videos, Bilder und Texte zeitgenössischer Denker, Akademiker und Künstler – alle rund um den Begriff ‚Performance‘ – fügen sich zusammen zu einer unmögliche Vorlesung, zu einem live vorgetragenen und vorgeführten Lexikon. Das Publikum kann kommen und gehen, wann es möchte.

Installations / Installationen

Red Room
(Performance installation / Performance-Installation)
P: Will Waghorn. C: Forced Entertainment, Hugo Glendinning, Will Waghorn.
CO: ICA Live Arts/Showroom Gallery, London (GB).
30. 11. 1993, Showroom Gallery, London (GB).

Visitors equipped with torches explore a dark room and its contents in detective style. Photographs show the performers in fragmented scenes set in urban spaces – telephone booths, stairwells and the backseat of a car. Entering the second room of the gallery, visitors find performer Will Waghorn, who is constantly processing new photographic prints and generating new texts to accompany the images.
Mit einer Taschenlampe ausgerüstet, durchsucht der Besucher wie ein Detektiv den dunklen Installationsraum und seine Objekte. Fotografien zeigen die Performer in Szenenbruchstücken aus urbanem Kontext – in Telefonzellen, Treppenschächten oder auf dem Rücksitz eines Autos. Wer in den zweiten Raum vorstößt, findet Will Waghorn, der Fotoabzüge und neue Texte dazu erzeugt.

Ground Plans for Paradise
(Installation with occasional performance/Installation mit gelegentlicher Performance)
P: Robin Arthur, Richard Lowdon, Claire Marshall, Cathy Naden, Terry O'Connor. C: Hugo Glendinning, Forced Entertainment. CO: Leeds Metropolitan University.
15. 3. 1994, Leeds Metropolitan University Gallery & Studio Theatre, Leeds (GB).

The architectural models, street names, photographs and occasional performances of this multimedia installation conjure up images and hidden narratives contained in a vast city. Innumerable models of high-rise buildings, each of them named and illuminated from within, create a desolate atmosphere. The performers sit at a chalk-covered table. Blindfolded, they draw streets in the dust, creating new paths through the city.
Häusermodelle, Straßennamen, Fotografien und gelegentliche Performances beschwören in dieser Multimedia-Installation Bilder und versteckte Geschichten einer riesigen Stadt herauf. Unzählige Hochhausmodelle, jedes mit einem Namen versehen und von innen erleuchtet, schaffen eine einsame Atmosphäre. Die Performer sitzen an einem kreidebedeckten Tisch und zeichnen mit geschlossenen Augen Straßen in den Staub und erschaffen so immer neue Wege durch die Stadt.

Hotel Binary
(Five-channel video installation / Fünfkanal-Videoinstallation)
P: Robin Arthur, Richard Lowdon, Claire Marshall, Cathy Naden, Terry O'Connor. C: Tim Etchells, Hugo Glendinning, Forced Entertainment.
28. 3. 2000, Site Gallery, Sheffield (GB).

Five projections. In one, people sat in hotel lobbies and airport lounges speak lists of their fears. The other four projections show slowed down glimpses of bodies, landscapes and locations – a dual carriageway by night, two people sleeping together, a hotel carpet. This series of outtakes forms a glancing relationship with the spoken lists of fears, at times confirming their contents and at other times, undermining them.

Fünf Projektionen. In einer sitzen Leute in Hotellobbys und Flughafenhallen und zählen ihre Ängste auf. Die anderen vier Projektionen zeigen verlangsamte, flüchtige Blicke auf Körper, Landschaften und Orte – eine zweispurige Fahrbahn in der Nacht, zwei Menschen, die miteinander schlafen, ein Hotelteppich. Die Aufnahmen gehen flüchtige, mal korrespondierende, mal widersprüchliche Beziehungen mit den gesprochenen Aufzählungen von Ängsten ein.

Scar Stories
(Installation)
C: Tim Etchells, Hugo Glendinning, Forced Entertainment.
5. 5. 2000, KunstenFESTIVALdesArts, Brussels/Brüssel (B).
Interviews conducted in Brussels, on the theme of scars as physical reminders with an emotional echo, are the base material for this installation and the beginning of the theatre performance with the same name. For the installation, fragments of interviews and images of scars are presented on the floor of a disused parking garage.

In Brüssel geführte Interviews zum Thema Narben als physisches Souvenir mit emotionalem Echo, sind das Material dieser Installation und der Ausgangspunkt der gleichnamigen Theaterperformance. Die Installation präsentiert Ausschnitte der Interviews und Bilder von Narben auf dem Boden einer leer stehenden Parkgarage.

Digital Media / Digitale Medien

Paradise
(Internet project)
C: Tim Etchells, Forced Entertainment. Digital Author: Mary Agnes Krell
CO: Lovebytes as part of the Channel Metropolis series, funded by Arts Council England.
23. 4. 1998, http://www.lovebytes.org.uk/paradise.
The interactive project *Paradise* was developed from the installation *Ground Plans For Paradise*. An online city, consisting of a thousand buildings, accessible through maps and a street index. Each visitor has the opportunity to add narratives and characters to the buildings and to read what others before him have written.

Aus der Installation Ground Plans For Paradise *entwickelte Forced Entertainment das interaktive Projekt* Paradise. *Eine Stadt im Netz, bestehend aus tausend Gebäuden, die über Pläne und Straßenverzeichnisse zu erreichen sind. Jeder Besucher kann Geschichten und Charaktere zu den Häusern erfinden und eingeben. Oder lesen, was andere vor ihm geschrieben haben.*

Frozen Palaces
(CD-ROM)
P: Robin Arthur, Tim Etchells, Richard Lowdon, Claire Marshall, Cathy Naden, Terry O'Connor. Guests: Nicky Childs, Mark Etchells, Tim Hall, Cathy Phillips, Justin Westover, James White, Tony White. C: Tim Etchells, Hugo Glendinning, Forced Entertainment. ST: John Avery. Digital Author: Mary Agnes Krell.
1999, published in/publiziert in ArtIntact 5, Zentrum für Kunst und Medientechnologie (ZKM), Karlsruhe (D).

A large house with one scene set in each room. The viewer navigates the photographed spaces which contain diverse events – love scenes, murders and parties. The inhabitants of this space are frozen in time, suspended in banal or significant moments, while the viewer alone has the option of wandering through the house, forming his own connections between the scenes.

Ein großes Haus, in jedem Raum eine andere Szene. Der Betrachter navigiert durch die fotografierten Räume und Ereignisse, durch Liebesszenen, Mordfälle und Partys. Die Bewohner dieser Räume sind in der Zeit erstarrt, gefangen in banalen oder signifikanten Momenten. Nur der Betrachter hat die Freiheit, durch das Haus zu streifen und sich seinen eigenen Reim zu machen.

Nightwalks
(CD-ROM)

P: Robin Arthur, Tim Etchells, Richard Lowdon, Claire Marshall, Cathy Naden, Terry O'Connor. T: Tim Etchells. C: Tim Etchells, Hugo Glendinning, Forced Entertainment. ST: John Avery. Digital Author: Mary Agnes Krell.
2. 10. 1998, Site Gallery, Sheffield (GB).

Panoramic photographs of frozen nocturnal scenes create a landscape which lies somewhere between urban England and a fictitious film set. The viewer is free to explore, exiting the scenes through key objects (hot spots) and inventing his own subjective narrative along the way. The work creates a poetic landscape, in which geographical logic does not apply.

Panoramafotos erstarrter Szenen nächtlicher Orte: eine Landschaft irgendwo zwischen urbanem England und ausgedachter Filmszenerie. Der Betrachter streift frei umher, verlässt die Szenen über gefundene Schlüsselobjekte (hotspots) während er seine subjektive Geschichte findet und erfindet. Eine unwirkliche, poetische Landschaft, die keiner geographischen Logik gehorcht.

Spin
(CD-ROM)

P: Robin Arthur, Richard Lowdon, Claire Marshall, Cathy Naden, Terry O'Connor. Guests: Martin Bailey, Neil Bennett, Huw Chadbourn, Peter Flannery, Tim Hall, Jenson Grant, Michelle McGuire. C: Tim Etchells, Hugo Glendinning, Forced Entertainment. Digital Author: Mary Agnes Krell. ST: John Avery.
2. 2. 1999, Sleuth/Barbican, London (GB).

The interactive CD-ROM shows the frozen end scene of a fictitious film. At a scrap-metal yard in the middle of the night, a man is dying from gunshot wounds, surrounded by his killers. The viewer is free to examine this moment endlessly, unable to prevent the unfolding events. A playful investigation about the subjective construction of narratives in film as well as in real life.

Die interaktive CD-ROM zeigt das Ende eines ausgedachten Films. Auf einem Schrottplatz, mitten in der Nacht: Ein Mann stirbt an seinen Schusswunden, seine Killer stehen um ihn herum. Der Betrachter kann das Geschehen endlos untersuchen, aber nicht verhindern, dass es passiert. Eine spielerische Spurensuche, über die subjektive Konstruktion von Erzählungen – im Film und im wirklichen Leben.

Imaginary Evidence
(CD-ROM)

C: Tim Etchells, Forced Entertainment. In collaboration with/In Zusammenarbeit mit: Mary Agnes Krell, David Jennings. PH: Hugo Glendinning.
1. 10. 2003, Sheffield (GB).

Fiction, home movies, anecdotes, theory, interviews and texts which together reflect the poetics and work process of Forced Entertainment. The CD-ROM allows the viewer to browse through the conceptual universe informing the works and also contains an extensive information archive on all Forced Entertainment pieces to date.

Erfundene Geschichten, home movies, Anekdoten, Theorie, Interviews und Texte, die zusammengenommen das Werk und die Arbeitsweise Forced Entertainments widerspiegeln. Die CD-ROM erlaubt dem Betrachter das konzeptuelle Universum der Arbeit zu durchstöbern und enthält zudem ein ausführliches Archiv mit Informationen zu allen Stücken Forced Entertainments bis zum Erscheinungstermin.

Photographic Projects / Fotografische Projekte

Cardboard Sign Photographs
(Photographs/Fotografien)
P: Robin Arthur, Richard Lowdon, Claire Marshall, Cathy Naden, Terry O'Connor. C: Hugo Glendinning, Forced Entertainment. PH: Hugo Glendinning.
8. 12. 1992, ICA, London (GB).

Five performers pose holding cardboard signs from *Emanuelle Enchanted*, staging situations for the camera in front of real locations in and around Sheffield. The locations take on the role of film or theatre backdrops.

Mit den Pappschildern aus Emanuelle Enchanted *posieren fünf Performer vor Schauplätzen in und um Sheffield für die Kamera. Die Schauplätze wirken dabei wie Filmsets oder Theaterkulissen.*

Hotel Photographs
(Photographs/Fotografien)
C: Hugo Glendinning, Forced Entertainment. PH: Hugo Glendinning.
19. 11. 1994, The Gantry, Southampton (GB).

Glendinning's photographs, set in an anonymous Novotel hotel, seemingly capture unobserved moments during a fictitious photo shoot – moments without activity, in which people are sleeping, waiting, staring blankly. The images were created during early *Hidden J* rehearsals at a point where the piece was exploring the idea of a group of people hiding out in hotels for prolonged periods of time.

Im anonymen Umfeld eines Novotels fangen die Fotografien Glendinnings scheinbar unbeobachtete Momente während eines fiktiven Foto-Shootings ein. Momente, in denen nichts passiert, Leute schlafen, warten, starren vor sich hin. Die Bilder entstanden während ersten Proben zu Hidden J, *als man der Idee nachging, sich mit einer Gruppe von Menschen zu beschäftigen, die sich für lange Zeit in Hotels versteckt.*

Looking Forwards
(Artist pages/Künstlerseiten)
T: Tim Etchells. PH: Hugo Glendinning.
Spring/Frühjahr 1996, Performance Research Vol. 1, Issue 1 (GB).

Photographs of people (bus drivers, cashiers, policemen) thinking about the future, set in their everyday surroundings.

Fotografien von Menschen (Busfahrer, Kassierer, Polizisten), die in ihrer alltäglichen Umgebung über die Zukunft nachdenken.

Rules of the Game
(Text and photographs/Text und Fotografien)
P: Robin Arthur, Richard Lowdon, Claire Marshall, Cathy Naden. Guests: Tim Hall, Mary Agnes Krell. C: Tim Etchells, Hugo Glendinning and Forced Entertainment. PH: Hugo Glendinning.
28. 3. 2000, Site Gallery, Sheffield (GB).

Bizarre text and photographic document of a very personal performance. An invented drinking game, played while watching television news broadcasts. Drinking, undressing and sexual acts abound in the game, regulated by complex rules and intricately linked to events shown on the television news. *Bizarres Text- und Fotodokument einer sehr privaten Performance. Ein selbst erfundenes Trink-Spiel vor laufenden Fernsehnachrichten. Trinken, Ausziehen und sexuelle Handlungen gehören zu diesem Spiel, das nach komplizierten Regeln funktioniert und auf verwickelte Weise an die Ereignisse gebunden ist, von denen die Nachrichten berichten.*

Video / Film

Many of the works in this section are solo projects by director Tim Etchells, or collaborations between him and Hugo Glendinning, produced by Forced Entertainment.
Viele der in dieser Rubrik aufgeführten Arbeiten sind Soloprojekte von Tim Etchells oder Zusammenarbeiten zwischen ihm und Hugo Glendinning, die von Forced Entertainment produziert wurden.

DIY
(Short film/Kurzfilm, 10 Min.)
P: Michael Atavar. D: Tim Etchells, Hugo Glendinning. C: Tim Etchells, Hugo Glendinning, Michael Atavar. Produced by/produziert von Life Size Films, Forced Entertainment.
12. 7. 1997, Channel 4, UK (GB).
Gay artist Michael Atavar visits places connected with the playwright Joe Orton – the house he died in, or the library in which he wrapped books in homemade pornographic covers. The film explores the changing nature of England from 1967 to 1997 and comprises a personal search for traces of past and cultural life.
Der homosexuelle Künstler Atavar sucht Orte auf, die mit dem Theaterautor Joe Orton in Verbindung stehen – dessen Sterbehaus oder die Bücherei, in der er Bücher mit selbstgemachten, pornografischen Umschlägen versah. Der Film zeichnet Veränderungen in England von 1967 bis 1997 nach und ist zugleich eine persönliche Suche nach Spuren von Kultur und Vergangenheit.

Filthy Words & Phrases
(Video, 420 Min.)
P: Cathy Naden. D: Tim Etchells, Hugo Glendinning. T: Tim Etchells. ST: John Avery.
31. 1. 1998, International Film Festival Rotterdam (NL).

A lone woman in an evening dress stands in front of a blackboard in a deserted school. For seven hours, she writes a list of dirty words: insults, crude and obscene terms for sex acts, body parts and bodily functions. In their endless succession, the words form an absurd and comic sex film without a plot as the performer drifts between fascination, boredom and exhaustion.
Vor einer Tafel in einer verlassenen Schule steht eine einsame Frau im Abendkleid. Sieben Stunden lang schreibt sie eine Liste schmutziger Wörter: Beschimpfungen, dreckige und obszöne Begriffe für sexuelle Handlungen, Körperteile oder -funktionen. In scheinbar endloser Folge zeigen die Worte einen absurden und komischen Sexfilm ohne Handlung, während die Performerin zwischen Faszination, Langeweile und Erschöpfung schwankt.

Kent Beeson Is a Classic & an Absolutely New Thing
(Video, 12 Min.)
P: Kent Beeson. D: Tim Etchells, Hugo Glendinning. T: Tim Etchells.
10. 3. 2001, Showroom Cinema, Sheffield (GB).

A spiralling twelve-minute monologue, exploring one man's ambitions of show-biz affluence in America, but the dream crumbles as it runs up against the reality of an actor who does not know his lines.

Ein Schwindel erregender zwölfminütiger Monolog über das Streben eines Mannes nach amerikanischem Show-Biz-Reichtum. Aber der Traum verpufft, als er mit der Realität zusammenstößt: einem Schauspieler, der seinen Text nicht auswendig kann.

My Eyes Were Like the Stars
(Video, 8 Min.)
P: Cathy Naden. D: Hugo Glendinning, Tim Etchells.
10. 3. 2001, Showroom Cinema, Sheffield (GB).

Cathy Naden – drunk late at night – struggles to recall a text that she has previously learned. The video is a collection of the material shot between takes – hysterical laughter, pauses, memory losses – as the text is attempted, remembered, forgotten and ultimately discarded altogether.

Cathy Naden kämpft betrunken und spät in der Nacht damit, sich an einen Text zu erinnern, den sie zuvor gelernt hat. Das Video ist eine Sammlung des Materials, das zwischen den eigentlichen Aufnahmen gemacht wurde: hysterisches Gelächter, Pausen, Gedächtnislücken während der Text gesucht, erinnert, vergessen und letztendlich zur Gänze verworfen wird.

Starfucker
(Video, 12 Min.)
T/D: Tim Etchells. ST: John Avery.
10. 3. 2001, Showroom Cinema, Sheffield (GB).

Another short solo project from Tim Etchells existing in live and video versions. Phrases and images in white text fade in and out of a black background on screen, comprising endless images of Hollywood celebrities caught in bizarre, violent or sexually graphic acts. The images, accompanied by John Avery's score, like those in *Dirty Work*, unfold only in the mind of those watching.

Ein weiteres Soloprojekt von Tim Etchells, das es als Live- und als Videoversion gibt. Phrasen und Bilder werden als weißer Text auf schwarzem Hintergrund ein- und ausgeblendet: Unzählige Bilder von Hollywoodstars bei bizarren, brutalen oder sexuellen Handlungen, die – wie bei Dirty Work *– zur Filmmusik von John Avery nur im Kopf der Zuschauer entstehen.*

The Last Mile Home
(Video, 10 Min.)
P: Claire Marshall. D: Hugo Glendinning, Tim Etchells.
10. 3. 2001, Showroom Cinema, Sheffield (GB).

In a dark cellar, dressed only in underwear and a tutu, Claire Marshall performs her melancholic dance from *Pleasure*, with a knife held to her own throat.

In einem dunklen Keller, nur mit Unterwäsche und einem Tutu bekleidet, vollführt Claire Marshall mit einem Messer am Hals ihren melancholischen Tanz aus Pleasure.

Everything

(Video, 14 Min.)

D/T: Tim Etchells.

22. 1. 2003, Xing Festival, Bologna (E).

Like its predecessor *Down Time*, this video shows Etchells' face deep in thought, recorded as he sits on a train late at night. In a spoken commentary, he attempts to reconstruct what went through his mind as he considered the topic of 'happiness'.

Wie sein Vorgänger Down Time *zeigt auch dieses Video Etchells' Gesicht tief in Gedanken versunken, aufgezeichnet während einer nächtlichen Zugfahrt. Im gesprochenen Kommentar versucht er sein Nachdenken über das Thema ‚Glück' zu rekonstruieren.*

Mark Does Lear

(Video, 35 Min.)

P: Mark Etchells. D: Tim Etchells, Hugo Glendinning.

30. 3. 2003, Tate Modern, London (GB).

Late at night, Mark Etchells attempts to recollect and narrate the plot of Shakespeare's *King Lear*, after a single reading of the play during a train journey from Devon to Sheffield. His meandering and at times inaccurate version of the narrative is recorded in this single-take video.

Spät in der Nacht versucht Mark Etchells sich an die Handlung von Shakespeares King Lear, *den er lediglich einmal während einer Zugfahrt von Devon nach Sheffield gelesen hat, zu erinnern und sie nachzuerzählen. Seine umherirrende und zeitweise ungenaue Version der Erzählung ist auf diesem ohne Schnitte gedrehten Video festgehalten.*

Miles Magic

(Video, 4 Min.)

D: Tim Etchells. With the particpation of/unter Mitwirkung von Miles Etchells, Seth Etchells.

6. 6. 2003, Festival Des Ameriques, Montreal (CDN).

Miles Etchells (aged 7) performs a well-known magic trick while Seth (aged 2) stares at the camera.

Miles Etchells (7 Jahre) vollführt einen altbekannten Zaubertrick während Seth (2 Jahre) in die Kamera starrt.

Miles Titanic

(Video, 1 Min.)

D: Tim Etchells. With the particpation of/unter Mitwirkung von Miles Etchells.

6. 6. 2003, Festival Des Ameriques, Montreal (CDN).

Miles Etchells (aged 5) briefly recounts the story of the famous sinking.

Miles Etchells (5 Jahre) erzählt eine Kurzfassung des berühmten Untergangs.

So Small

(Video, 12 Min.)

P: Katie Ewald. D/T: Tim Etchells.

6. 6. 2003, Festival Des Ameriques, Montreal (CDN).

A performer addresses the camera directly in a stream-of-consciousness rush of language, describing how she imagines her own death, her funeral, the reactions of friends and family. The text also featured in the performance *The Voices*.

In direkter Ansprache der Kamera schildert die Performerin wie einen inneren Monolog ihre Vorstellung vom eigenen Tod: ihr perfektes Begräbnis, die Reaktionen von Freunden und Familie. Der Text stammt aus der Performance The Voices.

Erasure
(Video, 8 Min.)
P: Nicholas Cooke. D/T: Tim Etchells.
27. 11. 2003, Künstlerhaus Mousonturm, Frankfurt (D).
In a forest, a sixteen-year-old boy speaks a monologue, uncut, directly facing the camera. The text, which also features in *The Voices*, is a description of his dream of disappearance, of being able to live without leaving a trace in the world.
Ein sechzehnjähriger Junge spricht im Wald einen Monolog, ungeschnitten, direkt in die Kamera. Der aus The Voices *stammende Text schildert seinen Traum, einfach verschwinden zu können, zu leben, ohne eine Spur zu hinterlassen.*

Forced Entertainment receive regular funding from Arts Council England. Their projects have also received support from the British Council, Arts Council Lottery Funds and the Esmée Fairbairn Foundation. *Forced Entertainment wird kontinuierlich gefördert durch das Arts Council England. Einzelne Projekte wurden außerdem unterstützt durch das British Council, Arts Council Lottery Funds und die Esmée Fairbairn Foundation*

Forced Entertainment Bibliography / Bibliografie

Beneke, Patricia. „Verschärfte Unterhaltung". In: *Theater Heute* 6 (1995): 60–61.

Callens, Johan. "Forced Entertainment: What You See Is Seldom What You Get". In: *English Studies: Publications du Centre Universitaire de Luxembourg* 9 (2000): 13–30.

Etchells, Tim. "Eight Fragments on Theatre & The City". In: *Theaterschrift* 10 (Dezember 1995): 300–325.

Etchells, Tim. "The Broken World: A Short Story". In: *Janus* 12 (2002): 33–40.

Etchells, Tim. *Certain Fragments: Contemporary Performance and Forced Entertainment*. London: Routledge, 1999.

Etchells, Tim. "Diverse Assembly: Some Trends in Recent Performance". In: Theodore Shank (Ed). *Contemporary British Theatre*. 2ND Edition (with alterations). London: Macmillan, 1996. 107–122.

Etchells, Tim, Richard Lowdon. "Emanuelle Enchanted: Notes and Documents". In: *Contemporary Theatre Review* Vol. 2, Part 2 (1994): 9–24.

Etchells, Tim. *Endland Stories*. London: Pulp Faction, 1999.

Etchells, Tim. "Good Places". In: *artintact: CD-ROMagazin interaktiver Kunst* 5 (1999): 53–63.

Etchells, Tim. "Here are 26 letters". In: Tilmann Broszat, Gottfried Hattinger (Hg). *Theater etcetera. Zum Theaterfestival '97*. München: Spielmotor e.V., 1997. 70–73.

Etchells, Tim. "Losing & Finding". In: *TransEuropeenes: Theater & the Public Space*. No. 11 (Automne 1997).

Etchells, Tim. "Manifesto on Liveness". In: Adrian Heathfield (Ed). *Live: Art and Performance*. London: Tate Publishing, 2004.

Etchells, Tim. "More and More Clever Watching More and More Stupid". In: *ArtPress: Speciale: Danse* 23 (2002): 82–91. Edited version in: Adrian Heathfield (Ed). *Live: Art and Performance*. London: Tate Publishing, 2004.

Etchells, Tim. "Nights In This City: diverse letters and fragments relating to a performance now past". In: Nick Kaye (Ed). *Site-Specific Art: Performance, Place and Documentation*. London, New York: Routledge, 2000. 13–24.

Etchells, Tim. "No Title/No Theory: Ten Short Stabs at Authenticity". In: *tidsskrift for teori og teater* 5 (1998): 16–21.

Etchells, Tim: "Not part of the Bargain". In: Tilmann Broszat, Gottfried Hattinger (Hg). *Theater etcetera. Zum Theaterfestival SPIELART.* München: Spielmotor e.V., 2001. 113–120.

Etchells, Tim. "On The Skids: Some Years Of Acting Animals". In: *Performance Research* Vol. 5, No. 2 (Sommer 2000): 55–60.

Etchells, Tim. "Permanent Midnight". In: *Small Acts: Performance, the Millenium, and the Marking of Time.* London: Black Dog Publishing, 2000. 28–33.

Etchells, Tim. "Preparing to Write: Six words on Franko B". In: *Still Life.* London: Black Dog Publishing, 2003.

Etchells, Tim. "Repeat Forever". In: Adrian Heathfield (Ed). *Shattered Anatomies: Traces of the Body in Performance.* Bristol: Arnolfini Live, 1997.

Etchells, Tim. "Replaying the Tapes of the 20th Century: Talk to Ron Vawter". In: *Hybrid Magazine* No. 3 (Jun./Jul. 1993): 12–14.

Etchells, Tim. "Say it Now". In: Tilmann Broszat, Sigrid Gareis (Hg). *Global Player. Local Hero.* München: Epodium, 2000. 120–126.

Etchells, Tim. "Some thoughts on *Who Can Sing a Song to Unfrighten Me?*" In: Tilmann Broszat, Gottfried Hattinger (Hg). Theater *etcetera. Zum Theaterfestival SPIELART.* München: Spielmotor e.V., 1999. 73–78.

Etchells, Tim. „Valuable Spaces". In: Nicky Childs, Jeni Walwin (Ed). *A Split Second of Paradise. Live Art, Installation and Performance.* London, New York: Rivers Oram Press, 1998.

Etchells, Tim. "Words for a New Theatre". In: Fiach MacConghail (Ed). *Performance – The Project Papers.* Dublin: Project Press/Project Arts Centre, 1998. 17–28.

Falke, Christoph. „Forced Entertainment – beobachtet". In: *Flamboyant: Schriften zum Theater* 4 (Sommer 1996): 31–33.

Forced Entertainment. "A Decade of Forced Entertainment". In: *Performance Research* Vol. 1, No. 1 (Spring 1996): 73–88.

Forced Entertainment. "Emanuelle Enchanted: Notes and Documents." In: *Contemporary Theatre Review: British Live Art.* Vol. 2, No. 2 (1994): 9–24.

Forced Entertainment. "Speak Bitterness: Text Fragments. Text From the 1995/6 Performance". In: *Language aLive* 1 (1996).

Geiersberger, Ruth. "Bemerkungen zum Probenprozeß *Who Can Sing a Song to Unfrighten Me?*". In: Tilmann Broszat, Gottfried Hattinger (Hg). *Theater etcetera. Zum Theaterfestival SPIEL-ART.* München: Spielmotor e.V., 1999. 79–82.

Glendinning, Hugo, Tim Etchells, Cathy Naden. "My Eyes Were Like the Stars". In: *Women & Performance: A Journal of Feminist Theory.* Vol. 12:2, No. 24 (2002): 57–66.

Glendinning, Hugo, Tim Etchells. "Forced Entertainment: The Red Room." In: *Art & Design* New Performance Issue (October 1994): 92–95.

Glendinning, Hugo, Tim Etchells, Forced Entertainment: "Ten games". Artists' page. In: *Performance Research* Vol. 6, No. 3 (Winter 2001): 44–45.

Goulish, Matthew. "Compendium: A Forced Entertainment Glossary". In: *Performance Research,* Vol. 5, No. 3 (Winter 2000): 140–148.

Heathfield, Adrian. "Bitterness and Betrayal". In: *Language aLive* 1 (1996).

Heathfield, Adrian. "Out of Sight: Forced Entertainment and the Limits of Vision". In: *Void Spaces.* Sheffield: Site Gallery, 2000. 20–23.

Heathfield, Adrian. "End Time Now". In: Small Acts: *Performance, the Millenium, and the Marking of Time.* London: Black Dog Publishing, 2000. 104–111.

Forced Entertainment
Bibliography / Bibliografie

Heathfield, Adrian. "Performing Questions: Forced Entertainment, Desperate Optimists, Reckless Sleepers and Blast Theory". In: *Art & Design* Vol. 10, No. 3/4 (March/April 1995): 58–67.

Kaye, Nick. "Art into Theatre. Performance Interviews and Documents". Interview with Tim Etchells und Richard Lowdon. In: *Contemporary Theatre Studies* 16 (1996): 233–251.

Kaye, Nick. *Site Specific Art: Performance, Place and Documentation.* London: Routledge, 2000.

Keidan, Lois. „Die Regeln beugen: Neue Performances in Großbritannien". In: *The Next Generation: Junges Theater aus GB, Irland und den USA.* Berlin: Berliner Festwochen, 1998. 37–43.

Matzke, Annemarie. „Come In and Look at My Life: Selbstinszenierung als Versuchsaufbau". In: *Forum Modernes Theater,* 17 (2002): 19–27.

McGuire, Michelle. "Forced Entertainment on Politics and Pleasure". Interview with Robin Arthur, Claire Marshall and Cathy Naden. In: *Variant* Vol. 2, No. 5, (Spring 1998): 13–14.

Oddey, Alison. "From Process to Product: Relationship and Practice". In: *Devising Theatre: A Practical and Theoretical Handbook.* London, New York: Routledge 1996. 73–104.

Phelan, Peggy. "The Space of Performance". In: *artintact: CD-ROMagazin interaktiver Kunst* 5 (1999). 64–70.

Phelan, Peggy. "Performing Questions, Producing Witnesses". In: *Tim Etchells. Certain Fragments: Contemporary Performance and Forced Entertainment.* London, New York: Routledge, 1999. 9–14.

Primavesi, Patrick. „Rhythmus/Unterbrechung". In: Hajo Kurzenberger, Annemarie Matzke (Hg). *TheaterTheoriePraxis.* Berlin: Recherchen, 2004.

Shaughnessy, Robert. "Ruined Lear". In: Robert Shaughnessy. *The Shakespeare Effect: A History of Twentieth-Century Performance.* Basingstoke, New York: Palgrave Macmillan, 2002. 182–93.

Sommer, Astrid. "When Tomorrow Comes: Some Notes on Forced Entertainment, Cities, and the Context of Interactive Media Art." In: *Void Spaces.* Sheffield: Site Gallery, 2000. 6–9.

Tushingham, David. "How Long Do You Have to Have Lived Somewhere Before You're Allowed to Lie About It?". Interview with Tim Etchells. In: *Live 4. Freedom Machine.* London: Nick Hern Books 1996. 51–58.

Tushingham, David. „Reisen in fremde Territorien: Forced Entertainment im Gespräch." In: *Festival Theaterformen: Programmbuch.* Berlin: Theater der Zeit, 1998. 43–47.

Quick, Andrew. "Searching for Redemption with Cardboard Wings: Forced Entertainment and the Sublime". In: *Contemporary Theatre Review* Vol. 2, Part 2 (1994): 25–35.

Quick, Andrew. "Stills of the Night". In: *Performance Research.* Vol. 4(2), (1999): 107–108.

Quick, Andrew. "Taking Place: Encountering the Live". In: Adrian Heathfield (Ed). *Live: Art and Performance.* London: Tate Publishing 2004.

Quick, Andrew. "Time and the Event". In: Scott Lash, Andrew Quick, Richard Roberts (Ed). *Time and Value.* Oxford: Blackwell 1998. 65–87.

Winnacker, Susanne. „Die Welt soll leer sein: Der reale Schauspieler ist unmöglich". In: Tilmann Broszat, Sigrid Gareis (Hg). *Global Player. Local Hero.* München: Epodium, 2000. 54–61.

Selceted Newspaper Articles / Ausgewählte Zeitungsartikel

Brennan, Mary. "*Pleasure*". The Herald (12. Dec. 1997).

Brennan, Mary. "*Showtime*". The Herald (9. Nov. 1996).

Etchells, Tim. "*Elvis Lives*". City Limits (1.–8. Mar. 1990).

Etchells, Tim. "*I Wanna Be Adored: ICA Live Arts On Tour In The USA*". The Guardian (1996).

Etchells, Tim. "*These Are a Few of Our (Half) Favourite Things*". City Limits (9. Feb. 1988).

Gardner, Lynn. "*Dirty Work*". The Guardian (3. Feb. 1999).

Gardner, Lynn. "So good it hurts". *The Guardian* (24. Jan. 1998).

Halliday, Robert. "A Show of Force". *Lighting and Sound International* (March 1995).

Kimbrough, Andrew. "Photo-Performance in Cyberspace: The CD-ROMs of Hugo Glendinning and Tim Etchells with Forced Entertainment". *Postmodern Culture*, Vol. 13, No. 1 (Sept. 2002). Online Journal. http://muse.jhu.edu/journals/postmodern_culture/toc/pmc13.1.html

Klett, Renate. „Trauer Made in Sheffield". *Die Zeit* 38 (14. Sept. 2000).

Kühl, Christiane. „Die Tonspur zum 20. Jahrhundert". *die tageszeitung* (24. Feb. 2000).

Laudenbach, Peter. „Bitte eine typische Handbewegung". *Frankfurter Allgemeine Zeitung* (9. Okt. 2000).

Levy, Deborah. "Forced Entertainment: Emanuelle Enchanted", *Hybrid*, Pilot Issue, (Nov. /Dec. 1992).

MacDonald, Claire. "Unpicking Kentucky Fried City". *New Socialist* (Jan. 1987).

Malzacher, Florian. „Fortuna am Ende der Hunderennbahn". *Frankfurter Rundschau* (30. Sept. 2002).

Malzacher, Florian. „Sheffield ist überall". *Frankfurter Rundschau* (27. Nov. 2003).

N.N. "Reality Bites: Forced Entertainment, the creators of the first pop theatre". *The Guardian* (14. Dez. 1996).

N.N. "Stage scraps". *Arts & Culture* No. 199 (16. Sept. 1996).

Schmidt, Christopher. „Call-a-Leben". *Süddeutsche Zeitung* (29. Jan. 2003).

Siegmund, Gerald. „Warum ist unser Leben so schrecklich?". *Frankfurter Allgemeine Zeitung* (5. Feb. 2000).

Slater, Ben. "Addicted to Real Time." Interview with Tim Etchells. *Entropy* Vol. 1, No. 3. (1997).

Timms, Steve. "Working class". *The Big Issue in The North* (18. Jan. 1999).

Tushingham, David. "Pleasure centre?" *Time Out* (21. Jan 1998).

Digital Media / Digitale Medien

Etchells, Tim, Forced Entertainment. *Imaginary Evidence*. Sheffield: Forced Entertainment, 2003.

Etchells, Tim, Forced Entertainment, Agnes Krell. *Paradise*. 23. 4. 1998, http://www.lovebytes.org.uk/paradise.

Forced Entertainment. *Forced Entertainment*. www.forced.co.uk.

Forced Entertainment, Hugo Glendinning: *"Frozen Palaces"*. In: *artintact: CD-ROMagazin interaktiver Kunst* 5 (1999).

Forced Entertainment. *Paradise*.

Glendinning, Hugo, Tim Etchells, Forced Entertainment. *Nightwalks*. Sheffield: Forced Entertainment, 1998.

Glendinning, Hugo, Tim Etchells, Forced Entertainment. *Spin*. Sheffield: Forced Entertainment, 1999.

Video / Film

Etchells, Tim, Terry O'Connor, Helen Russell. *Making Performance: The Forced Entertainment Education Video*. Filmed by Rob Hardy, Mark Perkin. Sheffield: Vision Mix, 1999.

Kelly, Alexander: "On Pleasure." *The South Bank Show: Young directors*. TV-Documentation. ITV (20. July 1997. 23.10 h).

Patricia Benecke (London)

is a graduate of theatre studies and founder of the London based theatre group Dialogue Productions. Apart from her directing for Dialogue Productions she directed at the Horizont Theater Cologne and was nominated for the Cologne Theatre Award. Benecke is London Correspondent for the journal *TheaterHeute* and *Neue Zürcher Zeitung*.

ist Theaterwissenschaftlerin und Gründerin der Londoner Theatergruppe Dialogue Productions. Neben ihren Regiearbeiten für Dialogue Productions führte sie auch am Horizont Theater Köln Regie und war für den Kölner Theaterpreis nominiert. Benecke ist Londoner Korrespondentin der Zeitschrift TheaterHeute *und der* Neue Zürcher Zeitung.

Tim Etchells (Sheffield)

is an artist, director and writer best known for his work with Forced Entertainment. Etchells himself makes works in text, photography, video, performance, installation and digital media. He has also collaborated with a wide range of other artists and has published three books *The Dream Dictionary (for the Modern Dreamer)*, *Endland Stories* and *Certain Fragments: On Contemporary Performance and Forced Entertainment*.

ist Künstler, Regisseur und Schriftsteller, bekannt vor allem durch seine Arbeit mit Forced Entertainment. Etchells selbst arbeitet in den Bereichen Text, Fotografie, Video, Performance, Installation und digitale Medien. Außerdem Zusammenarbeit mit zahlreichen anderen Künstlern. Etchells hat drei Bücher publiziert: The Dream Dictionary (for the Modern Dreamer), Endland Stories *und* Certain Fragments: On Contemporary Performance and Forced Entertainment.

Hugo Glendinning (London)

has been collaborating with Forced Entertainment for 18 years. Their collaboration ranges from using still photography and text through film and video to interactive new media. Alongside his work as collaborator and artist, Glendinning works in professional photography publishing and is exhibiting internationally in the fields of dance, performance and magazine editorial.

arbeitet seit achtzehn Jahren mit Forced Entertainment zusammen. Die Zusammenarbeit reicht von der Verwendung von Szenenfotos und Text über Film und Video bis zu interaktiven neuen Medien. Neben der künstlerischen Arbeit werden seine Tanz-, Performance- und Magazinfotografien international publiziert und ausgestellt.

Matthew Goulish (Chicago)

is Co-Founder with Lin Hixson of the Chicago performance group, Goat Island, in which he has been working and touring as a performer and author to the present day. He teaches writing at the School of Art Institute of Chicago. A collection of essays was published under the title, *39 Microlectures: In proximity of performance*, by Routledge. Co-founder with Tim Etchells of the Institute of Failure.

ist Gründer der Performance Gruppe Goat Island, Chicago (gemeinsam mit Lin Hixson), mit der er bis heute als Performer und Autor arbeitet und tourt. Er unterrichtet Schreiben am School of Art Institute/ Chicago. Routledge publizierte seinen Sammelband mit Essays, 39 Microlectures: In Proximity of Performance. *Gemeinsam mit Tim Etchells gründete Goulish das Institute of Failure.*

Adrian Heathfield (Nottingham)

is a writer and curator. He is the author of numerous articles and editor of several books on performance. He co-curated *Live Culture* (Tate Modern/London) a four day performance series and international symposium, the national performance series *Small Acts at the Millennium*, and *Marathon Lexicon* the durational performance lecture with Tim Etchells.

ist Schriftsteller und Kurator. Er publizierte zahlreiche Artikel und ist der Herausgeber mehrerer Bücher über Performance. Er co-kuratierte Live Culture *(Tate Modern/London), eine viertägige Performance-Reihe mit internationalem Symposion, die Performance Reihe* Small Acts at the Millenium *und mit Tim Etchells das* Marathon Lexicon, *eine* durational performance lecture.

Judith Helmer (Vienna)

is a graduate of theatre studies and works as a freelance arts section journalist in Vienna (Austrian Press Agency, etc.). She is currently writing a doctoral dissertation on Forced Entertainment's *Who Can Sing a Song to Unfrighten Me?*.

ist Theaterwissenschaftlerin und arbeitet als freie Kulturjournalistin in Wien (Austrian Presse Agentur etc.). Sie schreibt an einer Dissertation über Forced Entertainments Who Can Sing a Song to Unfrighten Me?.

Hans-Thies Lehmann (Frankfurt/Main)

is Chair of Performing Arts at the University of Frankfurt. He is the author of the much-discussed book, *Post-Dramatic Theatre*. Further publications: *Theater und Mythos, Das Politische Schreiben* and *Heiner Müller-Handbuch*.

hat einen Lehrstuhl für Theaterwissenschaft an der Universität Frankfurt inne. Er ist Autor des vieldiskutierten Bandes Postdramatisches Theater. *Weitere Publikationen:* Theater und Mythos, Das politische Schreiben *sowie das* Heiner Müller-Handbuch.

Florian Malzacher (Frankfurt/Main)

works as a freelance theatre journalist (Frankfurter Rundschau, taz, TheaterHeute, etc.) and as an independent curator (e.g. International Summer Academy at Künstlerhaus Mousonturm; RePublicAction at Festival Theaterformen; Unfriendly Takeover).

arbeitet als freier Theaterkritiker (Frankfurter Rundschau, taz, TheaterHeute, etc.) und unabhängiger Kurator (u. a. International Summer Academy am Künstlerhaus Mousonturm, RePublicAction beim Festival Theaterformen, Unfriendly Takeover).

Annemarie Matzke (Berlin)

is Assistant professor at the department of theatre studies at the university of Hildesheim. She is a Member of the performance-group She She Pop, having worked as an actress and dramaturge in numerous theatre projects.

ist Assistentin am Institut für Theaterwissenschaft an der Universität Hildesheim und Mitglied der Performance Gruppe She She Pop. Matzke arbeitet als Schauspielerin und Dramaturgin in zahlreichen Theaterprojekten.

Andrew Quick (Lancaster)

is Senior Lecturer at the University of Lancaster, author of numerous essays on contemporary performance and co-editor of several performance books; member of the British performance group, Imitating the Dog. He is currently completing a monograph entitled, *The Event of Performance*, to be published in 2005.

ist Senior Lecturer an der Universität Lancaster, Autor zahlreicher Beiträge zur zeitgenössischen Performance und Mitherausgeber mehrerer Publikationen zur Performance Art. Mitglied der britischen Gruppe Imitating the Dog. Derzeit arbeitet er an der Monografie The Event of Performance, *die 2005 erscheinen wird.*

Anke Schleper (Frankfurt/Main)

studied philosophy, is an antiquarian and member of the independent group of curators Unfriendly Takeover.

studierte Philosophie, ist Antiquarin und Mitglied der freien Kuratorengruppe Unfriendly Takeover.

Gerald Siegmund (Gießen/Frankfurt)

wrote his doctorate on *Theatre as Memory*. In 1998, he joined the staff of the Department of Applied Theatre Studies at the University of Giessen, where he is teaching now. Since 1995 he has been working as a freelance dance and performance critic for *Frankfurter Allgemeine Zeitung, Ballettanz* and *Dance Europe*. He has published widely on contemporary dance and theatre performance.

promovierte mit dem Thema Theater als Gedächtnis. *Seit 1995 arbeitet er als freier Tanzkritiker für die* Frankfurter Allgemeine Zeitung, Ballettanz *und* Dance Europe. *Seit 1998 ist er Wissenschaftlicher Mitarbeiter am Institut für Angewandte Theaterwissenschaft an der Justus-Liebig-Universität, Gießen. Gerald Siegmund hat zahlreiche Essays zum zeitgenössischen Tanz und Theater veröffentlicht.*

Astrid Sommer (Karlsruhe)

is a graduate of theatre studies and works as a freelance editor and dramaturge. She has been associated with the ZKM/Centre for Art and Media Karlsruhe since 1993, and with the dance company commerce since 1999.

ist Theaterwissenschaftlerin und arbeitet als freiberufliche Redakteurin und Dramaturgin, u. a. seit 1993 für das ZKM/Zentrum für Kunst und Medientechnologie Karlsruhe und seit 1999 mit der Tanzcompagnie commerce.

Investigative Journalism

An Interview with Philip McKenna, Landlord of The Rutland Arms, Sheffield.

When did you first meet Forced Entertainment? Eleven years ago, when I took over the bar. They were much younger then and didn't have families. They used to come here for a meal at lunchtime or in the evening and for beer, of course. They discussed here what they were going to do. **How did you get to know them?** Because they were the naughty ones … no – only joking. But they always came as a group, and so you would get to talk to them and find out what they were up to. Well, in the beginning, they were here more or less every day of the week and when they had a show they wouldn't come at lunchtime, but if they had a performance across the street, they would come rushing in for a drink afterwards. And the audience would come too. Then all the sudden you would find them missing for a month: they were touring the continent. Then they reappeared. And then there is a new one with them, and one says: "That's my wife now." I don't know who she is but that's fine. **How often are they here?** It's less now, because they are touring more, but when they are in town, they come. And now they come even with their children in summer in the garden. **Can you tell from the outside how their work is progressing?** If they are feeling affluent it will not be a sandwich it will be a meal and not half a beer but a pint. **So how do you like their work?** I have never seen a performance. Because when they are playing on the stage, I am here in the bar. **So, what kind of theatre do you think they are doing?** I think it's very modern. And I think it's not my theatre. My theatre would be a good murder, Agatha Christie or something like that. A theatre with a proscenium arch and a curtain. Not theatre in the round or with no props, but I think they are good at what they do. **And would you like to see one of their shows?** I think it's better I don't. Not for them, but for me. I'm old-fashioned. And what they do is very modern. **How do you know?** From what I see from the photographs and the advertisements. I look at it and say: Well, it's not my generation. It may be for a lot of people, but it's not for me. **Could you imagine your bar being part of one of their performances?** Oh yes, I think they could portray the bar. Very modern and maybe with no beer.